Constructive Evaluation of Literate Activity

Constructive Evaluation of Literate Activity

Peter H. Johnston

State University of New York at Albany

Longman

New York & London

Constructive Evaluation of Literate Activity

Longman, 95 Church Street, White Plains, N.Y. 10601

Associated companies:
Longman Group Ltd., London
Longman Cheshire Pty., Melbourne
Longman Paul Pty., Auckland
Copp Clark Pitman, Toronto

The tape that accompanies this textbook was designed to be used with Chapters 10 and 11, and with Appendix A. The examples on tape and instructions for their use in learning to make running records all appear in those sections of this textbook.

Executive editor: Raymond T. O'Connell
Development editor: Virginia L. Blanford
Production editors: Kathryn Dix and Halley Gatenby
Text design adaptation: Lee Goldstein
Cover design: Lee Goldstein
Production supervisor: Anne P. Armeny

Library of Congress Cataloging-in-Publication Data

Johnston, Peter H.
    Constructive evaluation of literate activity / Peter Johnston.
      p.   cm.
    Includes index.
    ISBN 0-582-29035-X
    1. Literacy—Evaluation. I. Title.
    LC149.J64 1992   91–19787
    302.2′244—dc20   CIP

1 2 3 4 5 6 7 8 9 10-HA-9594939291

For my parents,
Betty and Bruce.
For my family,
Tina, Nick, Emily, and Samantha.
And for my grandmother,
a truly grand lady,
Rebecca Dagger.

Contents

PART III   **THE FOCUS OF EVALUATION: NOTICING THE DETAIL
OF LITERATE ACTIVITY**   **163**

PART IV   **WHAT WE VALUE IN EVALUATION**   **247**

Acknowledgments

If I were to list all to whom I owe a learning debt, this book would be long indeed. Yet there are people whose contributions should be acknowledged, like my editor, Ray O'Connell, whose patience I have sorely tried. When I began writing this book, I thought I might have something to say about evaluation, but most of what made me think that has since been thrown away, resulting in a couple of years' delay in the completion of the manuscript. I am guardedly grateful for Ray's quiet nagging. I am also grateful for the supportive efforts of Ginny Blanford and Kathy Dix in putting the book together.

Terry Crooks and Richard Barham made it possible for me to do graduate study. David Pearson and George McConkie got me into this domain of study and sent me on the road to my present position. Marie Clay and Don Holdaway were mentors of mine well before they were aware of it. And to Peter Winograd and Peter Afflerbach, I owe personal and intellectual debts.

My many wonderful colleagues at the University at Albany have provided me with a particularly stimulating environment. I have worked closely with Dick Allington, Anne McGill-Franzen, Rose-Marie Weber, Lil Brannon, and Cy Knoblauch, each of whom has had an impact on my thinking. Alan Purves organized the Center for Writing and Literacy, which made some of these discussions possible. I have also gained from discussions with Frank Vallutino and Frank Hodge. I have been privileged, here at Albany, to learn from a wonderful group of graduate students at both the master's and doctoral levels. I would like to acknowledge the material contributions of Joan Watson, Donna Singleton, Rhoda Spiro, Dennis Mike, and Paula Weiss. I also owe thanks to Mary Unser, our department secretary, who against all odds keeps my work life relatively sane.

Many intellectual debts are born of the struggle to solve practical problems while worrying incidentally about philosophical ones. The students in our practicum course over the years have insisted that I learn in this way. Susan Harmon has kept me up-to-date and arguing about practical political problems. Faith Schulstrom, curriculum coordinator for the Guilderland Central School District, has made it possible for me to loiter in the schools, and Bob Oates and Martha Beck have allowed me to loiter in their particular schools. Kathy Oboyski-Butler, Pat Colfer, Trudy Warner, and Ellen Farnsworth have allowed me to be in their classrooms as an aide and observer for extended periods of time, and to talk interminably about teaching. I have also learned a great deal from my visits with Helena Spring and the folks in the Ithaca School District. I have doubtless omitted important people from this list, but I hope the many people from whom I have learned will see bits of themselves in these pages.

Many people contributed examples for the book and I am most grateful. I particularly appreciated the reading of Nick, Emily, Sam, Amanda, and Billy.

Much of this book has to do with the entanglement of values, feelings, knowledge, and human action. In attempting to give recognition to intellectual debts, I have found them stubbornly difficult to untangle. Some are not obviously intellectual. It only recently occurred to me that my late father's ethical commitment and persistence, my mother's empathy and caring, and their collective sense of humor had anything to do with science. I have been very fortunate in my heritage.

While writing and reading, it is not always obvious that one is working. My family have put up with my being in the basement writing, in the evenings and on weekends, and rarely questioned that I am in fact working. I doubt that they have enjoyed sharing me with this book, though they have complained only sufficiently to keep me aware that, whatever the contribution of this book, it is likely to be small in comparison to the contribution of a sane and playful family. Nonetheless, for my part, I have not enjoyed the guilt of occasional neglect.

The family's contributions to the book have been enormous. Aside from the obvious reading and writing examples contributed by Nicholas, Emily, and Samantha, witnessing the miracles of birth and childhood in triplicate and surviving the miracle of parenting have changed the way I think about children, learning, and what is to be valued. Studying parenting and partnership under the tutelage of my wife Tina, a wonderful teacher, has contributed to this book immeasurably.

PART I

BASIC ISSUES

In this first section of the book I try to convince you that evaluation is not so much a technical problem as a people problem. It has to do with what people learn when they evaluate, and what others learn as they are evaluated. I argue that evaluation is always interpretive, that we *make* sense of literate activity, and that evaluation is always a social interaction in which evaluators give as much information as they get. I describe the importance of self-evaluation. I argue that if evaluation is to be improved, then we must start with teachers and students, and we must create conditions in which they will be likely to critically and constructively evaluate their own literate activity. I emphasize two kinds of knowledge that will help teachers in their evaluations of children: knowledge of what makes reading and writing more or less difficult, and knowledge of how to make sense of children's (and their own) errors.

CHAPTER 1

Introduction

There are some very odd things happening in this country in the name of evaluation. Consider some of the following examples:

1. In many parts of the country, children are being tested to see whether they have learned enough to be able to enter kindergarten.

2. Not far from where I live, a school was cited by the state department as being one of the worst schools in the state because of its students' performance on the state tests. Two years later it was cited as one of the outstanding schools in the state for its performance on the state tests. This small miracle was performed by the simple expedient of classifying about a quarter of the children as disabled (using tests) and excluding them from the testing sample.

3. In another district, a similar improvement in test scores has been obtained. The cost? Nearly two-thirds of the students have been retained[1] by the time they reach third grade.

4. Although "grade level" is statistically defined as the performance of the middle child in a national sample of children taking a test designed to produce as wide a range of scores as possible, many believe that schools should have no children reading below grade level. For example, a conference announcement from Harvard University trumpeted that "Recent NAEP findings show that, despite progress in the last fifteen years, children from low-income families are still at risk of being below grade level in language skills and literacy."[2] At the same time, when it was found that every state reported that its average test score was above grade level, there were howls of protest that schools must be cheating.[3]

5. A local elementary school student, having just read comfortably from his class textbook to the Committee on the Handicapped, was nonetheless classified as reading disabled on the basis of psychological tests. He was placed in a resource room with other students considered similarly disabled so that he would be more able to learn to read.

6. In many states, my own included, Realtors sell houses and attract industry with school test scores under their arms—a situation which ensures that the rich get richer and the poor get poorer. In some states, the average test performance of students in each classroom is published in newspapers. Teachers are judged by administrators, the public, and their peers on the basis of these scores.

7. Each year the average elementary school student loses four days of instruction to standardized tests. An upper primary grade student loses six days, and junior and senior high students lose approximately ten days.[4] These figures are actually gross underestimates because:

☐ Administrators underreported test use. For example, the Milwaukee Public Schools Assessment Task Force found that test use was five to eight times higher than administrators reported for the survey, about five per year per student not counting the tests in the basal reading program.[5]

☐ They do not include optional tests such as college placement tests. Neither do they reflect those tests included in basal reading programs (indeed, I have argued elsewhere that the entire basal program *is* a test).

☐ They do not reflect the time spent preparing for these tests, which is probably somewhat proportional to the stakes involved.

Sooner or later this madness has to stop. I hope this book will provide some rationale and method for alternatives to the current state of affairs. In our zeal to produce new and improved evaluation instruments, we have forgotten that the object of the exercise is to improve the learning experiences children have in school so that fewer children will become casualties of our sincere efforts to help them become literate. It is easy to lose sight of this purpose. Many people who have specialized in assessment or evaluation are not provided time to spend in classrooms with teachers and children. Thus they easily lose contact with the central reason for the existence of their specialization. This book is my attempt to restructure the evaluation of children's literate activity so that the improvement of their instruction is the central goal.

HOW THIS BOOK WORKS

The book is organized rather differently from others in the same area, so let me briefly explain my logic. In Part I, "Basic Issues," I set out to establish some common ground by elaborating on the definitions and premises to which I subscribe, and the social and educational bases of evaluation. In Part II, "Recording and Keeping Track," I plunge directly into the "how to" of evaluation by introducing some basic techniques for gathering and recording information about reading, writing, and teaching. Along the way I describe the effects these techniques have on students' learning and the conditions that will make them most useful. Chapters 10 and 11 of this section have a companion audiotape of children reading. The taped examples match the text as co-author Marie Clay and I teach you step-by-step how to take running records of oral reading.

In Part III of the book, "The Focus of Evaluation: Noticing the Detail of Literate Activity," I describe in more detail the nature of the literate activity we are evaluating. It may seem more logical to do this before describing observation procedures, but getting comfortable with some of the techniques in Part II takes considerable time. Introducing them first allows more practice time so that you might become more comfortable with them more quickly.

In Part IV, ''What We Value in Evaluation,'' I discuss issues related to the interpretation and use of data, and how to put that information together in the most useful forms. I try at the same time to untangle some of the misconceptions about evaluation that underlie what currently goes on in schools.

Finally, in Part V, I propose some ways to restructure what we are doing in schools. I try to describe ways to recognize and break out of the beliefs and assumptions that keep us doing basically the same old thing in evaluation.

The appendixes at the end of the book contain examples for illustration or practice. Appendix A contains additional practice examples of running records to go with Chapters 10 and 11 and the audiotape that accompanies the book. Appendix B contains an assortment of interview questions to explore following your reading of Chapters 12 and 13. Appendix C is a simple checklist to record a child's alphabet knowledge. Appendix D provides examples of reports of children's literate activity.

SOME DEFINITIONAL ISSUES

I hope that your dialogue with me during your reading of this book (I have left wide margins) will help you to responsibly evaluate literate activity. Since that is the focus of this book, let me briefly describe what I mean. For me, literate activity is not simply an isolated set of skills, but rather a very complex way of interacting with the world and oneself.[6] It cannot be separated from the rest of a person's life or from his culture. I will be more descriptive in later chapters, yet I will not attempt any complete, definitive definition of such a simultaneously cultural, historical, political, and personal concept. Indeed, such a definition would soon be out of date since the term continues to evolve, to change—and it must do so. To be literate today is not the same as being literate fifty years ago. To be literate in one culture is not the same as being literate in another. However, I would like to highlight the fact that being literate is more a role than a skill: something one *is* rather than something one *has*. Further, I include in literate activity what teachers do in classrooms that helps children develop their literacy.

I have used the word *evaluation* rather than terms such as *measurement* and *testing,* for a good reason. These other terms have connotations from their derivations or use that have made them unsatisfactory. *Testing,* for example, is too restrictive. Most of what I describe does not involve tests in the modern sense at all. The derivation of *test* is actually instructive. It came to us from Latin via old French with the meaning ''a piece of burned clay or skull'' from the practice of testing metals by incineration in a clay vessel resembling a skull. Current tests are not so far from this origin.

Measurement, too, is restrictive in that it implies a concern for comparability and standardization, and a belief that the measuring process is somehow amoral, nonreactive, and linear. Testing, as it is currently done, is about as non-reactive as vivisection. Evaluation carries more useful connotations.[7] *Evaluation* shares a common root with *value,* which recognizes overtly the value-laden nature of the activity. Actually, the Latin root is *e* meaning "from," and *valere* meaning "strength" or "worth." Throughout the book I shall stress the importance of valuing strengths. Indeed, the word *constructive* is in the book title for two reasons, the first of which is its meaning "positive and helpful" as in "constructive comments." The second reason is because of its connection with social constructivist theories of knowledge. The essential point behind these theories is that through language we name the world we live in. We make and order our knowledge of the world with language, and we do so in interaction with others. We each construct our versions of the world and live within these realities.

I also use the term *responsible* as a contrast to the term *accountable.* Responsibility comes from the individual. A teacher or other learner *is* responsible, whereas he is *held* accountable. This distinction is critical in its implications. It requires that the individual (teacher or learner) become reflective about his own practice, and about students' learning. If he is not reflective, then someone else will be required to hold him accountable. It is possible to be held accountable but at the same time not to be responsible.

The title of the book originally contained the word *diagnostic.* The roots of *diagnosis* are Greek and are very relevant to my view of evaluation. *Diagnostikos* means "able to distinguish between," and is built from *dia* meaning "through" or "between," and *gignoskein,* meaning "to know." Really knowing a child and how this child differs from other children and across time, is part of our responsibility as teachers. On the other hand, the term has connotations of disease and the medical model of a powerless patient and an all-powerful, impersonal scientist. It is tied to the word *clinical* which has the Latin root *clinicus,* meaning "bedridden." I dislike these connotations of the word *diagnostic* when applied to gathering instructionally useful information about a child.

Throughout the book I have tried to emphasize the common metaphors in teaching, learning, literacy, language, knowledge, and evaluation. As an illustration, one day our two-year-old, Samantha, came to me and said something like, "I e a hou?" to which I replied, "You want to eat a house?" She hesitated then said, "Yes!" and giggled uncontrollably. The big joke lies in her realization of the power of language. With language, she realized, you can construct a world that could never exist.[8] Because of language we are not condemned to live in a cell of sober reality imposed by someone else. This ability to create multiple realities is central to language, but it is also at the heart of reflective teaching and evaluation. It is this ability that allows teachers to do mental experiments to consider the possible consequences of particular changes in their instruction. In his book *The Reflective Practitioner* Donald Schon points out the importance of the teacher's "capacity to hold several ways of looking at things at once without disrupting the flow of inquiry."[9] This ability to construct multiple realities is also what Mihalyi Csikszentmihalyi defines as wisdom, which, he says:

> . . . does not lie in becoming mesmerized by that glimpse of reality our culture proclaims to be ultimate, but in the discovery that we can create various realities.[10]

SOME ALTERNATIVE GROUND RULES

Several premises have guided my writing about evaluation. The first of these is the understanding that evaluation (indeed perception) is interpretive: *we only look with our eyes: we see with our minds.* In other words, what appear to be simple acts of perception are actually interpretive acts. We don't see children "as they are"; we see them as we have learned to see them, and always through a veil of language. Meaning does not lie in the world ready for our eyes and ears to scoop it up, we *make* meaning out of the world. Perhaps it is better to say, we make our own versions of the world and we live within them. My version will certainly not be the same as yours, although there will equally certainly be many similarities.

This constructive view of human perception is not new.[11] However, its implications for evaluation, and for concepts of knowledge and literacy, are critical. It implies that each child constitutes the world in a different way. Literacy, learning, and various literate activities mean different things to each child. Stories have different meanings for each child. The differences may or may not be substantial in particular cases, but they are there. One day when my eldest daughter, Emily, was four, she painted a picture of which she was rather proud. The entire paper was various shades of orange. I had to admit that I was at a loss until she explained that it was the peach in *James and the Giant Peach,* a book by Roald Dahl. I guess I just wasn't standing as close to the peach when we read the story a week or so before. Perspectives differ in very consequential ways. As teachers, part of our job is understanding the students' perspectives— and our own.

Teachers (and other adults involved in children's literacy development) imbue children's behavior with meaning differently, depending on how they have constructed their own knowledge of children and of literate activity. Two teachers can watch a child do something and describe her in completely different terms, partly because they use language differently, and partly because they "see" and value different things. It is not just that they all see different aspects of what is really going on; rather they all see things differently. Their observations are not simply complementary. They are governed by the structure of their own knowledge, experiences, language, and values. In this way, *each evaluative act is at once social and personal, and, because of its consequences, political.* Evaluation is a profoundly human and value-laden activity, like all human science. The most important thing is that we understand it, that we are careful and reflective in our efforts to document literate activity, and that we invite dialogue. There is no single right way to evaluate. Rather, every way has its consequences, and some will view as good the same consequences others view as bad. Because evaluation is interpretive and multiple interpretations and consequences are possible, *a critical reflectiveness is absolutely the most important dimension of an evaluator's expertise.* It is this attribute which produces learning and self-correction, and allows dialogue.

In many ways, *evaluating is just like reading and writing: it involves noticing details and noticing themes and patterns.* Good writers are able to describe believable characters because they notice the details of people's behavior and have a wealth of observations to draw on. Good readers construct detailed meanings from a similar wealth of observations. Good writers write with audiences in mind and readers read with authors in mind. They also read and write with a concern for the consequences of the meanings they construct. These are all equally true of good evaluators.

By the same token, *learning to evaluate is like learning to read and write.* It involves a socialization of values and of attention to the most relevant details. We can never attend to everything that goes on at the same time. We must be selective. Learning to be literate involves learning which things to attend to in print and in the world which will best inform literate activity. This learning can take place only in a social situation in which the learner is immersed in literate activity and in which feedback on his own attempts is available. Learning to evaluate involves these same conditions.

Literacy is a social activity. In order to evaluate someone's literacy development, we must carefully describe the social conditions in which the person engages in literate activity. People build their literacy in social interaction, and in order to understand literacy, we need to describe the social interaction and how the individual contributes to that interaction. We cannot know what the "failure" of a child means without situating it in his normal classroom interactions and his perceptions of them.

In order that we might easily observe literate activity in its social context, we might bear in mind that *the more independent literate activity that is going on in the classroom, the easier and more consistent evaluation will be.* The more students are reading and writing, and talking about the reading and writing, the more examples are available to be observed, and the less critical it is for the teacher to notice every single one. In addition, the more commonplace it is for students to talk about their literate activity, the more capable they become of participating in their own evaluation. In a classroom in which students are supposed to work quietly on their workbooks, briefly read to the teacher in a reading group, and do only single sentence response writing, a teacher will be hard-pressed to talk coherently about students' literacy development.

The word *independent* is critical in this principle because the most useful information is obtained in one-to-one conferences with students, and from stepping back and watching how students make choices and manage their literate activity when they are self-directed. Both of these types of information require students to be able to manage themselves independently. If they cannot, they forever will be trying to butt in on teacher-student conferences to get help, and they will not be able to allow the teacher to step back and observe classroom literate activity uninterrupted. The word *independent* also implies the making of choices. Indeed, *the more students have options to choose among, the more useful information they will provide about their reading and writing processes.* The process of making choices among books, strategies, topics, audiences, and so forth, yields a great deal of useful information. When a teacher is required to use a basal reading program, the students will be unable to demonstrate their interests in particular types of literature. They will be unable to demonstrate their ability to choose material they can manage. When teachers tell students what to write about, they lose the opportunity to understand what children are interested in writing about and how they choose topics.

Another critical premise of this book is that *self-evaluation is the most important evaluation.* Any process needs feedback to direct it. Imagine being deaf and blind, and trying to live a normal life with a hearing person on one side giving you feedback and a seeing person on the other. Being dependent on others to know how you are doing is neither as efficient nor as effective as doing it yourself. If children are unable to evaluate their own literate activity, then we have failed in our instruction. They will be dependent. If teachers cannot evaluate their own teaching, they cannot be professionally responsible, and a case can be made for holding them accountable.

Not only is literacy a social activity, but *evaluation, too, is a social interaction between people or groups of people.* In evaluative (or any) social interactions, evaluators convey information about their beliefs and values regarding the other person, and the nature of the literate activity they are engaged in. When we put this principle with the previous ones, we conclude that *the consequences of evaluation are the first thing to consider when establishing the validity of an evaluation procedure.* Although workers in the fields of measurement and evaluation have often asserted that validity is dependent on the use of the information, in practice that has usually been the last thing to be considered. It is generally only given lip service. But I will assert, for example, that evaluation which fails to promote self-evaluation is suspect in terms of its validity.

American children are the most tested in the world.[12] Children in some schools are tested more than children in other schools. Some children are tested substantially more than other children in the same class. What is the point of all of this evaluation? If I were to ask a selection of teachers, administrators, and laypeople, I would be given an enormous variety of reasons for the evaluation going on in their particular school. I have based this book on the premise that *there is one central reason for evaluating children's literate activity, and that is so that we might ensure optimal instruction for all children.* All other reasons are secondary to that goal. For example, if we evaluate in order to group children, the grouping is simply so that we might better serve the children instructionally. If the grouping is counterproductive, then the evaluation is counterproductive (it is actually invalid). If the evaluation does not contribute to improving the learning of students and teachers, then we should seriously question the need to evaluate at all. Ordinarily, ensuring optimal instruction will require learning on the part of all stakeholders in the child's educational development: students, teachers, parents, administrators, and the general public, but particularly students.

Given these assumptions, then, I argue that we should *seek the most instructionally useful information* and *use the most instructionally useful strategy for obtaining it*. Any evaluation procedure that interferes with or reduces optimal instruction to any child should be regarded as highly suspect, probably invalid, and generally unacceptable. Furthermore, any information gathered should be in a form that is helpful to teachers and students and likely to be used by them. To have value, it must influence the teacher's teaching or the student's learning.

Since the bulk of educationally relevant decision making takes place in the classroom, on a moment-to-moment basis, that is where we should focus our evaluation concern. The teacher makes instructional decisions in the classroom at an alarming rate, and most frequently without recourse to formalized sets of data such as files and test scores. Thus our major efforts in educational evaluation need to be directed toward helping teachers to make these decisions in the most productive and thoughtful way possible.

These are the major emphases of this book. I think it is clear that, from my perspective, *evaluation is not so much a technical problem as a people problem*. The problem is to arrange conditions, so that all parties are able to learn as well as possible about teaching and learning. For example, it will behoove us to remember that people who are nervous and defensive are not good learners, regardless of the quality of the data placed before them. Indeed, I shall argue later in the book that posing evaluation as a merely technical problem in many ways *is* the problem.

CHAPTER 2

Being a Constructive Evaluator

A couple of years ago I was speaking to a group of teachers and saying disparaging things about basal readers. One of the teachers, a young man, stood up and said, "I know basal readers are a problem. I use one and I would love to get rid of it, but quite frankly I'm scared." My first reaction was to try to convince him that he was not throwing away much, but I realized that my answer was rather lame. If he knew little about children's literacy development or how to keep track of it, he would be unable to see learning take place or to set conditions within which a sensible curriculum could develop. Unable to recognize the fruits of his labors, as the end-of-year tests loomed larger he would panic and return to the basal reader and be much more cautious about leaving it the next time. In order to take control of his instruction, he would need to become more knowledgeable in some very specific ways.

The required knowledge does not have to do with the giving and interpreting of tests. It has more to do with knowing how not to feel the need to use tests. Tests generally do not assist professional classroom evaluators very much. Indeed, some test makers have been forthright enough to say that to us, though we have not been inclined to listen. For example, in the manual of a popular test, its publishers advise us that test results:

> should be viewed as tentative until substantiated by additional information. . . . Accept the test results as a challenge to your ingenuity in finding out why the class or individual pupils obtained certain scores. . . .[13]

A reasonable, if slightly cynical, translation of this would be:

> Here are some test scores. We cannot say what they mean, but you are the expert, you have the data there, you figure out what they mean.

I could not agree more. You must be the expert, and you must know how to gather useful data. A test may give you a score, but even that must be interpreted. You might as well interpret the more direct evidence of literate activity available in your classroom in the first place. To make good instructional decisions, you need to understand why the class and individual pupils do the things they do. Since the test makers in this case admit to being unable to provide that information, I am not sure what they felt they were contributing.

Evaluation does involve expertise, and research has told us something about what it means to be an expert. Much of what has been learned has come from studies of problem solving, and of activities such as playing chess. Experts differ from novices in the extent and structure of their knowledge. Experts know more about their domain, which in this case includes literature, literacy, children's development, and procedures for keeping track of their development, and they tend to know it in a more coherent, integrated way than do novices.[14] They also know when and how to use particular knowledge, more of their knowledge is automatic, and they monitor and strategically use their knowledge. When they are problem-solving, experts are not distracted by the surface features of the problem, but instead recognize the underlying principles needed to solve or redefine the problem.

In order to make this a little more concrete, let me use the analogy of the chess expert. A chess master recognizes about 50,000 board configurations, a good club player about 1,000, and a novice only a few.[15] These patterns can be recognized quite quickly and acted upon. A master chess player can look at a pattern of pieces on a board for a few seconds and be able to replace the pieces in their original positions if the board were upset—a very functional skill for those of them who have young children. However, if the pieces are placed on the board in a way that could never occur in a game, the expert can no longer replace the pieces. Only familiar patterns are recognized and remembered. If we view children as engaging in patterns of literate behavior which teachers might recognize, then teachers are faced with a similar task. It is these patterns to which the teacher responds, and if they are not recognized, they will not be responded to or remembered. The idea is to see patterns and not to treat them as exactly the same as each other, but as a way of organizing domains of experience and ways of responding. One pattern is not seen as *identical* to another, but rather as a good metaphor to explore for this child in this situation. The broader the range of possible patterns and responses available, the better and more flexible the problem solving, and the better the ability to envision possibilities and to predict their consequences.

The analogy between expert teacher and chess player is closest in the special case when the chess expert plays exhibition matches against 20 or 30 club players simultaneously, going from board to board around the room. Even master chess players lose some of these games. However, the expert teacher's job is even more complex since chess masters have to attend to only the board and the inert wooden pieces. Teachers are dealing with people, whose actions and thoughts are influenced by the contexts of their lives. For this aspect, bird-watching expertise provides a better analogy. A bird-watcher recognizes a yellow shafted flicker on the basis of a small flash of yellow of the bird in flight and the pattern of the flight, or the size and red head when not in flight, and so forth. But bird-watching requires not only rapid pattern recognition on the basis of partial information, but also a knowledge of where and when to look for a particular bird. If you want to see a snowy owl it is not enough to know what it looks like; you will need to know where to look for it. You might hang around California for a long time looking for one without success, but it would be unfortunate to conclude that they do not exist. In other words, a teacher can fail to see a student's development if he does not know what development would look like, but he will also fail to see it if he knows what it would look like but is unable to set a classroom context in which it is likely to appear. For example, independent literate activity will not be seen if there is no opportunity in the classroom to engage in such activity, or if there is time but an unsatisfactory supply of appropriate books.

The point is, then, that both an expert and a novice might look at a child's activity, but the expert is likely to see more patterns and relationships in it—to make more meaning out of it. Again, people only look with their eyes. They see with their minds. The novice might look at the sample of a child's writing shown in Figure 2.1 and see only scribble, whereas the expert might see a letter written in spelling which is partially invented and partially derived from visual memory, with appropriate opening and closing, and a message (a rainbow) in the middle. The expert might also observe that the child has used print for those parts of the letter for which only print can be used, and graphics to convey a message that, converted into words would simply be too laborious to produce. In this case, a picture may, in fact, be worth a thousand words.

Experts are distinguished not only by the extent of their knowledge but also by the structure of their knowledge and their way of going about making it. Two experts on a controversial issue like nuclear power plants may each know a

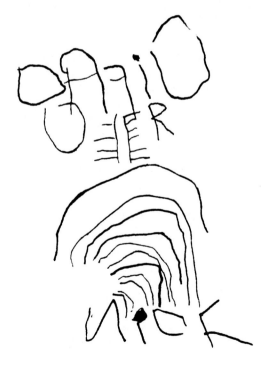

Figure 2.1. Rainbow letter: An example of a young child's writing. (From Peter H. Johnston (1987). ''Teachers as Evaluation Experts,'' The Reading Teacher 40(8), p. 746. Reprinted by permission.)

great deal, but their knowledge will be organized differently. When they both visit the same new power plant, what they each see, remember, and report may very well suggest that they had visited entirely different places. Teachers with many years of experience in the classroom have a lot of knowledge. But sometimes it is not organized into theories of how children learn to become independent readers and writers, but into theories of how to control and organize children to learn a series of skills. This is a different kind of knowledge involving different kinds of patterns. To return to the chess example, the expert chess player can put all the chess pieces back in their right places only if they could have been in those positions in a game. If the pieces are put in impossible positions, the pattern recognition falls apart. Consequently, a teacher viewing a classroom from the perspective of "time on task" and "efficiency" will very likely not listen to the patterns of the dialogue in children's classroom talk, since she will mostly be concerned about the fact that there is too much talk.

In part this difference is cultural. Just as children's attention is socialized toward particular aspects of their literate environment, and their language reflects that socialization, so teachers' attention is socialized toward particular features of children's literate activity, and their descriptive language reflects that socialization. Whereas mainstream Americans have a single term for green, but separate words for green, orange, and purple, the Shona divide up greens but not red, orange, and purple. Similarly, the Inuit have an extensive language for describing snow, whereas mainstream Americans, even skiers, have rather limited descriptors. In part this attention is determined by the functional value of the shades of meaning, and in part it is determined simply by one's experience.

As an example, some teachers recently showed us how their knowledge of literature makes a difference to their evaluations of children's development.[16] A teacher who knows literature well tends to see children through that lens. For example, a teacher who had a substantial knowledge of children's literature described to me in these terms the literacy development of a student whom she knew well:

> So he would stick to those kinds of books or these kinds really, you know *Three Bears, The Business letter*—those kinds of books. Then gradually he branched out a little bit to the . . . *Fortunately* is one of Mercer Mayer's books, and the *Clifford* books, and that type of thing. [Later] he was again sticking with the things that he felt secure with, like *Frog and Toad Together*. . . . And now, I guess he'd have to be considered one of the Patricia Riley Giff experts. Because those books are not real easy for him. But he just likes the character so much. I think he's in love with Ms. Rooney—with her classroom—that he's willing to spend that extra time getting to know more about those children in that room, in that book, and he really tries very hard to be very self-sufficient reading those books of hers. . . . He's tried the mystery ones that she's come out with . . . [and that was only one quarter of the description of a single child].

Another teacher, whose knowledge of literature was more limited, described to me a child she knew well as:

> From the beginning of his coming into my room he could not read. He's eleven years old, in third grade, and very little sight vocabulary. Now he's able to read, not fluently, but he can read. And he's real proud of himself. He's made progress. He'll still be placed in special ed in a couple of weeks, but I do see progress. [This was the entire, prompted, description]

I hope you can see that knowledge of literate activity is what drives teachers' pattern recognition, and that for this reason alone it is important for teachers themselves to read and write regularly and diversely. This kind of knowledge is also critical if a teacher is to provide optimal instruction for students who approach learning in a variety of different ways. Without this knowledge, the teacher will be forced to assert absolute control so that things are done the only way he knows how to do them.

Other conditions also impact on the pattern recognition aspect of expertise. For example, another teacher who had a substantial knowledge of children's literature, but whose classroom was dominated by the district's insistence that students complete the basal reading program with all its workbooks and tests, described a child without reference to literature at all. When prompted, however, she was able to describe what the more able of two students was reading. The reason for the difference was that children were able to do free reading only after they had finished their workbook assignment. Thus, only the more able readers got to read and talk about books. The less able readers never finished their workbooks. What the teacher sees and remembers of the students' development is what influences her interactions with the students, and the relationship is reciprocal.

In addition to recognizing patterns of literate activity and development, the expert evaluator knows how to look and listen. By looking and listening, I do not mean just scrutinizing with a more intense ''scrute'' than usual, but actively looking and listening. And listening involves not just cocking an ear, but opening it to the many possible things to hear, tuning it to the speaker, and responding in such a way that the speaker tells a detailed, accurate, and focused story. For a classroom teacher it means making polyphony out of cacophony.

Evaluation also involves describing the learner and his development. We do this for a variety of audiences, and the manner in which we describe the learner influences how those audiences treat him in the future. There really is a difference between describing a cup as half-empty or half-full. If we give the learner the role of a failure, he will tend to fill that role for us. In contrast, if we give him the role of a successful learner and a literate individual, then that is how he will generally respond to us. Thus, our job as evaluation experts is to describe the learner through his strengths, and in order to do so we need to put him in situations in which he will feel literate.

Literate activity is highly dependent on the context in which it occurs or is expected to occur, and evaluation is part of that context. Evaluation, too, is dependent on the context in which it occurs. A teacher who is required by mandate to use materials that specifically preclude children's choosing literature to read, will not evaluate those children through their selection and reading of literature.[17] The children in such a class will learn a very narrow and controlling concept of literacy.

There is one final, and critical, aspect of constructive evaluation. A constructive evaluator is aware that she constructs her own knowledge, as do others concerned with children's welfare. She realizes that none of them has a corner on the truth, and that one responsibility to themselves and their children involves listening to each other and critically evaluating their own evaluations as well as those of others. The constructive evaluator's responsibility requires her to maintain for herself a situation of undefensive "intelligent unrest,"[18] in which she is constantly reflective on her own evaluations. In other words, pattern recognition is just fine, but what if the patterns that we see are inaccurate, stereotypical, or incomplete? Part of our expertise, then, involves being able to collect good data that will help us to confront our own knowledge, and actually being able to confront and restructure our knowledge. *This critical reflectiveness is absolutely the most important dimension of a constructive evaluator's expertise,* since it is the one that produces development in the other dimensions, and produces self-correction.

CHAPTER 3

It Takes Two: Evaluation as a Social Interaction

Whenever we evaluate we are engaged in a social interaction. The interaction can take a variety of forms, but it is always a social activity in which each participant constructs an understanding of what is going on. Consider the following scenario.[19] Mary is a white professional in her early thirties. She is also a literacy volunteer who is meeting her client Raymond for the first time. Raymond is an unemployed man of color who can neither write nor read with facility. They sit down opposite each other at the table and introduce themselves. To begin their first learning session, Mary uses a test to discover at what level Raymond is reading. The test materials fold up in the middle of the table between them so that Mary can see the questions and answers, and Raymond can only see the text he has to read in order to accurately answer the questions Mary asks. Raymond reads what he can and answers the questions as best he can until he has demonstrated (and experienced) a level of consistent failure. Following the test directions, Mary then decides what "grade level" he is on and "diagnoses" his "problem." Her analysis of the test results suggests that his "phonic analysis is weak."

What understandings have been constructed in this situation? Mary has constructed an understanding of Raymond as being "a nice man who is nearly illiterate—well, reading at a low first-grade level—and whose problem is deficient phonics, particularly in medial vowels." This understanding is quite laden with affect. Mary has volunteered her time and effort in order to help another human being and she can see that Raymond really needs her help. Her understanding is colored with a certain amount of pity, but at the same time with feelings of power in the awareness that she knows more than this person, and may be able to give him the gift of literacy, which will give him access to work and perhaps to the pleasures of literature. Mary records the numbers from the test in the record book so that her supervisor or some other person who was not present at the time, can construct some understanding of Raymond and his "needs."

Raymond is also busy constructing an understanding of the situation. Although he and Mary began with a difference in social status, with each step in the process the power difference between them became greater. Raymond begins to understand that in this situation he is powerless, and even more incapable and ignorant than he thought (as incapable as a first grader). He colors this with anxiety, a certain amount of frustration at being unable to demonstrate some things which he thought he could do, a certain amount of oppression, and later perhaps some anger. He begins to understand that whatever he learns in their instructional sessions, his relationship with Mary is likely to be perpetually embarrassing and demeaning. His role will be to receive knowledge from this person to whom he must remain indebted since he has nothing to offer the one-sided relationship. He also learns that this reading stuff is even harder, less comprehensible, and less interesting than he thought, and there appears to be less reason than he thought to engage in it and learn about it.

There are consequences to these understandings that Mary and Raymond have constructed. On the basis of her diagnosis (in the medical sense), Mary begins an intensive phonics instruction program which requires Raymond to alter his dialect towards hers in order to participate in the instruction. This in turn requires him to essentially deny his cultural heritage in order to take part in the activity. On the basis of the understanding he constructs, Raymond quits the program. Mary, in self-defense, decides that Raymond is unreliable and not particularly motivated to become literate. But at the same time she has a nagging doubt about her own ability as a teacher. In other words, in the course of the evaluation interaction the participants constructed knowledge about themselves, each other, their relationship, and about the nature of the activity in which they were engaged. Their subsequent actions were guided by these understandings.

The example may seem a little extreme, but in fact similar ones occur all the time in schools. Children generally do not have open to them some of the possible responses, such as physically leaving (though they can mentally leave), but they will respond to the understanding they construct. At first glance, it may seem that group tests are immune to these problems. However, this is not true. Most of us at some point have experienced some sort of test along with the feelings that accompany it. These feelings often have to do with beliefs about our own self-worth, and are easily compounded by fears that our performance will be made public.

Group tests are a form of social interaction as well, and understandings are constructed from them and the context of their administration. Institutions are socially composed, and quite capable of conveying messages to other institutions or social groups or individuals. For example, when a standardized test is given to students to evaluate their performance and that of the teachers, the students will construct some understanding of what school is about, what reading (if it is a reading test) is about, what kind of knowledge is valued, and possibly something about themselves as learners, knowers, and who controls what. The teachers may construct knowledge about themselves, about the kind of knowledge that is valued, and about their relationship with those who are responsible for the administration of the test. For example, they may come to learn that administrators (and possibly the public) believe that teachers are not capable of monitoring their own performance or not responsible enough to do so. The largely female teaching community might construct knowledge about its relationship to the largely male community of administrators, and about the "place" of women. The administrators might construct knowledge about the quality of particular teachers, about their power over the teachers, and about their prestige in the community or the security of their jobs given the test scores. "Objective" testing can have the effect of depersonalizing the evaluation inter-action, and hence the relationship between the participants. People behave differently in personal and enduring relationships than they do in impersonal objective relationships. Evaluations are not simply outcomes, they are part of the process and product of social activity.

Many of the evaluative interactions that take place in school easily pass unnoticed. A kindergartner brings to her teacher a story she has written. The story looks like "AATLLLcpNoOWWIX" but sounds like "Yesterday we went to the beach and I went swimming with my sister and we went in a boat and caught a fish." The teacher, hoping to preserve the oral version of the story, writes it correctly underneath the child's writing. This may not be intended as an evaluative act, but *under certain circumstances* it very easily can be interpreted as one by the child—ample evidence that she did not do it right, with the outcome being a lack of desire to try it again.[20] A good analogy to this situation is when an eighteen-month-old infant speaks to us with her best attempt at language. To repeat it back to her correctly would not encourage continued conversation, which is central to development. Just responding to what she has to say will provide a correct model of the language, along with a motive to attend to it, and a set of beliefs about the uses and value of language.

ROLES

We can think about evaluation relationships in terms of the roles the partici-pants occupy. Donald Graves has termed one set of role alternatives for the evaluator as those of either an *advocate* or an *adversary*.[21] The adversary sits opposite the student in a higher chair, takes the student's writing without waiting for it to be offered, and makes little eye contact. In reading, we might add that the adversary has all the right answers and is clearly the center of the value part of the evaluation. Such a role places the student in a defensive position in response to threat, particularly ego-threat. If I have a large investment in my work and someone criticizes it, my likely response is ego-defense and entrenchment in my position, or retaliation. By comparison, for example, the response to self-evaluation is quite different and is more likely to produce change.

Consider now the role of the advocate. In Graves's view, an advocate is likely to sit next to the student, at the same height, make lots of eye contact, and wait to be offered the student's writing. In reading, the analogy holds rather well too. We might also add that the response is nonjudgmental, calling for self-evaluation. And it is not as simple as it may seem to be nonjudgmental, especially if the student is used to judgmental teachers. If that is the student's expectation, then reflective comments such as "uh-huh," or "so you feel that

. . ." are likely to be interpreted as equivalent to saying "wrong!" or "oh boy!" However, even this expectation can be overcome if the student is treated as a real, literate person in genuine dialogue. To remember what this feels like, discuss a book with another adult. Try one that you have both read, and one that only one of you has read. Reflect on the kinds of questions you asked, if you asked any, your feelings, and the nature of the whole interaction. (You might try tape-recording it some time for this purpose, but notice how the taping affects the conversation.) We have to remember that our dialogue with the students tells them who we think they are, what we think learners should do, and what we think it means to be literate (or how literate people behave).

CHAPTER 4

Evaluative Messages

The messages conveyed through evaluation interactions are very important. Even young children figure these out. They are not carried so much through what we say, but how we say it and the context in which we say it, including the nonverbal cues we provide. If we regularly praise particular children's handwriting neatness, we can say to the class until we are blue in the face that handwriting neatness is unimportant, but the students will know otherwise. Children are very good at reading nonverbal and incidental cues. Consider the very common individualized reading test procedure in which the evaluator sits opposite the student, higher up, and holds the answers the student is to match. The *Woodcock Reading Mastery Test*[22] is an example of this type of test, but the opposing position is almost universal. Rare exceptions to this are the *Concepts About Print* test and Running Records designed by Marie Clay (running records are described in more detail in Chapters 10 and 11), in which evaluator and student sit alongside each other, share the same book, and share the same activity.

John Austin talks about three aspects of linguistic communication.[23] The "locution" is the linguistic form of an utterance with its linguistic meaning. For example, in the sentence "The dog's name was Spot" words have been placed in relationship to one another in such a way as to convey a particular attributive relationship. However, in any particular context the utterance has an "illocutionary force," which is the type of social action intended by the speaker. For instance, an evaluator might have intended this sentence as a question of clarification after a child's inaudible response. However, the utterance also has a "perlocutionary force," which refers to the meaning constructed by the listener. Thus, even though the evaluator intended the sentence as a genuine question of clarification, the child may interpret it as meaning "The dog's name was Spot! Boy, are you stupid!" We might say things that we think are absolutely clear, yet the child understands them in a way quite different from what we had intended. The foundation of clear communication is basically a trusting relationship along with shared cultural knowledge. Each person must assume that the other understands something about how the other understands the situation, and that they are both after the same ends.

The cooperativeness of the communication depends on the participants' sharing a definition of the situation. Unfortunately, schools and current evaluation procedures work directly against this meeting of the minds. Rather, the adversarial nature of the interaction sets conditions for mistrust and suspicion of dishonesty.

We certainly do not want to be suspected of being untrustworthy. If we are, then the student may deliberately avoid the obvious definition of the situation and search for an alternative, more devious definition. If we think we asked a simple question like "How did you feel about the mouse?" but the student suspects us of duplicity and hears, "What am I thinking about the correct feelings you should have about the mouse," then the entire communication (and hence the evaluation) will be misleading. If we lose the trusting basis of the interaction, then all is lost. We no longer have a way of drawing reasonable conclusions about what the responses mean, but we are also likely to have done some additional damage to such intangibles as the student's self-esteem or our instructional relationship—all through the interpretations the student has made of our questions and we of her responses.

If we view evaluation as a type of social interaction, then we must begin to think about how the relationship develops between the people involved. Uri Bronfenbrenner reckons that when two people start paying attention to each other's behavior, they are likely to become engaged in the same activity together.[24] You may start by watching each other, but you tend to become involved in the same activity as a consequence. Such a relationship between a teacher and a student has an effect on the student's development. The extent of this effect is determined by the extent to which the relationship involves positive feelings towards each other and the extent to which there is a gradual shift in the balance of power in the relationship in favor of the student. Within the teacher-student evaluative interaction, the dimensions of interest are attention, reciprocity, the balance of power, and the affective relationship. Implicit in this relationship is a valuing of the child and her responses. Several terms are currently being used in the literature to reflect this valuing. Don Graves and others talk about the writing "conference." Don Holdaway talks about the "professional-client" relationship, and Tom Nicholson talks about "interviewing" and "getting alongside children."[25]

This valuing makes it possible for children to ask questions. Indeed, the frequency with which children are prepared to say, "I don't understand," or to admit as much through their questioning is probably a reasonable indicator of the health of the teaching/learning relationship for some children. The reciprocity of the relationship is critical to the assurance of the credibility of the evaluation. The evaluator's goal is to understand the subjective reality of the task and situation for the learner. This is so much easier if the learner is willing to, where possible, correct the misconceptions of this reality that the evaluator is developing.[26] The essence of the relationship is active listening. The supportive listening role that the evaluator models is what becomes internalized by the students. One type of reading involves actively listening to what the writer has to say, and constructing a meaning from it. The important thing for this type of reading is for the child to internalize this listener role, which the evaluator is modeling.

DIMENSIONS OF THE EVALUATION INTERACTION

Given that the evaluation interaction is a social interaction, how can we go about it in such a way that it maximizes the benefits for all concerned? To begin with, I must clarify the directions in which I consider "maximum benefits" to be found. I will be looking for interactions that produce greater reflectiveness or self-evaluation, greater confidence and commitment to proceed, and increased understanding of the learner and learned by both parties. At the same time I think it important that trust be maintained between the participants. Some of these issues will appear again in other chapters, particularly the chapter on talking and listening.

Power and Relationship

It is very important to try to balance the power in the evaluation interaction, to try to minimize its importance, and to acknowledge whatever power differential is unavoidable. There are some simple principles that can help accomplish this.

To begin with, body posture and orientation say a lot. A more powerful status is taken by standing or sitting in a higher position, and emphasized by standing with hands on hips or with arms folded, for example. Avoid these postures. Sitting next to someone is more comfortable and less confrontational than sitting opposite. Thus it is important to sit next to each other rather than across from each other in most interactions to minimize differences in power status. Nonetheless, there *is* a power difference between teacher and student in the classroom. The trick is that this difference need apply only to certain domains and in certain situations. In the role of maintaining physical and emotional safety in the classroom, the teacher has a clearly dominant position. Steps can be taken to minimize this problem through clear community-agreed-upon rules and through maximizing community responsibility. Under most other situations, the relative power positions are up for negotiation. Power differences can be minimized by treating students' views as seriously as you expect them to treat yours.

Questioning is a common activity for teachers in order to gather information. Indeed, the format of testing and instruction that is based on it (such as basal readers) demands extensive questioning. However, questions have at least two different sides to them. One is to request information; the other is to demand a response. Only when children consider the question genuine do they focus on the request for information. If there is a likelihood that the question will be misinterpreted, then we can help students to focus on the information request by providing them with sufficient reason for our interest in their response. Maximizing the trusting relationship also goes a long way. In other words we are likely to get a better response to a question if the student understands and accepts our need for, or genuine interest in, the information requested.

It is worth remembering, too, that questioning is not the only way to get information, and giving information can frequently be better. For example, to respond to a student's writing with "The part in the middle about the horse made me feel very sad, but I felt a bit confused about the part where you were going home," can have a more helpful effect on the student's writing than asking, "Why did you write the part about going home in that way?" The statement at once gives a reason for clarification and shows respect for the writer and the piece of writing without necessarily invoking a power differential.

Timing and Taking Turns

Timing is a big thing for people. When two people talk to one another, each has to decide when the other has finished taking his turn. There are cultural differences in the times people will wait for further comment, and there are substantial individual differences within cultures. Each of us also waits a different amount of time before responding, depending on our interpretation of the other person and the social situation we are in. For example, teachers are generally more prepared to wait longer for responses from students who are seen as more able than for those who are seen as less able. This can easily be interpreted by the student as an indication of her self-worth, or expected ability to respond. Her interpretation is likely to be more or less accurate.

When we do not allow the student enough time to respond, we adopt a more dominant position. This will set students up to say little, be defensive, and often enough to feel inadequate. So it is important to take your time with students—to wait that extra few seconds for a response to your statement or question. This can be hard, especially with students who are not doing well. We often are inclined to jump quickly to the conclusion that such students will not be able to respond, and with best intentions we jump in quickly to save them from embarrassment, thereby rendering them powerless. On the other hand, timing is a very fine balance. No one likes to be left with the floor when there really is no response. This makes it imperative that we reduce the likelihood of such situations arising, and that the relationship allow the student to get out of such situations—for example, by saying "I don't understand." In other words, "I don't understand" must be an obviously valued, and not socially punished, response.

One other aspect of turn-taking seems critical to me. As I have already noted, most evaluation takes place in the classroom. That means that other students are present. But I have also implied that a great deal of the important evaluation interactions must be one-to-one. A common problem we have when attempting such interactions is that other children suddenly realize that they need our attention immediately. If we are engaged in an activity with an individual child—a reading or writing conference or whatever—and we allow ourselves to be interrupted by another child, then the child with whom we had been engaged can easily feel that we do not value the interaction with him. It also breaks the flow of the conference in which you were engaged. That is a great loss. We and our students operate optimally when there is total involvement in an activity. It is during those times of involvement that we lose any ego-defenses, because we are totally taken up by the activity—we are "into it." It is very important, then, to set conditions so that the other children can and will continue to be independent and to resolve their difficulties without interrupting the conference you are having. Generally, explaining this to the students and then assiduously avoiding even acknowledging their presence when they try to interrupt will develop independence quite quickly. It also helps if each student knows that he will get his personal time with the teacher, because it is scheduled, and that he does not have to compete for this attention.

In an evaluation situation, the social interaction itself can alter the timing of responses that in turn alter the interaction itself. Ann McGill-Franzen and Peter McDermott have provided a particularly clear example of this in an analysis of the timing of interactions between an adult and a student in a test situation.[27] The evaluator was "administering" a test (the *Diagnostic Reading Scales* by George Spache) to a young student. The test involves a series of subtests and requires oral and silent reading. The major finding of the study is that as the pair proceeded through the test, the timing of the adult's responses to the child's activity became increasingly rapid. It seems that as the adult began to feel that the task was becoming more difficult, he gave the child the answer or a prompt with increasing speed. As the examiner increased assistance, the student began waiting longer for assistance instead of making an attempt, thus leading to an increased error score. The main point made by this piece of research is that the ultimate diagnosis was essentially "negotiated" by the adult and the child through their interaction, and it is essentially a performance shaped by interpretations, expectations, and behaviors on both sides.

Making Meaning

Whenever we interact with a student, we send messages, or rather the student constructs meaning from what we say and do. What the student constructs is strongly determined by his perception of our relationship and of the context. For example, it is common practice to ask students "factual" questions about what they just read out loud to the teacher. The teacher responds with "good" or "correct" or "no." This is clearly a testing situation in which there is an obvious power differential. The intent is obviously to find out if the student got THE meaning. Students are likely to thus come to understand that the teacher has access to the single privileged meaning that is in the text. Such a view of reading eliminates the basis for dialogue about the book or story. Such questions can also tell the student that the question to which they responded was not a genuine question, since the teacher already had the answer, and that probably most of the other questions will not be genuine either and should be responded to as test questions with their implicit power differential and limited latitude of response. At the same time, the timing of our response tells the student something about our opinion of their ability to respond.

Of course many students come from homes in which asking such questions is considered normal even for trustworthy parents.[28] These students may not interpret such questions as indicating anything to do with trust. An interesting example of these issues is when teachers ask children for a "retelling" of a story which has either just been read out loud to the teacher, or which the student knows the teacher has read. More capable readers are inclined to give fairly complete and organized retellings, whereas less capable readers do not. However, as Connie Bridge and her colleagues have shown, this may not mean that the child does not have the information to do so, since he can supply nearly half as much information again when directly asked for it.[29] It seems likely that the less able readers, many of whom come from a different social class from the teacher and the more capable readers, respond to the retelling request as they would to a normal social interaction about a common experience. More able readers appear to understand that this is a particular form of social interaction—a test—that has a different set of rules. They do not find this particularly threatening since they are commonly successful in such situations.

It seems that if a student understands that the situation is a test situation, clearly marked off from other social interactions, there is a greater chance of getting useful information in both testing and non-testing situations. This will be particularly so if the test situation is not threatening, and is continually overtly being turned over to the student as a self-checking activity that can be shown to be of personal benefit to the student. The best advice seems to be to simply try to be straightforward and genuine, and always an advocate for the child as an independent learner.

CHAPTER 5

The Bases and Consequences of Evaluation by Self and Others

I guess I could be called a "late bloomer" (a Leo too).[30] My youthful academic career was not healthy for quite a long time. Figure 5.1 is a copy of the last of my high school report cards. Some years after I received that report card, at the insistence of my younger brother, I reluctantly attended a high school reunion. My math teacher, a Scotswoman, a little tipsy, approached a small group of us, most of whom had been in her class. She asked us each in turn what we were now doing. At the time I was teaching undergraduate statistics—not very well— but that was what I was doing. Her amused response was "Pull my other leg, it's got bells on it."

I cannot blame her or the other teachers for their evaluations, written or oral. They were trained in particular ways and were caught in a system that was not conducive to alternative views of evaluation. And I was not the kind of student that inspires teachers to look for positive attributes. There was a time in my schooling (around eighth grade) when the most important evaluation for me, and the rest of my group, was the number of notches in my belt, which indicated the number of times I had been caned by the principal or vice-principal. By the end of high school my criteria had changed. I had moved on to more inventive pranks. My evaluation of my schooling career was actually quite positive, based on the principal's call to my parents the night before the graduation ceremony asking for their assurance that I would not pull any pranks at the ceremony. How could I count that as a failure?

Alas, others were looking at my *academic* performance as an indicator of the success of my schooling (or rather as an indicator of *my* success in schooling). They took my grades to be important indicators of my academic prospects. Things did not improve quickly either. Ultimately, the University of Wisconsin at Madison rejected my application to their doctoral program in Educational Psychology because of my undergraduate grades. Indeed, I too evaluated myself academically in similar terms. I had applied to do doctoral work only because when I returned to the university for graduate work after teaching, my advisors believed that I was capable of doing doctoral work and had so advised me.[31] I applied to doctoral programs out of a sense of responsibility to them with no expectation of being successful.

The point of this story is that others evaluate us and we evaluate ourselves, and the two evaluations are related to one another, sometimes in subtle ways.[32]

HUTT VALLEY HIGH SCHOOL

REPORT FOR ½-Year ENDING _13 Dec. 1968_   NAME: _Peter H. Johnston_

Half-days Absent: ___6.___   FORM: ___6A___

	Number in Form	Place in Form	Term Marks	Exam. Marks	Remarks	
English	15	14	41	48	Has difficulty getting his good ideas down on paper.	ItH.
French						
German						
Latin						
Greek						
History						
Geography						
Mathematics	19	18	37	20	Has made little effort to improve this subject.	VP
Additional Mathematics						
Physics	32	31	26	22	Not a good effort.	hLh.
Biology	10	8	84/44	43	Appears to have made little effort. Results are poor	AM
Chemistry	13	9	55	31	Often somewhat puzzled, but has made some genuine attempt	DJC
Bookkeeping						
Economics						
Com. Law						
Physical Ed.						

Conduct: _____

General Comments: _____

Form Master/Mistress: _HJM Henderson_   _JJ McLea_ Principal

Figure 5.1. My final high school report card. Relevant names have been removed to protect the relatively innocent.

Sometimes, for survival, we reject the criteria others apply to us, but we usually reject more than just the criteria. In the long run, the most critical evaluation for any learner—teacher or student—is self-evaluation. When we evaluate others' literate activity, we need to be concerned about how our evaluations impact upon their evaluations of themselves and their learning. In our classrooms we need to be helping children to become independent, literate individuals. Central to both independence and literacy is the ability to monitor and evaluate one's own literate activity and to reflect on what that activity and changes in it mean. When children come to our university reading lab, a very common feature of their reading and writing is their failure to monitor and self-correct. As soon as they attempt a word, they turn to the tutor to see if they did it right. They do not feel capable of evaluating their own responses. When these children write a first draft, it is final.

Our efforts to evaluate should be designed to develop and encourage self-evaluation, for several reasons. First, such independence in literate activity is part of our long-term goal. Second, it is eventually more efficient if the children are self-evaluating since it saves our having to worry about evaluation to the same extent. Third, self-discovered problems are most amenable to change since they are "owned." In other words, they must be dealt with in order for us to become more fully who we are. Fourth, when you discover a problem for yourself, there is a greater likelihood of responding to it constructively than when someone else points it out. When someone else pokes holes in your teaching, if you have any insecurities, your first response is likely to be defensiveness, entrenchment, and rejection of the other person. Fifth, unless a student is self-evaluating, he may develop a misconception or an inefficient strategy that we do not notice; and since he is not keeping track of the coherence or efficiency of his reading, he may practice it to the level of automation. Automated processes are hard to change.

How can we help students (and ourselves) to become good self-evaluators? To begin with, let us look at the obstacles to self-evaluation. We can readily prevent children from self-evaluating. If we continually correct them as soon as they make errors, we will prevent them from reflecting on their responses. In reading, when a child becomes stuck on a word or reads it incorrectly, if we immediately leap in and give the correct response, we will deprive the student of the opportunity for self-correction, and he will gradually become passive in this respect.[33] If we continually make it clear that students are incapable of self-correcting, that we have the correct way and theirs is simply a poor imitation, they will always look to us for evaluation. In a way, they will evaluate themselves as being incapable of that function. Thus, our way of interacting with the student can make him self-evaluative or not.

ENCOURAGING SELF-EVALUATION

We can encourage self-evaluation by recognizing it. When a student becomes aware of a problem, we can say, "I like the way you noticed that yourself. That is a sign of a good writer." Praise is a tricky thing really. In this case we might be considered to be giving praise, but most importantly the information conveyed is that self-evaluation is important to becoming a better writer. General praise such as "Good work," "correct," and so forth, mostly makes it clear that you hold the criteria for what counts, and often helps children base their motivation in external rewards. They read for praise rather than for what the reading does to them and for them along the way.[34]

Pointing out the effectiveness on an audience, or the consequences of particular strategies, or the value of the feelings aroused by the reading, is much more important than the praise itself. When discussing a student's writing, it is different to say "I don't understand this part here," or "These two parts seem to be in conflict. What happened after you rode down the hill?" than to say "Clarify these terms." The latter type of comment does not suggest reflection at all. Neither does it call forth any existing reflection within the framework of responsive literate communication.

We can encourage self-evaluation by encouraging learners to have a go, to predict, and to check their predictions, attempts, and so forth. Seeking students' advice about your own writing will also have a salutary effect—for example, presenting students with two versions you have written, asking for advice on which they prefer and why. Similarly, we can encourage self-evaluation through encouraging peer dialogue and making it easier to self-evaluate than to consult peers, and easier to consult peers than to consult adults. In other words, making the consequences of these selections favor self-evaluation, and making the costs (such as delays) favor it too.

Self-evaluation can be encouraged within a relationship by reflective responses that turn questions back to learners. Jack Easley and Russell Zwoyer talk about "questions that teach."[35] For example, when a student looks to me for evaluation, I might ask, "What do you think?" Of course if she hazards an opinion to which I respond "wrong" or something similar, she is likely to avoid such invitations next time and to feel insecure in her self-evaluations. A question such as "How could we check whether that is correct?" might provide more assistance since it opens up one or more strategies for self-checking. The student's response is also likely to give us information about the strategies which the learner has available. In other words, such questions do double duty. They prompt self-evaluation and also tell us what strategies the student has available.

Reflective questions can at once prompt and focus self-evaluation. For example, Marie Clay suggests prompting in children's oral reading with "Does that make sense?" or "Can we say it that way?" or "You said ———. What letters would you expect to be there?" or "Does that look right?" These reflective questions focus the child's attention on sense, structure, print detail, and letter-sound relationships respectively. If a child does not monitor his reading to be sure it is making sense, it will be helpful to ask him to reflect on the sense. However, asking, "Does that make sense to you?" only when it does not make sense is exactly the same as saying, "That does not make sense!" Consequently, it is important to ask such questions when it does and when it does not make sense. It is also important that the student understand what is meant by "making sense."

When children are encouraged to be reflective about their learning they become able to talk about it. Thus, Jane Hansen has been able to ask children,

"What have you learned most recently in writing?" and "What are you work-ing on next?" and they have been able to talk intelligently about these things.[36] Even quite young children are able to write such things down. Indeed, there is little reason why children cannot write at least half of their own report cards, and several reasons why it would be advantageous. It would blatantly place value on self-evaluation, and it would make available children's self-evaluation criteria for discussion with the teacher.

Reflectiveness can also be overtly valued by making portfolios a central part of classroom evaluation. A portfolio can include items from the semester (year, quarter) selected by the student to represent her development. Each item can have attached to it a statement of why it is important, or what it represents in terms of her development. This gives the teacher information about what the student values, and *requires* the student to be reflective. In doing so it encour-ages greater commitment.

But in order for children to become self-evaluating, they must feel them-selves to be able knowers and evaluators. As teachers, the way we talk can make us appear to have all the knowledge and appear to be the all-powerful final ar-biters, or it can suggest that the children are knowledgeable and able judges of their own learning. For students to be self-critical and to develop reflective com-mitment to their reading or writing, they need to have confidence and self-respect, and they need to value their own knowledge. These conditions are likely to occur only when children feel that they have something to contribute. In other words, they must feel that their experience is important and worth talking about. This feeling tends to come when people actually listen to them. They must feel that their ideas are not less valuable than those of the teacher or their peers. This arises most commonly when it is agreed that multiple perspectives are possible. From such a position, the teacher can help the student develop "intelligent unrest" from which learning is most likely to take place.[37] But a student must first feel intelligent. Thus evaluations must emphasize the positive aspects of responses. This emphasis builds a positive basis for the relationship and allows the learner to attend to problems from a position of strength.

At the same time, it is easier to help students to focus on the positive if there is a lot of positive. In other words, ensuring that evaluations take place in, or directly following, an activity in which the student can perform expertly is very important. This is why it is helpful always to have students begin any read-ing evaluation sessions reading material which they can read confidently. And I don't mean a brief experience of success followed by extensive difficulty. The majority of a session that is specifically concerned with evaluation should be spent engaged in activities the child can manage more or less comfortably. Marie Clay, in describing tutoring sessions focusing on accelerating the reading growth of children experiencing difficulty with beginning reading, talks about spending several sessions "roaming the known."[38] By this she means engaging the student in activities that will require no teacher intervention—in which the student explores and becomes more comfortable with what he already knows and can do. This is sage advice.

THE REFLECTIVE LENS

But suppose we manage to help children become serious self-evaluators. There is still a hitch. When we look in a mirror, many things influence what we see. The kind of mirror we use makes a difference in what we see. Sometimes we end up looking into distorting mirrors like the ones at fairgrounds that make us look fat, thin, or dumbbell-shaped. Sometimes the mirror is small and lets us see only bits at a time. Sometimes it is hanging on a wall leaning forward, making our feet small and our head big. Reflection is rarely through a perfect full-length mirror; and even if it is, we rarely see ourselves that way. In reflecting on our teaching practice, we focus on certain aspects: sometimes, self-consciously, we end up focusing on the pimple on our nose or the mole on our neck, not even seeing the rest of the image. It rather depends on whether we are going on a first date with a person we think is perfect or whether we are going out to build a fence in the backyard: whether the principal is observing us or whether a trainee teacher is observing us. In other words, the tools we choose to help us reflect reveal and hide aspects of ourselves to us, and the context in which we view ourselves makes a difference to what we see. But serious distortions can easily occur. Anorexics can see themselves as fat regardless of the mirror in which they view themselves.

The focus of our reflection is determined by many factors, but chief among them appears to be the way others interact with us. If we happen to have only one arm and that is the first thing everybody notices and people tend to treat us as disabled, then this feature is likely to dominate our view of ourselves. It is one thing to be a *blind person* who reads and quite another to be a *reader* who happens to be blind. In writing, if the major feedback we get focuses on neatness, then that is likely to be distorted into the largest part of the image we see— rather like the teenager going on a date whose pinhead pimple has expanded in his mind to the size of quarter. If he is not confident in the first place, this distortion may cause him to cancel the date.

As learners we can focus on many different things. For example, we can focus on the ways we went about doing an activity. We may pay particular attention to the specific strategies we used to solve a writing problem. Alternatively, we can focus on our feelings. For example, we might remember how terrifying it was to read our piece of writing to the class. Or we might focus on how others responded to our piece of writing, or how it compared to the writings of others. Each of these different foci is possible, and our responses to children influence quite strongly the shape of the mirror they hold up to themselves. Each of these different criteria has consequences for the student's subsequent motivation, their perception of the difficulty of the activity, and the way they go about it in the future.

Within our view of literate activity, we can try to encourage students to reflect on their work through a thoughtful, non-normative understanding of literate activity. We can try to see in detail what the student has done, and hear the motives and feelings that come with it. From this we help the student attribute to himself the best that is there. Nel Noddings, puts this most clearly when she says:

> What the teacher reflects to [the student] continually is the best possible picture consonant with reality. She does not reflect fantasy nor conjure up "expectations" as strategies. She meets him as he is and finds something admirable and, as a result, he may find the strength to become even more admirable.[39]

CHAPTER 6

Self-Evaluation: Conditions of Reflectiveness

Self-evaluation usually involves bringing activities to consciousness to examine them. But there can be one small problem with this. If I become highly conscious of my typing while I am typing, my fingers tend to trip over one another. Conscious awareness can be incompatible with fluent complex activity—like reading or writing, for example, or intense discussion such as might occur in a classroom. As anyone who works on computers or microcomputers knows, the machines occasionally "crash" or go "down" or "become inoperative." The only hedge against this is frequently saving (making a copy of) the file you are working on. In that way if the machine destroys your work, it destroys only the part that has not yet been saved. I work on a wretched machine that happens to quit on me frequently. So I try to save my work often. However, as fate would have it, when I am doing my best work, my most creative work, I am totally taken up by the composing activity. I might work for an hour with such involvement that the time seems like five minutes. In accordance with Murphy's Law, after fifty-nine minutes the machine quits, and I lose all my work. During those fifty-nine minutes, however, my involvement has been such that I have been unable to maintain a part of myself as a "watcher" whose job it is to step back and reflect on my work and to remind me to save. Thus in some ways involvement and conscious reflection can be temporarily in opposition. Reflection then tends to occur after the fact. "I should have saved." This reflection is often with the clearest of visions—20/20 or better.

We can cripple children as learners by preventing them from self-evaluating. On the other hand, we can help children become self-evaluators, but help them set crippling standards for themselves that make them repeatedly define themselves as having failed, or worse, as being failures. But we can also cripple them by making them so reflective that they lose integration of their activity. Only so many things can be reflected upon at once without overwhelming the learner. This is just as true for teacher learners as for student learners.

We have only limited control over most of these factors. Among other things, some children are simply more compulsive than others. There are differences between children relevant to birth order in the family and to many other factors outside a teacher's control. A child who learns about the separate sounds that make up spoken words, and about print detail, before muscle development allows easy control of a pen, can easily set for himself evaluation criteria that will make writing particularly frustrating. A child who is simply unaware of that level of detail may find it easier to set more manageable performance criteria.

Similarly if teachers feel that there is only one way to teach, that there is a single correct way to evaluate progress, then they will be very likely to feel that they do not have it, but that someone else does, or at least that one of their colleagues is better at it. This breeds insecurity, which tends to deprive them of the conditions necessary to talk comfortably about their own practice and to be self-critical. Insecurity produces defensiveness and, in turn, back-biting which is destructive in every way. It must be clearly understood that *everyone* can improve their teaching practice and that there are many ways to do a good job. This is exactly what we would want our students to understand about their literate activity. Teaching is like writing a novel. There is more than one good thing to write about and there is more than one good way to write about it.

REFLECTION IN ACTION

It is also important that there be models against which to compare one's own practice. Some of our criteria for evaluating our writing come from the writing of others that we read. Some of the criteria for evaluating our teaching come from our observation of other teachers' teaching. The models need not be "better" in any sense, just different. It is the juxtaposition of one's own practice against someone else's that produces the tension needed to rethink, especially when there is a situation for dialogue about the differences and similarities and the theory underlying them. Usually just videotaping my own teaching produces a situation in which what I think I am doing is juxtaposed against what I see myself doing, and that is enough to produce change. Actually, I often don't even need to listen to or watch the tape. Just being aware that the machine is running causes part of me to step outside myself and observe while I am teaching. This situation has the effect of making some parts of our activity that are normally automatic and not in our awareness, available for conscious reflection. In a way this awareness is like the awareness children develop about language that assists them so much in their learning to read and write—when language stops simply being the window through which they view the world and they actually become aware of the presence of the glass in the window: the language itself. Similarly we become aware of our teaching practice as an object of study and reflection.

The most common way in which this ''reflection in action'' comes about is when something we do results in something we did not expect. Normally, we predict what will happen, without being conscious of doing so; and when it happens just as we predicted, we carry on without thinking about it. However, surprise, whether pleasant or unpleasant, often brings to awareness something we had previously left unexamined. If we create situations in our schools in which teachers cannot afford to be surprised, then they will not look for surprise. The same is true for children. If classrooms do not allow the savoring and studying of surprise, then opportunities for reflective self-evaluation will be lost.

Part of the self-evaluation process involves finding other ways to make automatic activity, things we now do without thinking, conscious or nonautomatic. Becoming aware of our practice through our own eyes is very important, and just inspecting our practice from that perspective and aiming for coherence between our beliefs and practice can also be facilitated by having a colleague visit our classroom and observe. I recall having a friend visit my classroom and watch me teach. While she was in the classroom, part of me watched myself teach through her eyes. It was not necessary for her to say anything negative about my teaching for me to see grounds for improvement. Knowing her and her approach to teaching and watching myself through that lens gave me a different image of my own practice. In a way it gave me a greater depth of vision—essentially stereoscopic vision.

A further perspective can be added if I have to talk to my colleagues about a video of my practice. In that case I view the video of my practice in a slightly different way, and the need to talk about my practice helps it to have greater coherence for me. I am most likely to be secure about this if I can choose the particular part of a video I wish to show and talk about. Indeed, the process of deciding which section to show and how to discuss it is a learning experience, in part because we must approach our own work from the perspective of a new audience. We might take this concept of audience and look at self-evaluation through that metaphor. Good writers write with an internalized idea of their audience, which they gather either from numerous responses from their audience or from knowing well particular people whose responses they can imagine. Teaching, as I note elsewhere in this book, is a composing activity in which we also can engage in revising and editing our efforts. We build our compositions from the collected experiences we have had in the past.

Having a colleague come in to observe our teaching gives us a particular kind of audience—one that is detached somewhat from the assumptions that make up our lens, and one that has comparable status to ourselves. This audience is also a reciprocal audience. If we have put our necks on the line for them to watch us, they must be open to the same—''You show me yours and I'll show you mine." In a way, as I have tried to explain, it is more a case of "You show me mine and I'll show you yours." But there are other audiences too. Most important, of course, are the children. The context we set in the classroom, and the extent to which we encourage them to think about how the learning community operates, will determine how overtly they give us our feedback. Figure 6.1

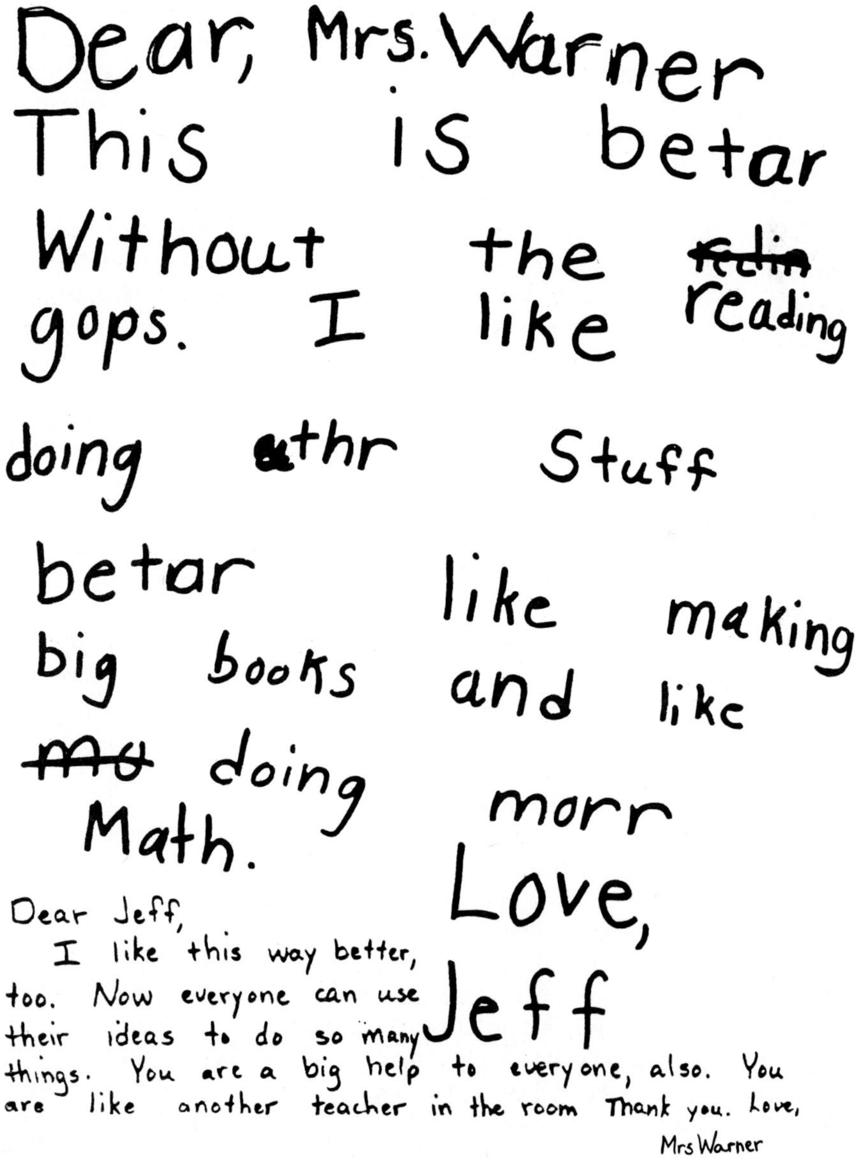

Dear, Mrs. Warner
This is betar
Without the ~~fcdin~~ reading
gops. I like
doing ~~a~~thr Stuff
betar like making
big books and like
~~And~~ doing morr
Math. Love,
Jeff

Dear Jeff,
  I like this way better, too. Now everyone can use their ideas to do so many things. You are a big help to everyone, also. You are like another teacher in the room. Thank you. Love,
Mrs Warner

Figure 6.1. A letter from a first-grade student to his teacher commenting on a change in classroom practice, and his teacher's response.

is an example of the feedback that Trudy Warner, a first-grade teacher, received from her students when she switched from using a basal reader and grouping to basing her program on children's writing and their choice of children's literature. The letter gives a clear evaluation of the change in classroom procedures. Trudy and her students freely write letters to one another and also have a discussion wall for writing things on. Trudy's response in the letter is a good example of the type of response that will maintain extensive and informative dialogues. In the chapter on talking and listening I expand on these conditions.

Sometimes getting children to take the step of reading their own work out loud to themselves helps them to hear things they hadn't heard before. We can help them remember to do this by having a little list in their folders or on the classroom wall which includes this strategy. Similarly, we often forget to read our own teaching aloud to ourselves (or perhaps watch a videotape) before being observed by an outside audience. We often forget the outside audience step too, of course, except when an observation by an administrator is required. Such conditions are less than optimal for change, especially given the fact that the administrator is almost certainly less qualified to observe, let alone pass judgment on, your teaching practice than is a competent teaching colleague or yourself.

If you keep a journal about your own teaching practice, you almost cannot help being reflective. Whenever we write down something that is on our mind, it allows us to take a step back from it and view it from another angle. Thus if you are having trouble with a student in your class, write down what the problem is, in terms of what you see, and your feelings, so that you can share the problem with a colleague. But you may find that simply writing it down helps you think your way through the problem. Indeed, the student with whom you are having a problem is very possibly classified, or going to be classified, as "learning disabled." Such students are notoriously unreflective and impulsive. Involving them in writing is a powerful way to influence their reflectiveness.

OTHER CONTEXTS FOR EVALUATION

Different contexts make self-evaluation more or less likely to occur, and alter the focus of the evaluation in important ways. For example, when children have writing folders in which they collect their writing, they are encouraged to examine their own development simply by the presence and use of the collection. They will be confronted with more and less successful efforts that are not simply good or bad, but each of which has good features and bad features. Indeed, we can obtain great insight into children's evaluative criteria by asking them to describe to us why they rejected certain pieces of writing. These pieces have already been removed from ego-involvement, and the criteria are much easier to talk about. Indeed, talking about it can help the students to clarify their criteria for themselves and think about ways to carry the work past those criteria. We can certainly encourage children to reflect upon their own work and how and why it changes. Teachers can make their own criteria more explicit and available for reflection by trading students' writing folders with another (trusted) teacher and discussing what they each see in the writing.

Competitive contexts, on the other hand, reduce the likelihood of reflection. When reflection occurs, it is rendered useless because it focuses on aspects of learning that are irrelevant to development. In competitive contexts, learners do not consider their own previous performance, and they concern themselves less with the process than with the outcome.[40] But it is reflection on the *process* that will help them to improve their performance. This is true for teachers and for students. The ego-threatening situation produced by competitive contexts has nothing to recommend it, yet the assessment systems used in schools, basal readers, and the standardized tests invariably produce competitive contexts by reducing literacy to simplistic linear scales.[41] Tests and basals are not the only way to produce competitive contexts. Valuing the best interpretation, the most books, the hardest books, the longest books, or the longest writing will have the same consequences in a classroom filled with children's literature.

In many ways, reflectiveness, or self evaluation, is critical to being an independent learner. Failure to monitor your own progress means that you are dependent upon someone else for your learning. Any process, and that includes learning processes, needs a feedback system to give it direction. If the feedback system is taken away, then the process is without guidance and is dependent on someone else to provide that guidance. It is thus critical that children monitor their own activity and reflect on what it means. Similarly we teachers must monitor our own teaching and reflect upon it to improve it.

CHAPTER 7

What Makes Literate Activity Easy or Difficult?

It is possible to construct not only experimental studies but "real-life" situations that make people (or pigeons, for that matter) look stupid or clever, generative or passive, combinatorial or rote.

Jerome Bruner

An evaluation expert must know how to set up situations in which students will behave in their most literate ways, and then describe these ways and the context and materials that helped to produce them. In order to have a learner perform like an expert, an activity must be selected that she can manage adequately. It would not be a good idea, in general, to ask a first grader to read from a college physics book so we could discover how she went about reading. There are several ways in which this relative level of difficulty can be altered. These and their consequences are the focus of this chapter and the next.

READABILITY

A major problem to which teachers and other researchers have sought solutions is "How can I tell how difficult this text is so that I can find easy enough material for my student?" Readability formulae were invented in the 1920s in a simplistic attempt to solve this problem.[42] The idea was that if we can test a student and find out how difficult a text she can read, and if we have measures of how difficult the texts really are, then we can match student and text perfectly. A 3.3 grade-level text should fit a 3.3 grade-level student, and a 3.1 grade-level text should be easy reading for her. On the surface, this idea is intuitively appealing. However, I will try to show that it has little to offer us.

The recipe for making a readability formula is as follows. First, select a set of texts that seem more or less difficult from one another. If you want your formula to work well, choose texts that range from extremely easy to extremely difficult. Second, have a large number of people read these texts and get some measure of their ability to read them. The wider the range in age, the better your results will appear. The reading measure will usually be either comprehension questions or cloze (fill in the missing word) activities. Third, describe the texts with as many different numerical indicators as possible. You will need measures of word difficulty, sentence complexity, and any other factors that might seem important. For example, you might include the number of:

    words per sentence
    letters per word or sentence
    syllables per word or sentence
    polysyllabic words
    low frequency words (not on high frequency word lists)
    percentage of words over a certain number of letters
    abstract words
    pronominal modifiers per 100 words

Now feed all this information into a computer and ask it to find out which set of these numerical indicators will best predict people's scores on the comprehension questions or cloze test. This will give you a formula like:[43]

$$\text{Grade Level} = 0.39(\text{average words per sentence}) + 11.8(\text{average syllables per word}) - 15.59$$

Some states still use formulae such as this to decide whether or not basal reading companies have made their reading materials at the appropriate level of difficulty. The U.S. military services also use such formulae to decide whether their suppliers are writing manuals that are easy enough for the armed forces to read.[44] We can also find printed on the cover of many children's paperback books a grade-level indicator based on these formulae so that, for example, as an eighth grader I will know what I should and should not be able to read.

    The general notion behind readability formulae makes so much intuitive sense to so many people that it seems almost foolish to question it. It is so logical and scientific. Indeed, these formulae, applied to books in general can produce a rank ordering of difficulty that will apply to the *average* performance of a large number of people who are reading things in order to answer questions about them. Unfortunately, there are large differences between individuals, so that for any two individuals the ordering might be quite different. This is particularly true in kindergarten and grade one. It is one thing to talk about an average level of difficulty for a large number of students and quite another to apply that ordering to a particular student. It requires arguing *ceteris parabis—all else being equal*—which is simply never the case between individual students. This and other problems with readability formulae will become apparent presently as I describe the numerous factors that cannot fit into formulae.

THE RESPONSIBILITY OF CHOICE

In spite of the well-documented problems with readability formulae and tests,[45] their rationale makes so much sense that we keep thinking there must be a way to do it right. But even if it were possible or sensible to have some test provide a clear measure of a child's reading "level" and to measure readability "levels" of books accurately, it would be inefficient and likely to produce too many problems.[46] Besides, it is simply too much responsibility for the teacher to bear. Currently, too many children are misplaced on materials that are far too difficult for them or far too easy. The most likely to be misplaced are the less able students, who are generally placed on material that is too difficult.[47] Indeed I have heard principals assert that every student in their schools reads grade-level material. They are not allowed to read off grade-level. Apart from being inhumane, this is a terrible misunderstanding.

Another way to match readers with texts is to have the student try the book and either listen to his oral reading or simply ask him whether or not it is too difficult. Alternatively we could use the library model and just let students choose their own texts. This seems almost too simple to be taken seriously. The diagram shown in Figure 7.1 gives some idea of the practical comparison between the approaches to matching a reader with a text.

How did we get ourselves and our students into such a fix? The belief that children are incapable of making reasonable choices and knowing what's good for them has been pervasive for a very long time. It fits very well with the belief that teachers have the knowledge that they are to give to children and that children are sitting around waiting to absorb. Suppose the local librarian took it upon himself to determine the reading levels of all patrons before allowing them to take out books (which of course would have to have readability indices to match)! This plan would not be received well by the general public. Yet we try desperately to accomplish this match in schools. It turns out that, by and large, children are quite good at selecting books of an appropriate level of difficulty if they are given the chance and the options.[48] Actually, if a book is too easy, a child is likely to get bored and put it down. If a book is too hard, the child is likely to get frustrated and put it down. The trick is to keep track of what *is* being read, and to make sure that when one book is put down another is picked up. There are, of course, conditions under which children will make unsatisfactory choices, and I will discuss these in the chapter on choosing and erring.

WHAT MAKES LITERATE ACTIVITY EASY

It is helpful to understand why an activity is more or less difficult for a student, and how to make it more or less easy. For example, Terry was asked, "How do you decide what books to read?" His response included that it has to be "easy, but not too easy," and that it should have "not too many words on the pages—and a few pictures to make it interesting." When asked about type of book, he

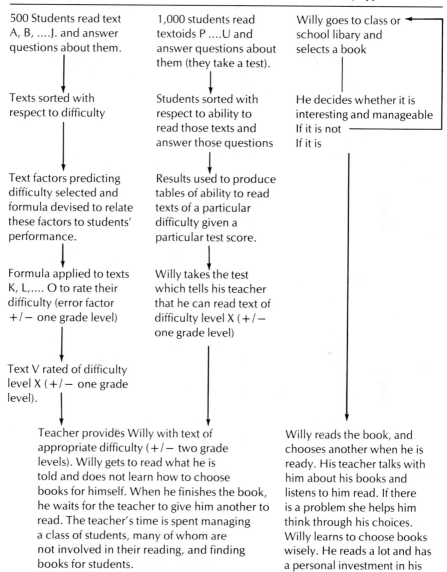

| | **Readability Approach** | | **Library Approach** |

500 Students read text A, B, ...J. and answer questions about them.

1,000 students read textoids P ....U and answer questions about them (they take a test).

Willy goes to class or school libary and selects a book

Texts sorted with respect to difficulty

Students sorted with respect to ability to read those texts and answer those questions

He decides whether it is interesting and manageable
If it is not
If it is

Text factors predicting difficulty selected and formula devised to relate these factors to students' performance.

Results used to produce tables of ability to read texts of a particular difficulty given a particular test score.

Formula applied to texts K, L,.... O to rate their difficulty (error factor +/− one grade level)

Willy takes the test which tells his teacher that he can read text of difficulty level X (+/− one grade level)

Text V rated of difficulty level X (+/− one grade level).

Teacher provides Willy with text of appropriate difficulty (+/− two grade levels). Willy gets to read what he is told and does not learn how to choose books for himself. When he finishes the book, he waits for the teacher to give him another to read. The teacher's time is spent managing a class of students, many of whom are not involved in their reading, and finding books for students.

Willy reads the book, and chooses another when he is ready. His teacher talks with him about his books and listens to him read. If there is a problem she helps him think through his choices. Willy learns to choose books wisely. He reads a lot and has a personal investment in his reading.

Figure 7.1.   A comparison of two approaches to the selection of books for children to read.

said, "Oh, less than 100 pages maybe, but with chapters so it would look hard. . . . It has to look like the books the other kids are reading, but I'll really know it's easy enough for me."[49]

As a second example, Steven was not enjoying writing at school. His writing was done in booklets which the teacher had made up. He mentioned his dislike to his teacher and she asked him why. He said that it was just too much to write. "There are too many pages." His teacher, discovering the confusion, pointed out that he did not have to fill all of the pages; he had to write only what he wanted to write. Later when the children were asked what they had learned in writing that day, the children offered all sorts of suggestions, but Steven said, "I learned that writing is fun." The apparently small change in his concept of the goal of the activity was Copernican in its consequences. For a while it was popular to talk about "time on task." Indeed, in some circles it still is. But children, as many have noted, are always on task. The important question is, what is the task? In Steven's case, the change in his understanding led not so much to a change in the time on task, but to a change in the nature of the activity engaged in, and the feelings associated with being engaged in it.

Knowing how a literate activity can be made more manageable to a novice is useful for both instruction and evaluation. For example, if a student is struggling with a book, it helps to know that reading it to him first might make it something he could read for himself. It is also useful if we can show that a student is able to manage increasingly difficult reading. Then we can make an argument that he has learned something. For example, *if it were* possible to come up with measures of text difficulty, there is the promise of being able to monitor progress by showing that a student is able to read more difficult books.

There are numerous different ways for text to be easier (or more difficult) for children to read. Simply reading the book to the child first will make it easier to read. The more readings, and the more recent the readings, the greater the memory for the text and the easier the activity becomes. If a child knows a lot about farms or dirt bikes, then farm books or dirt-bike books are likely to be easier to read than books about which she knows little. A well-illustrated book will generally be easier than one without illustrations.[50] These factors and many others are listed in Table 7.1. Knowing what makes text easy means that it is virtually always possible to obtain a sample of reading, even when a student is relatively new to literacy. For example, when a text is read to the student first it will make it easier, especially if it is short, predictable, melodic, and interesting. Similarly, even relative novices can read back a sentence that they have just dictated, especially if the criterion for success is preserving the meaning of what was dictated rather than exactly replicating the words.

If I read about Taoism having never encountered the term before, I will have a difficult time understanding the material. Similarly, if I have not experienced the joy of reading a tax form many times, I will have considerable trouble with that. The more times I read a given tax form, the easier it is to read it the next time. The more experience I have reading tax forms in general, the easier they will tend to become as a whole. A four-year-old child can "read" all 1,500

TABLE 7.1 Some Factors Influencing the Ease of Reading Activities

History	Familiarity of the specific text from previous readings
	Familiarity of the concepts in the text
	Recency of the experience with the concepts or the text itself
	Successful experience with the text or related text
	Extent of own relevant personal experience
	Familiarity with book language
	Familiarity with the structure (e.g., the commonalities in narrative pattern across familiar stories)
Language Used	Complexity and diversity of the syntax
	Match between book language and reader's language
	Repetition of sequences of language
	Melody and rhythm of the language
	Pattern of the language:
	-rhyme
	-cyclical patterns
	-size of unit in cycle
	-cultural patterns (counting, days of the week, months, etc.), idioms
Structure	Narrative vs. non-narrative
	Plot complexity
	Inference load (especially causal and motivational)
Vocabulary Used	Simplicity of the vocabulary
	Decodability of the vocabulary
	Repetition of vocabulary
	Density of new vocabulary
	Vividness or memorableness of vocabulary
Format	Lines per page
	Complete message on each page (Theme book) vs. each page only part of narrative
	Diversity and complexity of page layout
	Sheer quantity of print/number of pages
Illustrations	Aesthetic stimulation
	Contextual support
	Intellectual stimulation
Immediate Functionality	Practical objectives such as construction, or to make peers laugh, or select menu items
	Relationship to desirable activities
Reader Reaction	Desire to return to the text/context
	Intellectual stimulation
	Aesthetic stimulation
Audience Reaction	Interest
	Support
Personal Control	Of reading rate
	Choice of material
	Choice of response

(continued)

TABLE 7.1 Continued

Context and Goal	Comparative versus cooperative focus of class
	Public performance vs. private experience
	Definition of success or failure, e.g., word level accuracy versus meaningfulness
	Consequences contingent on success or failure
Teacher Intervention	Prompting strategy use, monitoring, etc.
	Supplying missing information
	Highlighting success

Source: I have drawn heavily here on the following works: Don Holdaway (1979). *The foundations of literacy.* Sydney: Scholastic; Barbara Peterson (1988). *Characteristics of texts that support beginning readers.* Ann Arbor, MI: University Microfilms International; and New Zealand Department of Education (1980). *Early Reading In-service Course.* Wellington, NZ: P. D. Hasselberg, Government Printer.

odd words of Bill Peet's *Cowardly Clyde* if he has been read it enough times so that the memory of it is almost perfect. Similarly, a child can read material that is substantially beyond her normal range if she rehearses it. Children are very sensitive to the natural rhythms and melodies of the language, and as they internalize these, they can use them to help them know, for example, how many syllables should be there. "Patty cake, patty cake, baker's man" is readily distinguished from "Twinkle, twinkle little star," aside from the words, and the knowledge that allows this distinction can be used to support a child's reading of many kinds of books. The rhyme of the words at the ends of the lines, too, makes them much easier to read. The predictability that comes from these rhythms and patterns is the same kind of predictability that makes the familiar patterns of oral language initially more readable than the less familiar patterns of "book language."

In writing, we find some children take a story they have read and essentially change the names of the characters to make a new story. Other students may take the characters of a favorite story or television series and, knowing how those characters normally do things, have something different happen and let them respond, thus producing a new story. These strategies may result in a more coherent, perhaps "better" story than that produced by the student who wrote her own piece of fiction, inventing plot, characters, and all; but the level of "difficulty" of the activity may be comparable in the sense that all were completely involved in their literate activity for a similar amount of time with total resistance to external distraction.

CHAPTER 8

Controlling the Ease of Literate Activity

There are several reasons why educators try to control the ease of literate activity. First, there is the problem of placing children in material of appropriate difficulty. Second, there is the psychometric problem of attempting to produce two activities that are not the same but that are equally difficult. This is the problem of producing parallel or alternate forms of a test, which we return to in Chapter 29. The intention is to create tasks which are different from one another in content but comparable in difficulty in some absolute way in order to evaluate the progress of a group of children. If they do better in the isomorphic (equal form) activity after a period of instruction, then we are inclined to say that development has taken place. This is not a difficult thing to do for groups of children. We can examine how groups of children perform on activities and say that *on average* the two activities are comparable in difficulty for two groups of children, and there is a very large branch of measurement theory busily engaged in trying to accomplish just that.

However, I hope it is clear by now that we will never accurately be able to say in advance that two activities will be equally difficult for two different children, or even for the same child. We can estimate in a number of ways and come reasonably close, but we will never be highly accurate particularly because *the student* can change from day to day. *After* children have attempted an activity, we can more easily make some statements about it. Beforehand it will be quite difficult without knowing something about the child's concept of the task and his background. This is one reason why a teacher's knowledge of his students and of literature are critical. If a teacher has knowledge of the student's background and his knowledge and strategies, as well as knowledge of literature, she can suggest particular books that are both manageable and interesting. If the relationship between teacher and student is good, the student will help correct errors of judgment. In general, however, there is no reason for the teacher to take on the responsibility of placing children in books, taking away their choice and independence. It is sometimes appropriate to require the reading of certain material, but motivational trade-offs will be made virtually always.

Nonetheless, helping children choose among the various literate activities and literature is part of a teacher's job. Children learn most when they are operating in what Lev Vygotsky called the "zone of proximal development." By this he meant those activities which a learner can do with some support: the area between what he can do independently and what he cannot do even with support.[51] Not only do children learn most when operating within the zone, but as they do so, they display the most instructionally useful information about their learning. Consequently, part of a teacher's job, and the third reason for knowing how to control the difficulty of literate activity, is setting up contexts in which children will frequently find themselves operating within this zone. The various factors which I described in the last chapter can be used by teachers in their attempts to arrange for these situations.

However, using these factors to control difficulty is not entirely straightforward. A predictable story such as *The Gingerbread Man* places quite different demands on a reader from a story that is written with controlled phonic regularity, such as *Dan Can Fan the Man*. Reading text which includes many complex words is different from reading text containing very simple, common vocabulary like "go," "stop," "the," and "to." Reading a poem is different from reading an instruction manual or a newspaper article. Each of these is more or less difficult depending on the context in which it is read and the reason for reading it.

CONTEXT, MOTIVES, AND GOALS

The same story, or any literate activity, presented to a given reader can be made easy or difficult by the teacher simply by changing the context or the goals of the activity. Consider the following two cloze activities A and B. Which is more difficult?

   A.   *We went to the shops to buy some _____.*
   B.   *We went to the shops to buy some b_____.*

The answer depends on what is required. If we simply require a response that fits the information given in the text, then A is easier because there are fewer constraints to be satisfied. There are many possible answers for A, and fewer for B. If however, the child thinks the task is to find the *right word,* the one that the teacher has in mind, then B is easier than A because there is more information available to find the right answer.

These situational effects can generalize beyond the immediate situation if children repeatedly find themselves in that kind of situation. For example, I have seen few children so reluctant to write as Jimmy. Jimmy was in third grade and was assigned to me to improve his reading. We were working together in a small room and after reading *Teach us, Amelia Bedelia,*[52] we began a session on writing. I told him that we were going to do some writing and I asked him if there was anything he could think of to write about. He began to talk about his summer vacation in New Brunswick. Until that point he had said very little without prompting, but he sallied forth into a lengthy description of his vacation. It clearly meant a lot to him. So I expressed great interest in the topic and set about finding and writing down my topic by thinking out loud about some ideas. I told him that the rules for writing were that we had to concentrate on writing the story and that we could spell words any way we wanted. Spelling didn't matter. He said, "Okay." Then, while I wrote, he began to make thoughtful, composing faces at the wall while not touching his paper. After a while the pretense wore off and he just stared blankly. I looked up from my work and asked, "What's the problem?" He said, "I can't write."

> "You just told me a fascinating story, Jimmy. Remember what you told me about?"
>
> "My vacation"
>
> "Okay," I said. "Write that down as best you can—my vacation."
>
> I began to write again, but again he just sat there, staring. After a few minutes, I said "Are you having trouble?" and he said, "We had to write a story about this before, but my Mom had to help me with all the words like New Brunswick and stuff." I asked him if he did any writing in class and he said that he did. I asked him what he did when he came to a word he didn't know. He said, "We can look it up in a dictionary or the teacher will tell us." I explained that we do things differently here and that spelling really doesn't matter to us when we are composing our story. "You can write the words any way you like. We can clean it up later. This is just a draft."
>
> He began to write, but had erased the first word three times before I explained that writers are allowed to be messy. I showed him my paper which had crossings out and corrections, but he was clearly uncomfortable about risking invented spelling. So I suggested he just leave blanks for the words he didn't know. While I wrote, he wrote the following:
>
> *My _____ of the _____.*
> *i _____ in a _____*
>
> I took a break from my writing to help him deal with this problem. He read it to me. "My vacation of the year. I left in . . ." But he could not remember what he intended for the last blank. Then he realized that he had meant to write "on Sunday" and began to erase in. I suggested he just modify the word. We then began to figure out *left*.
>
> "What letter might start the word?"
>
> "L"
>
> "Can you hear any other sounds in the word?"
>
> "F"
>
> "Okay."
>
> "E"
>
> "Left—how could you end it?"
>
> "T."
>
> And so we got *lFet*. We moved on to *Sunday*.
>
> "How would you start it?"
>
> *S* (writes, pauses) *U* (writes, pauses) *N* (writes, pauses, then writes *day*). He spelled the word accurately, conventionally. We moved on to "vacation." He wrote *Vak* and then was stuck. I said, "va-ca..." and he said, "I already have the A" (it is part of the name of the letter K). So I asked, "shin—what would start that?"

"C. No—S." He then wrote C.

"And what does it end with?"

"shin—N—I N G"

So we ended up with Vakcing[53] and moved on to *year*. With no prompting he wrote *yere*.

He then proceeded to extend the story with *i dov for 7 or 8 orers* [I drove for 7 or 8 hours].

Jimmy made quite clear at the outset his definition of the activity and his criteria for success, or rather for failure. To misspell a word constituted failure at writing, and his goal was the avoidance of failure rather than the achievement of success. Avoiding failure meant not misspelling any words. Jimmy's definition of the task, which arose from the context in which he normally wrote, made it extremely difficult for him. Another perfect example of this was Micky, who began writing *I have a dog*, all words he thought he could spell. He wrote *I have a go* and realized he had gone wrong. Instead of crossing out *go* and writing *dog*, he said, "Wait—g-o-d—that's a word. I have a god. [He finished writing it] There!" Having selected a low-risk sentence to write, he was content to sacrifice even its intended meaning in order not to mess up the page. To make writing easier for these students involves changing their definition of what it means to write.

THE CONSEQUENCES OF CONTROL

The factors I described influence not only the ease or difficulty of the reading, but also the manner in which the reading is done—the strategies that are used along the way. For example, if a child reads a text for amusement, that is a different goal from reading to find specific pieces of information, which is different again from reading to answer questions about the text, or reading it aloud to an audience. Writing a list because of a textbook requirement is different from writing one to make sure that you take all the things you need to camp. Writing something professional within a time limit is likely to produce a judicious choice of words that are easily spelled, unless you have a competent secretary or a spelling program on your word processor. When the goal of reading or writing is different, or the context is different, the strategies the reader or writer uses are likely to be different.

Because of the interrelatedness of goals, contexts, and strategies, controlling the difficulty of literate activities can result in problems for the unwary. Educators have tried various combinations of these ways of making texts easier for a long time. Sometimes, however, they have overrelied on particular techniques, and children's reading development has become distorted in that their way of viewing reading and the strategies they use to read can become restricted. For example, a child who has been learning to read in a text controlled for phonic regularity is likely to read example A with some ease, yet have difficulty with example B because her decoding strategies are simply not adequate for handling the words.[54] Similarly, a child whose reading experience is limited to material like example B, will probably have difficulty reading example A because the prediction strategy to which he is accustomed simply will not work. Neither will his self-correcting from meaning since text A is not highly meaningful.

    A.   The man and his cat can get in the pit.
          The tan fan is in the can.
          The man and his cat can not get at the fan.
    B.   Rachel ran up the stairs.
          Rachel knocked over chairs.
          Rachel tore out her hairs.
          When the ghosts came out on Halloween.

    At the same time that we control difficulty by one means, such as the highly decodable words in example A, we can deprive the reader of interest (and hence motive), meaningfulness, and relevance of prior knowledge, and increase concern over the accuracy of word pronunciation. Thus overall we are achieving an increase in the difficulty of the activity, and possibly of such activities in the future. The material read also can act as a model of authorship for the reader; thus we can get spillover into students' writing that will make it look like the kind of text they are reading.[55] I will return to this in a later chapter.

    The context of the activity is very important. Even texts such as "The man on the land can get tan fog from the log" can have their place. If they are read as nonsense, which children enjoy immensely, they are fine and may well encourage the children to play with the language more themselves. Indeed, it may heighten their comprehension ability by allowing them to explore possibilities, and by helping them to define more clearly the boundaries between sense and nonsense. If, on the other hand, such texts are read as serious reading material, children may conclude that they are a true sample of reading and that reading has little to do with making sense. Alternatively, they may try desperately to make sense out of the nonsense and produce oral reading errors which reflect that. Systematic control of children's reading material through any simple means is rather like the Japanese art of bonsai: it systematically distorts the growth of a child's reading. The consequence is rather less attractive in a child's reading than in a houseplant.

    Another way to alter the difficulty of the task is for the teacher to provide some support. Teacher intervention as part of evaluation has been advocated recently by many researchers in the name of what is called "dynamic assessment" or "interactive assessment."[56] A common term for such assistance is "scaffolding." The idea is that an activity that would normally be out of reach of a student can be accomplished if the teacher helps by providing certain kinds or support or instruction until the student can take over these functions. For example, when a student is reading and cannot figure out a word, the teacher could provide the word or prompt with ''What would make sense there?'' or ''What does it start with?'' or ''How could you figure that out?'' Each of these kinds of support is appropriate in certain conditions, but supplying support always has its catches. Under certain conditions, it can easily end up in dependency just as with the overuse of any difficulty controls. Students who use only predictable language material can easily end up overpredicting, being overdependent on the predictability of the language, and not using or developing their knowledge of the details of print. Similarly, students who learn on only phonetically regularized text can easily become overdependent on the decoding aspect, failing to look for and use the larger patterns in the language. Students who are continually told the word without having to work it out for themselves can readily end up dependent on the teacher for such words, and at the same time with their confidence eroded. Loss of confidence makes any task psychologically more difficult. This problem occurs most commonly in a basal reading program in which the teacher controls most of the reading. Where children spend a fair amount of time reading material that they select for themselves, the context is such that the teacher cannot help them all, and they have substantial motive to figure things out for themselves—both because there will be less disruption of the story, and because it is *their* story and they are involved in it.

The goal of helping children engage in manageable literate activity is to help a child to know what it feels like to learn within her zone of proximal development, and to distinguish that from the feeling of literate activity that is too difficult. This means setting situations in which the student often becomes involved in literate activity at a level just beyond what can normally be managed alone. And this is just as true of teachers as it is of students. If a teacher attempts something well beyond his current capacities, he will very likely become frustrated. Frustration leads to changes in emotional, and hence cognitive, activity that lead to reduced effectiveness and ability to solve problems, and hence a destructive cycle.[57] On the other side of the zone, as individuals continue to attain goals that require no new learning, their behavior becomes increasingly repetitive, routine, and primitive. Their freedom of choice is also reduced, with predictable consequences for motivation.[58] In the long run, we want children to take responsibility for managing the difficulty of their literate activity, and understanding the consequences of the choices they make.

CHAPTER 9

Choosing and Erring

Choice is important. It is important to us and to our students, both motivationally and for the information that our choices yield about ourselves and our students. We do not always make good choices, nor do our students, but errors are generally informative. The more each of us understands our choices, the reasons for them and the consequences of them, the more we will understand ourselves and our students as readers and writers, teachers and learners. In this chapter I will first discuss choice in general, and then proceed to the important issue of erroneous choices.

CHOOSING

It feels quite different to do something because you are forced to or because you have no options, than to do the same thing when you have chosen to do it yourself. When children are able to choose the books they read, choose not to complete reading a book, and choose the interpretation they wish to make of the book, they will read in a different way than if they do not have these choices. They will also generally read more often. The same is true of writing. When I began writing this book, I signed a contract with Longman to complete it in approximately two years. I said at the outset that I did not want a deadline, but they had paid me some money as an advance on the royalties so that I might buy myself a word processor to write with. As the deadline for the completion of the book approached, I found myself forcing myself to write. I walked around with a stoop from the burden on my shoulders, and I ultimately found that I could not write anything at all. Finally my wife, Tina, and I talked about the problem and decided simply to take a loan from the bank, pay back the money I had been advanced, and write the book on my schedule instead of Longman's. As soon as we had made this decision, I was able to write again. Freedom to choose, or at least the perception of freedom, is important. Students who experience this freedom will read more and with greater involvement than those who do not experience it. Remember that it is the *feeling* of free choice that matters. Thus it is possible for a teacher to tell a student what to do, offering no choice, and for the student to do it joyfully because he has chosen to trust that teacher's judgment.

When readers and writers make choices, they reveal important information about what it is for them to be literate, about how they deal with constraints, what knowledge they have about audiences, about conventions, and about strategies. When you highlight the reasons for choices, and help students consider the reasons for their choices, they become more aware of the possibilities open to them and more able to choose wisely in the future. They become more in control of themselves as literate people. Thus a large part of our job as teachers is to help our students increase their options, to predict the consequences of their choices, and to attend to the choices they make as valuable objects of study.

When people write and read, they exercise their intentions by making choices within their set of beliefs and a framework of socially sanctioned language conventions. They make choices among letters, words, sentences, books, authors, strategies, topics, audiences, goals, genres, information to include and leave out of their writing, pieces of writing to include and leave out of their portfolio, pieces to finish and not to finish, and so forth. A student who reads the sentence ''We all rushed into the pool'' as ''We all raced into the pool'' is not so much demonstrating her inability to decode the word ''rushed'' as her intention to make meaning predominate over her desire to match all of the conventions of printed language. The same is true in writing. When a person writes, he intends to accomplish something and makes use of his language and the conventions of the discourse community in which he wishes to participate (to the extent that he is aware of these conventions). A big part of a teacher's role is to help students accomplish their intentions by making sensible choices, and by having options among which they can choose.

People do not always make the best choices. In general, students are quite capable of choosing their own books, and they are likely to choose ones that are interesting to them and of an appropriate level of difficulty. They even know to choose an easier book to read aloud than they would to read to themselves.[59] However, children who have been in the bottom reading group for the bulk of their school career are unlikely to be reading independently outside of school. They only read what they are told to read in school. Thus, not having had the experience of choosing, trying, and rechoosing books, they will not be good at choosing.[60] Furthermore, being in the bottom group, they very likely have been placed on material that is too difficult. As a consequence, they may never have experienced the feeling of reading something which is manageable and satisfying. With only the reading group experience of reading to guide them in their decisions they are likely to make unhealthy choices.

Other situational factors can also influence their choices for better or for worse. In some literature-based classrooms, a nasty rumor gets spread that there are such things as ''baby books.'' This is most likely to occur in competitive classrooms and in classrooms in which there is a clear (and inappropriate) transition, for example, from illustrated books to chapter books. Children who are not finding reading satisfying for one reason or another, or who are feeling insecure, will find success or security in placing themselves above other children who appear less competent. Children who are not reading well in those classrooms will either choose books that are too difficult for them or will (more frequently) choose not to read at all. Both choices are unhealthy ones. Any situation which produces a simplistic linear ranking of ability and of texts will create this sort of problem.

Sometimes students will consistently choose "low risk" books—books they know that they can read well. Thus they do not challenge themselves to struggle with more difficult ideas and more complex language. Most children will be inclined to do this at times—adults too. It is not a problem unless a child chooses never to venture into more challenging books. In these cases, teachers can encourage children to choose "challenging books" or "brave books," and to have more than one book going at once.[61] But as Nancie Atwell demonstrates, when students trust your judgment (a trust which, I'm afraid, you have to earn), they are very likely to read the books you suggest for them even though they could easily choose something else.

The decision-making process speaks of the learner's priorities. For example, when a child chooses a word which he can spell, rather than misspell the word he intended, or look it up in a dictionary, or ask someone, it says a great deal about his concept of the task in which he is engaged. This type of choice is one thing in a form letter and quite another in a draft of a piece of expressive writing. Understanding the thinking behind choices is thus instructionally indispensable. Listening to children think through their choices can be especially informative. For example, Jane Hansen listened to a student trying to decide which book to share with the class, Donald Hall's *The Man Who Lived Alone* or Patricia MacLachlan's *Arthur, for the Very First Time.* Mark said:

> If I share *The Man Who Lived Alone,* I could read it all, but *Arthur* has some funny parts and they might like it better.[62]

In thinking through his choices, he tells us what he thinks his options are, and on what grounds he is making the choice. He tells us that he understands the concerns of his audience, the constraints of time, and the trade-offs between wholeness and sampling. A child telling us that he has chosen not to continue with a piece of writing because it did not have enough action, or a child who chooses to keep a character description and discard the rest of a piece of writing because "I can really feel myself being Betsy, and I just think that she would never do what I had her doing" tell us about what they think counts for readers and authors. Jane Hansen quotes another student explaining the basis for her choices:

> I like both [writing with someone else and by myself]. If I'm writing about my kittens or my family I'd rather write by myself, unless a friend was along with me on a trip. If I'm writing a mystery or something, it's fun to have a friend.[63]

This comment shows an awareness of the consequences of particular choices of topic and writing situation. The process of thinking through the decision process is usually informative to both teacher and learner.

When people make choices in their writing, they are choosing in order to accomplish some particular intention. Asking a student at the beginning of a writing conference, "What are you trying to do with this piece?" or "Where are you with this piece?" will get the intention out on the table. Once we understand the intention, we can help them accomplish that intention. But that is not all. Simply asking the question also asserts that you expect that they are trying to do something with this piece, and that your role is to help them realize their intentions. When choices do not accomplish intentions, or have unintended consequences, then the choice might be considered an error. If we intended to write using conventional spelling and form, but failed to do so, then we erred. If we did not intend to write using conventional spelling and form, but the social situation (a job application) calls for it and we consequently fail to accomplish the purpose of our writing (getting the job), we erred again.

The intentions we ascribe to people have a lot to do with how we perceive their command of the conventions. In other words, it matters whether we think they can use language conventionally and choose not to, or if we think that they cannot and are therefore incompetent. A first grader taking the liberties with language typical of the poetry of e. e. cummings is unlikely to receive comparable acclaim. The first grader is likely to be seen as erring, but it is a bold critic who suggests cummings has done so. Indeed, when we read books we look for voice in the way the writer uses and violates conventions and in the choices she has made.

ERRORS

If "to err is human," then why are people so afraid of making mistakes or, having made one, so keen on calling it something euphemistic? Error is often the consequence of exploration. Error-free learning is very rigid learning. The big advantage of mistakes is that you stand to learn something new when you have made one and noticed it. In fact, a good way to improve your teaching is to make a point of documenting at least three interesting errors you have made each week. This takes the edge off making errors, and at the same time makes them instructional. Students too, might be interested in this approach. *For teachers, the most useful aspect of errors is that people do not make them randomly.* There is always a reason for them. If you can figure out the reason, then you know where to use your instructional expertise without further confusing the student. Children's choices are based on the hypotheses they have developed in past and present literate activity, and on the various motivations and goals in their literate lives.

In order to learn from errors, you have to assume that others do not experience the world the same way you do, and then set out to see what it is like in their particular universe. We often make the mistake of assuming that children think like small but erroneous adults. But in many ways, children actually inhabit a different world put together with a different set of assumptions (in teenage years this is referred to as the "generation gap"). Although we often mistakenly assume that children have the same logic as we do, it is even easier to assume that adults hold the same logic as we. But small cultural differences produce big differences in ways of thinking about people, the world, and literacy. The logic and intelligence of students' errors can be impeccable, but relatively inconceivable from the teacher's perspective. Consider this story dictated by a three-year-old:

> My old cat was dead because he was probably sick. He was sick because I was not born yet. When I wasn't born yet, he wanted three children, so he died.
>   We had three cats. One was my parents' cat and now, one we have right now. I liked number one better than number two.
>   My mom's parents' cat died and Opa ran over it. Opa was sad because that cat did not scratch.

The story points out the limitation of our own systems of thought, and the sheer impossibility of imagining the situation in which the child conceives of these relationships. Yet children do this sort of thing all the time, and teachers are faced with exactly that imaginative challenge.

Standing where the learner stands in order to see his world is not easy, and it is something you must want to do. This is no more than we ask of students when we ask them to write (understand their audience), to read (understand the author's use of language), and to edit their writing from the perspective of a person who uses conventional language. The critical parts of understanding errors and choices, then, are:

- [ ] the knowledge that people understand the world, and literacy, differently,
- [ ] the mind-set to look for intentions and patterns of choices or errors,
- [ ] the imagination to envision how a pattern of choices or errors could be related to those particular intentions,
- [ ] the understanding that *error* does not mean *failure,*
- [ ] learning without error is learning without exploration and is likely to be very narrow and inflexible learning.

Teachers often reach a point at which they understand intention and the positive nature of error, but lack the imagination to construct the possible ways in which the error could have occurred. This imagination develops as many different students explain the stories behind their particular errors.

We learn from our students' errors by reading them to understand their meaning, in just the same way as we might make a careful reading of a book, attempting to make meaning of the particular uses of the language the author has made: the way in which the author has pressed the language into the service of her intentions. In doing so she has used the uniqueness of her own language along with the conventions of the culture which she has available. When a teacher knows how a student knows the conventions, she can be helpful in straightening out misconceptions (best done one-on-one) and introducing new knowledge about conventions and techniques (often best done in a group).

The critical thing for understanding errors is often inferring intent, which is harder to do from a cold piece of writing than in talking with the writer shortly after she produced the writing. The intention is what organizes the writing. Thus, error analysis involves being able to take the perspective of the student so as to be able to imagine what produced that particular pattern. That is why a writing conference is often begun by asking the author to talk about the piece and what she is trying to accomplish with it. Intention also organizes reading, and intentions must be inferred in order to make sense of patterns of reading errors.

Suppose a child writes, "U kld my frg. I hat U and U ar suped." and gives it to her friend. Her friend throws it on the ground and won't play with her the next day unless the letter is destroyed. Did the writer err? She may have not spelled the words conventionally, but the letter probably served her purposes well without requiring her to take special steps and time to spell words conventionally. At the same time, her choice to put it in writing rather than simply saying it speaks to the child's awareness of the powerful and permanent nature of print. If a child writes, "A cat is on a bus. A hat is on a man." has he erred? If he writes this after talking at length about an exciting event in his life, which he was keen to communicate, then he has probably erred. His error is either in misperceiving the function of writing, or in having a teacher who focuses on convention over meaning. In other words, he may have accurately perceived the nature of literacy in his classroom, and the error may not really be his.

In analyzing errors, there is lots of room for error. If we analyze incorrectly, we may end up reinforcing the source of the error. For example, consider a student who tries to "sound out" each word when he is reading orally, but is not particularly successful. If we interpret his performance as representing a particular kind of decoding problem such as "has trouble with consonant blends and medial vowels," and set about trying to rectify this problem, the probable result will be that he will focus even more on phonic analysis than on the construction of meaning. Alternatively, we might equally well interpret it as an erroneous perception of the nature of reading. The problem to be solved, then, is how to help him to have the intention of making sense rather than the intention of sounding out each word correctly. On the other hand, if we look further, we might find that the error lies in the selection of books that are too difficult, making for too many errors and the loss of even the intention to make sense.

Intentions come from social interactional history.[64] Often adults who are having difficulty in reading and writing identify the problem they want help with as a spelling and decoding problem, which is what they were taught they were not good at in school. While their central intention in writing is to learn to spell, it will be a hard and unsatisfying road to becoming literate. Nonetheless, the sensible teacher will concede instructional time to the individual's perceived problem, rather than deny the value of that perception, and do it within a framework of the separate role of editing rather than composing.

It is very important to know which errors a student knows how to detect and correct. Errors which the student can detect and correct, need practice so that the correct form or choice becomes more automatic. Errors which can be detected but not corrected are the perfect place for instruction. But although these are important, it is equally important to know whether there are strategies in place for detecting and correcting errors. For example, reading their paper aloud helps some writers, reading it from the bottom to the top helps others, reading it to another student with the understanding that their partner say nothing helps others. We look for the kinds of error a student can detect unaided, or within an identified sentence, and whether he has a feeling for the types of error that he commonly makes. When a student is aware of the kind of choices and errors he is likely to make, he can proceed to locate them and subsequently prevent them. When he is aware that he is inclined to leave *ed* off the end of words, or to run sentences together, he can make an editorial pass through his work looking specifically for that type of error. He might even keep a brief, and changing, list of these personal hurdles. Such a list and its changes will be most useful for evaluation purposes. When he is aware that some authors use only a handful of words to write big and interesting ideas whereas other authors use many words, or that the existence of illustrations in books do not make them for younger or less able students, he may make different choices. Getting students involved in studying their own reading and writing puts them more in control of themselves as language users, and makes them less likely to be used by a language which they do not control.

Some of the errors evident in young children's writing, such as the confusion of word boundaries in *our next store nabor,* are still to be found in the writing of graduate students who do not read widely. For example I recently encountered the term *fact simily.* Each student has a particular pattern of errors, the basis of which needs to be decided before instruction begins. For example, a decision to be made on the basis of error analysis is whether individual or group instruction is warranted. Glynda Hull differentiates between "those things that the majority of students don't do in their writing," that are appropriate for group instruction, and "those things that they do incorrectly (which require both learning and unlearning)" that are better dealt with individually.[65]

One kind of error is simply produced by the mind going faster than the pen or the eye. Still other errors arise in writing when a student tries on a language, that he does not yet own. This can produce errors of all sorts such as *all of the sudan* and *imput.* (But of course the latter error might well simply be a typo.) In order to decide on the logic of the error, we need to talk with the author in the first place, and then expand the sample we have. For example, Glynda Hull provides an example of repeated use of a particular sentence pattern in a student's work:

1. My response to this story I feel work that SFC Robert Cooley had such a big influence in my work he always kept me busy "every" minute.

2. My response from this story I felt that she was pressured by her own peirs who never understood Ruth's Viewpoint.
3. My first impression toward Victor Bean I felt he was all right, but as work proceeded I got to know him and his emotions toward younger people.
4. My future employment, I want to advance myselv in the clerical or business field, because I feel their will be opoenings and advancement, high paying salary.[66]

Hull provides six additional examples of this writer's use of a "topic/comment" strategy in which he joins a topic to a comment on that topic spatially but not syntactically.

Other kinds of error arise when a student either generates or is taught problematic rules. Mike Rose has provided some lucid examples of this in his analyses of writer's block.[67] He describes Ruth who learned a decision rule in high school, that an essay must always grab the reader's attention immediately. This, along with her rule that you always begin writing at the beginning, and her rule that ungrammatical sentences are a no-no, effectively shut down Ruth's composing process. Making choices which meet all of these constraints at once would be extraordinarily difficult. Martha, on the other hand, has learned to plan essays. She will not write a draft until she has spent several days preparing an outline which looks, Rose says, "like a diagram of protein synthesis or DNA structure." Unable to convert this complex outline to a short essay, she would reach her deadline, scrap the whole thing, and throw together whatever she could. Her failure to translate her outline into an essay was made a certainty by another rule which asserted that humanities papers must scintillate with insights, images, and ironies.

The notion of an error arises from the contrast between an intended text and an actual text. In writing, teachers have to imagine what the intended text would look like—what the student was trying to accomplish—in order to infer the misconceptions which underlie different patterns of errors. I can only assume that the more extensive the teacher's experience with a particular student's writing and the better the teacher knows the student, the more likely it is that the analysis will be accurate. We need to ask ourselves, "What does she know and what did she do that produced the error?" We must assume a logic and set out to find what it is. Error is not to be feared, but ennobled. As Donald Schon puts it:

> . . . the formation of new concepts treating the new as the old can perhaps best be understood as a form of error. Coming to form a new concept involves in several ways making a mistake. A new hypothesis, however fruitful, is typically at least partially wrong. The account of a discovery is typically partly false. . . the formation of new concepts typically leads to error. Every good new scientific theory is surrounded with error, as appears abundantly in retro-

spect. It is typical of insights that they are overstated. What is more, error often leads to the formation of new concepts.[68]

And we must not assume that error is the privilege of children. Analyses of the errors of teachers, administrators, and parents are best done in the same way. Often simply describing the error in as much detail as possible sets the conditions for developing a deeper understanding of it.

In the next two chapters I will describe a way of recording and interpreting children's oral reading errors.

RESOURCES

Some good resources for studying error analysis are:

David Bartholomae (1980). The study of error. *College composition and communication, 31:* 253–69.

Glynda Hull (1986). Acts of wonderment: Fixing mistakes and correcting errors. In David Bartholomae and Anthony Petrosky (Eds.), *Facts, artifacts and counterfacts: Theory and method for a reading and writing course.* Upper Montclair, NJ: Boynton/Cook, pp. 199–226.

Mina Shaughnessy (1977). *Errors and expectations: A guide for the teacher of basic writing.* New York: Oxford University Press.

Notes and References for Part I

1. Retention is achieved by screening children out of kindergarten, by placing children in "transition rooms" ("pre-first grades"), by classifying children as disabled, and by outright retention.

2. Harvard University Graduate School of Education announcement of an institute on Reading, Writing, and Language, July 1986.

3. John Cannell (1987). *Nationally normed elementary achievement testing in America's public schools: How all fifty states are above the national average.* Daniels, WV: Friends for Education.
   Robert Linn, M. Elizabeth Graue, and Nancy Sanders (1990). Comparing state and district results to national norms: The validity of the claims that "Everyone is above average." *Educational Measurement: Issues and Practice* 9(3): 5–14.
   Lorrie Shepard (1990). Inflated test score gains: Is the problem old norms or teaching the test? *Educational Measurement: Issues and Practice* 9(3): 15–22.

4. These figures come from the National Center for Educational Statistics (1983) report *The condition of education.* Washington: U.S. Government Printing Office.

5. Reported in *Fair Test Examiner 3*(3): 8.

6. I base these comments on the work of Lev Vygotsky, particularly on the two translations of his work:
Lev Vygotsky (1978). Mind in society: The development of higher psychological processes. Michael Cole, Vera John-Steiner, Sylvia Scribner, and Ellen Souberman (Eds. and Trans.). Cambridge, MA: Harvard University Press.
Lev Vygotsky (1962). *Thought and Language.* Eugenia Hanfmann (Ed.), Gertrude Vakar (Trans.). Cambridge MA: MIT Press.

7. John Hayman and Rodney Napier (1975). *Evaluation in the schools: A human process for renewal.* Monterey, CA: Brooks-Cole. Hayman and Napier describe "process evaluation" as examining ". . . the reasons why events occur in a particular manner at a particular time" (p. 62). They describe process evaluation as being action-oriented, and collaborative from beginning to end, information being shared with those in the process as much as possible.

8. I probably would never have noticed this had it not been for my having read Kornei Chukovsky (1963). *From two to five.* Miriam Morton (Ed. and Trans.). Berkeley: University of California Press.

9. Donald Schon (1983). *The reflective practitioner: How professionals think in action.* New York: Basic Books, p. 130.

10. Mihalyi Csikszentmihalyi (1981). Some paradoxes in the definition of play. In Alyce Cheska (Ed.), *Play as Context: 1979 Proceedings of the Association for the Anthropological Study of Play.* West Point, NY: Leisure Press, pp. 14–25 (pp. 18–19).

11. A good reference is:
Peter Berger and Thomas Luckmann (1966). *The social construction of reality.* Garden City, NY: Doubleday.
A shorter, clear psychological perspective can be found in:
Kenneth Gergen (1985). The social constructionist movement in modern psychology. *American Psychologist 40*(3): 266–275.
These writers have used the term "constructionist," whereas I have used the term "constructivist." I use the latter to connect with the terminology of:
Mary Belenky, Blythe Clinchy, Nancy Goldberger, and Jill Tarule (1986). *Women's ways of knowing: The development of self, voice, and mind.* New York: Basic Books.

12. Daniel Resnick and Lauren Resnick (1985). Standards, curriculum, and performance: A historical and comparative perspective. *Educational Researcher 14*(4): 5–20.

13. Joanne Nurss and Mary McGauvrin (1976). *Teacher's manual, Part two: Interpretation and use of test results.* New York: Harcourt Brace Jovanovich, p. 16.

14. This analysis comes from:
Robert Glaser (1988). Cognitive and environmental perspectives on assessing achievement. In *Assessment in the service of learning: Proceedings of the 1987 ETS invitational conference.* Princeton, NJ: Educational Testing Service.

15. William Chase and Herbert Simon (1973). Perception in chess. *Cognitive Psychology 4*: 55–81.

16. Peter Johnston, Peter Afflerbach, and Paula Weiss (1990). *Teachers' evaluations of the teaching and learning of literacy and literature.* Technical report, Center for the Teaching and Learning of Literature. Albany, NY: The University at Albany.

17. Johnston, Afflerbach, and Weiss. *Teachers' evaluations of the teaching and learning of literacy and literature.*
I do not mean to imply here that teachers somehow "naturally" will develop a constructive practice based on children's literature. Indeed, there is every reason to

believe that unless they develop a constructive and critical way of thinking about literacy, this will not happen. All of their background with their own schooling and basal reading instruction will mitigate against it.

18. Donald Graves (1983) uses this term in his book *Writing: Teachers and Children at Work*. Portsmouth, NH: Heinemann.

19. This example is not in any way meant to detract from the efforts of dedicated and concerned folk like Mary or the organizations within which they work. It is intended solely to provide a real example of evaluative relationships.

20. This interpretation will only be constructed by some children in certain circumstances, which are more clearly described in later chapters. In particular this will tend to happen if a child develops the unfortunate notion that writing is representing words correctly ("getting all the letters right"). This can most easily be avoided by helping the children make a clear distinction between the different literate roles of composer, editor, bookmaker, and so forth. When such distinctions are clear, the composition role is unaffected by the teacher's writing the conventional spelling onto the child's text.

21. Graves. *Writing: Teachers and children at work.*

22. Richard Woodcock (1973). *Woodcock Reading Mastery Tests.* Circle Pines, MN: American Guidance Service.

23. This area of study is called "pragmatics" and seminal works in the area are:
John Austin (1962). *How to do things with words.* Cambridge, MA: Harvard University Press.
John Searle (1969). *Speech acts: An essay in the philosophy of language.* London: Cambridge University Press.

24. Uri Bronfenbrenner (1979). *The ecology of human development: Experiments by nature and design.* Cambridge, MA: Harvard University Press.

25. Donald Holdaway (1979). *The foundations of literacy.* New York: Scholastic.
Tom Nicholson (1984). You get lost when you gotta blimmin' watch the damn words: The low-progress reader in the junior high school. *Topics in Learning Disabilities 3:* 16–27.

26. As Bronfenbrenner notes:
"In the absence of persons able to recognize unwarranted interpretations based on misperceptions of fact, the unwitting investigator can, in all good faith, arrive at false conclusions. Once such persons are involved in the scientific enterprise, the risk of errors is appreciably reduced." (pp. 31–32)

27. Ann McGill-Franzen and Peter McDermott (1978, December). Negotiating a reading diagnosis. Paper presented at the annual meeting of the National Reading Conference, St. Petersburg, FL.

28. Shirley Brice Heath. (1983). *Ways with words: Language, life, and work in communities and classrooms.* Cambridge, Eng.: Cambridge University Press.

29. Connie Bridge, Mary Jane Ciera, and Robert Tierney (1978/79). The discourse processing operations of children. *Reading Research Quarterly 14:* 539–573.

30. In case you missed this very little joke, this is a reference to the children's book *Leo the Late Bloomer,* along with my astrological sign.

31. First Richard Barham, now at the University of Guelph in Canada, and then Terry Crooks, still at Otago University where I did my master's degree work, urged me to travel overseas to do a doctoral degree. I will always be grateful for, but puzzled by, the faith they had in me.

32. Terrence Crooks (1988). The impact of classroom evaluation practices on students. *Review of Educational Research 58Z*(4): 438–481.

33. Richard Allington (1983). The reading instruction provided readers of differing reading abilities. *The Elementary School Journal 83*: 559–568.
Stuart McNaughton (1981). The influence of immediate teacher correction on self-corrections and proficient oral reading. *Journal of Reading Behavior 13*: 367–371.

34. John Dewey cautioned us about this problem in 1913 when he noted that we should spend less time looking for reasons *for* activities and more time looking for reasons *in* them. *Interest and effort in education.* New York: Augustus M. Kelly.

35. Jack Easley and Russell Zwoyer (1975). Teaching by listening—toward a new day in math classes. *Contemporary Education 14*: 19–25.

36. Jane Hansen (1987). *When Writers Read.* Portsmouth, NH: Heinemann.

37. Graves. *Writing: Teachers and Students at Work.*

38. Marie Clay (1985). *The Early Detection of Reading Difficulties.* Portsmouth, NH: Heinemann.

39. Nel Noddings (1984). *Caring: A feminine approach to ethics and moral education.* Berkeley: University of California Press, p. 179.

40. Carole Ames and Russell Ames (1984). Goal structures and motivation. *Elementary School Journal 85*: 39–52.
Peter Johnston and Peter Winograd (1985). Passive failure in reading. *Journal of Reading Behavior 4*: 279–301.

41. The consequences of this in terms of children's evaluations of themselves are discussed further in Chapter 18, "Concepts about Being Literate."

42. For a historical review of readability formulae, and their uses and abuses, see George Klare (1984). Readability. In P. David Pearson (Ed.), *The handbook of reading research.* White Plains, NY: Longman, pp. 681–744.

43. This example is the Flesch Reading Ease formula, which can be found along with others in Klare's excellent review of readability research. I recommend this resource for further reading on the subject.

44. Klare also describes the specialization of these formulae for naval personnel and the like. it is interesting to note that the formulae are still prepared to produce a grade-level indicator for navy personnel who presumably no longer go to school.

45. See the chapter by Klare, for example, but also see:
Alice Davison and Robert Kantor (1982). On the failure of readability formulas to define readable texts: A case study from adaptations. *Reading Research Quarterly 17*: 187–209.
Although they have many flaws, you will see that I have had occasion to use readability formulae with due caution.

46. Some of the problems produced by this approach to matching are described in other parts of the book. However, the following are important:
  • Students must learn to do it themselves anyway and we restrict their opportunity to learn this by taking control of it.
  • When we take control of placing children in books, we cannot account optimally for interest as an important factor except in the sense of a general topic.
  • Personal choice is a motivating factor. To have chosen a book to read does not feel the same as being told to read the same book. Personal choice also makes the reading easier as a consequence.

47. Linda Gambrell, Robert Wilson, and Walter Gantt (1981). Classroom observations of task-attending behaviors of good and poor readers. *Journal of Educational Research 74*: 400–404.
Linda Gambrell and her colleagues found that in their sample of elementary students, children in the bottom reading groups were frequently placed on material which was well beyond their ability level.

48. Rhoda Spiro and Peter Johnston (1989). Children's selection of, and placement in, reading materials. Paper presented at the annual meeting of the National Reading Conference, Austin, TX.

49. This example came from Kristen Iverson-Cartwright, a teacher and graduate student in the Department of Reading at the State University of New York, Albany.

50. This generalization can easily be foiled. Some of the linguistic reader series, for example, deliberately used pictures rather than illustrations. The "authors" deliberately tried to make the pictures give no clues to the meaning of the text in order to force children to attend more to the print cues. Some children have learned not to seek meaning in reading; thus illustrations are in some ways irrelevant to what they consider reading to be.

51. Some researchers interpret the zone of proximal development as the area between what a child can do unassisted and what he can do with *adult* assistance. As I understand Vygotsky, it is not necessary to have *adult* intervention; collaboration with more developmentally advanced peers will do fine. In my opinion, I don't think it is even necessary for the peer to be developmentally advanced. When two children are writing together on a computer, it is quite common for one to take on the role of transcriber and the other to take more responsibility for composition. This support allows the individual to muster all of her resources on the one role, rather than having to split them between the two, and allows her to accomplish things which would not be possible without such aid.

52. Peggy Parish (1977). *Teach us, Amelia Bedelia.* New York: Scholastic.

53. This last part, going from *in* to *ing,* is a reflection of useful knowledge which Jimmy had. He recognized visually a common ending for words. His analysis of the sounds of the words took him so far, then his visual memory of the words took over. More on this in Chapters 21 and 22.

54. Recent work on the consequences of children's reading materials has included:
Connie Juel (1988). Learning to read and write: A longitudinal study of 54 children from first through fourth grades. *Journal of Educational Psychology 80:* 437–447.
Elsa Jaffe Bartlett (1979). Curriculum, concepts of literacy and social class. In Lauren Resnick and Phyllis Weaver (Eds.), *Theory and practice of early reading,* Vol. 2. Hillsdale, NJ: Erlbaum.

55. A good example of this can be seen in the work of Barbara Eckhoff (1983). How reading affects children's writing. *Language Arts 60:* 607–616. I have presented a clear example of this in Chapter 28 (Figure 28.4).

56. The idea of this kind of assessment has arisen in several different places recently with different interpretations. Vygotsky spoke of dynamic assessment:
Lev Vygotsky (1962). *Thought and language.* Eugenia Hanfmann and Gertrude Vakar (Trans.). Cambridge, MA: MIT Press.
Without reference to the work of Vygotsky, Reuven Feuerstein also came up with dynamic assessment.
Reuven Feuerstein (1979). *The dynamic assessment of retarded performers: The learning potential assessment device, theory, instrument and techniques.* Baltimore, MD: University Park Press.
Different approaches to dynamic assessment value different aspects of the process. Vygotsky and his followers value the performance of the student with assistance as a better estimate of ability than performance without assistance. They have also valued the difference between what is called static (unassisted) assessment and dynamic assessment. In the context of tests of intellectual competence, the difference between the two is proposed as an indicator of aptitude. I find this not particularly helpful because it assumes that the difference between the two is fixed. I find it more helpful to examine the assisted performance so that I can understand the na-

ture of what Vygotsky called the *zone of proximal development,* that is, the area in which instruction is likely to pay biggest dividends. Intervention of the kind I have mentioned also can provide indications of what strategies the student has but does not automatically use, those which he does not have at all, those which he has restricted use of, and so forth.

57. Chris Argyris and Donald Schon (1974). *Theory in practice: Increasing professional effectiveness.* London: Jossey-Bass.
They base this on the work of:
Roger Barker, Tamara Dembo, and Kurt Lewin (1941). Frustration and regression. *University of Iowa Studies in Child Welfare 18.*

58. Chris Argyris (1970). *Intervention theory and method.* Reading, MA: Addison-Wesley.

59. Fred Danner, Elfrieda Hiebert, and Peter Winograd (1983, April). Children's understanding of text difficulty. Paper presented at the annual meeting of the American Educational Research Association, New Orleans, LA.

60. Rhoda Spiro and I found that in classrooms in which children were placed in basals and spent virtually all their time with them, children were not as good at choosing appropriate books.
Rhoda Spiro and Peter Johnston (1989). Children's choice of, and placement in, reading materials. Paper presented at the annual meeting of the National Reading Conference, Austin, TX.

61. I like this term that I learned from Kathy Bidnell, a first-grade teacher. You cannot fail when you choose a brave book. Simply choosing it makes you brave. A ''more difficult book'' you can choose and fail because you were unable to read it. The latter term also assumes a linear scale of difficulty.

62. Jane Hansen (1987). *When Writers Read.* Portsmouth, NH: Heinemann, p. 160.

63. Hansen. *When Writers Read,* p. 223.

64. Although intentions come from social interactional history, two people with the same history (an impossibility) would just as likely have different intentions because individuals differ, for example, in their temperament.

65. Glynda Hull (1986). Acts of Wonderment. In David Bartholomae and Anthony Petrosky (Eds.), *Facts, artifacts and counterfacts.* Upper Montclair, NJ: Boynton/Cook, pp. 199–226. (p. 222)

66. See note 65 above, p. 209.

67. Mike Rose (1980). Rigid rules, inflexible plans, and the stifling of language: A cognitivist analysis of writer's block. *College Composition and Communication 31*(4): 389–401.

68. Donald Schon (1963). *Displacement of Concepts.* London: Tavistock, p. 26.

PART II

RECORDING AND KEEPING TRACK: CLASSROOM EVALUATION STRATEGIES

This section of the book describes some ways of gathering information, recording it, and generally keeping track of changes in literate activity. At the same time, I try to convince you that simply having a technique to collect data does not guarantee constructive evaluations. For example, many techniques work sensibly only in certain situations.

The section begins with two chapters on the recording and analysis of oral reading errors. These chapters are accompanied by a tape recording of children's oral reading so that you can have practical experience with the recording procedures. Subsequent chapters proceed through less time-honored procedures such as portfolios, journals, and thinking out loud. To the extent that there is a technical side to evaluation, this is probably it.

CHAPTER 10

Recording Oral Reading

Chapter 10 contains examples of running records that appear on the audiotape accompanying this book.

One of the problems with mature reading is that it is generally done silently within the privacy of one's own head. As far as evaluation is concerned, this poses a bit of a problem. Beginning readers, however, tend to read out loud quite naturally, even when asked to read silently. Oral reading has been used for many years to estimate the kind of linguistic processing taking place in the head of the reader. As Don Leu has pointed out, this parallel is a little hazardous, because the two are not the same thing.[1] They serve quite different functions for adults. However, there appears to be sufficient relationship between the two to make analyzing oral reading quite informative.

Detailed analysis of oral reading errors began seriously with the work of Ken Goodman and Rose-Marie Weber, though Goodman used the term "miscue" rather than "error."[2] Analysis of oral reading is a particular example of error analysis (hence my use of "error"). As with many other aspects of development, the errors suggest the kind of processing taking place. Each individual error by itself is less helpful than the patterns of errors. The clearer and more frequent the pattern, the more reasonable the inferences made from it.

Oral reading has had some bad press on and off for many years because it is not what mature reading usually involves.[3] In addition, oral reading as a classroom "round robin" activity presents a socially threatening situation for the less able reader. Oral reading is most appropriate in choral or shared reading, or in the context of "readers' theater" in which prepared reading can be done as a public performance. However, for purposes of evaluation, oral reading can be very helpful for both teacher and student, and need not occur in a stressful situation or with a frequency that suggests that it is the most important or only form of reading.

RECORDING ORAL READING ERRORS

An experienced teacher in the early elementary grades can often listen to a reader and get a good idea of the strategies being used and the state of develop-

---

This chapter is co-authored with Marie M. Clay and is based on her book, *The Early Detection of Reading Difficulties* (3rd ed.). Although this chapter is co-authored, the first person, singular voice is maintained for continuity of style in the book.

ment of the reader. However, generally it is not enough simply to listen to oral reading and depend on your memory. Memories are frail and are not much use as a sole source of information. You could tape record a child's reading, which is useful, and certainly has the advantage of fidelity, but in the long run is somewhat inconvenient. You don't have immediate random access to a particular reading and you can't focus on the important aspects without listening to the whole thing. It is much better to have a graphic record of the oral reading which allows you to get the important information at a glance, compare earlier and later performance, and keep conveniently filed and accessed records.

Many people have devised ways to record oral reading errors and each has its advantages and disadvantages. In this chapter, with the help of Marie Clay, I describe how to record children's oral reading by the use of "running records," a method she devised and presented in her book *The Early Detection of Reading Difficulties.*[4] When a child is reading out loud, you simply take a blank (or lined) piece of paper, and use a shorthand method to write down the child's reading behaviors. An overview of the shorthand recording scheme can be seen in Table 10.1.

I shall refer to some other methods of recording, including the commonly used Informal Reading Inventories (IRIs) later in the chapter. However, in order to avoid confusion in those readers who are already familiar with IRIs, I

TABLE 10.1. Recording Symbols for Running Records

General Format	Child's response | Final response	
	Word in the text | Teacher Prompt	
	During Reading	After Reading
Correct Response	✔	✔
Omission	–	– / text word
Insertion	spoken word	spoken word / –
Substitution	spoken word	spoken word / text word
Repetition[a]	R	R
Self-Correction	error | SC	error | SC / text word |
Attempt	at | attempt	at | attempt / text word
Appeal for Help	– | APP	– | APP / text word |
Teacher Prompt	–	–
tells the word	T	text word | T
asks to try		
section again	| TA	| TA

[a]Number of repetitions is recorded with a supersccript. Size of repetition is recorded with a line from the R to the beginning of the repeated section.

should note that running records are different from IRIs in one major way. To take a running record, unlike an informal reading inventory, you do not need to have a copy of the text to write on—just a piece of paper. This is very important because that is what makes running records more difficult to learn than informal reading inventory procedures. It is also the source of their major advantages. It allows you to record oral reading behaviors at any time from any book without any preparation such as photocopying or dittoing the pages, or having extra copies of the book available. This makes the recording system very flexible.

Running records have other advantages too. First, because it is not necessary to do anything except pick up a pen and paper when a child is reading, teachers are more likely actually to do running records. Second, running records do not set up a "test" situation. They can be done frequently on whatever the child happens to be reading. Third, IRIs are often taken to find out the "level" at which children are reading so that they can be placed on appropriate material in a basal. This means that a child's oral reading is recorded on text that is assumed to be comparable to the classroom texts on which she is to be placed. With running records it makes more sense to simply try out the books to be used in the classroom, or chosen by the student, and find out how the student manages.

So let's begin learning to record oral reading errors and figuring out what they might mean.[5] Each of the types of error is illustrated in the tape recording which accompanies this book. Starting at the beginning of the tape, the examples will be announced. The tape should be stopped after each example so that you can return to the book. Accurate running records for additional practice examples can be found at the end of the book in Appendix A. This chapter of the book will take some time and will produce a certain amount of frustration. The critical ingredient is practice. You would not expect to be able to learn to take shorthand overnight, so don't expect to learn to take running records overnight. Expect your facility to improve with practice. Fortunately, you can easily practice on the sly, and no one is likely to be looking over your shoulder. If you are a teacher and are practicing running records with your students, you will find that students are very understanding about your clumsiness. Always explain to them what you are doing at the outset and tell them that they can look at it afterward and you will explain it to them. This makes the whole process instructional and less threatening.

Often people learning to record oral reading tape-record it so that they can stop the tape and keep up, or go back and make sure they got everything right. Learning like this tends to produce a dependency on the tape recorder. If you become dependent on tape recorders, then taking the running record (or doing an IRI) takes at least twice the time it would otherwise, and there is a good chance that you will do many fewer of them or eventually none at all. Occasional recordings for self-checking and for repeated record-taking in order to build fluency (like repeated readings) can be beneficial. However, they become a hindrance if you continually stop and start the tape to try to keep up. Patience and practice are great virtues.

Identification Information

Always place at the top of the piece of paper the reader's name, the date, the book and page being read, and any special conditions which should be noted such as whether or how often the book has been read previously, or whether the book has been read to the child.

Words Read Correctly

Each word read correctly is represented by a check mark (✓). Thus the following rendition of a text by a child would be recorded as shown:

TEXT   Today the class went to the zoo.
            We saw an elephant and a monkey.
STUDENT   Today the class went to the zoo.
            We saw an elephant and a monkey.

**RUNNING
RECORD**   ✓ ✓ ✓ ✓ ✓ ✓
            ✓ ✓ ✓ ✓ ✓ ✓

Note that there is one check mark for each word, and that they are arranged in exactly the way the words are arranged on the page so that we can tell which check represents which word. (Your check marks will be bigger and more spread out than those shown here.) Now you try this with the following text, which is the first reading sample on the tape.

TAPE EXAMPLE #1

"Go home,"
said the hens.
"No," said Little Pig.
"Go home,"
said the ducks.
"No," said Little Pig.
"Go home,"
said the cows.
"No," said Little Pig.
"Go home,"
said the sheep.
"No," said Little Pig.
"Go home,"
said the butcher,
"or I'll make you into
sausages."
"Yes, I will,"
said Little Pig.[6]

Words Missed (Omitted)

Sometimes children simply skip over a word, sometimes deliberately and sometimes accidentally. We write this as a dash (–) and *after we have finished the record* we record the omitted word. The actual word in the text is always recorded on the lower line and the reader's omission or substitution (the next section discusses substitutions) is recorded above the line. A running record with omissions should be recorded as follows:

TEXT	There was once a jolly farmer
	who had a red tractor.
STUDENT	There was a jolly farmer
	had a red tractor.

**INITIAL
RECORD**
   ✓ ✓ – ✓ ✓ ✓
   – ✓ ✓ ✓

**FINAL
RECORD**
   ✓ ✓ <u>–</u>   ✓ ✓ ✓
    <u>once</u>
   <u>– ✓ ✓ ✓</u>
   who

Now try to record the second example on the tape.

TAPE EXAMPLE #2

**"I'm looking for a house,"
said the little brown mouse.**

Your first pass at the running record should look something like this:

   ✓ ✓ ✓ ✓
   ✓ – ✓ ✓ ✓

After you have finished taking the running record, add to it the details. Add the word omitted and a line separating the two.

**FINAL
RECORD**
   ✓ ✓ ✓ ✓ ✓
   ✓ <u>–</u> ✓ ✓ ✓
    the

It is very important to wait until the end to add in the actual word missed. It only takes a minute to add these finishing touches to the running record. If you try to do it during the reading, you will find that you miss a lot of other things. In all the examples in this chapter, the notations in boldface are added **after** the reader has finished reading.

Words Substituted

Younger readers quite commonly substitute a different word for the one on the page. Simply write down the word the reader says, and later fill in the word that was in the text. For example:

TEXT   Harry was a good boy.
STUDENT   Harry was a nice boy.
RUNNING
RECORD   ✔ ✔ ✔ nice ✔
            <u>good</u>

Now try your hand at recording the example on the tape.

TAPE EXAMPLE #3

**At the same time, Richard
and Claire, Henry and Huia and Billy,
were going up the road wearing
their dragon costume.**[7]

Your running record for this should look something like the following:

✔ ✔ ✔ ✔
✔ ✔ Harry ✔ ✔ ✔ ✔
      <u>Henry</u>
✔ coming ✔ ✔ ✔ ✔
   <u>going</u>
✔ ✔ ✔

Notice that although the words are substituted, the meaning has not been lost, and the substitutions reflect some of the print features of the author's words. The reader is striving to make sense and to match what he says with the print features.

Words Added (Inserted)

Sometimes children add words to the reading which are not in the text. These words are simply written into the record just as in the case of substitutions. Later, a dash is added underneath to indicate that there was no matching word in the text. An example of an insertion would look like this:

TEXT   I went to the shops.
STUDENT   I went down to the shops.
RUNNING
RECORD   ✓ ✓ <u>down</u> ✓ ✓ ✓
            –

Now take your turn at this recording with the example on the tape.

TAPE EXAMPLE #4

"Fantail, Fantail,
have some cheese."
"No. No. No.
I don't like cheese."
"Fantail, Fantail,
have some peas."
"No. No. No.
I don't like peas."
"Fantail, Fantail,
have some pie."
"No. No. No.
I don't like pie."[8]

The running record for this goes:

✓ ✓
✓ ✓ ✓
✓ ✓ ✓
✓ <u>do</u>   <u>not</u> ✓ ✓
  don't   –
✓ ✓
✓ ✓ ✓
✓ ✓ ✓
✓ <u>do</u>   <u>not</u> ✓ ✓
  don't –
✓ ✓
✓ ✓ ✓
✓ ✓ ✓
✓ <u>do</u>   not ✓ ✓
  don't –

The interesting and positive thing about this reading error is that Emily has substituted book language for the more natural language in the text. Books are more likely to have *do not* than *don't*. The down side of this is that she is not as concerned about matching one spoken word to one printed word as we hope she will become.

Self-corrections

When we make an error in our reading, often (though not always) we stop to correct it. This is a very important behavior because it is evidence that the reader is cross-checking one set of cues with another. Every time a reader does this she learns something. Self-corrections are recorded using the letters SC as in the following example:

TEXT   Once upon a time there
            lived a dragon.
STUDENT   Once upon a time there
            was lived a dragon.
RUNNING   ✔ ✔ ✔ ✔
RECORD   was | SC ✔ ✔
            lived |

This example suggests that the reader used her knowledge of syntax and perhaps of other stories, to predict that *was* would follow *there*. This is a reasonable prediction, but when she reached the word, she did not see the letters which would be there if the word were *was*. Instead, she saw the letters *lived,* which she then read correctly. *This is a healthy strategy.* She was being efficient in trying to predict what was coming, but she also showed a concern for accurate representation of the text. We call this self-correcting from print because the print clues led to the self-correction. The next example on the tape illustrates this type of self-correction.

TAPE EXAMPLE #5

He saw Squirrel.
"Squirrel, did you see
my old brown hat?"[9]

The running record for this should look something like:

✔ ✔ ✔
✔ have |SC ✔ ✔
   did
✔ ✔ ✔ ✔

This is not always the way self-corrections occur. Sometimes incongruities in meaning prompt the change. Consider the following:

The girls' hair was really quite ornate. Their bows for the audience were received with much applause.

In this sentence, you probably read the word *bows* incorrectly and returned to patch it up. You made a plausible reading but found that it later did not make sense. This is called self-correcting from meaning. Good readers will engage in both of these types of self-correction as needed, showing their awareness that reading requires a balanced use of the available cues.

However, interpreting self-corrections requires some cautions. First, not all self-corrections are made out loud. As readers mature, they are increasingly able to self-correct internally, without external signs. Second, self-correction is not always a positive activity. Some readers become overconcerned about rather trivial errors such as substituting *a* for *the*. It is rare that a reader should be encouraged to take the time to go back and correct such an error. Self-correction takes effort, and is disruptive to the flow of the reading. You can certainly have too much of a good thing, particularly when the reading does not involve life or death situations such as reading drug prescriptions.

Repetitions

Sometimes readers, having read a word or a sentence or some other segment of text, decide to go back and reread it. There are numerous reasons for this. For example, we might reread because what we read the first time did not seem to make sense, or we might reread to savor what the writer said, or to help figure out a difficult word, or we might reread to get a better flow if there were several difficult words in the sentence. Repetitions are recorded as in the following example:

> **TEXT**   The spider grabbed the fly
> and wrapped it up.
> **STUDENT**   The spider grabbed grabbed the fly
> the spider grabbed the fly
> and wrapped wrapped wrapped it up.
> **RUNNING**
> **RECORD**   ✓ ✓ ✓R ✓ ✓R
> ✓ ✓R² ✓ ✓

The letter *R* is placed next to a check mark to indicate that the child repeated that word. If it is repeated two or more times, as in the last line of the child's reading, a superscript indicates the number of repetitions. The repetition technique can be used to indicate repetition of a larger section of text as well as of a single word. The child's repetition, "the spider grabbed the fly," in the second line, is illustrated in the running record by the letter *R* and a line going back to the beginning of the repeated segment.

Try recording repetitions from the following text:

TAPE EXAMPLE #6

> **On Tuesday I rode my bike**
> **around the tree,**
> **over the bridge,**
> **under the branches**
> **and through the puddle.**[10]

The running record should resemble the following:

```
✔ ✔ ✔ ✔ ✔
‾‾‾‾|
✔ ✔ R ✔
✔ ✔ ✔
✔ ✔ ✔
✔ ✔ ✔ ✔
```

Now try the next example:

TAPE EXAMPLE #7

> **"Dad, the car is clean,**
> **and so are we," said Mark.**[11]

```
‾‾‾‾‾‾|
✔ ✔ ✔ ✔ ✔ R²
✔ ✔ ✔ ✔ ✔ ✔
```

PROBLEM-SOLVING

Often when a child does not recognize a word right away, he will try to figure it out, possibly making several attempts. These attempts are frequently made out loud, especially by younger students. You should try to record each attempt because the manner in which the student makes such attempts tells us a lot about her strategies for figuring out words. Consider the examples of readers reading the following sentence.

TEXT   She could see people swimming in the water.
STUDENT 1   She could see people s/sw/swim/swimming in the water.
STUDENT 2   She could see people sing in the water—swimming in the water
STUDENT 3   She could see people swing/ing/swim/swimming in the water.
STUDENT 4   She could see people—in the water—swimming in the water.

Each reader was successful in figuring out the unknown word, and each tackled the word in a different manner. Even a single example gives us some useful information, but a pattern of several examples gives us more dependable information.

Recording students' problem solving on words is done as follows:

TEXT	We all went to the fair.
STUDENT	We all went to the f/fire/far/fair.
RUNNING	✓ ✓ ✓ ✓ ✓ f| fire| far| ✓
RECORD	<u>fair</u>

Try your hand at recording problem solving using the next taped example, the text for which, starting on page 8, is:

TAPE EXAMPLE #8

> **The next morning, a boy named Richard**
> **said to his sister Claire,**
> **"Today's the dragon's birthday."**
> **"Everyone knows that," said Claire.**
> **"Poor dragon. No one is brave enough**
> **to go up to his cave and say,**
> **'Happy birthday'."**
> **"Perhaps we could go," said Richard.**
> **"It's too dangerous," said their mother.**
> **"He might frizzle you up."**[12]

Your running record should resemble the following:

```
8
✓ ✓ ✓ ✓ ✓ ✓
   ✓ ✓ ✓ ✓ cr |l |cr |cl-aire | ✓
                  Claire
✓ ✓ ✓ ✓
Even |SC ✓ ✓ ✓
Everyone
✓ ✓ ✓ ✓ ✓ br | af |braf |SC ✓
                  brave
✓ ✓ ✓ ✓ ✓ ✓ ✓
✓ ✓
P |Per |aps | ✓ ✓ ✓ ✓ ✓ ✓
Perhaps
✓ ✓ ✓ ✓ ✓
✓ m-ate | ✓    fr-e | ✓ ✓ ✓
   might        frizzle
```

This is not easy to learn. In fact, it may be the hardest part of taking running records. However, the information it provides is very important and worth the effort. It gives a record of the strategies the reader uses to figure out unfamiliar words. You will notice in this reading that Nick is very consistent in his attempts to figure out these words. One part of your record may have been different from mine. When Nick was figuring out *brave,* I recorded it as a self-correction rather than as a word which he finally figured out. Thus I put SC at the end instead of a check mark. I interpreted his intonation on *braf* as suggesting that he was satisfied that he had made a word. His voice had an air of finality about it. Having said it, he changed his mind. To me this is a self-correction. You may differ. Our difference on the matter is not particularly important unless we have hardly any other examples of Nick's reading. If this were the only example of self-correction and it was doubtful, that would be a problem. Multiple examples are important for establishing patterns.

Sometimes rather than "sounding out" words, readers will spell them. This is recorded with capital letters instead of lowercase ones. Sometimes we get to observe very complex strategies for figuring out words, and great persistence in doing so. Listen to the next example on the tape in which Nick figures out the word *midnight* in the following text.

TAPE EXAMPLE #9

. . . . **for his midnight swim.**

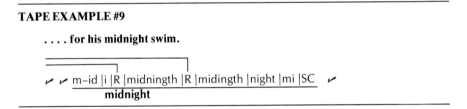

midnight

Instances like this may outfox you in the beginning, but you can simply make a side note later of some of the strategies that you heard. In this instance, he tried to figure the word out left to right, backing out to get the context and have another go; then he shifted to recognizing a sight word within the word which finally allowed the whole thing to come together.

TIME TO TAKE STOCK

The next example on the tape is to help you to begin to put together what you have learned so far. Nick is reading the following text:

TAPE EXAMPLE #10

page 2

Beside a pond, a beaver snacks on tall grass and weeds.
On land, beavers find trees to use for making their homes,

> **called lodges. They build the lodges in deep water.**
> **A beaver swims back and forth from its home to the land.**
>
> page 4
>
> **This beaver is busy building**
> **a dam to hold water back**
> **in a pond. Soon the water will be**
> **deep and will be a safe place**
> **for the beaver to build its lodge.**
>
> **With its sharp front teeth,**
> **the beaver cuts a branch in two.**
> **A hard orange coating on the**
> **teeth keeps them from chipping**
> **as the beaver bites through wood.**[13]

The running record should look something like the following:

2
Beavers | be | sid | SC ✓ ✓ ✓ ✓ ✓ ✓ ✓ ✓ ✓
Beside

✓ ✓ ✓ ✓ ✓ ✓ ✓ ✓ ✓ ✓

✓ ✓ The |SC beavers |SC |R ✓ ✓ ✓ ✓ ✓
　　They　　**build**

✓ ✓ ✓ ✓ ✓ ✓ ✓ ✓ ✓ ✓ ✓

4
✓ ✓ ✓ ✓ ✓
✓ ✓ ✓ ✓ ✓ ✓
✓ ✓ ✓ ✓ – ✓ ✓ ✓
　　　　　the
✓ ✓ ✓ ✓ s|SC ✓
　　　　　a
✓ ✓ ✓ ✓ ✓ ✓

✓ ✓ ✓ two |SC　　✓R ✓ ✓
　　　　–

✓ ✓ ✓ ✓ ✓ ✓
✓ ✓ ✓ ✓ keep |SC　✓ ✓
　　　　　on
✓ ✓ ✓ ✓ ✓
✓ ✓ ✓ ✓ ✓

Notice how the page numbers have been recorded on the top of the sheet for ease of reference at some later point.

You may have found yourself at or beyond your limit in attempting to take this record. This should not be surprising. You are essentially in the process of learning shorthand and should not expect to become comfortable with it in a few minutes. Fortunately, like reading, the more you do it, the easier it becomes. Indeed, you might like to rewind the tape and try the example again.

Just as beginning readers find rereading helpful for developing fluency, teachers beginning to take running records can develop fluency from repeating a record. Just be careful not to become addicted to tape recorders.

In recording the example, you might also have found that your running record was not the same as mine. Actually, there is more than one way to record this reading, depending on how you interpret certain reading behaviors. For example, Nick read one part as follows:

> **TEXT**   Soon the water will be deep and will be a safe place . . .
> **STUDENT:**   Soon the water will be deep and will be s - a safe place . . .

When I was making my record, I felt that the reader predicted the word "safe," and began to say it but encountered the word "a," noticed the discrepancy, and corrected his error. You might have interpreted the behavior in terms of the reader skipping over "a" to "safe," but then noticing the "a." This would be recorded as:

$$- \mid SC \qquad s \mid R \;\nearrow$$
$$\;\mathbf{a} \qquad\qquad \mathbf{safe}$$

Again, some differences in interpretation are to be expected, but in the long run should not have problematic consequences.

INTERVENTION

In general, when you are taking running records or evaluating any aspect of literacy development, you want to intervene as little as possible. You are interested in learning how the reader manages things himself. However, occasionally there are times to intervene. The major time to intervene is when the usefulness of your subsequent records or your rapport with the reader is seriously at risk. Sometimes children make a series of errors which compound themselves and stall their reading. When this happens, they either cease to read altogether or cease to read in a manner typical of their normal performance. It then becomes important to provide sufficient assistance to restart them in a productive manner. However, if we intervene, it is important that we record our intervention for future interpretation.

The first type of intervention is simply a prompt to reread. Usually we would say, "Why don't you try that again," and direct the reader to the beginning of the sentence, paragraph, page, or other meaning unit. This allows the reader to approach the problematic section with greater momentum. It amounts to a prompted rereading. If they are successful at rectifying the problem, then we have modeled for them a repair strategy, which we might later point out to them, and it tells us something about what they can do with some strategic support. This can be recorded simply by the letters TA (try again), as in the following example:

TEXT   Once upon a time,
     an old man planted
     a little turnip.
     He said to the little turnip,
     "Grow, little turnip!
     Grow bigger and bigger!"

STUDENT   Once upon a time;
     an old man p/panded/pandled?
     a little t/trip/turnip – turnip. [Try that again].
     Once upon a time,
     an old man p/planted
     a little turnip.
     He said to the little turnip,
     Grow little turnip.
     Grow big/bigger and bigger.

RUNNING   ✓ ✓ ✓ ✓
RECORD   ✓ ✓ ✓ p | panded | pandled? ⎤
          planted   ⎟ TA
    ✓ ✓ t | trip | ✓   ⎟
       turnip   ⎦
    ✓ ✓ ✓ ✓
    ✓ ✓ ✓ p | ✓
       planted
  ✓ ✓ ✓
  ✓ ✓ ✓ ✓ ✓
  ✓ ✓ ✓
  ✓ big | ✓ ✓ ✓
  bigger

Notice, that the whole repeated section is bracketed and marked TA for "try again." Notice too that I have used a question mark to show the questioning inflection in the reader's voice. Had he also looked up at me in an appeal for advice on the correct word, I would have annotated it as:

    p |panded | pandled | APP

An appeal to another person is another type of strategy for figuring things out and is important to note. If it occurs with any regularity on text that is not that difficult, then it is a sign of a lack of independence and confidence, and a cause for concern.

    The second type of intervention that will occur is actually telling the student the word. You will want to minimize the likelihood of having to do this, for example, by introducing stories well, including any particularly awkward words, and by knowing the student well enough to predict how he will manage particular books. However, sometimes it is clear that reviewing the context will give little or no support, or it is clear from your experience with the student that a particular word is out of his range. When you tell the child the word it is recorded with a T in the bottom corner of the record as in the following example:

TEXT   We cannot go back to
        the old quarry.
STUDENT   We cannot go back to
           the old [Teacher tells *quarry*]
RUNNING   ✔ ✔ ✔ ✔
RECORD: ✔ ✔ _____ –|
              quarry | T

The next example on the tape is for practice.

TAPE EXAMPLE #11

He could sing.
He could dance.[14]

Your record should look something like:

  ✔ ✔
✔ ✔ draw |d |d |drancee? | d
     dance | **T**

Some Other Comments

Other types of reading behavior may be important for different children. For example, pauses can be recorded as _____ although they generally do not provide much information. Some children do a lot of figuring out silently, and the pauses can highlight a child who otherwise appears not to be using many strategies. You may find it useful to code teacher assistance other than "try that again." For example, for a particular child you might prompt with "What word would make sense there?" or you might prompt with "Do you know another word that starts that way?" You may devise a code for these kinds of support. In general, it is more helpful to make notes and comments which elaborate the record with respect to context or teacher or child behavior. For example, I often find it helpful to comment on fluency, pace, any relevant student comments or nervousness, and expression. Instructionally, the most useful information in the running record would be answers to the following:

1. Is the object of the activity to make meaning? and
2. What kind of strategies are being used to make meaning?

CHAPTER 11

Making Sense of Records of Oral Reading

Chapter 11 contains examples of running records that appear on the audiotape accompanying this book.

We have already made an evaluative leap in order to decide which oral reading behaviors to record. However, having recorded them, now let us make sense of them and leap even further.[15]

ERROR RATE

Whatever the recording system, it will be important to decide how the student is managing. If students are choosing their own books or if we wanted to place them in books, we would want to make sure that they are reading materials that are manageable for them. But what is manageable? The first thing we consider is likely to be simply the error rate: the proportion of the words which were read incorrectly.

The error rate is simply the ratio of the number of words read incorrectly to the total number of words read. This seems like a reasonable measure of how difficult a text is for a child. It is not perfect, however, for a number of reasons. Many years have been spent with researchers arguing over what error rate indicates that a text is too difficult ("frustration level"), what error rate indicates very easy material ("independent level")[16] and what error rate indicates material that is just right. The arguments are actually futile for two reasons. First, all errors are not created equal. Some errors suggest difficulty with the text whereas others do not. Many substitutions of *a* for *the* and *shouted* for *said* and the like are not the same as substitutions of *jump* for *joker*. Self-corrections may take a lot of mental effort and disrupt reading substantially, or they may not. Hesitations may suggest increased mental effort. Second, some children seem to have a higher tolerance for different kinds of word level errors than others do. I have found that some children's reading processes seem to fall apart when they reach an error rate of about one in twenty (5%). Other children seem

This chapter is co-authored with Marie M. Clay and is based on her book *The Early Detection of Reading Difficulties* (3rd ed.). Although this chapter is co-authored, the first person, singular voice is maintained for continuity of style in the book.

to feel comfortable, showing healthy reading processes, even in material in which they have an error rate of one in eight (12.5%). Nonetheless, error rate is not a bad indicator of difficulty if we use it cautiously. Marie Clay suggests that an error rate of up to one in twenty (5%) indicates the text is generally easy enough to be read independently. She calls this *easy text*. Text read with an error rate greater than one in ten is considered to be *hard text*. An error rate of between one in twenty and one in ten is considered to be material which is at the edge of what a student can manage without assistance. This is often called *instructional level text,* but let's call it *learning text*. While it provides information useful for instruction, it is most important because children actually *learn* from it provided they are self-correcting appropriately.

In general, running records are of most value when the text is in the learning range because there are not enough errors to disrupt meaning, but it is difficult enough so that many of the strategies used by the reader are overt and able to be recorded.

What Counts As an Error?

Words are easy to count, but errors are less straightforward. Researchers have argued back and forth about what counts as an error, and this is reflected in the various oral reading tests on the market. Table 11.1 shows the differences between tests in this matter. In a way it depends on what we think we are counting. If we are counting "errors," then it hardly seems "fair" to count repetitions, words laboriously figured out, or self-corrections. However, if we are counting "indicators of difficulty," which is, after all, the major reason for counting them at all, then it is easier to argue for counting these and even extensive hesitations. Unfortunately, there is no sensible formula for doing this. There is no way to weight different types of errors. Is an omission as serious as a prolonged hesitation? Is a substitution as serious as an insertion? Is substituting "smell" for "small" the same as substituting "little"?

I do not see an immediate solution to this, and I don't think one is necessary for most situations. It is probably enough to have a consistent method for counting, and a way of making a reasonable argument when our knowledge tells us that the counting method has failed us in a particular case. The consistent method of counting allows us to make certain comparisons while being on the lookout for qualitative changes. Since I have used Marie Clay's method of recording oral reading behaviors, I will also use her method for counting errors, with minor adjustments.[17] This is as follows:

1. Omissions count as one error each.
2. Insertions count as one error each.
3. A word repeatedly read inaccurately counts as an error every time except when it is a proper noun. Proper nouns count only the first time.
4. Dialectical pronunciations do not count as errors.

TABLE 11.1. Oral Reading Behaviors Counted as "Errors" by Various Authors
of Diagnostic Tests

	Gray (1915)	Gates (1927)	Durrell (1937)	Gilmore (1951)	Spache (1963)	Clay (1975)
Omission of sound and/or word	X	X	X	X	X	X
Addition of sound and/or word	X	X	X	X	X	X
Substitution or mispronunciation	X	X	X	X	X	X
Repetition	X	X	X	X	X	X
Self-correction	X		X	X	X	
Word aided	X	X	X	X	X	X
Hesitation			X	X	X	
Punctuation ignored		X		X	X	

[a]One-word repetitions not counted.
Source: Richard Allington (1984). Oral Reading. In P. David Pearson (Ed.), *Handbook of Reading Research.* White Plains, NY: Longman, p. 836. Reprinted by permission.

5. Self-corrected words do not count as errors.
6. If a line is omitted, count it as one error but do not count the words in the line in the word count. This also applies to skipped pages.
7. An intervention with "Try that again" counts as one error and other errors are counted only in the rereading, not in the first reading.
8. If there are several ways to score a section, choose first that which fits with your interpretation of the pattern of errors. If that is not possible, choose the lowest error count.
9. Sometimes you will end up with more errors on a given line than there are words on it, but on any given page, do not score more errors than there are words. Usually in this situation, the child is creating his own text from memory or from the pictures, and there is little point in continuing the running record. Simply note the kind of picture-story match, the quality of the constructed story, and any demonstrated concepts about print.[18]

The error rate equals the number of errors, divided by the number of words in the text, multiplied by 100. For example, if a child makes 15 errors in a 192-word text, his error rate is 15 divided by 192 (which equals about 0.08), times 100, which equals 8%. This can be written as:

$$\text{Error rate} = \frac{\text{Number of errors}}{\text{Number of words}} \times 100$$

Accuracy rate is simply this figure subtracted from 100. In this case it would be $100\% - 8\% = 92\%$ accuracy.

For practice, calculate the accuracy rate for the running record of the "Beaver" story on pages 78–79. The correct calculations are at the end of Part II in the notes section.[19]

SELF-CORRECTION

At the beginning of the book I described the importance of self-correction. If a child is not self-correcting, then he learns nothing from his mistakes, runs the risk of not understanding the text, and may even practice errors to the point of having automatic incorrect word identification. If a reader is self-correcting, then there is a good chance that in a literate environment he will teach himself to read with relatively little help. Thus, it is helpful to have an index of how often the child self-corrects. Based on Marie Clay's work, we can calculate self-correction ratio as the number of times a child did self-correct in relation to the number of times he could (i.e., the number of errors plus the number of self-corrected errors). As a formula, the self-correction ratio is:

Self-Corrections : (errors + self-corrections)

which is symbolized:

S.C. Ratio = S.C. : (E + S.C.)

Calculate the self-correction ratio for the "Beaver" example on page 79. The correct calculations are at the end of Part II in the notes section.[20]

Within the learning range of text difficulty, the self-correction rate is a helpful indicator of the extent to which the reader is monitoring his own use of the different sources of information available to him. It is not a perfect indicator of monitoring since some readers will monitor their reading, find problems, but not correct them. Self-corrections are reflections of the reader's comparing different sources of information, finding them discrepant, *and* doing something about correcting the discrepancy. However, as I have mentioned before, some readers may correct themselves silently.

Not all self-corrections are equal. In particular, it is important to examine which sources of information are being seen as discrepant. Susan makes substitutions that do not make sense but that would, if they were written down, look a lot like the word on the page. However, she immediately realizes that what she said did not make sense, and she tries again, using both the meaning and the print detail. We can interpret Susan's running record as suggesting that she is attending most strongly to the print detail but comparing it with a strong internal notion of the meaning of the text. We call this self-correcting from meaning. It is as if she says to herself, "That doesn't make sense" or "That doesn't sound right."

On the other hand, Jane goes about her reading in the opposite manner. She most strongly emphasizes meaning, producing substitutions that make sense but do not fit well with the print, and corrects herself from the print detail. It is as if she said to herself, "No. That doesn't look right." We call this self-correcting from print.

When the text is very easy for a child, she will usually use all the sources of information necessary to get things right the first time. However, as things become harder, she will tend to abandon one or other source of information for a first attempt and then use the other to check up. As things become harder still, we often get a total neglect of information that the child is quite capable of using under normal conditions. Thus running records taken on material that is too hard tell us relatively little of any importance about the reader's strategies except how they break down.

PREDICTION

Prediction is at the heart of efficient reading. It is critical at all levels of reading activity mainly because it is hard to know how to interpret letters or words without knowing the context in which they appear. Jerome Bruner describes the problem as:

> Language, to whatever use it may be put, has the design feature of being organized on different levels, each level providing constituents for the level above which dominates it. . . . the distinctive features of speech sound are determined by the phonemes that they constitute at the next level up; phonemes are combined according to rules at the next level up, the morpheme, and so on.
>
> So too at the levels above sound, for morphemes, lexemes, sentences, speech acts, and discourse. Each level has its form of order, but that order is controlled and modified by the level above it. Since each level is dominated by the level above it, efforts to understand any level on its own have inevitably led to failure.[21]

Fortunately, oral reading errors can give us some insight into whether or not children are or are not predicting. Prediction is done on the basis of the extension of meaning or patterns into the future. Thus, if a child without hesitation makes, or begins to make, a substitution that would make good sense up to that point, but does not fit entirely with the print detail, then he is likely to have been predicting. For example, consider the following:

> **TEXT**   One day the teeny tiny woman
>   put on her teeny tiny bonnet
> **STUDENT**   One day the teeny tiny woman
>   wen- put on her teeny tiny bonnet

In this case he has made an error that is difficult to explain without assuming that he predicted the word *went* would begin the next line, but got there and did not find the letters he expected. There is nothing new about the recording here, only something important to notice for interpretation.

The next two examples on the tape illustrate prediction.

TAPE EXAMPLE #12

**There was
a little Indian.
He wished
he had a horse.**[22]

The running record should look something like:

Th | ✔ one | one | SC
there   **was**

✔ ✔R ✔
✔ ✔
✔ ✔ ✔ ✔

TAPE EXAMPLE #13

**Mum hosed the garden.
"Please will you hose me?"
said Helen.
"Please will you hose me?"
said Mark.
Mum hosed Helen and Mark.**[23]

The running record:

✔ ✔ ✔ ✔
✔ we |sc   ✔ ✔ ✔
  will
✔ ✔
✔ ✔ ✔ ✔ ✔
ask |SC   ✔
said
✔ ✔ ✔ ✔ ✔

In the first example, Emily predicts that the story will begin "There once was
. . . ," but she looks and either sees some letters there that disagree (*once* does
start the same as *was* but does not have an *n*), or she goes on to the next line and
sees *a* and realizes that you can't say "There once a . . ." so she corrects herself.
In the second example, we hear Nick predicting on two levels. Using normal
conversation, Mark asks a question, and the text should say "asked Mark," but
it doesn't, so he corrects himself. When he gets to the bottom of the page, however, he begins to predict where the story will go next, and seeks verification
when he turns the page. The most complete contrast to this is the child who is
substituting nonsense words or words that do not fit the context. It is unlikely
that such a reader is predicting.

It is always helpful to have several examples of a particular type of error in
order to be comfortable with what you are inferring. However, sometimes we
get a single example of an error that is almost certainly a result of prediction and
we can say, with reasonable certainty, that the student does, or can, predict
while reading. This is not a trivial assertion.

Prediction produces words that do not necessarily fit the letters on the page
but that certainly fit with the context up to that point. However, the error does
not necessarily fit with the context after that point. In other words, substitutions that make sense in context often suggest that the child has predicted. However, there are exceptions. For example, if a child comes to a word with which
he has difficulty, pauses, and then says a word which makes sense up to that
point and fits with some of the print detail, it is evidence that he is trying to
make sense, but not that he is predicting. Prediction takes place *before* you get
there, not after.

THE BALANCE AND METHOD OF INFORMATION USE

When I study children's oral reading, I am most interested in the information
they use and the manner in which they use it. When they are reading a book that
is not too easy and not too hard, I want to know whether they use the available
information from their language, their experience, and from the page in a flexible and active manner. I want to know whether they try to stay a little ahead of
what they are reading, and whether they check one source of information
against another. Sometimes problems occur. For example, some children over-
rely on one source of information to the exclusion of another. A child may rely
on her knowledge of the alphabetic generalizations in the language, without
checking against her knowledge of the language or her own experience. An oral
reading such as the following might occur:

TEXT   I cannot go out to play with you today.
STUDENT   I cannot go oot to play with you todda.

There are, of course, a number of possible reasons for this. She may not have the relevant experience, or her language pattern may be substantially different from that of the text and she may not have learned "book language." On the other hand, she may have come to doubt the relevance or adequacy of her own knowledge or language. Her interpretation of her reading instruction may have convinced her that reading has nothing to do with her own personal knowledge and language. Whatever the cause, we will try to encourage her to make more use of these other sources of information in conjunction with what she already uses. However, we will certainly be interested in seeing whether something in the classroom (or at home) is maintaining this situation. For example, if the books she has to read in class are too difficult, her error rate may make it impossible for her to construct meaning from the text. Consistently deprived of meaningfulness in those activities designated as reading, she may have developed unfortunate habits and even unfortunate misconceptions about reading itself.

Similarly, we get imbalances in the use of information sources in the opposite direction. Some children depend too heavily on their own knowledge and language patterns, more or less ignoring what is on the page. For example:

TEXT   Down came the biscuits
         and the book
         and the bucket
STUDENT   Down came the biscuits
         down came the book
         down came the bucket

It is true that reading is a constructive activity, and that the meaning must be constructed by the reader using his own knowledge. Some reading situations require limited concern over the use of exactly those words the author used, such as in reading a paperback novel. However, certain types of reading require detailed attention to the words the author uses, such as instructions for running expensive or dangerous machines. It is important to have flexibility in the use of the different sources of information, and we will be encouraging these readers to attend more to print detail, particularly when checking predictions. Such readers rarely are found not predicting; it is the verification of their predictions that is missing. It may be that the reader lacks the knowledge of print conventions or the alphabetic principles, or it may be that he has them but fails to use them for one reason or another, such as having developed reading habits that exclude the need for such knowledge.

Overattention to one or another cue source is very common for brief periods of time in children's development.[24] It is quite common for children just getting the hang of letter-sound relationships to devote an overabundance of effort to them, even to the extent that meaning is lost as attention is exhausted by the process. Rereading at such times makes a substantial difference to performance. Similarly a child who over-predicts often will perform quite differently when asked to read the text with her finger.

Although the balanced use of sources of information is important, it is also important that the information be used flexibly and strategically. If one strategy fails, are other strategies used? Are the strategies efficient? These are important questions to ask of running records. For example, we might see a reader rereading sentences, parts of sentences or paragraphs. This can be an effective strategy, but if it is used as the major method of figuring out unfamiliar words, it is quite inefficient. We might observe repeated rereadings of parts of a sentence to help figure out a word, in a situation where rereading from the beginning of the sentence would give more helpful contextual support. Sometimes we see readers who simply give up after one attempt at each problematic word. There are no hard and fast guidelines as to what constitutes efficient reading strategies, except to say that flexible use of strategies and information sources is likely to be most efficient, provided it is clearly directed toward the goal of constructing meaning.

SUMMARIZING ORAL READING

In order to talk about change over time, it is helpful to have summaries of the running records available. A summary sheet is shown in Figure 11.1. This summarizes, with relatively limited effort, most of the information you could want.[25] The name, date, book, and accuracy are self-explanatory, though it is important that the accuracy be roughly between 90 and 95 percent. The "times read" refers to whether and how many times the book has been read previously by the student. Under "self-corrections" I have filed self-correction rate, which I have already described, and the source of the self-correction, which requires circling any or all of the sources when an example occurs. The same is true for prediction. If an example occurs, circle it. I do not think that numbers of times each occurs is particularly critical here, since we are looking for balance, and since it is sometimes hard to tell the source.

Under "errors," I code the total number of errors, the number that is consistent with the meaning up to the point of the error, the number that is consistent with the grammar, and the match between letters and sounds. In the latter case I am interested in the general pattern, but two or three circles can be used to show variety. The strategies used are a little too complicated to indicate by a listing so I have listed the strategies of rereading and reading ahead. However, most informative here are the number of words figured out, and the number of times the student appeals to outside help. These are both good indicators of change. The use of print is more variable and should be described, along with how and whether the print, meaning, and grammar cues are integrated. Examples can be very helpful here. Fluency is also an indicator of change, and I have four categories: fluent (F), finger-pointing (FP) in which the child reads point-

Figure 11.1. Summary of Running Records

NAME: _____

BOOK: _____

DATE: _____   TIMES READ: _____   ACCURACY: _____

SELF-CORRECTION

Rate: _____ Source: print   meaning   syntax   Prediction

Comment: _____

ERRORS

Total: _____   Meaning: _____   Grammar: _____   L/S match: 1 2 3 4 5

Comment: _____

STRATEGIES
Words figured out: _____   Appeals: _____   Reread: _____   Read Ahead: _____

Print use: _____

Integration: _____

Examples:

Fluency: F   VP   FP   D   EXPRESSION: Y/N

CONNECTIONS
Author/Illustrator   Book   Experience   Style

Other: _____

ing with his finger at each word, voice-pointing (VP) in which the child does not use his finger, but separates each word as if he were using his finger, and dysfluent (D). The category dysfluent generally occurs only when text is too difficult, but it is there just in case. Expression is an area for advancement, and is one indicator of the sense which the student is making. The connections which the student makes with other books, authors, personal experiences, and the like are ways of comprehending the text. These can be addressed in discussing the book, and we will return to them in later chapters. Comparing summary sheets like this simplifies discussion of growth.

This summary is reasonably elaborate, and I am certain that a simpler version would suffice for many purposes. A simpler summary might include a simple list of books with their level of accuracy and self-correction rate, and a brief description of the strategies used and how the use of strategies and cues differed on the easier and harder texts. A different and simpler summary sheet might resemble that in Figure 11.2.

Figure 11.2. Oral Reading Summary

Student _____ Teacher _____ Date _____

Book _____

Comment _____

Accuracy Rate _____ SC Rate _____ Reading Rate _____

Strategies   **Comments**

Prediction _____

Self-correction (print) _____

  (meaning) _____

Word/word match _____

Rereads _____

Skips word and returns _____

Uses phonic analysis _____

Uses context (meaning) _____

  (grammar) _____

  (illustrations) _____

Talks sensibly about text _____

_____

_____

_____

_____

_____

SOME CAUTIONARY NOTES

Running records are not perfect reflections of children's oral reading, let alone perfect reflections of their reading in general. However, they do provide some extremely useful data that can both document change and direct instruction. They provide indirect evidence of how children are going about understanding what they are reading. A number of studies have shown that particular patterns of errors are strongly related to other measures of understanding: cloze tests and retellings, both of which will be discussed in later chapters. Increases in self-correction alone, given a comparable error rate, suggest a greater degree of understanding. However, more consistent indicators can be produced by adding together different oral reading behaviors.[26] In general, it is unnecessary to engage in mathematical exercises to show change, but it does help to know that studies do show a sensible and strong relationship between healthy patterns of oral reading behavior and other indicators of healthy reading.

Running records also have a couple of extra bonuses. In my experience, when I begin to take running records, the student generally wants to know what I am doing. I explain what I am doing and that I will show the student and explain it when he has finished the record. Students find it interesting and it is rather helpful to get them to think about their reading through the records. With running records it is easy to highlight the positive. To begin with, you have a page of check marks and a handful of other records, indicating all the words the student read correctly. Second, you can highlight the value of the strategies the student used. I think sharing the records with the student is an important thing to do.

In the beginning, when you are trying to learn how to take running records, you will need to skip sections occasionally so that you can keep going. But every now and then it is all right to ask a student if he will stop for a moment while you catch up because you are just learning and he is reading so fast. This is good news for a less able reader—he is shown to be doing well and you are shown to be a novice. Very good for the confidence, this!

Some students in the beginning are a bit concerned about the records, especially if they can hear you taking them. For example, if you use a pencil on a piece of paper on a wooden desk it is often quite easy to hear the difference between a check mark and some other record such as a substitution. If a student is nervous and becomes attuned to the sounds of the record rather than to his inner monitor, self-monitoring goes out the window because the monitoring is done through your pencil. A student who is thus concerned can be helped by discussing the records and sharing them, but also if a ballpoint pen is used on a pad of paper, some of this problem goes away. Also, if you are right-handed, try to sit on the right-hand side of the student; otherwise you will have the recording paper in a distracting position and you will likely be poking her in the eye with your elbow.

Before leaving running records, I would again urge you to get a copy of Marie Clay's *The Early Detection of Reading Difficulties,* which has a more thorough treatment of the topic. I have taught classes using the book for the past nine years, and I have yet to hear of anyone being able to buy a secondhand copy.

CHAPTER 12

Talking and Listening: Evaluation through Interviews

When we evaluate children's literacy development, we are interested in finding out how the young reader/writer engages in and thinks about literate activity and about herself as a literate person. In the past we have tried many devious ways of getting this information and I can hear my mother saying to me, "Why didn't you just ask?" This may sound like simplistic advice, but often it is the best way to get good information. Not only that, but when we ask good, honest, thoughtful questions, there are some instructional benefits that go beyond the usefulness of the information we receive. However, most questions asked in classrooms are not of this kind. They are short questions to which the teacher already knows the answer. Under these circumstances, students do not ask their own questions, and it is these that provide us with the most useful information. This is what makes it particularly distressing that students generally do not ask questions. Rose-Marie Weber found that, in over sixty reading lessons she analyzed, although students were asked up to 40 questions in a single session, in the entire body of data she collected, not a single student asked a question.[27] James Dillon similarly found in a study of 27 classrooms only 11 questions asked by students.[28] This compares starkly with David Yaden's studies of children being read to at home and not being asked questions. Under these conditions, children asked thousands of questions.[29]

Although just asking sounds straightforward, it is not a simple matter to get very important, accurate information from young learners, particularly if they are used to talking to *National Enquirer* reporters or Educational Gestapo. Adults are generally quite self-centered, or at least adult-centered, in their view of children and keep trying to understand children's activity in terms of adult views of how the world should be. Julie Tammivaara and Scott Enright describe the problem of "adult-centrism" beautifully:

> In many ways, any adult ethnographer[30] who traipses through a child's world smug in the certainty that the adult world is the highest known form of civilization and a distant goal that young children have just begun to strive for is not unlike the stereotypical "Ugly American" tourist invading the shores of exotic cultures only to find them quaint [in the case of children "cute"] but clearly inferior.
>
> Ethnographers who insist on visiting and studying children from the rigid perspective of adulthood will in the end understand the reality of childhood no better than tourists who visit another land and do their best to bring their

"home" along with them. *Respect* for children and their own knowledge about themselves, as well as the same willingness to suspend (adult) judgment and perspective in talking with *children* as in talking with adults are key components of the successful ethnographer's interviews and participant observation.[31]

The common use of the term "diagnosis" with its medical connotations has perpetuated and extended this view of the adult expert examining the poor unfortunate child afflicted with "reading disability" or the "illiterate" adult.

Although interviewing has a long history in the field of ethnography, it has only recently become looked upon as a credible perspective for gathering evaluation information in educational settings. This very likely has to do with the increased interest in ethnography among educational researchers, and the fact that process-oriented approaches to writing have gained popularity.[32] The purpose of an interview is to gain an understanding of how an individual understands and organizes her world or some domain of knowledge within it—in other words, to try to depict the world as it appears from the other person's perspective. When we approach the children in our classes in this manner, we find it much easier to provide appropriate instruction for them because they help us to see the curriculum as they see it. We tend to think only of the knowledge to be taught rather than of the child who is to learn and of her life. We think of the knowledge to be imparted in terms of what makes sense to us. We also tend to think of the important questions for us rather than trying to find out the important questions for the children.

There are many types of interview, some of which are permissible with adults and possibly older children but which do not work well with younger children. The "structured interview" does not work well with younger children generally, especially when the interviewer reads the questions. Adults have schedules and time constraints, and tend to understand such formalities better (though still do not always accept them). However, younger children have their own concerns, and pushing them to conform to your schedule and your set of questions makes it clear to them that you are an adult and are intent on pulling rank on them. Children will often then begin trying to figure out what you (the Adult) would like to hear. It is a game they play often. If they are good at the game they may be able to leave you satisfied but ignorant. This is generally a problem for structured interviews such as those often used in research studies. Researchers in such studies are usually trying to compare children with one another and are attempting to quantify responses and standardize interviews in order to do so. Even though the questions that are written down might be excellent questions (see for example those by Karen Wixson and her colleagues),[33] there is a great loss in the process of standardizing (as opposed to personalizing) the interview. However, classroom teachers (and most others concerned with the welfare of children) do not need to compare children one with another, so I do not suggest such procedures unless they are clearly necessary.

One of the most amusing examples of this standardizing procedure, which is still common in schools, in research, and in books on diagnosis, is the "Interest Inventory" in which children respond to a number of rating scales or multiple-choice questions on a standard form so that the teacher will be able to look at the form and find out what each child is interested in without talking to him. Interviewing a child is a far better way to get this information, along with conferring with him about his writing and the books he is choosing to read. This would be true even if we used "interest" in the narrow sense of the word meaning "horse riding" or "motorbikes" and the like, but it is so much more true when we are referring to the issues that occupy the child's thoughts such as the birth of a new sibling, feelings of failure, an impending plane trip to Grandma's, divorce, and so forth.

In this chapter and the next, I describe how to conduct interviews as part of your evaluation procedures. I discuss the conditions required for using interviews as an evaluation tool, their consequences for classroom teaching practice, some of the information that is available through interviews, and the kind of benefits that accrue from interviewing. Along the way I shall also talk more generally about listening in the classroom. But first, let us consider the information that we *give* in an interview because it will have a considerable influence on what we *get*.

INFORMATION WE GIVE IN AN INTERVIEW

To briefly review some of the comments in Chapter 3, an interview is a social interaction that can be seen as conveying various messages. The communication that takes place is two-way and is both verbal and nonverbal. Although the interviewer has the intention of learning particular things from the interviewee, the interviewer always conveys information to the interviewee about the rules of the social interchange, and the balance of power or status in the relationship. We convey most of this information quite unintentionally. Because of our status as adults and teachers, for example, many children will interpret even apparently quite neutral statements in terms of their normal relationships with teachers in particular and adults in general. Thus a simple question such as "Is this your classroom?" can be interpreted as a controlling statement, perhaps meaning "You are supposed to be in your classroom."

Consider the information conveyed in a standard testing situation. We show the child into a room and show him where to sit [directive]. We sit opposite him [confrontational position] in either a higher chair or a chair that is clearly for an adult [highlighting the power differential]. Then we take a test for which we have the answers the child is to try to get right. Next we have the child perform in such a way that he is guaranteed to fail at some point. There are clear status messages in this interaction. Whenever we give a command or are highly directive, we increase the status difference and decrease the likelihood that the child will tell us anything valuable, particularly about weaknesses and fears.

The kinds of questions that we ask also convey information about the kind of knowledge we think the interviewee has and the kind of information we think is important. For example, if we ask someone how many books he has published, we are suggesting that that is important. If we ask, ''What do you think the poet was trying to do with this poem?'' we presuppose that the student understands poetry as something written with a particular goal in mind. In a similar way, the responses we give can convey information that can change everything. For example, if we say ''good'' or ''okay'' or ''right'' in particular ways, it can be interpreted as evaluative feedback conveying a message about the nature of the activity—that there are right and wrong answers (or at least better and worse answers) and that we already know them.

The way in which we ask questions conveys a message too. If we use a standardization procedure, we can convey messages about implicit comparisons. We can also convey messages about the objectification we are attempting—about the negation of personalization in order to produce quantification. To the extent that we are seen as part of particular social groups, we can also be seen as representing their values. Thus, if we ask about the most recent book a reader read and it happened to be the Kama Sutra, or perhaps a Harlequin romance, we may or may not get the straight scoop depending in part on the extent to which we appear to be the sort of person who would approve or disapprove of the material, or the extent to which that is ambiguous. Of course the motives of the student will interact with that perception. For example, if the student supposes that we will not approve but he wishes to shock us, he will respond differently than if he wants to impress us or wants to participate in honest dialogue. We can never be exactly sure what messages are being conveyed, but these are important considerations. Children are not born with adult discourse strategies, and teachers play a part in developing these strategies. In a classroom interview with a young child, the teacher's questioning strategies begin to shape the child's developing patterns of discourse. In this way, our interviews with children shape their interviews with each other, and ultimately affect the way they view themselves. If we want them to interact as literate adults, then we must treat them as such from the outset. When two normal literate adults have both read a particular book, if one of them quizzes the other attempting to find out if she got ''the main idea,'' their interaction is likely to be brief and terminal. Literate adults normally discuss books with the expectation of gaining a different (not inferior) perspective.

CONDUCTING AN INTERVIEW

If an interview is to provide useful information, it is important for the student to do most of the talking. This seems reasonably obvious, but in my experience teachers (and I include myself in that category) often have the greatest difficulty keeping quiet. Learning how to keep others talking is not what teachers are usually taught to do. To the contrary, they are usually taught how to keep children quiet. Yet getting others to talk more is at the center of the skill of interviewing. You can do a simple self-check with a tape recorder. Record yourself interviewing a child. If the dialogue is unbalanced and you are doing most of the talking, then things are not going well and you may need a gag. Of course, it will depend somewhat on the focus and context of the discussion. For example, if you are each describing a book that you have read, you will want to spend an appropriate amount of time talking about your book, as you are also providing a model of the way literate people do things. But in general the more you listen, the more you learn (and often the more the student learns about himself). If the dialogue sounds stilted, like a test, then it probably was a test, and any information gained will be about as useful as if it had been gathered on a test.

Julie Tammivaara and Scott Enright suggest that with very young children it is helpful to build interview questions into familiar games or into familiar activities. In that way, they are familiar with the format, and there is less that is unfamiliar about the process. They suggest classroom activities such as having the children draw pictures of themselves doing happy things at school, and then discussing the pictures with the children individually. Writing obviously poses very helpful situations to prompt discussion, especially since it is in the context of print, and there are interesting, concrete things to discuss. This is particularly true if the child is writing about personal experiences in which there can be no challenge to his role as the expert.

A book that has been read can also serve well as the center of the exchange. However, the interview situation may be rendered useless by other social experiences. For example, children whose chief experience with text is in the context of a basal reading lesson are likely to treat book interviews in a similar manner and respond just as they would in that context. The basal reading lesson format is generally one in which there is a "right answer" that the teacher has and the student is to get. In such situations there is no room for discussion, and the student is clearly not the expert. In the same way, adults tend to insist that children understand literature just as they, the adults, understand it rather than trying to understand the child's understanding of it. If this is the format of your reading lessons, the interview will be more difficult for you, and you might consider changing your approach to teaching reading.[34] Strive for opening the mind and closing the mouth.

Using the child's own terminology is especially important in understanding his perspective. Apart from showing that you are listening and trying to understand, it reduces the likelihood of your putting words in his mouth, imposing your own meaning on what he is saying, and misconstruing his position. The time for translation into your language and that of other audiences (parents, administrators, etc.) will come later. In addition, you are likely to have him simply give back to you the description you gave to him, preventing him from being reflective. Reflectiveness is something which you wish to encourage both because it helps children self-evaluate, reducing your own role in evaluation, and because once children understand their role in your partnership, they will continually be collecting and analyzing information to teach you during your interviews. Reflective children can provide extraordinarily focused instructionally relevant information for teachers. For example, Jane Hansen asked some of her young students such questions as "What have you learned most recently about writing? What would you like to learn next?"[35] These questions work best over an extended period of time in which students become used to reflecting on such things (and having the time to do so), and the questions are those which they regularly ask themselves.

Often we are inclined to ask children what they mean when we have not grasped what they said. This is not a good tactic because we are asking them to rethink what they were talking about and try to tell it to us in our language. This is likely to make the message apparently clearer in the short term, but make our understanding less accurate in the longer term. At the same time, such questions convey a hint that we think the child is not good at expressing himself. He will then be more concerned about the form of what he says than the content. It is better to ask questions that will provide more information in his own language, which will help us to understand. Questions about use are helpful. For example, I might ask a second-grade student, "if a first-grade student were having trouble knowing when to use a comma, what could you tell him about how to use a comma?"

The objective of evaluation is to know a student well enough to help him with his learning. If you know a student well, you are more able to provide the most useful support with the minimum of intervention. Thus the student does as much independently as possible and has ownership of the learning. He then has something to talk to you about—something about which he is the expert. This situation is maximized when the student feels the classroom to be "home turf." Helping students feel the classroom is theirs involves helping them take responsibility for the generation of class rules, class decoration, and other such decisions. Teachers often spend part of their summer making next year's classroom beautiful with big illustrations and posters. Children's feelings of ownership and home turf might be stronger if they arrived to a bare classroom and began with a discussion of how they could decorate it and manage it, and then set out to do so.

ESTABLISHING RAPPORT AND TRUST

Before another person will give you any information of importance, you must establish a trusting and supportive relationship with him. This relationship is usually called "rapport." Rapport is established mostly indirectly. You can say, "Trust me. I want to help you. Think of me as your friend. . . . I really respect you," as much as you like but, regardless of your sincerity, you are not likely to reduce a student's anxiety or increase his trust. However, if you are relaxed, supportive, and show that you are interested in what he has to say, especially on topics of his interest, you convey much more powerfully the message that you respect him and find his remarks important. The principal message to be conveyed throughout is that the student is the expert from whom you wish to learn, and that you can be trusted with the information he gives you. Particularly the student must believe that his ego or self-esteem will be left intact, or even enhanced, by the interchange. It may help to point out explicitly that you are interested in his opinion or perspective, but these statements are of little use if not backed up with evidence. For example, simply restating to him parts of what he said in his own words gives evidence of your interest in and intention to understand what he has to say. Not allowing other children to interrupt conveys the importance of his message too. This is often difficult in a classroom, but it is vital to socialize children to be independent, and to understand that their wishes, interests, and concerns must take second place when two people are having a serious discussion. Children are much better at interpreting actions than they are at interpreting speech. They learned language in the first place because they were so adept at constructing meaning from people's actions and their context and then applying meaning to the patterns of speech sounds.

Establishing rapport will not only be different from person to person, but it will also be different for the principal, the school psychologist, the specialist reading teacher, and the classroom teacher. The classroom teacher has the advantage of extended contact in that she sees the child every day for most of the day. But there is the disadvantage of having many children and hence less opportunity for individual, uninterrupted conversations unless she specifically makes time for them by stressing independent and collaborative problem solving and self-evaluation. On the other hand, the classroom teacher sometimes has to take a controlling role in the classroom, and this works directly against the establishment of the balanced relationship within which a child will be an optimal informer. At the same time, the classroom teacher, because of her familiarity with the student, may find it more difficult to claim ignorance about the child and his learning, thus making it difficult for the child to adopt the role of "expert" in which he is likely to be maximally informative.

Nonetheless, the classroom teacher has the considerable advantage of being able to set up a predictable relationship. Within the security of this relationship, children speak more. This security also allows more challenging questions to be asked, including ones that cause a temporary loss of control. A child struggling with a difficult question, or a process he does not yet control, from a position of confidence is developing independence. Don Graves notes that such questions are particularly effective if accompanied by a reason or even a challenge such as "Do you think you are ready to handle a problem like this?"[36] These questions work only within the security of a trusting relationship based on frequent interactions.

Specialist teachers and support staff such as reading teachers and school psychologists often meet with smaller groups of children, even one-on-one sometimes. However, they also tend to have less contact time available, for example, meeting children in a "testing session." It would probably be better for a school psychologist to be spending time in classrooms each day so that she could be a familiar with some of the children in a noncontrolling setting, and able to do some of the interviewing in the class context. Indeed, federal regulations currently require documentation of students' classroom context.

It is helpful to have something to do together or something of common interest, perhaps an object, as the center of the interview. This allows for the development of a relationship which can then provide the opportunity for extension into the area in which you are interested. Books, particularly those selected by the student, can readily provide such a situation, if there is mutual interest and minimal power differential. Writing, too, serves as an excellent focus for interviewing. On the other hand, if the student has written on a topic chosen by the teacher there can be a power differential with the student not being the expert. However, if the topic encourages opinion and the children know that the teacher respects their views, this can still work well.

The most critical factor in interviewing is balancing the power differences between interviewer and interviewee. The major ways to do this are to establish that you are ignorant about the topic or that your view is in no way better than that of the student. Many teachers have difficulty with these, partly because their backgrounds have led them to believe that they must always be the expert and always be in control. Many teachers, for example, feel obliged to have read every book in the classroom before the students read them. Another difficulty for teachers is letting go of the idea that they must check to see whether the student understood each story. If you have trouble, as most of us do, I suggest reading interviews in which you and the student have read different books and you have not read the one that the student read. Then the student really does know more than you and will likely be able to talk about her book quite readily if you show interest in her description. Try this as an exercise and see how it feels. Once you have a feel for it, try a book that you have both read but give information first, perhaps about what you liked or what it reminded you of. When you have a writing conference or interview with a student, try to start with personal narrative writing if possible because the student, again, must be the expert.

ESTABLISHING THE NEED FOR INFORMATION

One of the informal rules of conversation is that you don't ask questions to which you already know the answer unless the student would like to be tested. Thus, if you are to avoid violating conversational rules and putting students on the defensive, you must establish that you are ignorant. It sounds a little strange to talk of being expert at being ignorant, especially for a teacher. Indeed, the problem is more one of establishing a legitimate need for the information or establishing the limits of the teacher's knowledge. Thus it will be particularly difficult for a teacher who has construed his role as being the provider of information for the children to learn. If the student does not accept the premise of the teacher's ignorance, she cannot provide information free of comparison. For example, children are often asked to retell stories to the teacher who has already read the story (or the child has read it aloud to the teacher). It is impossible for the teacher to establish ignorance under these circumstances. If the child thinks that the teacher is looking for specific correct answers, then the student's authority is questioned; either the interview will cease or the information provided will be only a reflection of what the child thinks the teacher thinks is correct. If we wish a student to tell us about what it is like for her to be a reader, she must feel that she is an expert on that topic. In other words, if anyone is supposed to have the "right answer" it cannot be the teacher.

In order for interviews to work, the classroom context must establish that no one has a monopoly on the correct interpretation of text, and only the student can be an expert on what it is like for her to be an author or a reader. Under these conditions, the student is the expert and the teacher is ignorant, allowing the expert to teach the teacher. Unless the primacy of individual perspective and group discussion are established in the classroom, this is going to be a perpetual barrier to the teacher's access to useful information. Probably a better way to think of it is that the student is an expert on her opinions and experiences, and the teacher is an expert on his. Each is a novice with respect to the other.

There are also ways for classroom teachers to get around the problem of shared knowledge (or apparent lack of ignorance). One way is to pose the issue in less personal terms. For example, instead of asking a second-grade student "How do you . . ." you might ask, "What would be a good question for a first-grade student to ask about how to do this?" or "What kinds of questions do some kids ask other kids about . . . ?" Actually, listening to the questions that children in the class do ask one another is a very important source of information. In the same way listening to children trying to sell other children on a book they have read can tell a great deal about what the book meant to the child.

A second way around the problem of assumed shared knowledge is to propose "what if" situations. For example, you might ask a student, "Suppose. . . . How would you . . . ?" This kind of question is useful in trying to find out how children understand stories, but it is also useful to find out how they understand being literate. For example, a second grader might be asked, "Suppose you had a younger brother who was just going to go into first grade. What things could you tell him about reading (or writing) that would help him to become good at it?" or "If you were giving advice to a first-grade student about this, what do you think would be most important to tell him?" Of course, the usefulness of this kind of question can be eliminated if it is followed by any suggestion that the response is wrong.

FRAMING THE INTERACTION

Whenever we engage in an interaction with another person we quickly try to work out what kind of interaction it is to be. For example, "How are you?" can be a genuine question or a formalized greeting that does not even require a response, let alone a lengthy treatise on the state of one's health. People can be offended when we respond inappropriately. The opening bars of the interaction say a great deal. For example, opening a discussion about a book you have both read by saying, "Tell me about the book," can frame the subsequent discussion as if you had said, "This is a test." This interpretation will be most likely when past classroom interactions have led to the expectation of a single correct interpretation and a power differential between teacher and student. It is radically different from saying, "What was your favorite part?" or "I really liked the part where . . ." These initial differences may appear to be small changes but they are small only in the sense that day and night only reflect a difference in the location of the sun relative to a person somewhere on earth.

Any particular interaction is framed by the history of interactions of each of the people, the history of their interactions with each other, the context of the particular interaction, and each individual's concept of the activity or topic of the discussion. For example, if a student is accustomed to being criticized for failure, or to being compared with others, he will find it difficult to admit to experiencing difficulty until he is convinced that this situation is safer than his usual predicament. If a student's concept of the reading process is such that there is a right way to, say, figure out a word, then that will often influence what she reports when asked about how she accomplished that activity. If the student has a history of nonthreatening, or even pleasurable, dialogues with the teacher, then the expectation of further such experiences will enter into the way the student interprets the framing of the situation.

MAINTAINING FLOW

Only insensitive or drunk people continue talking past the point at which someone's interest has obviously gone. If you want someone to keep talking about something you must continue to show interest. There are a number of ways in which people do this. Not yawning is a good start. Even occasionally saying such things as "I am interested in . . ." is fine. However, you must make it clear that you are interested in finding out the honest details rather than in being entertained. The last thing you want is an interesting, but marginally accurate story. Thus, the main thing is to show that you are following what the person is saying. Often a simple "Mhmm," or "I think I see," or a verbatim repetition of what the other person said, along with good eye contact, accomplishes this. Showing that you are checking on your own understanding is also useful. For example you might say, "So let me see if I have this right." However, whenever you make such statements try to use the *student's* words.

Otherwise you put words in his mouth and you may get them back without knowing then whether they are his or yours.

Although the objective is for the student to lead the discussion, you don't always want him to ramble on about things that are not relevant. On the other hand, you don't want to cut him off and indicate to him that you're the boss and are interested only in interrogating him about the particular item on your agenda. The younger the child, or the less able in a particular area, the more likely he is to be sensitive to adults pushing their interests upon him. However, there are ways to guide the development of the interview. For example, you can ask questions like:

> You said that the book made you sad. Can you tell me more about that?
> You said the book made you sad. What was it about the book that made you sad?
> I noticed that you said before that you . . .

Remember that the most important thing is to keep him talking. Once he quits, that's it. Try to choose something that he said and work from that toward what you are interested in so that you stay within his language and interests, and accommodate yours as well.

Keeping the student talking is fine advice, you might say, unless you are trying to operate a classroom. You can't have everybody talking all day. That is true, though not as true as you might think. The classroom can function quite well with quite a number of quiet discussions continuing. Nonetheless, in order for interviews to form a good basis for classroom evaluation, there need to be some rules and patterns established. First, children need to become used to operating independently. They must understand that if you are engaged in conversation with someone, they cannot ask you for help. If this rule does not hold, and you cannot devote your full attention to a given child, then you cannot demonstrate your interest, and the continuity and structure of your interview will be disrupted. As interviews in the classroom take on a certain predictable framework and focus on the children's reading and writing, they will increasingly become focused quite rapidly as the children come to understand that this time is their time with the teacher to talk about their reading or writing. The children will also have an ongoing relationship with the teacher, which maintains rapport, and some shared knowledge of one another's reading and writing.

It is probably worth noting that the kind of interaction you set up in interviews about books and about writing, will form the basis of those interviews that take place between students. Indeed, as students become more adept at independent discussions of books, it will become increasingly easy to gather useful information from their discussions. It will also become increasingly easy to have undisturbed time to have your own interviews.

When you have finished an interview with a student, remember to help him return to what he was doing, or to move to something new. If interviews end up being disruptive, then they lose their value (and validity). Jane Hansen suggests that a simple "Where were you when I came? Could you please read just a bit to me." will get students back into the flow.[37]

EQUALIZING THE BALANCE OF POWER

In several places I have commented on how power and status in relationships influences the kind of interaction that takes place, the kind of information that is likely to be given, and the meanings constructed. It is very important that we try to equalize power differences between interviewer and interviewee. As adults we are automatically handicapped in this from the beginning. Being teachers as well, we often have to work against stereotypes and the problems of control necessary to protect life and limb in the classroom. Fortunately, there are ways we can help to minimize these power differences.

If involvement, rather than information, is central to the social definition of literacy in the classroom, then there is less basis for status difference. If the most important thing in classroom literate activity is that students do it—read, write, and talk about their reading and writing—then power problems are less likely to arise. In the same way, if literacy is seen as a personal and a social activity, then only the individual can be an expert on his perspective, and differences between individuals must be seen as normal and worthy of discussion, which is the basis of the shared social knowledge. In other words, the view of literacy presented in the classroom provides a context that can make the teacher's task of getting good information about the children's literacy development either easy or nearly impossible. When a child is writing about something he knows well, particularly personal experience writing, he is indeed, the expert. The teacher cannot know this personal experience unless he chooses to tell her. The same is true in reading. If Jane's opinion and personal literary experience are respected, then she will likely be able to talk about her experience with a book and discuss that experience in an open manner since she is the expert, and there is no status difference. It must first be agreed that neither teacher nor student can know the author's intentions. Teachers who claim privileged knowledge of THE main idea or the author's intention will have difficulty with this. Remember that power differences arise easily. Just asking a question forces a response and can invoke a power differential.

In order to make interviewing effective in the classroom, we need to give up some control of the students because the controlling role has a built-in power differential. Giving up control does not mean leaving the classroom in chaos. Rather, it means that you must set conditions in which classroom rules set by the teacher and the students in cooperation, are clear and seen as community responsibility. Routines are also very helpful as they set a pattern that does not keep coming up for personal negotiation. It is like bedtime with young children. If there is a routine, then power battles do not have to take place each night along with their negative consequences on the relationship, and time is left available and uncluttered for healthy dialogue. Routines must, however, be balanced by choice; otherwise the routines also remove power from the students. Regardless of routines and negotiated rules, a teacher will sometimes be called on to take certain roles, such as judge, which involve asserting a power difference. If you are fair and consistent, and make the different roles you must take distinct, you can assert authority when it is necessary and not have the status difference spill over into your role as listener. The critical features of the interaction are trust and mutual respect, recognizing authority where it must exist, and minimizing the role of disciplinarian.

RESOURCE

As an excellent resource on talking with children *and* helping them manage their behavior, I recommend:

Adele Faber and Elaine Mazlish (1980). *How to talk so kids will listen and listen so kids will talk*. New York, NY: Avon Books.

CHAPTER 13

Learning from Talking and Listening: Making Interviews Work

I have discussed the importance of rapport and some techniques for establishing it. The establishment of rapport alone is likely to lead to the volunteering of some important information. Most important will be the questions that children ask if they feel comfortable enough asking them. One question from a child yields more information than his responses to ten questions from an adult. For example, if a child asks, "If we went in the car all day, would we get to the edge of the world?" he reveals a great deal about his knowledge of time and of the nature of the earth, among other things. Obviously it would help if we arranged for a trusting, noncompetitive classroom situation in which children would be likely to ask their own questions. Also, we can directly elicit questions. For example, we might ask, "What would be a good question to ask the author of this book?" Such questions will naturally come up when children are having their writing conferences.

When we do ask our own questions, we cannot always simply ask directly about the things we *know* are important. Much of the important information is tacit knowledge that is not consciously available to the student. This is particularly so for less able students.[38] Thus, the children from whom we need the clearest information are likely to need the most help in providing it. Yet we must help them to provide it without putting words in their mouths. They are also likely to have the most at stake in terms of defending their self-esteem, and to have suffered the most at the hands of the schooling system. Why should they trust us with what is often sensitive information? These are areas of expertise that are critical for us to be introspective about.

ASKING QUESTIONS

People who are involved in evaluation generally ask a lot of questions. Their questions may elicit a lot of information, more detailed information, more accurate information, and just as easily ensure no further information of any value, or worse, bad information inextricably intertwined with good information. The questions we use and how we use them are critical. There are essentially three types of questions that are most useful in gathering information: descriptive questions, structural questions, and contrast questions.[39] *Descriptive questions* are the ones of initial concern since they are most important for keeping the student talking—putting the student into the role of teacher.

Could you tell me what it is like for you to read at school?

What do you do when you read?

Could you tell me what usually happens in your reading group?

Could you study the next piece of your textbook just as you would do it at home and explain to me how you are doing it?

How do you use the classroom library? When do you use it?

Can you give me an example of when you might use that kind of strategy in writing?

If I were to sit in on your reading group, what kind of things would I hear kids say to each other?

Such questions can put the student into the role of teacher, with ignorance established on the part of the listener.

Actually, students can move into the role of teacher in other ways too. Young children given free-play situations in kindergarten and first grade, will take turns role-playing the teacher. Watching them is like holding up a mirror, or having someone draw a caricature of you. At the same time, if you listen to their language, you will hear them use key literacy terms in different ways that will reveal some of their knowledge about them. Listening to students being the teacher provides a great deal of information about their knowledge of the activity.

Descriptive questions might also be used to find out about reading habits. For example, part of the problem faced by adults whose literacy is not well developed, is the pattern of habits they have developed to avoid print. Since becoming more fully literate will involve increased participation in literate activity, often they will need to restructure the way they go about their daily lives. Descriptive questions, which James Spradley calls "tour" questions, can be helpful in finding out how the person's day is organized, and helping her to make small nonpublic adjustments to her schedule, which will allow the inclusion of literate activities. For example, a question might be "Could you describe the things you usually do in an evening?" "Could you give me a moment-by-moment description of what you did at work today?" "You mentioned that you have to read and write in the log book. Could you tell me everything that you did with the log book today?"

Structural questions are useful for understanding how aspects of the person's world relate to one another. For example, I might ask, "Is it okay to write in reading class?" "Can I say reading is part of writing?" I might ask, "Are there different kinds of books?" or "Are there different kinds of writing?" or "Are there different ways to write? Could you tell me what some of them are?" "Is reading a book and reading a poem a different sort of reading?" Answers to these questions tell us how people structure their world—how they relate concepts to one another.

Contrast questions are used to try to learn how the student (or teacher, administrator, parent) understands a domain. For example, I could ask a student how many different types of books he knows of. From the list he produces, I could then ask how two of them, say, folktales and mysteries, are the same and different. I might ask a student for a list of authors whom she has read and then we could play "Twenty Questions." For example, from the list of authors I could choose one and the student has to guess which one by asking questions to which I am allowed to respond only yes or no. The questions she asks will give a lot of information about the ways in which she knows these authors apart. I might restrict the kinds of questions to questions about writing style. Another ploy I could use would be to present three authors at a time and ask, "Which one is different from the other two? Is there any way to regroup the books so that one of the others is different?" In Appendix B I have included a selection of questions that have produced informative responses. You might explore some of these as a way to learn about what you can learn from different kinds of questions.

Much of the information that becomes available through interviews is not made available in simple, direct statements. Rather, it is embedded in the way things are said, the order in which they are said, and the kinds of words used. For example, the order in which someone describes features of something often reflects the importance of those features to him. Consider Ben's response to the question "Could you describe your classroom to me?"

> Well, I sit at the back behind Betty and next to Gerry and the teacher's desk is in the middle up the front. All our desks is separated. Um—We on the second floor and we got lots of windows. There's the chalkboard up front and the wall on that side's got pictures 'n stuff on it and that's about it.

What Ben leaves out of his description, like the shelves of books under the windows, is just as important as what he describes and the order in which he describes it.

EFFICIENCY AND PLACE OF THE INTERVIEW

From the description of the interview technique, you will see that it is, at the outset, time-consuming. You have probably already said, with good reason, "Fine. But when do I find the time for that?" On the face of it, interviewing seems like a highly inefficient way of gathering information. There are four major reasons why it is actually highly efficient.

1. Interviewing provides information that cannot be obtained any other way.
2. The information obtained is often most critical.
3. Over the course of the year, many (but not all) of the students move into the participation stage of the interviewer–interviewee relationship in which they understand their role as a teacher about themselves and about the literacy culture of the classroom. They begin to take it upon themselves to observe, reflect on, and analyze their activity in the classroom from their own perspective and to inform the teacher about these things during interviews. In other words, the process becomes increasingly efficient as rapport and role understandings become more developed.
4. The process also becomes increasingly accurate as teacher and student achieve a cooperative arrangement in which they understand each other's needs. For example, the student begins to correct the educator's errors of interpretation. The student also becomes more likely to offer more personal, and sometimes more painful, information. As you help them to teach you about themselves as literate individuals, they come to understand and be reflective about themselves and their literacy.

WHAT INFORMATION CAN WE GET FROM AN INTERVIEW?

Many kinds of information can be gathered from interviews. For example, we can find out how a person goes about doing things, how they conceptualize literacy and literature, how they feel about reading and writing, and how they understand themselves. Let us examine some examples of information that can be obtained through interview procedures and that cannot be provided through any other technique available to the classroom teacher. The most important information is usually tacit information—information to which the student does not have conscious access and which he does not know that he knows.

Becoming literate involves the development of complex sets of knowledge that are interrelated with one another. It is this knowledge which governs not only what we do but also what we see and understand. In other words, what I think I know today in some ways determines what I learn tomorrow. When I read or see something new, I attend to what seems to me to be the most important information, and what I already know or don't know plays a big part in determining that. Sometimes we see a student continually behaving in a way that we are tempted to describe as "bizarre." However, children behave one way or another for a reason and our job is to try to understand the reasons. For example, one adult who worked with me read the word "dwindle" as "windle." I asked him how he knew to pronounce it that way and he included in his response the fact that he thought that the *d* in that position would be "silent."

Such misconceptions are not uncommon and can make life difficult for the student. To repeat an earlier example, Stephen was not enjoying writing at school. His writing was done in booklets that the teacher had made up ahead of time. He mentioned his dislike to his teacher and she asked him what he saw as the major problem with it. He said that it was just too much to write. "There are too many pages." Once he learned that he did not have to fill the book, writing was easier, even enjoyable for him. His teacher also decided not to make up books for the students to draft stories in. We have encountered through interviews children who believe that when they are taking a test it is cheating to reread the passage after they have looked at the questions.

Tom Nicholson has provided a number of useful examples of other conceptual confusions which can become evident through interviews.[40] He describes from his interviews a junior high school student's understanding of what it means to "do research." The steps in doing a school research project turned out to be:

Step 1: Ask your friends for information.

Step 2: Check any magazines or books at home.

Step 3: Ask older siblings or your parents.

Step 4: If necessary, adjust your research topic to fit your resources.

Step 5: If steps 1–4 do not work, check with the teacher, or perhaps even try the school library.

Michael Cole and Peg Griffin report a student who revealed in an interview the use of what they call the "copy matching" strategy.[41] Their student was puzzled when she had to answer a question of the form, "Who was John Smith?" when the text contained the name John Smith three times. Her normal strategy of looking for the name and transforming the sentence in which it occurred had been foiled since there were three such sentences. She thus felt that the question was unfair. We can also learn about writing strategies. For example, you might ask, "Are there things you wrote in your story to help your audience learn about Chuck (a character)?" To which you are likely to get a response like:

> Yeah. Like, here I told how Chuck smells and how his clothes are trashed, and like, here when he pushes the kid off his bike . . .

Many other decisions that young readers and writers make can also be topics of discussion. For example:

> "Are there any other decisions you made while you were writing this piece where you tried to get the audience to think in a particular way?"
> "How did you come up with this way of writing the story [this plot, this topic, etc]?"
> "Does this story you have written remind you of any stories you have read?"

These questions lead us and our students to understand how their literary attention is being socialized by their reading and writing and the social interaction which surrounds them. At the same time, such questions socialize their literary attention.

In interviews we can learn what being literate means to a student, or what it means to be successful, or what it means to fail. These definitions are very important since they determine whether in the long run we consider ourselves a failure or a successful participant. When a student says he is not a good reader, he is often able to say quite clearly how he knows this to be so, and who is a good reader and why. The responses often give us information about how to restructure our classroom in order to change the criteria. For example, if he defines his reading ability normatively, we can reduce or eliminate the grounds for simplistic normative comparison in the classroom. If we can change the notion of successful reading from getting more words right than the other guy did to having a satisfying interaction with a book, we will change with it the extent to which the various children in the class feel that they were successful or otherwise and how they choose to spend their time.

In interviews we can learn about the affective and emotional aspects of students' developing literateness. While tutoring an adult and interviewing him along the way, I learned about stress. He told me:

> I was getting . . . for some reason something triggered me off before this that I was starting to get tense . . . and I could see, I could feel myself shutting

down. Like when I get this way I can feel my whole self tense . . . and I'm not absolutely, not even been . . . I'm not even . . . at one point there I wasn't even being able to . . . I had to force myself to concentrate because everything was going.

What it is, it's the old feelings. It's like, y'know, well . . . something will trigger it. Like when I was a kid in school and they would ask me to read, and the teacher didn't know that I couldn't read. Well, those feelings still can come back to me, and it's like feeling . . . never . . . I can't even begin to explain . . . It's like you completely feel isolated, totally alone . . .

Many other affective aspects of reading and writing such as frustration, elation, and depression, are also revealed in interviews.

Also available through interviews are people's explanations of their lives. People tend to try to explain away the things that happen to them. For example, a student who passes a test can attribute it to luck, an easy test, his brilliance, the teacher marking it in his favor, a clever study strategy, and many other possibilities. Similarly, a student who defines himself as being unsuccessful can explain it in terms of such things as his own lack of ability. These attributions have consequences for future learning. If a student attributes his success to luck, and his failure to his lack of ability, there is no reason for him to try harder or to attempt alternative strategies. On the other hand, if a student attributes his success to the strategies that he used, there is some incentive for him to feel responsible for the success and some motive for him to be strategic in the future. Thus, the definitions we have for success and failure and the explanations we give for their occurrence are important for our learning futures. For example, one adult explained to me in an interview:

Because you feel stupid . . . because they're smarter than you. And if you say anything then you're lower than them . . . idiot can't read. Y'know.

Other adults showed a similar pattern of attributions but in different ways. For instance, Jack commented "What's wrong with me that I have this problem?" indicating that he felt the source of the problem was within himself. He also showed a change in this perception in a later interview after his ability to read had improved considerably. He commented that:

I don't know if I should say this or not, but the last few months I felt a little resentment towards my mother because of the instruction, and that bothers me. I sort of at some point say, "Well, why didn't she intervene or why didn't she do whatever she could have done to make this not happen to me?" Because . . . see . . . prior to now I have always felt that there is a possibility that something was wrong. You know, maybe I was retarded. I think that was always in the back of my mind and that's a hard thing to live with.[42]

These comments suggest a different orientation toward the situation he is in, one which suggests that he has some degree of control.

Talking and listening to students can also help us to learn about our own classroom practices. Indeed, when honest questions are asked and honest answers given in return, a simple survey not only will tell a great deal but also can serve as an interesting class research project. Part way through the school year, Noemi Kraut decided to organize her fourth-grade literature groups heterogeneously rather than by reading performance level. At the end of the year she wanted to evaluate the change. Her very open relationship with the students allowed her to take her problem to them. The students generated the following questions with her:

1. Which literature group did you enjoy more, the early ones or the last one?
2. In which literature group did you learn more? Give some examples.
3. How did you feel working in mixed groups?
4. Give your opinion of some specific literature group activities. Consider the whole year's work.

Noemi added two questions of her own to the list:

5. What advice do you have for me?
6. Does it make a difference who the adult is who facilitates the group?

A small selection of responses to these questions can be seen in Figure 13.1. Most of the letters expressed strong opinions, and with them raised detailed issues for Noemi and her co-teachers to think about. The central issue is confounded with issues of which books were read when, what they did with the books, and even the fact that the students already knew themselves in terms of disparate ability. However, the responses are instructionally informative. I doubt that such informative responses could be obtained without a context of open, trusting dialogue.[43]

Sometimes it can be helpful for a stranger to the classroom to visit and interview children while they go about their classroom activities. This information can be related to the teacher later in a confidential discussion. For example, in one teacher's class I interviewed a couple of boys about the worksheets they were doing and they told me in no uncertain terms what they thought of them and why. However, a better way to accomplish this is for a teacher to visit another teacher's classroom and interview the children about some of the things they do. What she learns from such interviews is often transferred back to her own classroom.

SOME CAUTIONS

Always try to buttress interview data with observations of actual literate activity. Interviews are not perfect reflections of thinking, but they can give us much to go on. Thinking, to the extent that it is accessible, is described in language,

QUESTION 1: Which literature group did you enjoy more, the early ones or the last one?
Student 1:   Last one, becus I liked the book more and were doing a play.
Student 2:   I enjoyed both rounds of lit groups, because the books were well-written, and the lit groups
were well-organized.
Student 3:   I enjoy the last one. My brother the thief book. It's a good book. And it has alot of argements
in the book. And I like my group.
Student 4:   I liket the first ones beter becawes they were funer.
Student 5:   I didn't like the last lit. group very much because: I learned very little. I never got to answer
any questions, I didn't get enough work, and it went to slowly.
Student 6:   Well first of all, I didn't really like The trumpet of swan, because I did not learn as much as I
did in tuck Everlasting, because I did more work, and I under standed what I've done.

QUESTION 2: In which literature group did you learn more? Give some examples.
Student 1:   Last one, I learned how to express my opinyon in a jurnell.
Student 2:   I probably learned the most in Queenie Peavy since the author was quite descriptive, and
the book told a compelete story of what a girl's life might have been like at Queenie's time.
Student 3:   I learn more in my brother the thief. Sammple. Did Richard steal the creampitcher. they
have realy good Question.
Student 4:   The first lit groop I learnd more becawes we read beter books and mor fun books and more
egacashening books.
Student 5:   I learned more in the earlier lit group becasue we had more work and we got more done.
Student 6:   I learned more in tuck ever lasting than Trumpet of the swan Because I did harder work.
Like learning harder words, meanings and alot more.

QUESTION 3: How did you feel working in mixed groups?
Student 1:   I thought it was fun, becus I liked having mixsted levels.
Student 2:   I felt that it was good to have mixed levels since it was a good experience for all.
Student 3:   It's fine with me who ever is in my group. Because, As long as they like me and I like them.
Student 4:   I'd like it beder if there the same levle
Student 5:   [No response]
Student 6:   I thought it was fun. Because I learned there opinons, and discusing things.

*QUESTION 4:   Give your opinion of some specific literature group activities. Consider the whole year's
work.*
Student 1:   The play my lit. group did becus I enjoyed acting out parts of the book, and being Mrs.
Landon.
Student 2:   My opinion of the lit group activities was that it was good to let the kids write questions, and
it was fun to predict things, and to draw pictures. I do not like writing summaries or reports.
Student 3:   Ever time we rEad a chapter bruces gives use Work, Questions about the chapter. Harder
books make me a good reader.
Student 4:   I think the hole yers work of lit groop mostly was reading
Student 5:   I liked making upquestrions becuase it made lit. goup. In the first lit. group we argued a lot
but that gave us a chance to voice our opinions.
Student 6:   I liked the prediction. Because it was alot of fun learning the obervasion.

QUESTION 5:   What advice do you have for me [the teacher]?
Student 1:   You should still have chieled lit. group leaders and not have boring books think like a kid
and pick, or let the kids pick the book, divied kids by intrests.

(continued)

Figure 13.1.   Examples of students' responses to the survey they designed to evaluate the relative merits
of two approaches to grouping that they had experienced.

Student 2:   I would like to say that kids should be allowed to run lit groups more often.
Student 3:   Noe'mi you pick a good group for me. And in the begging I didn't like the book. Because it was hard for me to read. Then I got used to the book. And liked it alot. Thank you Noe'mi!
Student 4:   I liket is sort of.
Student 5:   Out of the people I'vs asked I realize that Q.P. [Queenie Peavy] folk are the only people who don't like the last lit. group but still, though I know I'm greatly out numbered, I'll say DONT HAVE MIXXED LIT GROUPS!!!!!!!!!!!!!!!!
Student 6:   I think you should try doing the same things that you taught us.

QUESTION 6: Does it make a difference who the adult is who facilitates the group?
Student 1:   lit. leaders are neded, to keep the kids in order, and give some edvice but thats it. [The reading teacher] was helpful in terms of learning.
Student 2:   [No response]
Student 3:   Bruce is nice and he made a game for are group. And it's fun.
Student 4:   [No response]
Student 5:   The importance of an adult varies with the kids. If teh kids are irrisponsible, they need an adult and if they are shy they won't know where to start but if they are responsible hard working kids that know what to do they don't need an adult. It doesn't matter what adult as long as they treat everyone equally (And hardly anyone does in mixed lit groups!)
Student 6:   I thought the teachers were important because they did hard work to make "get things" and put together lit groups. And it doesnen't matter which teacher I have because their all good. I really enjoyed having lit groups.

Figure 13.1 Continued

that is slippery even without the possibility of alternate motives. For example, I asked one adult how much he wanted to become literate and he held out his arms to me and said, "Take these." I am sure that he believed that. However, it transpired that even though he had the house to himself in the mornings with the children at school, he could never find time to read or write anything outside of our sessions. To tease apart the complex motivations and emotions would be very difficult indeed.

In a similar vein, it should be clear that one-shot interviews are less informative than multiple interviews or ongoing ones such as can occur in a classroom. You can look for patterns of consistency or inconsistency in what people say at different times. However, don't pounce on inconsistencies or you will get nothing further. Good rapport needs to be established before such conflicts are raised. With good rapport, such internal conflicts are the perfect situation for learning to take place. A teacher who sees a conflict in his practice is most likely to do something about it unless he is publicly confronted, which will often cause defensiveness and entrenchment and the termination of further learning exchanges.

Interviews, as you will have noticed, do not automatically leave by-products to which you can return. In some ways that does not matter so much. The things you learn tend to stick in your mind as you develop your understanding of the student being interviewed. Not all evaluation requires records accessible for the longer term. However, it can be quite helpful to jot down odd comments after the interview to be placed in your file or journal about that student. Perhaps a comment about a book that you would like to come back to later, or some other issue you wish to get back to in another situation. These comments will be useful in illustrating to parents the changes that have occurred in the student's understanding. At the same time, writing down direct quotes from students allows later reflection on them.

Group discussions as well as interviews provide lots of information. When children become involved in their own reading or writing conferences, their language tells a great deal about what they understand about literate activity.

In Appendix B I have listed a variety of questions that you might like to explore in order to get the feel for interviewing. But remember, there is simply no magical question or set of questions that will miraculously transform children's writing or produce a "successful" writing conference. The central feature of the interview is listening to what the child has to say and responding honestly to it. Probably the best way to find useful questions is to ask a child, once a piece of writing is complete, which questions were most helpful to her in developing her piece.

CHAPTER 14

Ways in Which Reading Outcomes Are Evaluated: Questions, Cloze, and Translations

Louise Rosenblatt distinguishes two types of reading, aesthetic and efferent.[44] Aesthetic reading is the kind of reading you do when you read a novel for pleasure. It is done for the feeling you get while you are reading it. Efferent reading, on the other hand, is done to remember what you read. Efferent is from the Latin *effere,* meaning "to carry away from." Both types of reading are legitimate activities that literate adults engage in. Unfortunately, schooling has put an end to aesthetic reading for many students by ignoring it and, for example, asking lots of recall questions about novels and short stories, forcing students into only efferent reading. It is not that literate people, having read a text aesthetically, do not remember what they have read, and talk about it with other literate people. Rather their reading of the book focused on their involvement first, and any trace left was incidental to the feelings of involvement. In efferent reading the reader's focus is the reverse. In both cases it is legitimate to ask questions about what the reader remembers. Literate people do that. However, with efferent reading *the reader* expects to remember particular things about the text and might be concerned if she didn't, whereas in aesthetic reading, recall of the text is incidental. These kinds of reading are not restricted to particular kinds of texts. For example, I quite often read aesthetically theoretical papers, cookbooks, and the like, which were written as exposition, not as narrative.

But how can we understand a student's understanding of a text so that we might be instructionally helpful? In order to evaluate a child's understanding of a text, we need some sort of response from the child. The possible responses are many, and most have been used by someone at some time. For example, tests have included both "open" and multiple-choice (including true/false) responses to questions, verbatim recall, free recall, summarizing, restoring deleted words, reordering pictures, drawing pictures, and selecting pictures.[45] Each of these responses tells us something different and is influenced by performance factors such as writing or artistic skill.

Every response is also a response to something. Generally, we are unsure of what that "something" is. The student may have read a book and we might think that the book prompts the response. However, the response is to a social situation, which includes the book, but which may or may not feature the child's understanding of the book. For example, the situation may be interpreted as one in which the student must guess the evaluator's interpretation of the book. Whenever we prompt a response we cannot specify the exact nature of the prompt because the important part of the prompt is how the individual interprets it—the subjective experience—to which we cannot gain direct access. Furthermore, any response is to the perceived audience, and we do not have access to how the audience is perceived. So there is always some uncertainty about what information we are getting from different responses. At the same time, we cannot specify exactly the message we have given the reader about herself, our relationship, and about literate activity.

We always have the problem of the frame of reference for the interpretation of the text. A child might understand the text on his own terms yet we judge the interpretation within the context of our own frame of reference. The same book can mean different things to different people. Robert Munsch's book *Love You Forever* tends to be heard by young children as a melodic cyclical story that appeals to the predictability prominent in their stage of development. Older children appreciate the book as a comedy, whereas many adults cry their eyes out over it. Other adults are left quite unmoved by it. Even writers change over time in their interpretation of what they have written as their own thinking changes. Our job is to understand children's understanding rather than to measure it. The question is not "How much did she understand it?" but "How did she understand it?" Note that *how* can be interpreted here as "how was it accomplished?" and "What is the nature of the outcome?" I mean it in both senses.

QUESTIONING

When we are trying to understand how children understand what they read, we often use questions. Legitimate questions can help us get some interesting insights into children's understandings and at the same time help them view themselves as more fully literate. In the chapters on social interaction and interviewing, I described some of the types of question and contexts for questioning that are likely to be productive. Unfortunately, these are not generally the kinds of questions that have been used in schools. The most frequent types of questions have been described by Dolores Durkin, Frank Guzack, and others,[46] and a quick look over a basal reader or a standardized test will provide ample examples. The questions usually ask for information already known by the teacher and they do not foster dialogue. In other words, we have tended to ask questions that would not be part of normal social interactions between literate people, and that address not *how* children understand, but *whether* they understand it the way we think they should. Questions have not called for reflection, but correction. Furthermore, they are often extraordinarily numerous. In one basal reader I counted one question for every seventeen words in the story the children were to read (and that wasn't even the part called the "test"). Such questioning techniques run the risk of being destructive. Rather like medical studies in which the rat must be killed in order to find out what physiological changes have occurred, the book, if not the teacher-student relationship, must be slaughtered to find out whether the student understood the text. Asking questions to which the asker already knows the answer can be done without these consequences if it is clearly understood that there is an important point to recalling information in the particular text and it is part of helping the students develop a review strategy. This can make sense when the agreed-upon reason for reading the book is efferent. In addition, if the situation is not competitive then problems are less likely to arise.

It is common to classify questions in different ways that are presumed to indicate underlying differences in the processes that are "tapped" by the questions. A most common distinction is that between "literal" and "inferential" questions. To demonstrate these question classifications, consider the following text and questions.

> The camping trip did not turn out as John had planned. The trip to the mountains that Friday was not bad, and they set up the tent easily. But on that first night the rain was so hard that the tent pegs pulled out of the soft earth. It didn't get better. In the morning the wind came up and he and Bill sat shiver-

ing in their damp clothes trying to hold up the tent. To make matters worse, their matches had not survived the night and they could not light a fire. They had plenty of food, but most of it needed to be cooked. They were cold, tired and hungry. At about two o'clock they began to face the facts. If they stayed another night they might not be alive in the morning. If they went home how would they feel? They had boasted about this trip for weeks and even called Steve a chicken for not coming.

1. On which night did it rain hard?
2. Why could the campers not light a fire?
3. How would they feel if they went home?

The first question would generally be classified as literal, meaning that the question and answer are "right there in the text,"[47] even in the same sentence. (This is not actually true, but we shall return to that matter presently.) The second and third questions would be classified as inferential, meaning that an inference must be made in order to answer them. In other words, this classification implies that the student, in reading and responding to such questions, will perform predictably different processes in response to inferential questions and literal questions. The argument is that an inference must be made in the one case and not in the other. But inferences must always be made. We cannot escape from them. Even the most bluntly "literal" question requires inferences to be made about the type of response expected, how the language is being used, why the question is being asked, and so forth. Nonetheless, varying degrees and types of inference must be made.

David Pearson and Dale Johnson have proposed an alternative classification system that takes into account both the question and the response given to it. For example, they propose that responses A and B to question 1 are both correct, but involve a different mental process.

1. On which night did it rain?
   A. On the first night of their trip.
   B. On the Friday night.

The combination of question 1 and response A is classified as "text explicit," meaning that the question and response are both explicit in the same part of the text. The combination of question 1 and response B is classified as "text implicit" because the reader had to put together different pieces of information from across parts of the text. When a reader uses information from outside the text to answer the question, that is termed "scriptally implicit," meaning that information from the reader's general knowledge or "script" about the particular topic has been used.

It has also been popular to talk about "higher level questions," and many references can be found to these in the professional literature. The problem of what counts as higher order, for whom, under which circumstances, is interesting to think about. Take, for example the "literal" question about a particularly small detail in a story. This can be very hard to recall when the text is unavailable to refer to, but easy enough if the text can be referred back to. In a detective novel, it is the burying of these details that make them important and potentially "higher level." A child who has been read to a great deal or who has been told many stories will develop a very good sense of the structure of stories, much of which can be left implicit yet will make easier question material than a literal question about a detail not central to the story plot. A child whose Sunday revolves around going to church will not need the word Sunday mentioned in the text to make the question "On which day of the week did the story take place?" a "lower level" question. The same question might count as "higher order" if he knows virtually no one who goes to church on Sunday—Saturday, perhaps, but not Sunday.

What count as higher and lower levels depends substantially on what you know, what you are used to, how you conceive of the question, and under what conditions you are answering. A classic example of this is shown in the following anecdote about the great mathematician J. von Neumann.[48] Apparently, von Neumann was asked by one of his friends the following question:

> There are two cyclists, a mile apart, cycling toward each other and each going at 10 mph. A fly flies from the nose of one cyclist to the nose of the other, backwards and forwards between them, until the cyclists meet. The fly flies at 15 mph. How far has the fly flown when it gets squashed by the cyclists' noses meeting?

Von Neumann is reported to have thought for several minutes before answering the question. In order to answer the question, von Neumann computed the distance that the fly traveled as the limit of a mathematical series. He did this mentally, which is a stunning feat well beyond the capabilities of even the most accomplished mathematicians. Had he conceived of the problem differently, all he needed to do was to calculate how long it would take the two cyclists' noses to meet, traveling a mile toward each other at 10 miles an hour, or how long does it take a cyclist traveling 10 miles an hour to cover half a mile (half the distance). The answer is three minutes. In three minutes, or 3/60ths of an hour, traveling at 15 miles per hour, the fly would travel three-quarters of a mile. Was the question a "higher level" one or a "lower level" one? It rather depends on what one knows and how one goes about answering it.

Questions are currently the main means of attempting to evaluate children's reading comprehension. Many different classifications of questions have been attempted, and it is possible that analyzing questions this way is helpful. In general, it is probably more helpful to ask readers how they arrived at the answer. It certainly seems risky to classify questions before knowing how the reader is going to understand what the question means. As you may have gathered by this point, my own preference is to think of the classification of questions in terms of the social event of which they are a part, which includes the reading of a given text, but also includes the relationship between teacher and student, and the context of the question. Often children will tell you more if you actually tell them something about your experience than if you ask them for information. Certainly there are ways to ask questions that are more productive than others, and these are discussed in the next two chapters. However, many other ways of evaluating understanding have been used and are still common.

CLOZE

The cloze procedure is one of the standard forms for assessing comprehension. The cloze technique, originally brought to us from Gestalt psychology, involves the ability to complete incomplete wholes.

> Once upon a _____ there was a little _____ called David who had _____ pet dog. David loved his dog _____ than anything in the _____ .

A person who is making sense out of mutilated text such as this is indeed performing many of the processes used by a person reading complete text. It is perhaps like reading text containing a number of very difficult words. On the other hand, reading a cloze passage is not the same as reading a normal text and thus, like all other means of studying the sense readers make of text, it is limited. The most functional use of the cloze procedure is when a reader talks about the reading as he goes along. This provides an understanding of how he arrived at his response, which is, after all, what we need to know to provide instructional support. However, in the first place this use is probably the least common. The most common use is in standardized tests, such as the *Degrees of Reading Power,*[49] in tests designed to prepare children for such tests, in basal end-of-unit tests and workbooks, and perhaps in certain kinds of detective work in which some of the words in a letter have been erased. In the second place, if we were to use cloze techniques like that, we might as well use unmutilated text in the first place.

Cloze activities take a variety of forms. They can have some letters r_ma_n_ng, they can have blanks of various lengths, and sometimes they are presented with response alternatives for the reader to choose among. The difficulty of the task can be controlled somewhat by controlling the difficulty of the alternatives. For example:

> Jack and Jill went up the _____ .
>   a) car   a) hell
>   b) at   OR b) rope
>   c) in   c) house
>   d) hill   d) hilt

When a cloze procedure is used as a test without providing response options, usually only exact replacement of the original word in the text is considered acceptably correct. For example, in the sentence

Their car was now rolling down the hill and the brakes appeared useless. They were terrified of what was about to _____.

If you wrote "unfold" you were correct. Increase your score by one point and your percentile rank by five. If you wrote "happen" or "occur" or "ensue," then go directly to jail, do not pass go, and do not collect $200. Exact replacement is required in order to obtain agreement among scorers, rather than from any belief about the impossibility of synonyms providing a reasonable response. In other words, if we allowed "explode" or "appear," some of our scorers would mark it correct and others would not. Enough of these scoring problems and pretty soon different scorers get quite different scores for the same student. We can't have that. What would the scores mean?

There has been considerable debate among researchers about whether the cloze procedure can provide information about the reader's understanding of anything more than a single sentence at a time.[50] Some claim that by careful selection of the words to be deleted, the procedure can require students to know the whole meaning of the text (assuming that only a single meaning can be acceptable). Of course, in order to feel a need to engage in these arguments, you have to feel that it is necessary to obtain some numerical indicator of a child's "ability to comprehend." If you do not feel such a need, then the cloze procedure simply remains a useful instructional technique for helping some children attend more to the use of context to figure out unknown words.

TRANSLATIONS

One common "comprehension assessment" practice for some time now has been to ask a child to retell what he has read. Various reading tests have required written reproductions of text since around 1914 when testing was really getting under way in this country. Some currently popular individual oral reading evaluations still require a child who has just read a story out loud to a teacher (or evaluator) to retell it to the very person who just listened to it being read aloud. This practice has seemed odd to me. It is certainly an unusual social situation. It is like two people coming out of a movie theater and one turning to the other and asking her to give an oral rendition of the movie they both just saw. This would be socially acceptable if the person asking for the retelling had slept through the movie, or had been involved in intense romantic activities and needed to be able to give a coherent story to inquiring parents; but in most other situations it would be socially unacceptable. One other interesting situation would make it socially acceptable among friends: if they had been assigned to watch the movie for homework and were to be tested on it in school, and they were helping each other out by preparing each other for a test on the content of the movie.

More and less capable readers retell stories differently. As Connie Bridge and her colleagues found out, more able readers are likely to retell the whole story even in sequence, whereas less able readers give a fairly truncated version of the story and nearly half of what they can tell has to be dragged out of them with questions.[51] There are, of course, several ways to interpret this finding. We could argue that less able readers are less able to attend to the coherence of the plot, or that they are unable to organize oral responses well, or several other possible causal arguments. My interpretation is that more able readers tend to interpret the retelling situation as the test situation it is and thus give the kind of retelling that is appropriate to such a situation. The less able readers tend to interpret it as a regular social situation and give a socially appropriate (less redundant) response to an audience that just witnessed the same incident. Alternatively, they talk about the most interesting or memorable event or character. Middle-class students are also more used to situations in which they are asked known-answer questions, and for other reasons are more likely to be among the more able readers. There are other possible interpretations too. Lower-class students are less likely to have been read many stories and are thus less likely to be familiar with the more common story structures in Anglo-American culture.[52] Different cultures have different kinds of predictable structures to their stories, and thus students may be more or less prepared for the kind of stories they read in school. Students who do not do well on the retelling may be shy in performance-on-demand situations. It is also possible that some such readers in some situations interpret the request to retell in terms of the controlling use of questions (discussed in Chapter 16, page 145) since it is clearly not an honest request for information, and simply refuse to be controlled in such a manner.

However, as I have suggested, there are situations in which retellings make social sense. For example, it makes sense for a person who has read a book to explain it to a person who has not, and to explain it in some detail and in appropriate order. Indeed, if a teacher has not read a book that a child has read, he will likely find that the child is happy to regale him with considerable detail. If the boot is sometimes on the other foot with the teacher retelling a story the child has not read, then the child's retelling is even likely to reflect the kind of retelling the teacher might normally give, including not giving away the ending so that the listener will be tempted to read the book. When a child can tell the teacher about a book the child has read and the teacher has not, the child has the luxury of being the expert and the teacher the novice. The teacher gets to ask legitimate questions about the book, questions that would otherwise quite blatantly be accountability questions (at the same time modeling useful questions). If a teacher cannot determine from such a retelling how a child understood the story, and this is rare, then the teacher can decide to read the story on the basis of the child's recommendation. This allows some evaluation of the child's understanding and at the same time provides the possibility of subsequent dialogue and possible legitimate rereading as part of the dialogue. The situation also provides a compliment to the student who was able to influence the teacher's reading, reflecting a level of trust and respect, along with the possibility of sustained intellectual engagement.

There is a second socially appropriate retelling situation that can be useful for getting information. Storytelling in the oral tradition is a process of retelling that is perfectly legitimate and has other social functions at the same time. In many cultures this has been, and is, a means of handing down culture and learning as well as entertaining. However, there is a difference between the oral tradition and the text tradition. One of the advantages and disadvantages of text is that it is, at least on the surface, linguistically the same each time.[53] Children learn this quite early and will correct adults who misread their favorite stories. In the oral tradition, on the other hand, personalization and transformation of the story are expected in the process of retelling. There are two points at which these traditions overlap. In oral cultures, there are ritualized stories that are repeated in considerable detail.[54] These usually occur in formal situations. On the other hand, there are written stories that were originally traditional oral stories. For example, there are many written versions of *The Three Little Pigs, The Teeny Tiny Woman, In the Dark Dark Woods,* and other such cultural masterpieces. Children who have examined such books can come to understand this personalization, and written retellings of stories can be done within this context so that a cumulative record of their retellings can be made over time. Something like this view of retellings has been used by Hazel Brown and Brian Cambourne in their book *Read and Retell,* which provides numerous examples of children's written retellings and the changes therein.[55] Actually, the ''folk process'' easily extends to the use of the same plot and different characters. Even when there is only one version of a modern story like, say, Tomie dePaola's *Now One Foot,* children can transfer it to the oral tradition, making it their own, by changing the people, the grandfather's illness, and so forth. In the process they will not only demonstrate their learning, but will develop brand new talents.

Oral retellings need not be restricted to stories either. They can fit quite nicely into expository text which is being read efferently. An interesting example of this can be seen in a cooperative studying procedure described by Donald Dansereau. Students divide their reading assignment in half, each being responsible for retelling their part to their partner. They then switch and read the other part. In the process of preparing for the retelling, they are likely to find that they cannot retell, which signals a need to return to the text. At the same time, one student's retelling to the other student prepares her for her own reading of the text and leaves open the possibility of their discovering discrepancies between their versions.[56]

Retellings done as a common procedure can function to help children take greater control of the schematic structures of stories. Thus the texts chosen for translation activities can be selected from quite diverse genres so that children come to explore types of texts and their functions with which they might otherwise not become comfortable. Biographies, fables, mysteries, exposition, essays, all are amenable in some way or another to these procedures. At the same time, these translation procedures provide students with a self-checking procedure for their own learning. In other words, they can help develop self-evaluation.

Translations into a variety of different modes and media can be used to help us understand children's understandings of particular texts. For example, children can dramatize stories as movie makers do when they make a book into a movie. Dramatizations can be done with others, to be acted out, or alone using small props. Pat Edmiston cut out shapes and colors to represent aspects of the book and their reading of it.[57] After first reading the story, students made some small paper figures to represent their favorite character, themselves as reader, and any other things they needed to portray their reading of the story. Some provided some setting, some made images for "I like to read," "I don't like to read," "remembering things," "I'm in the book," and "I have feelings." While rereading the text, these readers moved the pieces around paragraph by paragraph to represent the story, their involvement in the action, their stance, and aspects of their reading process. Some of the students became involved in role play ("If I were him I would . . .") and some constructed dialogue and thoughts for the characters ("She's thinking 'Boy, he's a nerd'"). This approach at once gives an indication of the translation outcome, and at the same time suggests some of the processes involved.[58]

The advantages of this dramatization technique are that the process of evaluating prompts a reflectiveness about the reading process on the part of the student, thus developing self-evaluation. The down side of such a procedure is that it is quite disruptive of the normal reading process and takes a substantial amount of time. It does not seem like an activity one would do often since it would drastically cut down the amount of text read by the student. On the other hand, it offers the possibility of intensive and instructional discussion in and about the process of reading. The strategy seems well worth exploring for its instructional and evaluative properties, especially for students who appear to be having some difficulty with understanding.

Translating stories into different media can be helpful. Indeed, young children commonly draw a picture first, then write a story about the picture. The picture helps them maintain coherence in the story as they struggle with phonetic representations of words. Visual representations can include charts, graphs, time lines, outlines, flowcharts, and the like. These are simply different symbolic representations of the concepts in print. Arranging pictures to represent the story and then talking about the arrangement is also possible but requires that there be appropriate pictures available or that the teacher be a reasonable artist.

Educators and psychologists have argued about the use of these various measures for a long time. The arguments against them have been that they confound the elements being measured. It is argued that when a child does a bad job of a written retelling, you can't tell whether it was because of inadequate writing ability or because of inadequate comprehension. These arguments have sprung from the perspective of people involved in constructing standardized diagnostic tests to portray subskill deficits and who don't want their deficits muddled. Such tests cannot allow interviews, or knowledge of normal writing performance in the classroom as part of the evaluative procedure since they would ruin the standardization aspect of tests. They can't allow writing either because it would both make scoring difficult and "confound" reading with writing. Confounding of response with writing ability may be less of a problem in classrooms in which children regularly write about their reading.[59] It is less of a problem if we are looking at students' being literate rather than how well they read or write. If students spent equivalent times on reading, writing, and artistic expression and interpretation, and each was valued as much as the other, I doubt that this would be seen as such a problem. We should encourage students to see the various symbolic processes as being part of the same process of construing the world and constructing representations of it. In a way it is a matter of being multi-representational (like multilingual, but lingual implies only "tongue"). The instructionally interesting information is about the process of making meaning and representing it symbolically.

The making of meaning from someone else's representation has been termed "comprehension" but people forget that comprehension is something we *do,* not something we *have.* They also forget that we are *always* interpreting representations. The human eye does not simply make an actual world in the human mind. It represents the world electrochemically and the brain takes these representations and constructs another representation. The ear, too, translates a mechanical representation into an electrochemical representation from which the mind, in turn, constructs a different representation. Each time we try to represent a mental representation or intention in speech, it comes out differently.

We could construe a good deal of children's literate activity as *translation*. We could, for example, think about the activity of translating sound into print in this way. Dictation is an example of this level of translation. Indeed, moving from any symbolic system to a different form of representation may be viewed as a translation activity. Following instructions (translating from print into action) can provide a good demonstration of understanding in a socially appropriate context. Not long ago, we were asked to evaluate a student who was about to start school and had been labeled "speech delayed." She was, nonetheless, reading quite well before going into kindergarten. The question we were to answer was: "Does she understand what she reads?" Her expressive language was not particularly well developed; but when she was presented with simple directions in print, like "Put the doll on the table," or sequences of such directions to follow, she was quite able to perform as the directions required. I might add, however, that this evidence of her language competence did not prevent her classification as learning disabled and her counterproductive placement in a class of children all of whom were classified as speech delayed.[60]

CHAPTER 15

Productive Trails of Literate Activity: Folders, Records, Checklists, and Portfolios

In recent years there have been arguments over the merits of evaluation focused on the "process" of literate activity versus evaluation of the "products" of literate activity. The basic argument is that information about the manner in which a literate act was accomplished is more instructionally useful than the number of questions which can be answered about it afterwards or the quality of the piece of writing which is produced. At the same time, the act of focusing on the process encourages learners also to attend to the process that helps them think strategically. The product approach is particularly represented by standardized tests that by purpose and design cannot provide information about the process. Advocates argue that it *does* matter whether or not a "good" letter is produced, or whether a student can answer questions correctly about a text, and that the product is at least as important as the process.

I think it wise to remember a couple of things. First, the real product of language activity is the response produced in the reader and/or listener, and not, for example, the letter that was composed. A letter judged as unpersuasive by an examiner may have exactly the desired effect on the reader the student had in mind when writing it. Furthermore, there are cultural and contextual differences in what counts as persuasive. Second, to stress literate processes over products is not to deny the product, only to say that the product cannot readily be interpreted for instructional purposes without knowledge of the process by which it was constructed. Indeed, the product is often the goal of the activity; and without knowledge of the product, it is hard for a student to reflect adequately on the effectiveness of the process. However, the product is not always the goal of the activity. Sometimes the process itself is the goal as, for example, in aesthetic reading. The current stress on the product of literate activity has a detrimental effect on the extent to which children and teachers consider aesthetic reading and journal writing, for example, valuable activities.

However, there are various artifacts which we produce as a consequence of our literate activity. We might call these the by-products of learning. For example, the writing which students and teachers do on paper—the various scribblings, notes, drafts, deletions, lists of questions, annotations, and so forth—are traces of their literate activity that have a useful permanence about them.

They can be used to keep track of one's own learning or someone else's. Sometimes literate activity that would not ordinarily leave such a trace can be helped to leave a trace by someone else or some instrument. For example, the running records we have already discussed, are a useful way for someone else to make a permanent trace of oral reading. A tape recorder would do just as well, of course, but the recording would have different properties. It would be more "true to life," but would lack the accessibility[61] and the analytic summary provided by the running records. There are numerous kinds of permanent records that can be made; each has advantages and disadvantages for particular purposes. However, it is important that teachers and students have some functional, accessible way of organizing and keeping track of these traces.

FOLDERS AND PORTFOLIOS

Folders, cumulative folders, and portfolios are useful tools for organizing paper trails. Quite simply, cumulative folders carry representative examples of the student's work over the course of her year and career. I think of writing folders as a place where students store all their bits and pieces of writing—a working file. On the other hand, I see the portfolio as a public demonstration of one's own development as a literate person or as a learner. The portfolio holds examples of the student's work that she sees fit to display and talk about to others in much the same way that an artist or architect keeps a collection of works. There are differences in that the portfolio in this case is a demonstration of both accomplishment as a literate person and as a learner. An artist generally has to demonstrate achievement only as an artist. To demonstrate achievement as a learner might require inclusion of pieces of historical importance, and the problem-solving that went into the production of a final work—all the drafts, revisions, and editing that took place along the way. Students are normally very proud of their work, and parents too as they understand students' development. Both are generally keen to take the folder home at the end of the year. Actually, there are probably few better uses of a copying machine than to copy the work to go into the portfolio so that the child can take home all her work.

A simple, useful strategy for keeping track of writing development is to have a box, file drawer, or some other permanent place where students keep their writing folders so that they can be readily accessible and so that tidiness is a somewhat public issue. At the same time, it allows the teacher to have ready access to the files so that he can review four or five each evening in preparation for scheduled conferences with the children the next day. Donald Graves has described writing folders and their operation very clearly in his book *Writing: Teachers and Children at Work,* which makes extraordinarily good reading.[62] Graves suggests that students not be allowed to take their work home in general, but that parents can have access to the whole folder by appointment. By special request folders may also be sent home in a manila folder to be returned the next day so that their use will not be disrupted. Students keep all of their writing in the file, and each piece must be dated by the student. These rules are critical. If work is not dated it will be hard (if not impossible) to document development, and similarly difficult for students to see their own progress. If only final copies are saved, or if final copies are sent home, it will be harder to reflect on and describe the development of composing, revising, and editing strategies. In addition, if final copies are sent home without the agreement to return them, the rest of the class will not have that author's work available to them as part of the reading material in the classroom. It will be harder for students to see each other as published authors if they do not have the published works accessible.

Within their folders, students can keep track of the topics they contemplate working on. These provide information on student interests and on the diversity of topics contemplated at the same time as they help the students prevent writer's block. Special topics, which are the ones on which the student would like to become particularly expert, might be underlined in color or kept on a separate list. These are topics that might involve some form of ongoing research. Some people use a prompting format for listing topics such as places I have been, things I have done, things I would like to know more about. However, many such prompts are possible. They might include such things as interesting metaphors, interesting people, people I would like to interview, word play, embarrassing moments, and so forth. These prompts might be kept on the classroom wall instead of in the folder, leaving the possibility of greater diversity in the folder. Indeed, the list on the wall can grow as the class discusses different books and how authors got ideas for those books.

Folders can also be used to keep track of the status of pieces of writing. A checklist can be used with space for topics down the side, and across the top checkpoints such as planning, lead, draft (which can have a number rather than a check), review, revise, confer, edit, publish. Many pieces will not go through all of these steps or even many of them, and the order of progression might be different for different pieces. However, having a place holder for something like "review" may well prompt an author to read it over to herself before sharing it with a different audience. On the other hand, unless the function of such a checklist is made quite clear, some children may feel pressure to go through all the steps with everything.

Nancie Atwell describes a procedure which she uses to keep track of students' status.[63] At the beginning of each class she has a "status-of-the-class" conference in which she calls each student's name and the students each respond with what they will be working on that day. For example, Bill might be working on the third draft of a poem about dirt bikes. JoBeth might be going to work on a draft of a letter to the editor of the local newspaper. Samantha might be going to have a conference with herself about her short story "Pimples." Atwell devised simple abbreviations for the possible things the students could be doing, including: drafts (D1, D2, etc.); self-editing; conferring with self; revising; rewriting for final copy; and conferring with the teacher, focusing on editing (ed. con.) or content (response). She also codes when a person is scheduled for sharing a piece with the group. The recording sheet is simply a chart with the names down the side and the page divided into five columns, one for each day of the week.

The extra benefit of this conference is that it helps the students set their own goals and represents a verbal contract with the teacher. This evaluation procedure is superb because it has several direct consequences. It helps develop commitment, focus, and planning. Rather than starting something and hopping around to other things, students are inclined to persist in solving the problems they need to solve. At the same time, it allows at-a-glance checking of students' progress and balance. For example, a student who never gets a piece to the point of editing, or who simply produces first drafts, or who writes only fantasy stories shows up readily. In addition, because of the predictability of the status of the class conference, students prepare in advance to be able to respond; thus they start the class ready to begin.

Students can also keep a list of "Skills I can use in writing" on the inside cover of the journal. This works especially well if children are encouraged to reflect on their writing and on their folders so that they become able to notice differences in the ways they go about their writing. An extra benefit is that when it comes to reporting to parents, children are able to describe the state of their learning. Indeed, when students are asked by parents, "What did you learn in school today?" their response may shift from "Nothing!" or "I don't know!" to a response more satisfactory to all concerned.

Whichever are chosen for keeping track, it is best to start with what is manageable for both teacher and students and what is understood. If you don't understand it, it's just clutter and wastes time. In schools where teachers are simply required to maintain folders of children's writing, without a good understanding of writing or the function of the folders, the folders are generally kept in a very perfunctory way and not consulted. It is also important to schedule use of the folders. You might have a checklist of children to schedule your examination of their folders and to plan conferences or interviews with them that are longer than the normal daily conferences. This schedule might be a simple chart with a row for each student and a column for each school day in two week blocks, allowing a little space for a coded comment.

In kindergarten, a very simple folder will suffice. Some children take a while to become interested in the idea of revising their writing. Figure 15.1 shows an example of kindergarten writing that has an added feature. On this sample the teacher has written a response to the student. These responses serve a number of functions. First, they help the teacher reconstruct the student's message at a later time. The response along with the picture, reduces the need to take more problematic options such as writing the correct version of the story underneath the student's writing. Second, the comments offer the beginnings of letter writing. Third, they make it clear that as part of the literate community, your writing gets a response. Fourth, the responses leave a trail of the teacher-student interaction that can be returned to by the teacher for reflection at a later date. This is the forerunner to dialogue journals, which are notebooks in which a teacher regularly responds to children's letters to her. Sometimes children also

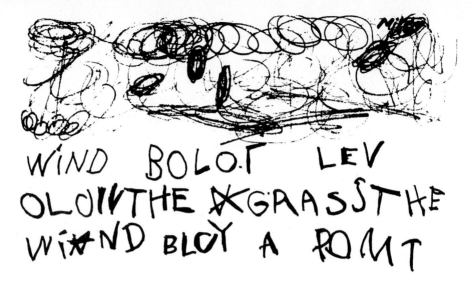

Figure 15.1. An example of a student's writing, with his teacher's written response.

write and respond to each other in them. These will be discussed in greater depth in the next chapter.

The most important point I wish to make here is that it is very helpful to all parties to have some means of making a paper trail of the child's development. First and foremost, it is helpful to the child to have access to her own history as a learner. When children are able to look at their own development as a reader or as a writer, it provides the possibility of looking forward to further learning. Learning becomes a draft of knowledge composition. Being able to reflect on one's own process and progress is also a partial antidote to competitive definitions of success and failure. Children tend not to attend to their own earlier performance, even when it is available to them, in competitive contexts.[64] Second, these trails give a method of describing and documenting development that is instructionally useful. They allow us to learn about important, but less obvious, aspects of writers' development. For example, if a folder does not contain abandoned pieces, then the student is not taking risks. Third, they are not exercises that take time away from teaching and learning. Rather, they increase the time spent learning and the quality of the learning. Fourth, they provide teachers with a means to see their own efforts mirrored, even though it is through somewhat frosted glass. Fifth, they provide something tangible as the basis of discussion among the various stakeholders in the educational enterprise who otherwise quite often drift off into abstract polemic. Sixth, the writing provides a means of increasing personal, individualized contact. Apart from anything else, this is likely to encourage greater participation and reduce the prospect of students dropping out. However, before considering any of this record-keeping, a reasonable time must be set aside for writing. A forty-minute period seems to be absolutely bare minimum.

LEVELS OF RECORDS

We might think of three levels of written records for students. At the first level there is the working folder of writing with various drafts and revisions, pieces set aside to be picked up later, some pieces marked up for editing, topics, ideas, reminders, and a list of books published or references to works with which the student has "gone public." This might also be accompanied by a journal of one form or another. In a more elaborate organization with older students there might be a spiral-bound journal with subdivisions for literature dialogue, a learning log, a personal response journal, and an observation notebook. These keep track of the day-to-day writing, reading, and learning taking place. But it is important to provide a regular stocktaking of where everyone is and where they came from. To accomplish this, we can use a second level of recording.

At the second level of records, we would have selections from the first level. Two to four times each year, each student (and teacher) might put together a portfolio which constitutes a public statement by each student of his or her development.[65] For example, the portfolio might have in it:

- ☐ pieces the student considers to be her best work of the semester or quarter
- ☐ a piece taken from draft through final form
- ☐ a sample taken at some earlier date and a later sample to show development
- ☐ some examples of diverse genres attempted
- ☐ a list (perhaps annotated) of books read with dates completed or abandoned
- ☐ a section from a literature log
- ☐ a copy of a letter written to an author
- ☐ a character extension
- ☐ a critical review of a book
- ☐ a parody of a book
- ☐ biographical background on an author

For each piece selected you might have the student write a brief comment on an index card or large "Post-it" describing why the piece was selected. This provides a good deal of information about what aspects of development the student is valuing. For example, one student wrote:

> This is my best piece because I put so much work into it. I did an enormous amount of research. I read five books about it.

About a second piece she wrote:

> I think this piece is good because the lead is good and because Jenny seems like she is real even though she isn't. I know I will finish this piece some time because it is too good to just drop.

The portfolio itself might take any number of forms. For example, it might be in a two-sided pouch folder with writing work on one side and reading work on the other, although there is no need to divide up writing and reading work in that or any other manner. It might be a time line or fold-out book, or a wall display of some sort. However, writing a reflective self-evaluation as part of the presentation is very important. This reflective work might be structured with a series of questions or prompts to respond to such as:

1. What has changed most about your reading (writing)?
2. Why do you think this has changed?
3. What change would you like to see in your reading (writing)?
4. How do you plan to make that change?
5. What is the hardest part of writing (reading) for you?

Questions 1, 3, and 4 are probably the most productive ones.

You might investigate different types of portfolio, splitting up these possibilities. Dennis P. Wolf describes three different types: biographies of works, range of works, and reflections.[66] The biography of a work involves a description, with documentation, of the development of, say, a piece of writing. The range of works is an attempt to demonstrate the diversity of activity engaged in—for example, documentation of the range of material read, or genres written. The reflection is a documentation or tape recording of the student's reflections on his work. For me, the reflective aspect is central and I hate to see it separated from any kind of portfolio.

The involvement of the student in the process of evaluation is absolutely critical. In the first place, it gives the student a goal and a time limit for putting together what amounts to a performance but gives control of the nature of the performance to the student.[67] Second, it gives clear purpose to the daily recordkeeping that the student is responsible for, in that it provides the basis for researching his own literate development. Third, it generates an ongoing reflective attention to development in one's own work. Fourth, it makes students historical, in the sense that they come to be aware that their concerns now (the insecurities of growing up and the level of skill with which they sometimes become frustrated) do in fact pass. This encourages personal growth and the development of a more grounded personal identity. A fifth important reason for the involvement of students in the development of the portfolio evaluation is that the choices they make and the reasons for the choices reveal what they value in their development as literate individuals.

Although it is critical that students select their own pieces for the portfolio and that they describe the reason for the selection, teachers too might contribute something. If the portfolio is a principal form of communication between home and school, perhaps in place of report cards, then, the teacher might add selections with reasons too, to illustrate aspects that the student is not yet able to see. In doing so, the student learns about other dimensions of his development. These selections might also be made in the light of particular concerns expressed by parents about their child's progress.

The third level of record might be archival. Although more parents and children are becoming aware of the value of keeping records of children's development, the school generally loses access to this work and hence its own instructional history. I cannot think of a better use of photocopying than to place on file students' end-of-year portfolios along with narrative descriptions by teachers. Better still, the use of microfiche or computer scanning would allow more manageable recordkeeping. With a computer scanner, we could store images of almost everything a child produces in her school career if we chose to. Apart from anything else, this would allow the school to systematically sample work over time in order to engage in serious self-study. I also have a feeling that such historical records would give graduates a stronger attachment to the schools in which they spent so much of their growing years, and that this would pay off in later support and respect for the efforts of the schools.

OBSERVATIONAL RECORDS

Often our best information on children's literate activity comes at the most unplanned time and in the most unexpected way. If we do not record it, then we will likely forget some important information. The things that we might keep track of using a checklist are extremely numerous. For example, in writing, we might use a checklist to take note of such diverse aspects as:

- ☐ topic choice—diversity, focus
- ☐ genre choice—diversity, knowledge of conventions
- ☐ selection of relevant details,
- ☐ willingness to revise
- ☐ willingness to edit
- ☐ focus of revision
- ☐ spelling using phonetic analysis
- ☐ spelling using visual analysis
- ☐ decision to discard or delete text
- ☐ decision to decide when to drop a piece of writing
- ☐ persistence with a given piece or topic
- ☐ persistence in problem solving

□ the use of self as audience
□ editing (numerous types of related behavior)

Many more items could be added to the list and most of the items could be broken into smaller items. Indeed, it would be hard to check off items like ''editing'' at any point since there is always room for improvement. Furthermore, breaking these down formally invites a broken-down curriculum.

Particular observations will often be critical for certain students. For example, some students do not contribute a great deal to discussions in teacher-directed groups. This is too often true of certain minority children. These students are often much more vocal and involved during peer group activities.[68] It is thus quite helpful to carry around a ring binder with a division for each student and one for general observations so that these observations can be recorded on the spot. For example, my records might include such observations as:

> Nick—Indep rding chose Mr McGee & My Cat—VERY easy—consistently choosing well below what he can manage.
>
> Tracy—asking Sam & Chuck for lots of help on writing—too much interruption for them.
>
> Sarah—rejected by group—no one conferencing with her.
>
> Andre—shared his writing with the group today—first time—big smile.
>
> Eric wrote hate letter to Franklin. U R SUPED I HAT U.
>
> Science corner unpopular.

Some of these observations will be written in the student's file, and others will be in a general class file to be used for planning. For example, the apparent failure of the science corner might suggest some immediate action after school, or during school the next day, or perhaps some interviews with the children, or the forming of a student committee to find out how it might be improved. Other observations might be transferred to the student's file at the end of the day. Further observations may be recorded on checklists of one sort or another.

CHECKLISTS

Some people like to use checklists as a help to make sure they have been thorough in keeping track of children's development, either by ensuring a systematic check on progress, or by ensuring regular checkpoints in children's development as a safety net, just as a shopping list helps us not to miss things at the store. However, lists can also represent the ''externalization of expertise.'' When children keep track of their own developing writing skills, they at once can admire and be admired for their knowledge, and be more consistent and responsible in its use, for example in their editing.

Checklists can be very helpful, but they do have catches. They lend themselves to misreading by other people. For a teacher to keep track of students' development and to ensure that some students do not get forgotten, they can be enormously helpful. However, when others come to look at them they are stripped of the richer context which the classroom teacher has and problems can arise. Often people who are short of time simply scan checklists. What do they scan for? They look for the missing check marks, scanning for abnormalities or negatives, and skip over the things that the child *can* do. This makes it likely that they will form a negative impression of the student rather than a positive one. I am sure that this is mostly a problem when teachers are under pressure from accountability testing and are nervous about children's poor performance on the tests. Using dates rather than check marks to show when a behavior was observed can also show whether development is taking place, and can suggest the need for closer observation. Similarly, leaving space for comments helps to alleviate the problem.

The most important thing about checklists is that they should be communally developed. When a group of teachers gets together to come up with a workable checklist, they have to negotiate within the following constraints:

- ☐ The possible list can be extremely long
- ☐ A workable list must be reasonably brief
- ☐ Everyone will have different priorities
- ☐ The checklist has implications for classroom practice.

The production of a working checklist is thus likely to produce lively discussion. The most interesting thing to me is that, having negotiated to the point of agreement on the final form of the checklist, the checklist itself could probably be thrown away. The process of negotiation will have essentially internalized the checklist for the participants and, at the same time, it will have helped each develop his or her view of literacy and learners. The second important thing about checklists is that they should always be thought of as drafts. As teachers transform their knowledge, they come to view children in different ways, and need to be able to change the structure of record keeping as they feel necessary.

CHAPTER 16

Dialogue in Print: Evaluation through Journals

Interviews are one form of dialogue in which the exchange is somewhat one-sided. The person who is being interviewed does most of the talking. In some situations interviews might even be considered a prompted monologue. As we move to a more balanced form of dialogue, in which both participants have equal contributions, with more balanced roles, each is able to fashion his own questions and answers, not only from the feedback, but from the model provided by the other party. In everyday talk, each person can take both the role of listener and speaker, questioner and responder. Each gets his agenda on the table. In most classrooms, dialogue like this is limited to student-to-student talk (if it is allowed at all) because of the large differences in power between teacher and students. If those power differences can be minimized or localized, real dialogue, rather than monologue, can take place. In dialogue, students ask questions as much as teachers, and in doing so, reveal a great deal about what occupies their thinking. In some ways, the most useful case of dialogue for evaluation purposes is that which occurs in the dialogue journal.

Dialogue journals are simply journals in which people write first draft letters to one another. For example, students write notes to the teacher in their journals, and the teacher takes time, usually at the end of the day, to respond to the children's entries. Students can write to each other in some dialogue journals too. All that is needed is a sturdy notebook that is large enough to write in easily and to see the letter continuity from page to page (spiral-bound is good), a box to keep the journals in, and a specific time set aside on a daily basis for the writing, although even that is not essential as it can be fitted into the regular reading/writing program. Your main responsibility as a teacher is to respond to the *content* of the student's entry, NOT to the conventions of spelling and punctuation, and to respond personally as another literate person, friend/mentor, or at least a decent conversational partner.

WHY DIALOGUE JOURNALS?

Dialogue journals provide a functional, self-motivated context in which students and teachers can share personal time and experiences while incidentally developing their writing and producing an historical record of the interactions and of writing development. Not incidentally, they also produce a lot of writing. For example, in David's journal we find:

DAVID: I wnt to the grat iscap wth my dad and we had iscrem and petsa. it was kul.

P.J.: I bet you had a lot of fun. Did you go on any rides? I have never been there. Would I have fun if I went? I really liked the toad you brought to school but I am pleased that you let him go again.

DAVID: I went on the stemn demn.it was rel scare. and I went on the wota slid that was neto. you wod love it I bet. I cot a slumndu in the lak.

The sheer quantity of writing produced and the communicative, dialogical nature of the enterprise ensures that a considerable amount of learning takes place. At the same time, students read the teacher's notes, which often provide models of ways of talking about books, conventional spellings and response structures, more complex language, and the like. Even better, the teacher's responses can provide provocative contexts that draw the student into making interesting analyses for herself.

Dialogue journal writing also provides a context that helps students move from conversation to essay writing skill. Indeed, Shirley Brice Heath describes the history of the essayist style as emerging from letters to journals to essays.[69] A central shift that takes place along the way is from the personal audience, or conversation, to the general audience, or what amounts to public speaking. One young student who was being tutored in our lab was quite quickly able to write in his journal to his tutor, beginning every entry "Dear Sharon," but he would not write stories. He would write the odd line and be unable to continue. He asked if he could start his stories with "Dear Sharon" and he found writing the story no problem, editing out the letter form at the end.

Dialogue journals allow children to engage in functional written language of quite a wide variety of types. For example, Jana Staton notes examples of: asking questions, reporting personal experiences, making promises, evaluating, offering, apologizing, giving directions, complaining, and giving opinions.[70] The journals provide a situation that allows a child to reflect on his audience's response to various ways of presenting ideas and arguments. At the same time these journals provide an excellent trail of artifacts of learning. For example, we can look at the way the students select and maintain topics and how they elaborate upon those topics. We can describe how they accommodate to their audience's response, the diversity of functions for which they are able to write, and many other possibilities.

On top of all these benefits, the dialogue journal provides a vehicle through which classroom management can be assisted. Students and teacher have a context in which they can write about the things that are bothering them in the classroom and they can communicate about them in a reflective way (which writing encourages) after reducing the emotion with which they might have been charged, or as a safe means of discharging that emotion. In interviews, students point out that they like dialogue journals for numerous reasons including being able to share problems, complain about things, have things explained that they did not understand, get action taken on class social problems, and many other functions.[71] The dialogue journals can allow students to raise questions which they would not ask in a more public forum. This, of course, applies to journals that are not used between students.

SOME HOW-TO'S

I have seen teachers use dialogue journals from first grade to eighth grade and in university (people are using them in high schools—I just haven't seen them).[72] Younger students may have difficulty getting under way, but Leslie Reed's solution is to give the students a sample journal entry at the outset. She allows them to copy it if they want, but encourages them to write their own. At the beginning one or two may copy it and some others will use parts of it and perhaps add to it, but quite quickly they become independent as they discover that they get a real response. She requires her fifth graders to write a minimum of three sentences per entry. Ms. Reed also gives some direction to her students' journal writing. During the first few weeks of school she puts on the board some made-up examples of journal entries and asks the students which ones they would prefer to read and why. She also points out to them that she is very busy answering so many letters each day, and she appreciates not having to go back to read earlier letters in order to understand what is being talked about today. In other words, she is helping the students gain some sense of audience, and the extra explicitness needed in writing.[73] The rules for use of journals are certainly something you should explore to find out what works better for you and your students.

There are some simple guidelines for responding to students' journals which will help make them work well. First, your response to their writing should be a genuine response to the content of their writing rather than its form. Apart from anything else, responding to the form would be like someone in a conversation saying, "You mean IS NOT able, not AIN'T able." Even positive comments on the form of their writing can be problematic. Telling them that they did a great job with their writing in their journal changes their understanding of the nature of the interaction and the motivation for participation. Responding to the content is what communication is all about. Second, your response should be friendly and supportive. This does not mean that you cannot express problems that you are having with the student, just that you do it in a friendly and supportive, non-blaming way, being understanding of the student's feelings. Third, your responses should prompt more writing. This hardly needs elaboration; but if you write interesting things they will want to get more, and if you ask relevant (to them) questions, they will often answer them. Fourth, you should not be forceful and demanding. Asking the student to do something or providing options for responses allows the student choice, and choice has many desirable properties.[74] For example, you might say, "Would you mind . . . ?'' or ''Perhaps you could . . . ?'' or ''Are there any other ways you could have done that?'' or ''Have you considered . . . ?''

WHAT'S IN THERE?

The dialogue journals provide a record from which you can draw many different pieces of information. In particular, in the dialogue lies a record of concerns (interests) and of change. The change can lie in many different areas. For example, a study by Jana Staton and Joy Kreeft shows change over the course of the year in students' selection of topics.[75] Toward the beginning of the year the topics tended to be closely tied to the classroom community—the shared context. Later in the school year the topics tended to be more personalized, reflecting the shared understandings and more developed relationship between teacher and student. The greater rapport that is developed between teacher and student is also likely to change the nature of the oral dialogue in the classroom, and the likelihood that the teacher is able to keep in touch with the students' development.

Jana Staton describes the development in dialogue journals of children's understanding of the conversational rules of elaboration in the context of a given audience.[76] Some years ago Paul Grice described two conversational maxims: Be informative and be relevant.[77] In other words, it is the speaker's or writer's job to convey information clearly, and coherently, but not so much information that the listener or reader is bored. These two desiderata of communication are not easily developed in children's writing. Dialogue journals provide a context in which students are motivated to consistently reflect on and develop the extent and nature of their elaborations on topics. Thus, there are likely to be changes in such things as the frequency of one-sentence statements, the reporting of specific new information, and the use of comparative and classificatory statements. All of these are documented in the journals, providing as ''hard'' data as one could wish for. On many dimensions, students' and teachers' writing tend to move closer together over the course of the year.

Students in interviews about their journals, or in the journals themselves, are very likely to comment on changes in their own writing. Comments such as the following are not uncommon:

> I use to do real short things but now I write alot because the more I tell her about what Im writing the more she understands what Im saying. Also the more she likes to read what I write. I think I write more stuff about less things than I use to.

Such self-evaluation is encouraged by the sheer presence of the continuous record of communication which the journals provide. I use dialogue journals in my university teaching and I actually require students to write an analytic memo reflecting on changes in their journal entries.[78]

Journals of even minimal scale can also be useful for documenting literate activity. Simply keeping a list of books read, completed and uncompleted (with dates), tells a great deal about what is going on in a student's reading life. Even unadorned, such a list is helpful as a basis of discussion and as a way of documenting progress. However, there are two major cautions with such lists. The length of the list should never become the focus of attention, and the lists should never become public. An interesting phenomenon takes place when the number of books read is the focus of public attention. Our baby-sitter one day asked me to sign up for a "readathon" our school district was having. The principle of the exercise is that the more books you read, the more money you make for the school or other charity. I asked Jenny what she was going to read. Her predictable response? "Oh, a lot of short books." If we place enormous stress on such outcomes, then we must pay the price.

A simple list of books tells us something about interests, amount of reading, and types of reading. However, an annotated list tells us more. For example, if as part of their routine students write something about the books they are reading, then we, and they, have a trail of what the reading has meant to them and the aspects of the literature to which they attend. This provides a way of keeping track, but the writing tends to become burdensome. There is no obvious reason for such monologue except for keeping track. This is what happens when students are required to write book reports. Monologues like this do not provide the conditions for learning to write or read in greater depth. We would commonly get only cursory comments, at best, in such journals. Writing for oneself as the audience can be very cryptic. For example, shopping lists usually have little detail about quantity, brand, etc. However, if we simply go one step further, we can have the comments about the books addressed to someone who can then write back to us. Dialogue journals provide a built-in motive for both writing and making the writing less than cursory. Furthermore, they provide for dialogue which is the basis of learning to be literate. Nancie Atwell's book *In the Middle* provides a wonderfully readable and practical account of the use of literary dialogue journals. Atwell describes the process and consequences of inviting her middle school students to engage in written dialogue with her, and each other, about books. These dialogues took place in spiral-bound notebooks that were numbered and filed alphabetically. The tone of their letters was informal, like notes to friends, and the conventions of spelling and grammar were not given overt attention. The idea was to create, in Atwell's words, a "dining room table" atmosphere. The consequence was literary talk written down.

There are two distinctions between the dialogue journals used by Atwell and those described by Staton and her colleagues. The first lies in the constrained domain of the discourse. Unlike Staton, Atwell and her students were writing only about their reading of books. The second distinction is that in Atwell's class, not all letters came to her. The students wrote to each other as well. Atwell's requirements were that students spend their reading workshop time reading, and then writing about their reading. She required at least one literary letter a week to be written to someone in the classroom community, and at least once every two weeks one of the letters should be to her. At least one letter a week should be analytic, going beyond simple plot descriptions. The letters were considered first-draft writing with consequently little concern over convention, just as in the dialogue journals of Leslie Reed described by Reed and her colleagues.

ADDITIONAL BENEFITS AND CATCHES

This practice of writing is habit-forming, and has the effect of leaving a paper trail of literary dialogue that yields volumes of information about the students' development through the language used and the way in which they analyze what they have read. At the same time, the different perspective of the teacher or student colleague prompts them to think of the books in new ways, and pushes them to develop their thinking. Others' comparisons with other books and writers and personal situations make for considerable development of the intertextuality (the building of connections) of literate understanding. Students' questions help to broaden the ways in which they talk about books. Better than that, the act of writing about their reading causes the students to step back from their reading and think more deeply about it than they otherwise would if they spoke only about the books. This helps them to become aware of their own knowledge and changes in it and to be able to talk about what they know and have learned; to move away from the inability to talk about what was learned at school. Indeed, if report cards must be done, students could write a good part of them themselves using their journals essentially as field notes. This would accomplish at once ownership, reflectiveness, and interest in development.

Students' literary journal entries tend to move from statements like:

I liked Charlotte's Web. It was great.

to

I cried over Tomie DePaola's "Now One Foot." The relationship which he builds up between Bobby and his grandfather is so strong and the way he has him do just what his grandfather did is—wow! Its alot like "A Special Trade" which Mrs. Sims read to us last year.

The journals provide student and teacher with insights about the activity of being literate; the kind of strategies and habits that readers engage in. For example:

I've sort of noticed "trends" or "cycles" in my reading. Right now I'm in a Paula Danziger "cycle." At the beginning of the year I was in a Science Fiction "cycle."[79]

Last night I fell asleep over Cold Moons. Again. Thats the 3rd time I've done that and I don't even get very far. I don't know whether to drop it and start a shorter book or just not read at home. It is so hard to find the time to read at home. I will drop it. Any ideas for a shorter book?

Letters also speak of students' emerging literary understanding and their developing sense of what makes for quality literature. For example:

To me, *Sea Pups* is more of an essay because there are more facts blended in than the number in a normal book. I think that *Sea Pups* is uniqe because I haven't read anything quite like it. I've read my brothers essays, of course, but no real essay like books.

I think that some of Auel's situations were a bit silly. One thing that bugged me was how Ayla discovered things, like building a fire with flint, riding Whinney, etc. You knew exactly what she was going to do next. When she gets on Whinney you just know that's going to lead to riding her, then using her to chase animals, then to hunt. She makes it so obvious! (Do you understand what I'm trying to say?)[80]

Not only are the dialogue journals habit-forming, but they are community-forming, and the dialogue journals hold a record of the developing interaction between teacher and student, and between others in the community of learners if they are involved in the journals. When dialogue is open and written, a wide variety of compelling evidence is available to document progress and guide instruction. A clear example of providing feedback on instruction was illustrated in Figure 6.1 (page 35).

Just because dialogue occurs in a journal does not make it any more nor less likely to be informative, however. The pattern of the interaction will show through, and sometimes we see reflections of different kinds of relationships in the journals. If a teacher is used to teaching children about literature by asking questions of them to guide them to a "correct reading," then he may well continue to ask those questions in the journal. For example, he might write:

I think you are really getting to understand the book, Steve. Why do you think the captain made that decision? What happened after they went ashore? What is the author trying to say with this book?

This maintains the power difference between teacher and student that is commonly evident in classrooms, and the journals become a test in which the students try to answer the teacher's questions correctly. There is a consequent loss of involvement, along with a loss of control and ownership.

A teacher friend of mine began using dialogue journals in his classroom. After a couple of months he asked me to help him solve a problem he was having with them. His students were writing very little in their journals and doing so reluctantly. So while the students were writing in their journals, I went around asking them about what they were doing. I asked what kinds of things they wrote and what kinds of things the teacher wrote. Every student I spoke to said that the teacher wrote questions. Having recently shifted from a basal reader, Tom had essentially transferred the "read the story and see if they got the meaning" format to the journals. When I explained what the students said, he decided to stop asking questions altogether. Instead he wrote comments about his own reading. Two to three days later, journal entries began appearing like "How come you aren't asking any questions? If you're not going to ask them, I guess I will." and "Since you haven't asked any questions I guess I'll tell you what I think." The most interesting part to me was that towards the end of the year, he was asking questions again, some of them the same ones he had been asking before, but the students were still writing a great deal with enthusiasm, and even answering many (but not all) of his questions.

To understand this paradox, it is helpful to know that there are two sides to a question: a controlling side and a request for information. When we ask a question, we control the topic of discussion and essentially force an answer. When Tom was asking lots of questions early in the year, the students understood them principally as controlling, which meant that the journals were essentially not theirs since topic choice and focus were taken away from them. When the questions stopped, they were able to establish their own topics and receive legitimate responses. Within this context, when questions arose again, they were viewed not as controlling but as requests for information arising naturally out of the dialogue.

Children can sniff out tests at forty paces. What appears as an insult to a teacher intent on having the students answer his questions may actually be a compliment in that the students feel comfortable enough to offer what they want to talk about and to decide which questions to answer when. Getting students to answer questions is secondary to getting them to reflect on and talk about literature and their reading. The basis of the enterprise is a trusting relationship.

Making comparisons yourself between authors is a good way to encourage students to see similarities and differences in their various readings. Certainly it is at least as effective as telling them specifically to do so. Teachers tend to dominate classroom interactions, particularly by asking questions. For example, Roger Shuy found that in the six elementary language arts classrooms he studied, 97% of all classroom exchanges were initiated by the teacher. Teachers ask most of the questions and by doing so control the topics of discussion and maintain authority and control.[81] Virtually all of the requests in the classroom tend to be made by teachers. The majority of questions by the teacher open interactions of the form: Teacher question—student response—teacher evaluative feedback. These are called "display questions," since the object of the exercise is for the student to display her knowledge or lack of it. The nature of teacher-student interactions tends to be different in dialogue journals.

There are several reasons for this difference. First, the journal opens up a different form of social interaction in which you can choose which questions to answer. It is all right not to answer questions, which takes away the power imbalance normally produced by asking a question that forces a response. Since students ask more questions in the journals, they gain greater control of the dialogue, and at the same time highlight their concerns more clearly. The kind of questions students ask tend to include requests about procedures, requests for information, requests for opinion, and challenges. Through these questions, many instructional and personal issues are resolved and a greater rapport develops as a consequence.

I find it most interesting that in an analysis of a classroom teacher's dialogue journal questions, the most frequently asked questions, about half of all questions, seek an opinion. Opinion questions do not carry the same power differential as other questions since your opinion cannot be correct or incorrect; rather, each participant has an opinion. The second most common question seeks unknown information. These are not display questions, which are quite rare. In other words, the teacher is commonly asking for expansion of the student's topic and thereby showing interest in it and helping to develop the elaboration aspect of written composition. The third most common type of question the teacher asked was reflective questions. These are the ones that I stressed earlier as developing self-evaluation and metacognition.

Journals allow teachers to step back and examine their own teaching in terms of the interactions between teacher and student. Self-evaluation is as critical for teachers as for students. The characteristics of the relationship in the journals may be reflected in such things as the formality of the language the student uses, the extent and nature of responses to questions, the frequency and nature of the questions that the students ask, and the extent to which the students tend to answer the questions the teacher asks. On the other hand, when the journals involve students writing to students, some of these observations may not be as relevant. In general, there is no such power differential between students. Introducing students writing to students as well as to the teacher opens the opportunity to look at the choice of dialogue partner for what it might say about what they get from each other.

An additional benefit of dialogue journals has been pointed out by Roger Shuy. According to his research, children asked twice as many questions through their journals as they did in the classroom, and the questions were more directly related to learning. Interestingly, teachers spent less time asking questions in journals than they did in their regular classroom talk—15% compared with 35%, and the questions which they did ask were genuine information requests rather than test-type questions to which they already knew the answers. Teachers also used fewer directives in their journal writing than in their regular classroom talk.[82]

Although dialogue journals give a wealth of information about students' literate development and about their interactions with the teacher, they also serve other functions useful to evaluation. Writing for, or talking with, parents about a student's development in reading and writing with concrete examples of their performance in hand is a good deal easier than doing it from test scores.

Documentary descriptions from such data are compelling and generally more understandable to parents. The journals show a knowledge of the student as a person, and they reveal some of the interaction between the student and teacher.

There is, however, another side to the use of dialogue, whether in journals or not, to understand children's literary development. The manner in which a teacher herself talks about books is likely to be reflected in both teacher and student language in the journals. If a teacher is unable to say more about a book than "It was a good book. I liked it," then the students are unlikely to talk with more insight about the books; and even if they did, the teacher would not be particularly likely to notice. In other words, the journals' usefulness, as with anything else to do with literacy, has a lot to do with what the teacher knows about literature, literacy, and her students. There is no avoiding the central evaluative problem of helping teachers develop their knowledge of literacy, literature, and of their practice.

RESOURCES

There is a growing body of research on the use of dialogue journals in a wide range of classrooms, including those in which English is being learned as a second language. It is, however, accumulating slower than it might, given the ease of data collection and the functional nature of the whole activity, both instructionally and for evaluation. Nevertheless, the following resources will prove useful:

Nancie Atwell (1987). *In the middle: Writing, reading and learning with adolescents.* Portsmouth, NH: Heinemann/Boynton-Cook.

Kathy Danielson (1988). *Dialogue journals: Writing as conversation.* Bloomington IN: Phi Delta Kappa Educational Foundation.

Toby Fulwiler (1987). (Ed.) *The journal book.* Portsmouth, NH: Heinemann/Boynton-Cook.

Joy Kreeft Peyton (1990). (Ed.) *Students and teachers writing together: Perspectives on journal writing.* Alexandria, VA: TESOL.

Jana Staton, Roger Shuy, Joy Peyton, and Leslie Reed (1988). *Dialogue journal communication: Classroom, linguistic, social and cognitive views.* Norwood, NJ: Ablex.

But dialogue journals are not the only useful journals. As a further example, Ann Berthoff describes a different kind of journal, the "double-entry" journal, or "dialectical notebook." These do not involve others writing in them, but students (or teachers) transcribe sentences on one side of the page opening, and comment on them on the other. This type of journal encourages deeper and reflective thinking about reading. It also leaves a useful trail. Berthoff points out a secondary audit function of such journals:

> . . . requiring a double-entry notebook is the only way I know to defend your-self against plagiarism, if you want to assign formal term papers.[83]

The principal value of these journals is, of course, the development of reflective inquiry, examination of one's own knowledge and its construction. Conse-quently, the double-entry notebook is also useful for teachers' learning about their own practice. On one side of the page may be observations from daily classroom activity, and on the other, comments upon them.

CHAPTER 17

Telling Thinking: Evaluation through Thinking Out Loud

If you have ever watched young children writing, you will have noticed that they write with their mouths. Their hands are working their pencils, but their mouths are doing all the work, exaggerating the sounds in the words so that they can be represented on paper. In fact, if you prevent them from doing this by getting them to bite or hold their tongues, they have great difficulty writing.[84] Similarly, young readers when reading "silently" often make quite a racket. The initial performances of literate activity (other activities also) are often done quite consciously. Later the brain organizes the activity so that it is done in an automatic sequence without involving conscious analysis. At that point, con-scious access to the process is often lost. Young children often think out loud, giving themselves instructions and going through planning and evaluative activi-ties quite audibly. The Russian psychologist Lev Vygotsky pointed out that this speech is often a reflection of the dialogue which has taken place with others as the social thought in dialogue becomes part of the child's use of language in thinking.[85] It is possible to ask students to make a point of thinking out loud for you. Under certain circumstances their think-aloud reports can help you understand how they go about their reading and writing and why they do it the way they do.

Thinking out loud does not simply go away as people get older. Indeed, when younger (and less verbal) students are asked to think aloud, they tend to produce less complete reports than older (and more verbal) students. However, thinking aloud does go away as people get more able at the activity or as the task becomes easier. Alexandr Sokolov's studies of "inner speech" show that when people are novices at a task, their processing becomes less automatic and more available in working memory.[86] Ake Edfeldt made three related observations from his work. First, more able readers engage in less silent speech than do less able readers. Second, less silent speech occurs when people read easy texts than when they read hard texts; and third, the more the print in a piece of text is blurred, the more readers engage in silent speech.[87] Thus, not just young children, but all of us tend to do things like read aloud, or at least subvocalize, when the reading becomes difficult or when we are trying to spell a difficult word. Try, for example, to read the following real but uncommon words, and watch yourself doing so—res gestae, internecine, parargyrite. For most people, the strategies they use to figure out these uncommon words will be available in part for reflection, unlike their reading of words like "the," "some," "happy."

This deautomation and externalization of thinking is useful for teachers in a number of ways. In the first place, it allows a window into the mind letting us glimpse, if briefly and incompletely, how the learner is going about what he is doing, and sometimes why. In the second place, it allows teachers to notice how their students go about managing difficult literacy tasks. Thinking aloud has been in use at least since the turn of the century, when Huey[88] and Marbe[89] were exploring its use in areas of psychology including reading. Though its use has been sporadic, recently it has undergone a revival in the study of reading and writing.[90]

Thinking aloud can occur accidentally as an unconscious by-product of a difficult activity or it can occur as a conscious attempt to make "silent speech" no longer silent. A classic example of unconscious thinking aloud occurs in oral reading. When a student makes several attempts at a word she is stuck on, it is reasonable to assume that the nature of these attempts actually reflects the kind of problem solving she is doing. Similarly, when a student reads a piece of her writing out loud and makes corrections and comments along the way, these are probably reasonable reflections of the thinking activity going on. Sometimes, then, asking students to think out loud can provide useful information about how they go about, for example, planning or writing a letter to a member of Congress, or reading their social studies textbook.

There are ways to increase the quality and quantity of think-aloud reports. Just asking people to think aloud does not guarantee that the talk they produce has anything to do with their thinking. When people are ego-involved, they are not likely to make their unedited thinking public unless they are enormously self-confident. In situations which produce ego-involvement, students are likely to report what they think the teacher wants to hear rather than what occurred.

Verbal reporting requires students to bare their minds to some extent, letting someone else be privy to their thought processes. When tasks are difficult, as they likely will be if automatic processes are to be made unautomatic, students may not feel secure enough in the reporting process to give an unadorned and unedited version of their thinking. For most people, actively trying to think aloud requires a trusting supportive context.

We have found that getting people accustomed to attending to how they do things makes them more able to report their thinking. In studies we have asked people to "watch themselves reading" whenever they can in the week preceding our think-aloud session. It is simply a habit of mind which can readily be developed in classrooms—taking one's own thinking as an object of study. The more people think aloud, or attend to their private speech, the more they are likely to be able to do it without thinking about it. That is, they become more able, and more likely, to take their own problem-solving strategies as an object of study with a view to improving them. In recent research this type of awareness has come to be called "metacognitive awareness." As people become aware of the effective strategies they use, they become more able to apply them in new and different situations.

There are many different ways of eliciting think-alouds. The basic principle is to have the student actually involved in doing whatever it is you are interested in learning about. When people talk about what they think they do, they provide different information from when they think aloud while actually doing the activity. For example, we asked children how they choose the books they read and how they know whether the books are right for them. Several of the children from one teacher's class said they used "the five-finger rule" which involved reading a page and keeping track of the problematic words on their fingers. However, when they actually chose books while thinking aloud, none of them actually did this. They used far more diverse and complex strategies.

When people are thinking aloud, they occasionally fall silent as they become completely absorbed in the task and forget that they are to think aloud. Sometimes it is necessary to prompt them with "What are you doing now?" or even a cough or something to remind them of your presence. Some researchers have used red dots at the end of each sentence to prompt readers to say something. Nonverbal cues are often useful points for discussion. Smirks, frowns, changes in eye movements, and changes in rate can all relate to understandings and puzzlements. You might use prompts such as these:

"You look puzzled. What's up?"

"Did you just realize something?"

"Wait a minute. I'm lost. How did you get from thinking about Chicago to thinking about potatoes?"

"I think I got something wrong here. I wrote down _____, but I don't think that's quite what you said."

You must always make it clear that it is *you* who is responsible for the misunderstanding. Once children understand that you often have this kind of problem, they begin to elaborate issues for you even before you have discovered the need to ask them to do so. At the same time, they begin to attend in more detail to the ways they are going about the things they are doing. This kind of evaluation pays dividends to all concerned.

Generally it helps if the child has confidence in her ability to perform that sort of activity adequately. Thus, for a classroom teacher engaged with a student learning about her reading strategies, a history of successful reading will help a great deal as they together work through the more difficult reading material which forms the basis of the thinking out loud. A person outside the classroom would do well to ensure that the student experiences comfortable success in their reading at least at the start and end of a think-aloud collaboration. Sometimes when a child cannot find the words to describe what strategies he used, he can be helped to do so by observing someone else, like the teacher, modeling the same activity, though not necessarily the same way. Provided the context does not lead the student to assert that the way the teacher did it was the way he did it, children can often describe how their strategies differed from those that were demonstrated.

There is always some trade-off with prompting. It increases the quantity of reports but runs the risk of changing the way the learners engage in the activity. Furthermore, if they do not actually have access to what they were thinking, they may feel obliged to make up something instead, thus reducing the quality of the information they provide.

There are even more complicated techniques for prompting think-alouds such as Charles Fillmore's technique of blocking off part of the text and asking questions systematically. For example the child opens the page and sees:[91]

Once upon a time xxxxxxxxxxxxxxxxxxxxxxxxxxxxxxx
xxxxxxxxxxxxxxxxxxxxxxxxxxxxxxxxxxxxxxxxxxxxxx

or possibly:

Dear Sir/Madame:
xxxxxxxxxxxxxxxxxxxxxxxxxxxxxxxxxxxxxxxxxxxxxx

The child is asked "What can you tell me about this piece so far?" "How do you know that?" "What do you think we might see in the next part of the story?" (read some) "Do you want to stick to your guess about . . . ?"

Such complex techniques are useful only in rare situations. Judith Langer has used them effectively to study how children negotiate their way though reading tests.[92] It should be obvious, however, that the time and effort involved would make such techniques prohibitive for classroom teachers and most others involved in practical educational settings. However, there are other reasons to be cautious of such techniques. The questioning involved in this type of think-aloud procedure produces an additional text for the student to "read"—the dialogue of the activity itself.[93] Furthermore, such techniques are very invasive and change drastically the nature of the activity the student is engaged in. For example, spreading a ten-minute story over half an hour does serious damage to the story. In the interests of learning how students comprehend, we may obliterate their comprehension. Having the student preread the story and then using the prompting as a stimulated recall ("What were you thinking when . . .") can help with this problem but introduces another in that it is a *re*reading, not a first reading. Strategies will differ in the two contexts. For example, prediction is preempted on the second reading.

Despite these cautions, a wide variety of interesting information about how readers read and how writers write can be obtained from think-alouds. The extent of students' monitoring of their understanding becomes evident—the click of understanding and the clunk of misunderstanding are louder. Similarly, their responses to these realizations become apparent. Readers report skipping ahead, rereading, rethinking the logic of an argument, changing their expectations about how much they expect to get out of the paper, mental imagery, and many other strategies. They reveal their predictions about where the text is going, and how they use text features such as signal words like "next," "first, . . . second . . . ," "because," and so forth. They report feelings about authors, and connections they make along the way with other books, authors, and personal experiences. The following part of a think-aloud is from an eleventh-grade student.

> *I'm not quite sure of this reference . . . so I need to go back to . . . to where I remember seeing the sentence on academic requirements . . . I'm re-reading that sentence . . . and it is the one . . . the reference . . . so it seems that the author is winding up his argument . . . for the importance of having academic standards for student athletes . . . and I expect that the final paragraph will re-state the author's thesis and perhaps give a strong example to back it up . . . that's what I expect.*

We can also gain access, through thinking out loud, to some of the difficulties readers experience in understanding the written word. For example, failure to use their own experience or lack of previous relevant experience will become apparent, as will overuse of their experience. Some readers expect a particular meaning and, in spite of the text, insist on clinging to that meaning. Readers often embellish and elaborate on the story they are reading. These elaborations (or lack of them) often become obvious in verbal reports and sometimes point to areas of difficulty in children's attempts to construct meaning from print. As a consequence of think-aloud reading and writing, both students and teachers tend to focus more on the processes of reading and writing than they had previously, a consequence that has many advantages.

Writers also are generally able to provide helpful information about their writing process through thinking aloud.[94] They will provide information on the reasons for the choices of words, punctuation, topics, style, plot, character, and the various other decisions they make along the way. Also revealed in the think-alouds of writers are their assumptions about audiences and about the goals of the writing activity.

Not only can readers' and writers' strategies become accessible, but also their attributions for the apparent success or failure of their performance. For example,

> *I'm losing it . . . shouldn't have partied so late last night. I knew it. I knew I'd screw it up . . . Idiot.*

Students often engage in self-instructions, at least more able readers and writers do.

> *No . . . wait . . . slow down . . . you're rushing this and losing it. Start over.*

Most students also engage in self-congratulation and accusation, cheering themselves on or criticizing themselves mercilessly.

> *Alright . . . now we're getting somewhere . . . O.K. we know where that fits . . . Damn . . . you always do that . . . you fool . . .*

They can be helped to become more inclined to cheer themselves on, which is what more successful students do, and within that context to become more constructively analytical.

Some of these decisions, strategies, and judgments made during the reading and writing processes will not be made consciously and will not appear in the think-aloud. Sometimes these decisions, strategies, and judgments are erroneous, or inefficient, or based on incorrect knowledge or assumptions. Knowing the source of the problem is most instructionally useful. Often simply raising a problem to consciousness is sufficient to allow the student to see the problem that needs to be solved. Without being aware of the problem it is hard to set out to solve it. Indeed, problem strategies that have become automatic generally *must* be brought to consciousness in order to be changed.

Pat Edmiston at Ohio State University has been using another interesting technique to help children externalize their reading processes.[95] After a student has read a book through, he then draws pictures of the characters in the book and himself, and cuts them out. Next he reads the book, paragraph by paragraph, moving around the players as if in a play. But there is also a player for the reader, who can move in and out of the performance as a spectator or participant. If the reader becomes one of the players, then the papers can be attached to one another. This approach offers considerable promise for understanding children's reading, and for children to become more reflective about their own reading. It offers the possibility of understanding point of view, and involvement.

Aspects of teaching, too, are accessible through thinking out loud. For example, when a teacher is grading papers, or writing report cards, he can think out loud into a tape recorder and go back later to try to understand how he has been going about this evaluation process. Experiences such as this can have a profound effect on one's teaching practice. Actually, just turning on the tape recorder and thinking out loud can make me so aware of the process that I do not need to go back and listen to the tape. The activity itself has made me sufficiently reflective and I have already learned enough to make some change.

Many teachers do not think of what they do when they write—what it is to be a reader and a writer. Just as children do not think about the language they use as an object worthy of study, teachers often do not take their literate roles such as readers, writers, editors, or researchers as objects of study. Thus the activity remains unanalyzed and it is harder for them to help children figure out their difficulties. It is also harder to do so in an empathic manner. Consequently, I have found it useful to have teachers themselves think-aloud while reading and writing. This makes them aware of themselves and the strategies they use when they are reading and writing. This in turn makes them more aware of writing and reading as strategic, constructive activities and helps them to think of their instruction in different terms. You will find reading think-alouds easier and more revealing if the reading is not very easy for you or if the goal of the reading is novel to you. To examine the possibilities for the think-aloud approach to learning about reading and writing, try thinking aloud onto a tape recorder while reading a book, particularly a difficult one, and try thinking aloud while trying to write a letter, research paper, report card, or whatever.

Think-aloud protocols also provide excellent grounds for discussion among school faculty. For example, a collaborative study of student think-alouds by some middle school faculty and some upper elementary school faculty would provide excellent grounds for them to talk about their goals and their instructional techniques. Such a collaborative activity would be rewarding for college and high school teachers as well since it would help them think more clearly about the nature of the academic discourse community and its expectations. These efforts seem desperately needed in view of analyses done by Linda Flower of the confusions of university freshmen in transition between discourse communities.[96] Such efforts would help both groups line up their instructional and evaluative practices and expectations.

Notes and References for Part II

1. Don Leu (1982). Oral reading error analysis: A critical review of research and application. *Reading Research Quarterly 17*(3): 420–437.
   See also:
   Jeanne Schumm and R. Scott Baldwin (1989). Cue system usage in oral and silent reading. *Journal of Reading Behavior 21*(2): 141–154.
   These writers found different rates of error detection in oral and silent reading at grades four, six, and eight, but not at grade two. They argue that the finding casts suspicion on diagnostic practices that assume similar word recognition processes in oral and silent reading. These differences may or may not be related to differences in the functions being served by the two types of reading, or to the methods used by these writers to study the two types of reading.

2. Ken Goodman, Dorothy Watson, and Carolyn Burke (1987). *Reading miscue analysis.* New York: Richard C. Owen.
   Ken Goodman (1965). A linguistic study of cues and miscues in reading. *Elementary English 42:* 639–643.
   Rose-Marie Weber (1970). A linguistic analysis of first-grade reading errors. *Reading Research Quarterly 5:* 427–451.

3. Richard Allington (1983). The reading instruction provided readers of differing reading abilities. *The Elementary School Journal 83*: 559–568.

4. Marie Clay (1985). *The early detection of reading difficulties.* 3rd ed. Portsmouth, NH: Heinemann-Boynton/Cook.
   Readers are referred to this definitive source for a more detailed treatment.

5. My use of the audiotape in this chapter is modeled on the superb *Early Reading Inservice Course* (ERIC) developed by the New Zealand Department of Education, which also develops the record-keeping system in greater detail.

6. *Little Pig* is written by June Melser and illustrated by Isabel Lowe. Auckland, New Zealand: Shortland Educational Publications, 1981. Published in the United States by the Wright Group, 10949 Technology Place, San Diego, CA 92127.

7. This text is from Margaret Mahy's book *The Dragon's Birthday,* illustrated by Philip Webb, published by Shortland Educational Publications, Auckland, New Zealand, 1984.

8. *Fantail, Fantail* was written by Margaret Mahy and illustrated by Bruce Phillips. It is published by Learning Media, the Ministry of Education, New Zealand, 1984, and distributed in the United States by Richard C. Owen.

9. *Who took the Farmer's Hat?* was written by Joan Nodset and illustrated by Fritz Siebel. It is published by D. C. Heath and Company, 1989.

10. *My Bike* was written and photographed by Craig Martin. It is published by Learning Media, the Ministry of Education, New Zealand, and distributed in the United States by Richard C. Owen.

11. *Saturday Morning* was illustrated by Lesley Moyes. It is published by Learning Media, the Ministry of Education, New Zealand, and distributed in the United States by Richard C. Owen.

12. This text is from Margaret Mahy's book *The Dragon's Birthday,* illustrated by

Philip Webb, published by Shortland Educational Publications, Auckland, New Zealand, 1984.

13. *Busy Beavers* was written by M. Barbara Brownell. It is published by the National Geographic Society Books for Young Explorers, 1988.

14. *Indian Two Feet and His Horse* was written by Margaret Friskey and illustrated by Katherine Evans. It is published by Children's Press, Chicago, 1959.

15. For an alternative (more detailed) treatment of the analysis (and recording) of oral reading errors, see:
Ken Goodman, Dorothy Watson, and Carolyn Burke (1987). *Reading miscue analysis*. New York: Richard C. Owen.
For more detail on the present approach, see:
Marie Clay (1985). *The early detection of reading difficulties*. Portsmouth, NH: Heinemann.

16. Except for George Spache, whose Diagnostic Reading Scales refer to what can be comprehended adequately in silent reading as "independent level."

17. This has been taken almost directly from the third edition of Marie Clay's book *The early detection of reading difficulties* (1985, Portsmouth, NH: Heinemann), to which I refer you for a more detailed treatment.

18. See Chapter 21 for explanations of the concepts about print.

19. There are 107 words and 1 error. The error rate is thus:

$$\frac{\text{Errors}}{\text{Words}} \times 100 = \frac{1}{107} \times 100 = 1\%$$

The accuracy rate, then, is simply $100\% - 1\% = 99\%$

20. There is 1 error (E) and 6 self-corrections (SC) in the "Beaver" example. Thus,

SC ratio = SC : (E + SC) = 6 : (1 + 6) = 6 : 7 = 1 : 6/7,
which is 1 : 1.2

21. Jerome Bruner (1986). *Actual minds, possible worlds*. Cambridge, MA: Harvard University Press, p. 21.

22. *Indian Two Feet and His Horse* was written by Margaret Friskey and illustrated by Katherine Evans. It is published by Children's Press, Chicago, 1959.

23. *Saturday Morning* was illustrated by Lesley Moyes. It is published by Learning Media, the Ministry of Education, New Zealand, and distributed in the United States by Richard C. Owen.

24. Andrew Biemiller (1970). The development of the use of graphic and contextual information as children learn to read. *Reading Research Quarterly 6*: 75–96.
Andrew Biemiller (1979). Changes in the use of graphic and contextual information as functions of passage difficulty and reading achievement level. *Journal of Reading Behavior 11:* 308–318.

25. More detailed summary procedures can be found in *The early detection of reading difficulties.*

26. Mark Sadoski and Sharon Lee (1986). Reading comprehension and miscue combination scores: Further analysis and comparison. *Reading Research and Instruction 25:* 160–167.

27. Rose-Marie Weber.(1985) Questions during reading lessons. A paper presented at the American Educational Research Association (April), San Francisco, CA.

28. James Dillon (1988). *Questioning and teaching: A manual of practice*. New York: Teachers College Press.

29. David Yaden (1984, December). 1000 questions about reading: A classification of

preschoolers' inquiries about print during story-reading. Paper presented at the annual meeting of the National Reading Conference, St. Petersburg, FL.

30. Ethnography is the study or description of different cultures. The idea is to describe a culture from the perspective of the culture itself.

31. Julie Tammivaara and Scott Enright (1986). On eliciting information: Dialogues with child informants. *Anthropology and Education Quarterly 17:* 218–238.

32. Though I have used the term "interview" here, most of what I have to say is similar to the writing "conference" described by Graves, Hansen, Calkins, and others.

33. Karen Wixson, Margory Lipson, Anita Bosky, and Nina Yokum. (1984). An interview for assessing students' perceptions of classroom reading tasks. *The Reading Teacher 37:* 354–359.

34. The use of basal readers creates many problems, some of which are explained elsewhere in this book. It is probably easiest to begin the transition away from basal readers with your writing program and then use that as a metaphor for your reading program. What you do in writing should be like what you do in reading. The following books on writing have been helpful to me:
Donald Graves (1983). *Writing: Teachers and children at work.* Portsmouth, NH: Heinemann, p. 116.
Lucy Calkins (1986). *The art of teaching writing.* Portsmouth, NH: Heinemann.
Jane Hansen (1987). *When writers read.* Portsmouth, NH: Heinemann.
Jerome Harste, Kathy Short, and Carolyn Burke (1988). *Creating classrooms for authors: The reading-writing connection.* Portsmouth, NH: Heinemann.
Donald Graves (1989). *Discover your own literacy.* Portsmouth, NH: Heinemann.
Donald Graves (1991). *Build a literate classroom.* Portsmouth, NH: Heinemann.

35. Jane Hansen (1987). *When writers read.* Portsmouth, NH: Heinemann.

36. Graves (1983). *Writing: Teachers and children at work.* Portsmouth, NH: Heinemann, p. 116.

37. Hansen. *When writers read.*

38. It has been reasonably well documented that less able readers have less metacognitive awareness. For discussions of this matter see:
Linda Baker and Ann Brown (1984). Metacognitive skills and reading. In P. David Pearson (Ed.), *Handbook of Reading Research.* White Plains, NY: Longman, pp. 353–394.
However, the reasons for this state of affairs are not well explored.

39. I base this on the following book which I have found exceptionally helpful:
James Spradley (1979). *The ethnographic interview.* New York: Holt, Rinehart & Winston.

40. Tom Nicholson (1984). Experts and novices: A study of reading in the high school classroom. *Reading Research Quarterly 19:* 436–451.

41. Michael Cole and Peg Griffin (1986). A sociohistorical approach to remediation. In Susan DeCastell, Alan Luke, and Kieran Egan (Eds), *Literacy, society, and schooling: A reader.* New York: Cambridge University Press, pp. 110–131.

42. These last three interviews are mostly from an earlier paper of mine:
Peter Johnston (1985). Understanding reading failure: A case study approach. *Harvard Educational Review 55*(2): 153–177.

43. Responses like these could be obtained through dialogue journals, which are discussed in Chapter 16, instead of through a terminal survey such as this. Indeed, dialogue journals would provide ongoing feedback so that problems could be solved along the way.

44. Louise Rosenblatt (1978). *The reader, the text, the poem.* Carbondale: Southern Illinois University Press.

45. For a good description of past attempts to test reading outcomes see:
David Moore (1983). A case for naturalistic assessment of reading comprehension. *Language Arts 60*: 957–969.
John Readence and David Moore (1983). Why questions? A historical perspective on standardized reading comprehension tests. *Journal of Reading 26:* 306–312.

46. Dolores Durkin (1978-9). What classroom observations reveal about reading comprehension instruction. *Reading Research Quarterly 14:* 481–533.
Frank Guszak (1967). Teacher questioning and reading. *The Reading Teacher 21:* 227–234.

47. Taffy Raphael has written about this kind of analysis of questions and its use in training students to answer test questions in:
Taffy Raphael (1986). Teaching questions-answers relationships, revisited. *The Reading Teacher 39:* 516–522.

48. I have taken this anecdote from a paper by Stephen Ceci and Kathleen McNellis, entitled "Entangling knowledge and process," which was presented at the annual meeting of the American Educational Research Association, Washington D.C., April 1987.

49. *The degrees of reading power* is used as the reading test for New York State Elementary Schools and is published by The University of the State of New York, The State Education Department, Albany, New York. In the Manual for Administrators and Teachers (1986), the makers assert that it is not a cloze test because, they argue, cloze uses blanks not multiple-choice alternatives to fill in the blanks, and because, they feel, the term "cloze" can apply only to texts in which every fifth word is deleted. Nonsense. The principle of clozure is the same, though they are right that the process used by the reader may not be the same. This test is referred to in the chapter "Evaluation mythology: A critical look at tests and testing." Issues related to its value can be found in:
Ron Carver (l985). Measuring readability using DRP units. *Journal of Reading Behavior 17:* 303–316.
Ronald Carver (1985). "Is the Degrees of Reading Power test valid or invalid?" *Journal of Reading 29*(1): 34–41.
Frederick Duffelmeyer and Shiela Adamson (l986). Matching students with instructional level materials using the Degrees of Reading Power system. *Reading Research and Instruction 25:* 192–200.
John Bormuth (1985). A response to "Is the Degrees of Reading Power test valid or invalid?" *Journal of Reading 29*(1): 42–47.

50. Timothy Shanahan, Michael Kamil, and Aileen Tobin (1982). Cloze as a measure of intersentential comprehension. *Reading Research Quarterly 17*(2): 229–255.
John Bormuth, J. Carr, John Manning, and P. David Pearson (1970). Children's comprehension of between- and within-sentence syntactic structure. *Journal of Educational Psychology 61:* 349–357.
Michael McKenna and Kent Layton (1990). Concurrent validity of cloze as a measure of intersentential comprehension. *Journal of Educational Psychology 82*(2): 372–377.

51. Connie Bridge, Mary Jane Ciera, and Robert Tierney (1978/79). The discourse processing operations of children. *Reading Research Quarterly 14:* 539–573.

52. I do not wish to invoke a stereotype here; indeed, such fallacies have been pointed out by:
Denny Taylor and Catherine Dorsey-Gaines (1988). *Growing up literate: Learning from inner-city families.* Portsmouth, NH: Heinemann.
Not all students from lower socioeconomic groups have been read fewer books, but *on average* more lower SES students will have been read fewer books.

53. It is not, and cannot be, interpretively the same each time—the nature of language will not bear that. And, besides, lawyers would be put out of work.

54. These differences have been described by Wallace Chafe. See:
Wallace Chafe (1982). Integration and involvement in speaking, writing, and oral literature. In Deborah Tannen (Ed.), Spoken and written language: Exploring orality and literacy. Norwood, NJ: Ablex, pp. 35–54.

55. Hazel Brown and Brian Cambourne (1989). *Read and retell: A strategy for the whole-language/natural learning classroom.* Portsmouth, NH: Heinemann.

56. Donald Dansereau (1987). Transfer from cooperative to individual studying. *Journal of Reading 30:* 614–619.

57. Patricia Edmiston (1990). From onlooker to activist: The nature of readers' participation in stories. Paper presented at the annual meeting of the National Reading Conference, Miami, FL.

58. Judith Langer obtained related descriptions of the cognitive processing through the use of prompted think-aloud techniques (see Chapter 17).

59. See for example:
Hansen. *When writers read.*
Nancie Atwell (1988). *In the middle: Writing, reading, and learning with adolescents.* Portsmouth, NH: Heinemann/Boynton-Cook.

60. Why is such a placement counterproductive? Given that we develop speech and language through interactions with other, more competent users, these children would be better placed in classrooms in which they normally interact with more competent peers. Placing such students together in the same classroom seems justifiable only under the dubious assumption that the children learn their language mostly through interaction with a teacher who knows best how to teach them to speak.

61. If random-access tape recorders were available, the access problem would be solved.

62. Donald Graves (1981). *Writing: Teachers and children at work.* Portsmouth, NH: Heinemann.

63. Nancie Atwell's (1987) award-winning book *In the middle: Writing, learning and reading with adolescents* (Heinemann) includes detailed descriptions of her record-keeping systems. I cannot recommend this book too highly. It is superb and will be referred to in several chapters of this book.

64. Carole and Russel Ames (1984). Goal structures and motivation. *Elementary School Journal 85:* 39–52.

65. A more detailed description of one approach to portfolios can be found in:
Robert Tierney, Mark Carter, and Laurie Desai (1991). Portfolio assessment in the reading and writing classroom. Norwood, MA: Christopher-Gordon.

66. Dennis P. Wolf (1989). Portfolio assessment: Sampling student work. *Educational Leadership 46*(7): 35–40.

67. Don Holdaway describes this performance phase as a normal part of natural learning following a phase of nonpublic investigation and practice. His model of natural learning is described in:
Don Holdaway (1986). The structure of natural learning as a basis for literacy instruction. In Michael Sampson (Ed.), *The pursuit of literacy: Early reading and writing.* Dubuque, IA: Kendall/Hunt.

68. Courtney Cazden (1988). *Interactions between Maori children and* Pakeha teachers. Auckland, NZ: Auckland Reading Association.
Susan Philips (1983). *The invisible culture: Communication in classroom and community on the Warm Springs Indian Reservation.* White Plains, NY: Longman.

69. Shirley Brice Heath (1987). The literate essay: Myths and ethnography. In Judith Langer (Ed.), *Language, literacy and culture.* Norwood, NJ: Ablex.

70. Jana Staton, Dialogue journals in the classroom context. In Jana Staton, Roger Shuy, Joy Peyton, and Leslie Reed (1988) *Dialogue journal communication: Classroom, linguistic, social and cognitive views.* Norwood, NJ: Ablex.

71. Staton, *Dialogue journal communication,* pp. 33–55.

72. To find people who are using dialogue journals in your kind of situation, write for back copies of:
    Dialogue: The Newsletter about Dialogue Journals. Write to: Dialogue, CAL, 1118 22nd Street, NW, Washington, DC 20037.

73. Leslie Reed (1988). Dialogue journals make my whole year flow. In Staton et al., *Dialogue journal communication,* pp. 56–72.

74. The advantages of choice are numerous and I refer to them more in Chapters 7, 8, and 9.

75. Jana Staton and Joy Peyton (1988). Topics: A window on the construction of knowledge. In Staton et al., *Dialogue journal communication,* pp. 33–55.

76. Jana Staton (1988). Dialogue journals in the classroom context. In Staton et al., *Dialogue journal communication.*

77. H. Paul Grice (1975). Logic and conversation. In P. Cole and J. Morgan (Eds.), *Syntax and semantics,* Vol. 3, *Speech acts.* New York: Seminar Press.

78. I learned this technique from Lil Brannon, who teaches in the English Department at S.U.N.Y. at Albany.

79. Atwell. *In the middle,* p. 173.

80. Atwell. *In the middle,* p. 173–174.

81. Roger Shuy (1988). The oral language basis for dialogue journals. In Staton et al., *Dialogue journal communication,* pp. 73–87.

82. See note 81 above.

83. Ann Berthoff (1981). *The making of meaning.* Portsmouth, NH: Boynton-Cook, p. 123.

84. Marie Clay notes that when one of Alexander Luria's colleagues had elementary school children hold their mouths open or hold their tongue still with their teeth while spelling, they made six times as many spelling mistakes.

85. Lev Vygotsky (1962). *Thought and Language.* Cambridge, MA: MIT Press.

86. Alexandr Sokolov (1972). *Inner speech and thought.* New York: Plenum.

87. Ake Edfelt (1960). *Silent speech and silent reading.* Chicago: University of Chicago Press.

88. Edmund Huey (1908). *The psychology and pedagogy of reading.* New York: Plenum.

89. Karl Marbe (1901). Experimentell-psychologische: Untersuchungen uber das urteil. Leipzig: Engelmann. Reprinted and translated in Jean Mandler and George Mandler (Eds.), *Thinking: From Association to Gestalt.* (1964). New York: Wiley, pp. 143–148.

90. The following are some examples of think-aloud research on reading:
    Peter Afflerbach (1990). The influence of prior knowledge on expert readers' main idea construction strategies. *Reading Research Quarterly 25*(1): 31–46.
    Peter Afflerbach (1990). The influence of prior knowledge and text genre on readers' prediction strategies. *Journal of Reading Behavior 22*(2): 131–148.
    Peter Johnston and Peter Afflerbach (1985). The process of constructing main ideas from text. *Cognition and Instruction 2:* 207–232.

Carl Bereiter and M. Bird (1985). Use of thinking aloud in identification and teaching of reading comprehension strategies. *Cognition and Instruction 2*: 131-156.

Susan Lytle (1982). Exploring comprehension style: A study of twelfth-grade readers' transactions with text. Doctoral dissertation, Stanford University.

91. Charles Fillmore (1981). Ideal readers and real readers. Proceedings of the 32nd Georgetown roundtable on languages and linguistics. Washington, DC: Georgetown University Press.

92. Judith Langer (1987). In Roy Freedle and Richard Duran (Eds.), *Cognitive and linguistic analyses of test performance*. Norwood, NJ: Ablex, pp. 225-244.

93. Not that this questioning, or the "reading" of this text, isn't instructional. Indeed, the whole procedure might make clear to a student what the teacher's idea of reading is.

94. Linda Flower and John Hayes (1981). The pregnant pause: An inquiry into the nature of planning. *Research in the Teaching of English 15:* 229-243.

Linda Flower and John Hayes (1983). Uncovering cognitive processes in writing: An introduction to protocol analysis. In Peter Mosenthal, Lynne Tamor, and Sean Walmsley (Eds.), *Research on written language: Principles and methods*. New York: Guilford Press, pp. 206-219.

95. Patricia Edmiston (1990). *From onlooker to activist: The nature of readers' participation in stories*. Paper presented at the annual meeting of the National Reading Conference, Miami, FL.

96. Linda Flower (1989). *The undercover work of task representation in reading-to-write tasks*. Paper presented at the annual meeting of the National Reading Conference, Austin, TX.

PART III

THE FOCUS OF EVALUATION: NOTICING THE DETAIL OF LITERATE ACTIVITY

This section is intended to give a rather brief description of the nature and development of literate activity—the thing we are trying to evaluate. This is itself the topic of many books, and I hope that you will take advantage of the more detailed readings, some of which I suggest along the way. It is common to organize material of this nature with details about print and the relationship of speech to print first, and then work through to the "higher levels" of comprehension later. My organization is different. I have begun with the larger issues like what it means to be literate, and what it means for people to make sense of and in print, and worked downward to details such as the relationship between speech and print, and the concepts about the conventions of print. I have done this largely in order to foil the belief that the details are the first things children should learn about literacy. The last two chapters in this section address the strategic aspects of literate activity, and the nature of development. I try to convince you that, although tests and curricula would have us believe otherwise, there is no nice, even sequence to development. On the other hand, there are predictable continuities and disjunctures.

CHAPTER 18

Concepts about Being Literate

What does it mean to be literate? One evening Samantha, at the time a two-year-old, sat at the table and produced the literary work shown in Figure 18.1. She worked with considerable earnestness, muttering "R S T oy M" and so on. These marks and mutterings were interspersed with numerous erasures and disgruntled comments of "I can't do it." When asked what she was doing, she replied, "I doing my homework." Apart from the pitch of the voice, it might have been a tape recording of her older brother doing his homework.

Children infer what it means to read, to write, and to be literate from responses to their reading and writing, and from the general pattern of literate interactions surrounding them. Nancie Atwell has her students fill out a writing and a reading survey at the beginning of the school year and then again at the end of the year.[1] The survey asks questions like:[2]

How do people learn to write?

What kind of writer are you?

What do you think a good writer needs to do in order to write well?

Why do people read?

What does someone have to do to be a good reader?

How do you decide which books you will read?

Who are your favorite authors?

Other questions are also relevant, such as:

What is the most difficult part of writing for you?

What is the most difficult part of reading for you?

Do you enjoy reading your writing to other people?

What is your goal in writing for the next two months?

What is your goal in reading for the next two months?

Whether or not a child views him- or herself as literate and what she thinks it means to be literate have critical consequences for what the teacher is doing and what can be done in the classroom. A third grade student who is having difficulty getting into reading may well believe that a reader is someone who thinks what she is told to think by the author rather than someone who tells what she sees and hears, and who has something unique and important to say.

Figure 18.1. Two-year-old Samantha's "homework."

The consequence will be a limited motivation to read or to think or say much at all about what is read. Her concept of authority will be something belonging to teachers and authors, neither of whom she feels she is. Children with these concepts read with the belief that reading is getting the words right or possibly getting *the* meaning. These concepts will show up in the way they go about reading (and whether they choose to) and they will often be revealed in an interview or even a questionnaire. Elizabeth Bondy, in studying first graders' concepts about being readers, found substantial differences between the concepts developed by children placed in high and low reading groups. Children in the high group viewed reading as primarily a social activity, a private pleasure, and a way to learn things. Children in the low group viewed reading as primarily saying the words correctly, as schoolwork, and as a source of status. (Two of the upper group children in this ability-focused setting also viewed reading as a source of status.)[3]

IN WRITING

In writing, sometimes children get the idea that writing is "getting the words right" (in the sense of getting them spelled conventionally). Under these circumstances, they are likely to produce writing such as that shown in Figure 18.2(a). In reading this piece, I feel no hint of the vibrant young person who wrote it. This writing has no voice at all. It is devoid of all traces of authority. Given the blank piece of paper, this child first drew neat lines, and then wrote ever-so-neatly the "story":

The Car

I have a car.
I like my car.
I ride my car.
I am going home.
Bye bye bye bye.

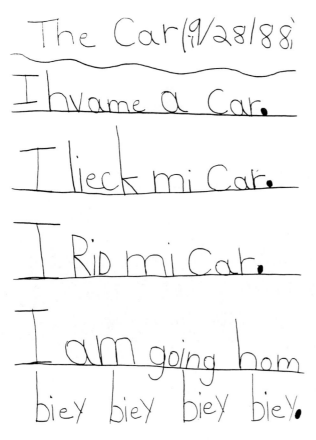

Figure 18.2(a). A sample of Nicole's writing showing her attention to convention more than to what she has to say.

Given Nicole's concept of what it is to write, these were the best (safest) words she could come up with. There is no voice in the writing; once the page is full the writing is complete, and the punctuation is about as terminal as you can get. These details tell us what Nicole thinks it means to be a writer, and what sort of writer she thinks she is.

However, when the response to Nicole's writing changes, so does her concept of authority, and her writing along with it. Figure 18.2(b) is a writing sample taken about a month after the beginning of twice-a-week tutoring by a tutor who responded only to the content of the writing, not the form. This story reads:

My New Friend.

I have a new friend. His name is Patrick. I like him very much. He and I write letters back and forth. He is funny sometimes.
The end.

Nicole's writing has begun to reflect her changed concept of what it means to be a writer. As she wrote this piece, the decisions she made along the way reflect

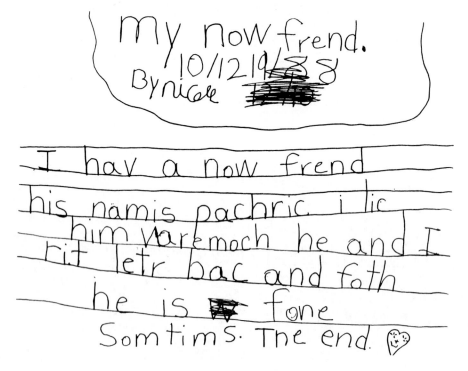

Figure 18.2(b). A sample of Nichole's writing one month after the sample in Figure 18.2(a) showing her increased attention to content over convention.

commitment to content more than convention. The lines are not so carefully drawn, the little punctuation that is used is much less terminal, there is crossing out (the first indication of changing something to make it better represent what she intended it to say), and there is the beginning of voice. The bottom of the page is still the end of the story, and it is even formally closed with the words "The end." However, there is clearly a change.

Another month later, Nicole wrote the story in Figure 18.2(c), on pages 170–171. It reads:

The Trip to the Palace.

I am going on a trip to the Palace.
My friend is going too. Her name is Kari. She is my best friend in the world.
We are going to sit on the balcony. Our Moms are going to sit below us. And we will be funny too. We are going to have food.

Several developments are apparent in this piece of Nicole's writing. On first glance, the lines are gone and the print is smaller and less neat. As we read it we see that it has been revised in a couple of places without fear of the mess. The piece is longer (though it was written in a similar amount of time to the first piece). It has substantial detail and there is a clear voice. You really get a sense of the author and that she has something to say (and feels she has something to say).

IN READING

In the same way, children's concepts vary with respect to what it means to be a "good" reader, and even whether such a term has any meaning at all. Some of the questions Rhoda Spiro asked first- through third-grade students revealed these concepts.[4] She asked, "Suppose you had a pen-pal in another school who was the same age as you, and you wanted to find out about him as a reader. What questions would you ask?" Children's responses differed depending on their classroom context. Some children wanted to ask, "What group are you in?" or "What book are you on?" whereas others wanted to ask, "What type of book do you prefer?" or "Do you read a lot?" The former type of response suggests a belief in a comparative, stratified notion of literate activity. This was more common in basal reader classrooms. The latter type of response generally occurred in the absence of a basal. There are many ways to structure such contexts. The one kind of response emphasizes a criterion of ability—you have varying amounts of it. The other type of response emphasizes a criterion of involvement as being indicative of literate people.

Children's concepts of being a reader and of being a writer can be interre-

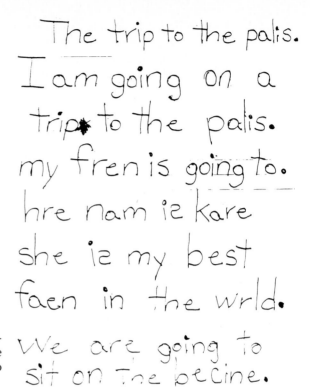

Figure 18.2(c). A sample of Nicole's writing two months after the sample in Figure 18.2(a) showing even more attention to content over convention.

lated. For example, Tom Newkirk quotes Allan, a second grader, on the matter of critical reading:

> Before I ever wrote a book I used to think there was a big machine, and they typed the title and then the machine went until the book was done. Now I look at a book and know that a guy wrote it. And it's been his project for a long time. After the guy writes it, he probably thinks about questions people will ask him and revises it like I do and xeroxes it to read to about six editors. Then he fixes it up like they say.[5]

The consequences of these concepts are very important. If a reader cannot apply criteria such as these, and cannot ask questions about what was included by an author and why, then he is what Newkirk calls "deferentially literate." There is a time to read deferentially, but it must be by choice, just as in any social situation, there is a time to ask awkward questions and a time not to. If a person does not know how to ask the necessary questions, then he is likely to be trampled upon by those who wish to impose their own agendas.

Some instructional contexts allow children to develop quite separate notions of what it means to be a reader and a writer. As one student commented,

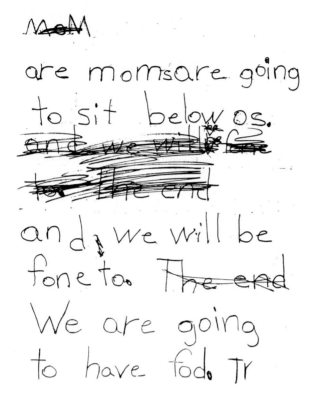

are momsare going
to sit below os.
and we will be
fone to. The end
We are going
to have fod. Tr

Figure 18.2(c). Continued

Writing is too slow and boring and it's too easy to make mistakes. Reading is more fun and people can't always tell if you miss a word like they can when you write.[6]

These criteria will make a difference to the way children engage in literate activity—indeed, whether they engage in it voluntarily at all.

MOTIVATIONAL CONSEQUENCES

This motivational aspect is critical. We infer motivation from requests, choices of activity, and expressions of expectation. For example, if a child frequently asks to be read to, we can generally infer that he enjoys it. Early on, requests are likely to be quite specific to have particular books repeated over and over. Later, he will become increasingly interested in new books rather than repeated experiences. Given free choice, children will role-play literate activity which may include reading (telling a story with reference to a book), writing (may look like scribble), and teaching-learning activity (e.g., playing teacher with a big book). Later these activities will include requests (of teachers or fellow students) for assistance with words or some other aspect of the detail of literate activity. Children also begin to develop an expectation that books will be read. For example, if no book happens to be read on a particular day, then the child might point this out. Disappointment may be shown when reading is interrupted for some reason. As children develop in their literate expectations, they will be found actively participating in literate activities such as predicting what will happen, predicting words, commenting on pictures, asking questions. Any of these indicators is grounds for making note in a child's file.

The overall concepts of what it means to be literate are closely tied to children's motivation. These notions include the amount of time literate people spend reading and writing, when and where they do it, for what purposes, whether worthy bonded people (as opposed to just "other people") engage in literate activities, and what kind of an activity it is. A difference in the overall goal of the activity can change the entire reading and writing process. Behavior is organized around goals and roles. When a writer's goal is strictly to make money, she proceeds with her writing in a different way than if her goal is to write a book of which she will be proud, or a book that expresses to her satisfaction the personal nuances of her life. An individual who sees writing as a solitary act, will clearly be engaged in it in a different way from the person who views writing as a community activity. Similarly, if a person views reading as a competitive activity, he will go about it in a different way from the reader who views it as an aesthetic or involving experience. This process will be conditioned by whether or not the person feels he is a good reader and by what criteria. The binge reading of specific authors, which is typical of good young writers (and readers), is something to be sought after, and it is not motivated by external threats or requirements.[7]

But there are more specialized literate concepts to be learned too. Many deal with the way a literary community works. For example, in order for it to work at all, there must be some conventions that everyone can take as given— just as in order for roads to work, there must be some arbitrary rules about which side of the road to drive on, when to stop, who gives way to whom, and so forth. The concepts about how written language is organized are similar (see Chapter 21). Concepts of how readers and writers respond to each other must be worked out too. These are social conventions that the literate community must be able to count on in order to explore written language with confidence. And there is an elaborate language to be learned that reflects and allows interpretation of these social conventions. The more students can divide up and name their literate activity, the more precise will be their learning and the less misinterpretation is likely to occur. When students have an undifferentiated concept of "writing," without separate notions of editing and composing, they will interpret comments on their spelling and other conventions as telling what you value in *writing,* not just in *editing.*

Without this more elaborate understanding, students get the idea that there is essentially only one writer role. Nicole's writing partly reflects this in the beginning in that she has not separated the role of editor from that of composer.

As long as a student feels that a writer is the one who writes a correct final version of a paper, he will have difficulty writing. Unless composer and editor are seen as different roles, any instruction on spelling and other conventions will have a direct impact on composing since the composer feels simultaneously responsible for the spelling and so forth. This added responsibility can make an otherwise involving activity burdensome.

A young writer can readily get the idea that writing is something that is "done" when the page is full. This was evident in the first two examples of Nicole's writing, reflecting her concepts of authorship. As another example, one inventive young writer, halfway through writing his single sentence, realized that it would not fill the page, so he wrote the word IN large enough to fill most of the page, and then stuck the last three words down at the bottom of the page. A similar concept often persists into graduate school and is represented by the "How many pages does it have to be?" request about assignments. Some of the concepts about being literate that can be found now in first graders often have not even been developed in adults who generally consider themselves literate. For example, many adults do not understand that part of a reader's responsibility is to respond, or that reading involves translating text into a language that is not really that of the text nor, at the time, the reader's own. Many adults do not see as part of literate activity the development of self-definition: learning where society ends and you begin.[8] This is the political nature of literacy instruction. It has considerable bearing on who people think they are and what they believe they can and should do.

These concepts are arrived at through the student's interaction with the literate environment, both physical and social. For example, the presence of a time and an organizational structure for conferring about writing is a critical part of children's growth in knowing that part of revising is getting feedback about one's work from a particular audience. Similarly, the presence of an editing table with editing paraphernalia in the classroom is a physical reminder that editing is important, but at the same time, not part of composing.

The social environment is particularly influential. The kind of feedback that a student gets has an impact on her understanding of what it means to be part of a literate community, and who she is as a writer. For example, saying to a student, "I don't understand this part here," or "These two parts seem to me to be in conflict" is different from saying "Clarify this part." They differ, particularly in the messages about the point of the activity, and about who is in control.

REFLECTIONS OF ADULT CONCEPTS

The concepts that children develop about themselves as literate individuals reflect in interesting ways the conceptualizations of literature held by the adults who have literate interactions with them. For example, the phenomenon of first and second graders coming to view illustrated books as "baby books" as opposed to "chapter books" (the real thing), is a result of an overemphasis on the word as the central symbolic medium, making it the medium of prestige. In such classroom contexts, many children either will choose not to read or will choose material which they cannot read. To break away from such concepts of literate activity, children (and adults) must understand that illustrations in books are not there just, or necessarily at all, to make the story easier. Literacy, as Dennis P. Wolf and Martha Perry put it,

> involves much more than accurate inscription . . . [It involves] understanding how writing, like other forms of record making, involves sustaining a process, making thoughtful choices among symbolic languages, and being mindful.[9]

Indeed, when children come to understand the function of graphic symbolization in these terms, they can discuss illustrations as an integral part of composition, and discuss the relationship among the symbolic representations. In the "real world," these symbolic representations are thoroughly intertwined.

Because the child's concept of what it means to be literate is highly dependent on the teacher's concepts of literateness and how it develops, the conceptions and misconceptions held by the adults in a child's life are important. And there are many misconceptions. For example, a quite common misconception about symbolization and literacy is evident in a recent letter to the editor in a local paper from a school board member. She noted that "the essential fact about writing . . . is that there is a unique relationship between a letter and a sound." As you will see in Chapter 22, this relationship is far from unique, and only in alphabetic languages is there any relationship at all. No, the "essential fact" about writing is that you can use it to express yourself, to overcome the limits of memory (also time and space), to be reflective, and to assert control. *In that context* it is also important that there are *reasonably predictable* relationships between print and speech.

While we, as teachers, conceive of literacy in simplistic ways, so will children, and even if they do not, our eyes will not be able to see their development. Dennis P. Wolf and Martha Perry suggest considering literate activity in terms of the ability to sustain a recording process from inception through editing, the ability to "tune" records to particular demands, and the ability to see oneself as a mindful author capable of making a thoughtful, useful record. They give an example of a book written by Lisa Marie, a second grader, conceived of in these terms:[10]

> To begin, Lisa Marie writes a short description of a salient event; "The boy has a hat he was playing with it." She is not satisfied with this rendition and uses the facing page to illustrate it, adding the dialogic "O boy" under the picture. Returning to her book later, Lisa Marie adds many more events and then comes back to the first page, adding a title ("The boy") and prologue ("This is the boy who his a yelllo hat here goes the stoy").
> Still later, when she reads her text over as a part of editing, she recognizes it

can't be read straight through and make sense. She adds the heavy horizontal lines which set off title, prologue, and text.

These overall concepts relating to what it means to be literate are critical. They involve understanding both the goal of the activity and the role of the individual, and these are what organize the way the learner engages in reading and writing, and when and why she does so. There are similar concepts relating to being a teacher. A teacher conceiving of teaching as primarily to help all students learn, with her role being as a model of a literate learner with the responsibility of developing a literate community, will teach differently from a teacher who sees teaching as a solitary activity primarily to do with imparting knowledge to those students whose learning is not impaired. Similarly, a teacher who teaches toward the ability to use a fixed set of rules will teach differently from one who teaches toward an ability to generate a set of rules to cope with particular purposes and contexts.

CONCEPTS OF THE DEVELOPMENT OF LITERACY

To foreshadow the chapter on development, let me describe the consequences of one contest between two different concepts of literate activity and its development. Recent research on children's literate development has used the term *emergent literacy,* a term coined by Marie Clay, that presents becoming literate as a developmental continuum in which many complex kinds of knowledge and ways of responding are being developed. Much of this knowledge is constructed before the children start formal schooling. From this perspective, development of literacy is essentially like the development of language. It requires social conditions which nurture it, such as good role models, good available and manageable literature, a clear valuing of literate activity, and a supportive, responsive context. There is no critical developmental point which makes a child ready to become literate, except perhaps passage through the birth canal.

By way of contrast, consider the ever-popular concept of "reading readiness." In the 1920s, following the application of Darwin's work to the concept of intelligence, Arnold Gesell (1925) and his colleagues popularized what might be called the botanical theory of human development. The basic premise of this theory is that there are sequences of physical, physiological, and cognitive development through which individuals pass in the process of development, and that these stages are largely genetically fixed and not to be hurried. The overall process is one of neurological "ripening." Children are not ready to "blossom" into reading until their nervous system has reached an appropriate stage of development, and trying to hurry them along will only result in harm.

In 1931 Mabel Morphett and Carleton Washburne discovered that within the reading program they offered in Winnetka, Illinois, children who began instruction in reading [after attaining a "mental age" of six years six months] were more likely to show progress on their reading materials and vocabulary lists than were children who began instruction before attaining that "mental age."[11] This they interpreted to mean that reading should not be taught until the children had reached that mental age—blossom time. They felt that the neurological maturity necessary for learning to read was reached at that mental age. So convinced were they that they had commented proudly that teachers in Winnetka had charts on their walls showing when each child would reach the golden mental age of six and a half and thus be eligible to begin reading. The mental age was calculated on the basis of the old IQ tests, which figured mental age (MA) from the test performance, and then divided it by chronological age (CA) and multiplied the outcome by 100.[12]

The consequence of all this is the reading readiness test which still enjoys enormous popularity. Current examples of such tests emphasize the lower, most countable aspects of literacy; include items that have nothing to do with literacy (such as finding the odd-one-out in a set of complex, meaningless figures); and provide a pronouncement on the extent to which the individual is ready to receive literate knowledge. A premise underlying all of this is that literacy is actually a cognitive skill that one has (or has not), rather than a social activity in which one can participate. From this perspective the defining, and initial part of the literate skill is decoding—mastery of the alphabetic principle of the language. This makes for a rather narrow view of literacy, but also roughly describes what a child will be able to do when he is literate and how he will be taught to become literate. Societies with nonalphabetic languages would be hard pressed to use the same definition of literate activity. However, once one has decided to define literacy in this manner, there really is a prereading and a reading stage. Furthermore, once the decision is made to teach this alphabetic principle first (possibly the most abstract part of the activity), there really is a chance that children might not be ready to learn from such instruction.

More recently, it has become clear that children develop literate activity in a variety of different ways, and that many of the "higher" aspects of language such as internalized "story schemas" are usually quite well developed before any alphabetic knowledge is developed, and that the ability to write, and read one's own writing, can precede or be coincident with the development of alphabetic knowledge. It is also now clear that children can read books with which they have some familiarity before they have developed a great deal of knowledge about print invariances. In this way literate development is like language development, the big things tend to come first. Take my youngest daughter, Sam, for instance. One of her first uses of language was "Dad" (approximately), used mostly around two in the morning. This sounded like a word, but to Sam it was just a use of the voice that worked. Although she gained three or four more such utterances, she did not find words for a long time. However, she began talking to us in sentences. We didn't know what they meant, but they were sentences. They carried all of the intonation patterns typical of adult language: appealing, questioning, asserting, complaining, commenting. Though she attended to some of the smaller parts of speech, she did not notice that words were in there. Thus she would sing *Twinkle twinkle* with the melody intact, and consequently the syllables separated (one syllable being essentially one musical beat), and the rhyming sounds on the end, but no other words. It went "ih hi ih hi ih hi har, ih hi ih hi hi hi ar." Then she discovered some more words, like "juice," and once she discovered a handful more of these, she could make two word sentences to convey intentions: more juice, I too, watch me, I go, I do-it. But many things just refused to fit into two-word sentences, so she continued to give us lengthy unintelligible sentences using the intonation patterns that she knew conveyed intention. However, having discovered words, the number she used began to increase at an alarming rate. Not all our children developed speech in this order; indeed, there is enormous individuality even within one family. However, Sam was a communicative person (and saw herself as one) long before she had the words to be seen as verbal. At the same time she already had favorite books and would sit and look at them, or turn their pages and make reading noises.

With a more complex view of literacy emphasizing the social nature of the activity, comes a greater reluctance to say whether or not an individual is or is not literate or ready to become literate. Indeed, if literacy is a social activity, and socially generated rather like speech, then the child can be thought of as always ready to learn more about the activity if placed in an environment that will support participation in the activity. Very young children generally, though not always, learn in their homes aspects of literateness such as the fact that print carries a message, that books go only one way up and you go left to right through them, and so forth. In other words, if the school reading program is flexible enough, then any child is ready for it. Thus we should talk about programs being ready for children rather than the other way around. Perhaps rather than having tests for reading readiness, we might consider evaluating literacy programs as to their readiness to accommodate particular children. In other words, depending on our view of literateness and how it develops, we structure schools and classrooms and organize our evaluations of children and our other interactions with them. If we have a very rigid notion of a reading program, we can be certain that some children will not profit from it and thus will not have been ready for it. However, if our program can accommodate considerable diversity in the nature of the children's literate development, then it is likely to be ready for the children.

I present, then, only partly with tongue in cheek, my program readiness test (or rather checklist) which is shown in Table 18.1. This is to be a self-administered test in the spirit of self-evaluation. I have no norms for this test nor data on any aspect of its generalizability or validity in particular contexts. However, I would be interested in the consequences of your use of the procedure for the purpose of self-evaluation. This test presents a good opportunity to point out the value-bound side of evaluation, which I will keep referring to in this book. While some readers will agree that most of the items on the test measure the construct "program readiness," others will contest many of the items, and still others will contest the premise of program readiness as being a reasonable construct at all.

TABLE 18.1. Readiness Test for Beginning Readers' Classrooms

	YES	NO
1. Children read to often.	___	___
2. There is abundant, well displayed, familiar children's literature, a good portion of which has a rhythmic or predictable quality to the language.	___	___
3. Children are invited, not forced, to participate in shared reading of books, often enlarged ones.	___	___
4. Books represent a range of cultures, and characters in a range of roles.	___	___
5. Storytelling, singing, and role-play are encouraged, along with reading and writing.	___	___
6. Language is used playfully in the classroom	___	___
7. Writing and art materials are readily available.	___	___
8. Invented spelling is encouraged when writing.	___	___
9. Invented reading (reading from illustrations and memory, and possibly some use of print) is encouraged when reading.	___	___
10. The classroom organization is noncompetitive, and literacy is *not* presented as a linear scale of sequentially more difficult skills or books to be mastered.	___	___
11. The classroom focus is on involvement not on ability.	___	___
12. If children are grouped, it is rarely on the basis of "ability."	___	___
13. Exploration and experimentation are encouraged.	___	___
14. Errors are seen as interesting events from which one can learn.	___	___
15. The teacher encourages diversity in: response to books, kinds of writing, and interests.	___	___
16. Children talk with each other and the teacher a lot.	___	___
17. The teacher listens to the children—each of them—and faces them at their own level.	___	___
18. Some teacher time is spent with individual students and some with larger groups.	___	___
19. Within a month of school, the teacher is able to describe the literate development of individual children in the class in some detail.	___	___
20. Children are encouraged to treat themselves and each other as authors, readers, and illustrators.	___	___
21. Children are encouraged to help one another and to seek help as they need it, but to be independent when possible.	___	___
22. Children are encouraged to be persistent and strategic in solving their problems.	___	___
23. Feedback to children about their activity is focused on *how* something was done, and is framed positively.	___	___
24. The classroom provides a caring, safe environment.	___	___
25. Children do not spend large portions of time sitting at desks unless by their choice.	___	___

CHAPTER 19

Recognizing and Connecting, Revising and Reflecting

A major difference between experts and novices is that experts automatically recognize, without effort, patterns that novices have to laboriously figure out. In Chapter 2 I gave the example of the expert chess player being able to recognize the patterns of pieces on a chess board so fast that with a brief five-second look she can quickly replace all the pieces of a knocked-over chess game. Expert readers are just like that with words, themes, styles, and arguments. The same is true of the expert teacher who is able to instantly recognize patterns of student behavior.[13] Once patterns begin to be recognized automatically, they actually take an alternate route through the brain, one that does not require conscious attention.[14] After that we recognize the patterns even if we don't want to. Since expert evaluators need to selectively manage a large amount of information, and to view it from multiple perspectives as their inquiries proceed, automatic pattern recognition is very important.

Recognition can become so detailed and automatic, that we don't even need to see the whole pattern for it to be recognized. Advertisers sometimes use this principle to increase effectiveness for lower cost. An initial television advertisement might be an expensive thirty-second vivid narrative presented several times in prime time to the widest audience. These images then become shared knowledge, which subsequently require only a two- or three-second fragment of the original to invoke for the viewer a version of the whole original narrative. Context can help too. When we are near a shopping mall, though it be in an entirely different part of the country, just the top half (or even less) of a chain store's label seen in the distance will allow us to recognize (read) it. Indeed, as readers develop, their recognition of individual words reaches a point where it is so fast and automatic that it generally does not benefit from context.[15] This does not mean to say that they do not constantly seek contextual agreement— just that recognition proceeds so very quickly and accurately that they do not generally need to. Thus, a very simple indicator of one part of reading expertise is the number of words recognized instantly. As an indicator, it is aided by the fact that word recognition expertise is developed by reading a lot, which means that good word recognition implies a considerable amount of other knowledge too. In a similar way we read, or rather recognize, entire story structures and other familiar elements of our culture.

For readers, the extent of pattern recognition ranges from recognition of letters, through letter patterns, words, word patterns, plots, characters, styles, stories, and lines of argument, to feelings. Five-year-old children can recognize different authors' styles of writing.[16] If they have had sufficient experience with, say, Bill Peet's writing and Dr. Seuss's writing, a new book by one of those authors can readily be identified with the author. Clearly if they have not experienced these books they will be unable to distinguish between them in the same way. If they have been read the books without having the authors identified, they may recognize a difference but will be unable to label the difference as relating to different authors' use of words. However, if they are used to attending to differences in authorial style and they are read two new books by different authors, they are likely to still notice a difference in style.

This type of recognition develops from two sources. First, lots of experiences of seeing the pattern, and second, knowledge of the significant features that distinguish one pattern from another. One without the other will result in only slow growth. There is no substitute for reading as a means of getting better at recognizing these patterns. This is also true of the patterns of letters that occur in words, as Connie Juel has demonstrated.[17] For example, let's say Karen's basal reader program contains more words with the letter patterns *fl* and *oun*. Daryl, on the other hand, is in a program that has more words with the patterns *thr* and *rd*. It should be no surprise that these two students more readily recognize those letter patterns they have seen more frequently.

However, simply encountering the patterns is not always enough. People can be surrounded by flowers every summer and never learn to recognize a single one. Most people cannot read flowers. However, if they spent their time planting or arranging flowers they would soon come to recognize more of them, and more of the details of each. Of course, it helps if you spend time with someone who has an interest in, and knows a lot about, flowers and you have the opportunity to ask questions of that person. Just so with reading and writing. Reading and writing *together* help highlight the significant features of the patterns to be read (and written). Spending time with a valued person who is interested in and knows a lot about literate activity also helps develop pattern recognition. But once you know the salient features of a new pattern, just the increased exposure to it makes the difference. Once a child knows to attend to letter order, simply reading more words will increase her recognition of the patterns of letters that commonly occur and the locations at which they occur.

What happens when people with culturally different experiences and values encounter the same text? The closer we are in terms of literary community, the less sign detail is needed to invoke particular shared images. But two readers with different cultural experiences can easily create two quite different meanings for any given text. The only way to assert that one of these constructions is less adequate than the other is through a belief that one culture is more authoritative than the other. This can be enforced at the same time as being camouflaged if a test is used, since the test is generally seen as the product of science rather than of (and for) people. In this situation, cultural convention is masqueraded as noncultural fact.

RECOGNIZING AND REASONING

When a pattern cannot be recognized, what strategies are used to render it recognizable? How do readers maneuver themselves into positions in which they can recognize the familiar aspects of text or make connections with their own experience? How do they choose the connections? For example, when a child has the strategy of looking for words he already knows in order to figure out words that he does not know, he has a strategy for learning more patterns. When teachers take the time to watch each other teach and to talk about what they see, they have a strategy for learning to recognize more patterns in their own teaching. The other side is, of course, how do writers make connections with very specific aspects of the reader's experience? How do teachers do this with children as they write the curriculum?

If we come across the word *resgestae,* most of us will have to stop and figure out what it represents, probably using context and our knowledge of the roots of words. Similarly, to the extent that an author's symbolism does not match our knowledge of the world and of text, reading becomes more of a reasoning process involving the use of various strategies to solve the problem of creating meaning from text. This is why reading textbooks is often difficult. Generally people read textbooks to gain knowledge they do not already have; they are thus likely to have difficulty recognizing words, arguments, and relationships, remembering names for which they have no referent, and making the inferences necessary to hold the meaning together. Lack of relevant knowledge to allow recognition makes the whole enterprise more effortful, less meaningful, and less memorable (except for the memory of the difficulty of the process).

The most useful information about students' construction of meaning is how they went about it. This is not to deny the importance of the meaning they constructed. Indeed, denying its importance will land you with a bunch of students who cannot read with authority, who lack a belief in their own ability to construct meaning. It is not that information about the consequences of their meaning construction is unimportant, but rather that information about the process is most useful *instructionally.* As I discussed in the chapter on errors, without knowing how a construction was reached, it is very difficult to know how to respond instructionally.

PREDICTING AND MONITORING

Pattern recognition also forms the basis of the feedforward and feedback mechanisms that serve to make us fast and accurate in our perception. At the heart of the reading process, indeed the perceptual process, are the processes of predicting, monitoring, and self-correcting. Our minds try to predict what will happen next from what we already know; and when we get there, our minds check to see whether this is where we expected to be. If it is not, then we begin to consider what could be wrong and what to do about it. The predicting and monitoring parts of this process are both dependent on recognition. They generally happen without awareness, although if there is a mismatch, and when recognition is not automatic, they produce awareness. This is the "click" of comprehension and the "clunk" of comprehension failure.

Imagine for a moment that you have just walked out of the woods after a week of rather wet backpacking. You are starving, but your attire and state of cleanliness will not allow you to dine at Maxim's, so as you pass a McDonald's you decide to indulge before getting home and becoming more civilized. As you enter the McDonald's you notice that it is decorated with subtle lighting, plush carpet and upholstery, and there are waiters in tuxedos. An entire set of knowledge that you earned through visits to a wide range of restaurants suddenly yells at you, "STOP!" Why does it do this? Before you entered the restaurant your mind had formulated an image (a version of reality) of what would be expected inside. This is the feedforward mechanism. As you enter the place, the image is shattered by the feedback mechanism that finds no place for tuxedoed waiters in the image that has been created. If you had no knowledge of restaurants at all, no expectation would be violated. The nature of our expectations has a lot to do with the structure of our knowledge. When we are reading, we are using the text to help us construct these images.

Predicting and monitoring are both critical processes. Prediction gives us speed because it helps us to already be there before we actually get there. However, prediction must always be held in check by monitoring—cross-checking with what is now on the page. Linda Fielding found in her research that teaching children to predict did not help their understanding unless it was coupled with monitoring.[18] Indeed, sometimes those who were not monitoring were led astray by their predictions, remembering predictions that conflicted with other parts of the text. Comprehension monitoring has often been discussed under the rubric of "metacomprehension," but I believe that it is properly part of comprehension itself and not separable from it. It is part of the composing process. In writing, we do not talk about editing and revising as "metawriting," and I think it proper that we do not. Comprehending is a process and, like all other processes, must have feedforward mechanisms in order to be efficient and feedback mechanisms in order to be effective. Both predicting and monitoring are essentially automatic in familiar material. Sometimes the source of conflicting feedback is a parallel pattern. For example, sometimes we write a word and think, "That doesn't look right." Our visual pattern recognition provides a mismatch. Other times we write it and halfway through writing it, without even looking at it, we think, "That didn't feel right." Sometimes we consciously use these conflicts. For example, we try two or three ways to spell a word to see if one stands out as recognizably correct, or we try writing it with our eyes closed to see what feels right.

CONNECTING AND EVALUATING

Recognizing means making connections with previous experience. Any given reader usually has a variety of possible experiences with which he can connect, and it matters which ones are selected. Children learn which connections are relevant through their literate social interactions. When a teacher makes a connection between one author and another, and possibly highlights a stylistic feature that exposes the connection, some students begin to attend to that kind of connection in the future. Comparisons and contrasts are how children develop their knowledge of the world, and highlighting these distinguishing features is the way literary knowledge develops. But children do not always apply this strategy to the literary domain. They will be more likely to do so if it is foregrounded for them in discussions.

I have seen the making of connections formalized in a worksheet to be filled out after reading a book. The worksheet has spaces to comment on such things as:

The part I liked most was: _____

A question I have for the author is: _____

Connections: _____

The point of the worksheet is to have a means of keeping track of children's developing understanding of books through their comments about them and the development of the connections they make with other books, authors, and experiences. But any worksheet contingent on finishing a book can be daunting to young (and older) readers, especially if the form of their response is dictated. I am similarly cautious about commercial chapter guides for trade books. I am inclined to believe that a dialogue journal will serve the function better, particularly in the context of rich discussion. The dialogue will highlight important connections, and others sharing their own connections will open up a breadth of possible connections. That the journal is written accomplishes the permanent reference aspect.

There are several ways in which pattern recognition is related to evaluation. For the teacher, it can be helpful to see which words are recognized by a particular child, particularly in the context of words previously recognized. This can be done using a simple word list of high-frequency words. If you need to keep detailed track of children's word recognition, a list such as the Dolche list of high-frequency words might be helpful. If you are using a basal reader, these have such lists included. However, these lists are less personal, more comparative, and less helpful for children's learning than their own personal lists. For example, young children can keep their own lists of known words either in a "word bank" box as Sylvia Ashton Warner used,[19] or in their own reading/writing folder as words which they control (they can both read and write them accurately and quickly). This can be a useful, and motivating, indicator of growth for both student and teacher—but not by itself.

It is also helpful to know what kind of connections a child is making with what he is reading. Does he see patterns of style, word choice, theme, and structure? These will show up in discussions of books he is reading. We will listen for his use of them in his writing when he explains what made him choose particular ways of selecting and addressing his topic, and why he quits a particular piece of writing. On the other side of this, if the teacher does not recognize these patterns herself, she is not likely to highlight them for the children, or see development in their recognition. An observer in her classroom, or her own tape recording of her classroom will reveal no trace of her highlighting of these features. When a teacher cannot recognize development when it occurs, the experience of reading the classroom, hence teaching, can become unsatisfying in much the same way as would reading a novel she did not understand.

But our experiences and values influence the patterns we recognize. For example, a teacher who has interests in writing and literature gave this impromptu description of one of her student's literacy development.

> Kurt has a very definite sense of whether he wants to write a personal narrative experience, or if he wants to write a fictional story, and when he writes he has multiple characters often. He doesn't usually give them fictional names, but he'll call them, say what they are. If they're animals, they're The Dog, The Rat, and The Fox, something like that. There's a lot of dialogue in his stories, and he has a lot of action and he has a very clear sense of setting a beginning of his story, and there's some kind of event, and sometimes multiple occurrences and a chain of events, and there's often a real conflict, and somebody's going to come out on top of solving a problem. And a very definite ending, very good closing to what he writes. He is able to create his own story. He doesn't just take from the literature, for example, as other children are still doing. . . .

This extensive recognition of patterns of literate activity allows this particular teacher to see and appreciate small changes in development.

REFLECTING, RE-COGNIZING, AND RE-VISING

In making sense of children's literate activity or the literate activity of a classroom, in reading what a writer has written, or writing our own thoughts, we recognize patterns and relationships. We *re-cognize,* that is we *know again,* these patterns and relationships. To experience one's thoughts again by writing them down is to know them again. To see a word on a page that we have seen before is to know it again. Since our experiences have a heavy hand in determining the patterns we recognize, we generally have options with respect to the experiences with which we make connections. Often a new metaphor brings to realization a set of patterns we had not noticed.

A new metaphor is simply a device for helping us make connections we had previously not made. Many teachers view their reading instruction primarily through the reading instruction they experienced in school, and through the basal reader. It is not that they lack other experience with which to make connections, it is just that those are the habitual connections. Breaking away from those habitual connections and trying a different metaphor makes for critical reading. Thus, becoming critical means reflecting on, and taking control of the connections we make—being able to create virtual worlds that we have not experienced but that may be possible. Reflection allows us to realize the diversity of possible metaphors and experiences, that our metaphors and experiences are merely a small sample of those possible, and that other people have important and often habitual metaphors drawn from their different experiences.

Reflective teaching involves constructing a virtual world in which aspects of the teaching-learning situation can be manipulated and examined.[20] This ability to construct virtual worlds is at the heart of comprehension (whether of texts, classrooms, or students). Readers create virtual worlds based on what a writer has written, and writers create virtual worlds and describe them in words. Thus, imagination is an important aspect of reading, writing, and teaching. Imagination allows the reflective practitioner to engage in a "reflective conversation" with the classroom situation, with students, and with parents. As Donald Schon puts it:

> the reflective practitioner's relation with his client takes the form of a literally reflective conversation. Here the professional recognizes that his technical expertise is embedded in a context of meanings. He attributes to his clients, as well as to himself, a capacity to mean, know, and plan. He recognizes that his actions may have different meanings for his client than he intends them to have, and he gives himself the task of discovering what these are. He recognizes an obligation to make his own understandings accessible to his client, which means that he needs often to reflect anew on what he knows. (p. 295)

Understanding the connections that we have made in, or that others make from, our writing is what allows us to revise—to see again—what we have written. We can see again through our audience, as we might in a writing conference, or we can see again our reading through the visions of other members of our literate community. We can also see our teaching through the eyes of our audience and our colleagues and thus consider revising our practice. Alternatively, we can see again through the person we are now, older, with more experience, and in a different situation than we were before. This type of reflection is encouraged through the use of what Ann Berthoff calls the "double-entry notebook," which is simply a notebook or journal in which you keep a record of thoughts and observations on one side of each page opening, and leave the other side open for later reflective comments.

Helping others revise usually means helping them to see what you saw, so that they might evaluate whether that was what they intended or would like to intend. Revising is not something which must happen to all pieces of writing. Only some are worth revising, and sometimes a first version needs only editing. Any piece of writing can be revised. On the other hand, it would be nice if we could write perfect first drafts. It certainly would have saved me a couple of years on this book. Young people (and grown-ups) can be helped to accomplish this by learning to tell their story to several other people before putting pencil to paper. Many of the bugs are removed in this process. Robert Munsch writes his books with little revision after orally telling the stories many, many times.

Revision is an important literate ability, and we should celebrate when a child has been able to take that step and have that level of investment. But sometimes, we get carried away with the importance of increased revision. Melanie, a fourth grader, showed me a piece of her writing. It went:

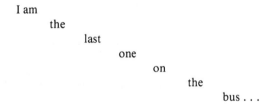

Melanie was somewhat isolated from her peers and she was not particularly happy. When she showed it to me it was written in rough, heavily pressed pencil printing—smudged. Actually it wasn't written in the form I have written it. It was written as simply: "I am the last one on the bus"—which was easy to think of as the first line of a story, and hence in need of considerable development or revision. But whether or not this piece needs to be revised, and in what way, rather depends on Melanie's purpose in writing it. It may be of interest whether and how often someone revises a piece of writing, but what is more interesting is how and why.

Sometimes revision in writing, teaching, or reading takes place because of the awareness, through reflection, of inconsistencies in our knowledge or practice. Some time ago I was involved with a group of teachers who had recently become engaged in the "process" approach to teaching writing as described by Don Graves, Lucy Calkins, and others.[21] However, many of these teachers were still using basal readers and thus organized their reading program on entirely different, often antithetical, principles. Even though they knew that reading and writing are related, they had never chosen to view their reading instruction through their experience with writing instruction. I asked them to write down the organizing principles of their writing program. Having done this, I asked them to translate these into reading instruction principles by changing some of the words. This generally produced a lot of "Aha!" experiences along with some discomfort as new patterns and conflicts were seen. The same type of phenomenon can be obtained by examining the teaching of art or music (both involving symbolic representation and interpretation). Without this experience of writing instruction to connect with—an entire metaphor of experience—they would have been very slow to detect patterns and make changes in their reading instruction. But with that experience and the accompanying feelings of satisfaction and success to connect to, they re-cognized different patterns, and were able to make changes in reading instruction much more rapidly.[22]

Being flexible with metaphors and having options, allows more diverse connections and allows contrasts between interpretations. This, along with reflection on the sources and consequences of the options is, again, the basis of critical reading.

CHAPTER 20

Constructing

Reading, writing, and teaching are all acts of construction, of putting together, of making meaning. As writers, we make sense of the world, and in doing so we classify, compare, and contrast things one with another. It is these classifications and comparisons that produce (and are produced by) our naming of what we see. Readers use these same processes, relating stories to the general pattern of stories heard before, contrasting authors' and illustrators' styles, and arranging together the ideas and experiences in different ways for different reasons. In the same way, teachers make sense of their classrooms as they "read" their students and the classroom itself. Teachers contrast students' work with their earlier work. They compare patterns of development with those they have seen before. A teacher, in interaction with her students, constructs the curriculum—the text of the classroom.

The first part of construction is collecting good pieces to put together. Authors must know how to observe, label and record, take notes to reinstate their memories, and to sort out what is significant among those pieces. Readers must know how to select information from text, perhaps take notes to reinstate their memories, and know how to observe authors. Teachers must know the kinds of knowledge and ways of thinking that are involved in reading, writing, and teaching in order to recognize these patterns when they occur. We need to know how a writer constructed a particular piece, both so that we might seek to understand why she constructed it, and so that we might construct pieces that will accomplish what we intend. For example, we can look at the way authors make characters speak in their distinctive voices, or how they make their own voices heard in their writing, their use of metaphors, their economy in the use of words, how they choose what to say and what not to say, their use of novel or surprising expressions, their focus, and their use of concrete examples.[23] We can look for the same things in the work of the young authors in our classrooms. We look for the feeling of being hooked by the opening lines, for the feeling of surprise, for the feeling of knowing, or of being compelled. Then we try to describe, with the composer, how the effect was produced. If it was not produced by earlier constructions, this may be evidence of increased flexibility and control in written construction, increased ability to assert authority.

AUTHORITY

Through their careful weaving of language, authors exercise control over readers' understandings and emotions. But authors never have complete control over readers, and readers should exert their authority to construct their own meanings. Language, because of its metaphorical nature, will not bear the assertion of singular meanings. Authors try to convey meaning using their writing, but meaning does not lie in their writing. We might try to infer what the writer had intended, which is one kind of reading, but we will never be able to assert a singular meaning for a text. Language is used to communicate, but the communication is not direct. Language is always ambiguous, even when we point to something. Indeed, an early missionary pointing to a tree and asking, "What's that?" was likely to be told, "Your finger."[24]

Neither can we assert that there is a singular main idea contained in a particular text and that it can be found by cleverly putting together the pieces as an archaeologist might. Composers, be they readers or writers, seek forms in language and thought that produce a satisfying match. The negotiation of this matching involves both concessions to the beliefs and conventions of the community and the author's and reader's rights to assert their own individual experience and vision. There are no rules for a simple match. Even if everyone had the same set of experiences, there are still only conventions which either party can ignore at will, if they are willing to pay the price in the negotiation of meaning. Reading to "get *the* main idea," then, is a test to see whether the reader is willing and able to make concessions to the group's vision of reality. Indeed, teenagers deliberately select their own language conventions and change them frequently in order to assert their *individual* rights to the language and to meaning—"That (attractive outfit) is really *nasty.*"[25] Even in a particularly positivistic world, meaning cannot be reduced to a "propositional base." Values, affect, and knowledge are inseparable, not propositional, and not weighable on any simple scale.

Indeed, as soon as we assert that there really is a single main idea, all value is lost in the main idea metaphor—the idea that authors use language forms to try to assert particular meanings. If children are taught to read to "get *the* meaning" (or main idea), they are being taught a way of knowing themselves as knowers as well as a way of knowing literacy. Barring intervention from other contexts, they will learn to view themselves as what Mary Belenky and her colleagues have called "received knowers" as opposed to "constructive knowers."[26] Such people do not see themselves as active authors of meaning, but rather as passive receivers of it. Under these circumstances, students who are doing research and gaining most of their information from writing often have difficulty separating themselves from the text and making the knowledge their own. They copy a great deal. As they get older, this starts to be called plagiarism. Authority is to do with feeling the right to construct knowledge, and it is hard for someone who lacks authority to write or to read well.

Teachers who are dependent on external sources of information such as tests for their knowledge of their classroom practice fall into this category, too. They tend not to value self-knowledge as valuable knowledge, and they avoid uncertainty. A constructive knower is more comfortable with the certainty that things can be uncertain. For example, one constructive teacher's description of one of her student's literacy development included the comment:

> In reading he is still struggling in some things, say in a basal, and this is where
> I have trouble. Again, like maybe I'll want to be assessing him and I'll get out
> a primer, and he may be having some difficulty, and yet my gut feeling is that
> he's a much better reader than this, because his writing reflects so much more.

She is comfortable with this uncertainty, knowing that she is still working on building an understanding, and she concedes credibility (not certainty) to her "gut feeling."

AUTHORS AND AUDIENCES

Although as readers we are free to construct our own meanings, we do need to be aware of the kind of meanings others are likely to construct, and the consequences of making the kinds of meanings we make. Knowing others and their responses is an important organizing framework for composing writing, reading, and teaching. Empathy does not sound like much of a literacy "skill"; but when we read novels, the extent to which we can empathize with the characters in the story has a lot to do with how we appreciate the story. Indeed, Gordon Bower has shown that when people are depressed they tend to identify with a depressive character in a story, and when they are happy, they tend to identify with a happy character.[27] When we read "nonfiction" the extent to which we can put ourselves where the author is with respect to the particular domain of knowledge makes a big difference to the meaning we construct from it. When we write, we make choices about what to include and what to leave out, in part depending on our intended audience. Simply writing down our inner speech will not reach much of an audience. Inner speech is very cryptic indeed.[28]

We construct our writing for different purposes and different audiences. For example, we can write to find out what we are thinking and where our thinking can take us. We can write in order to remember a scene, a detail, an experience. We might write in order to persuade, but how we go about doing so depends on our audience. To persuade academic audiences to buy your theory, formal argumentation is essential. But to persuade someone to buy your car on the street, sometimes it is best to create the illusion of casual indifference. Of course, anyone streetwise enough to use that strategy in a test requiring written persuasion would probably fail the test because of the privileging of formal, abstract argument.

If students are to know how to construct writing for different audiences, they must come to predict the kind of knowledge that audience has and the kind of response particular forms and arguments will draw. They must know what it is like to talk with that audience, which is one of many reasons for insisting upon cultural diversity and talk in classrooms. The available audiences are many, for example:

> Peers
> > in class
> > in other classes
> > in other schools
> > pen pals
> > famous peers
> > younger kids
> > older kids
>
> Teachers (as examiner vs. trusted adult, vs. expert?)
> Parents
> Principal
> Local newspaper
> Authors
> Potential employer
> Executive of company
> Government body

If students are to write for different purposes, they must know how much to say about what and in what form. In the same way, their reading will develop as they become able to understand why authors make the decisions they make. Readers, writers, and teachers make critical choices as they compose, and there are many tensions. For example, there is the tension between inclusiveness and specificity. Children move from the "everything I know about x" construction and the "bed-to-bed" story to more focused pieces as they extend the detail of their work through exemplification, providing reasons, showing cause and effect, and specification. But these same patterns and changes can be seen in the writing of graduate students struggling to come to grips with issues and audiences.

The same tensions occur in reading. Once we are aware of how authors make decisions in the face of such tensions, we can stand back from the text and ask, "Why would someone write this? How does this relate to the work of other writers on this topic? What else might they have put in here? What did they leave out and why? Can I recall the details of this?" Authors make choices about what to illustrate and what to symbolize with words. Compare, for example, Tomi DePaola and Richard Scary. Young authors make similar decisions. In Nick's letter to David on page 13 (Figure 2.1), the rainbow is performing something the text cannot. He cannot put this into writing. The writing has its part in the construction; the illustration has its part.

FORMS

Composing is a matter of seeing, naming, and ordering relationships, and then representing them. In exposition, for example, we might look at how writers portray relationships among and between ideas and entities. Because of the social nature of language, and the social development of thought, there are some commonly occurring rhetorical structures in English language and Western thought, which include:[29]

Subordinate relations:
part-whole
class-member
entity-characteristic
term-definition
Coordinate relations:
cause-effect
problem-solution
evidence-conclusion
negation
sequence
comparison
addition
alternate

These relationships are connected to standard logical forms of reasoning. For example, standard mathematical logic uses terms to describe relationships: THEN, IF THEN, AND, OR, NOT, EQUALS, THEREFORE. These represent the patterns of: sequence, consequence (and cause-effect), addition, alternate, negation, and equivalence (also definition). Also we have, from set theory, SET, SUBSET, MEMBER, and ELEMENT, representing part-whole, class-member, entity-characteristic relationships. Social logic is also important. Children and adults make arguments based on social norms (all the other kids have them), on precedent (John was allowed to), on exception (yes, but these circumstances are different), and by appealing to hierarchies of values (yes, but x is more important than y).[30]

I list these habitual ways of thinking with some apprehension. Such listings have historically been converted to curriculum organizers and frameworks for scoring writing. I want to stress that these structures are not exhaustive, and that they are abstractions of habitual ways of thinking *in the rationalist tradition*. To impose them as criteria of performance, and to teach them as abstract forms in the name of "metacomprehension," is to trivialize both thinking and writing. Flexible use and organization of these and other ways of thinking *in the service of real intentions* is the central issue. To score a piece of writing on the basis of the extent to which it conforms to an abstract "story grammar," is to miss and to repress both individual and cultural variation in the telling of stories.

Narrative is another common way of composing the world. Jerome Bruner argues that it is a different way of thinking which is, in some ways, opposed to the forms which I have just described.[31] "Expository" or "scientific" thinking and writing is directed toward abstract, objective principles, separated from context, feelings, and motives. Narrative thinking is, in many ways, the reverse. It is directed toward concrete, involving, context-bound interpretations that recognize and include human motives, values, and feelings. Young children are exposed to narrative more than to the other ways of construing the world. Partly because of this, along with its more personal and affectively involving nature, and its association with oral rather than literate culture, narrative is not valued as highly in this culture as are other ways of composing the world. This undervaluing of narrative actually has many roots, none of them admirable, and most relating to dominance and suppression.[32]

If a student cannot construct worlds in terms of these various relationships, all of her teachers, not just her English or language arts teacher, should look carefully at their teaching. These are not simply paragraph structures: these are ways of construing the world. They are also ways of appealing to and persuading other audiences. Evaluation too can be a matter of making a persuasive argument to an audience to impact a decision. We might be arguing to an administrator or parent that a student needs a particular kind of instructional situation. Or we might be arguing with ourselves about whether or not a particular instructional strategy we used with a student was successful. Or we might be trying to persuade taxpayers that their money has been well spent. These audiences often require different kinds of argument. Indeed, they currently require different kinds of arguments for different age-groups of children. For example, currently, parents still find narrative description of cognitive development compelling with younger children, but less so with older children.

RECONSTRUCTING

Of course, these relationships and forms are not all separate. For example, saying that something is not A or is opposed to A is another way of talking about what A is. These are all ways of classifying and naming the world that are critical to both reading and writing. We might find it instructionally helpful to know whether students have acquired these forms of logic, and the means of expressing them in language, and we can find these out in dialogue. If students know of these alternative expressions, reconstructing to make a translation is a good study strategy and, at the same time, a good indicator of how an exposition was understood.

A good story can persuade better than impeccable formal logic under certain circumstances and for particular audiences. So can a good metaphor. However, for other audiences and under other circumstances, narration is not persuasive. Negotiation is at the heart of persuasion, and the availability of alternative forms and arguments is critical. Children whose only solution to problems is to appeal to force or to higher authority, such as the teacher, are not well prepared for adult literate activity. Children who learn to work out their problems with one another have a better chance at developing multiple forms of argument, and an awareness that different arguments work with different audiences. Children who have such an opportunity also *display* this knowledge so that it can be observed, recorded, and capitalized on in teaching.

When students have to reconstruct their knowledge, perhaps what they have been reading about, for a different purpose or audience or using a different form, they reveal a great deal about their understanding. Indeed, reconstructing is an excellent tool for students to learn for their own self-evaluation. If they want to learn about how they know something, they might try changing their audience, explaining the topic to someone who knows absolutely nothing about it, for example. They might try using what they have learned about pollution to persuade a state legislator to vote in a particular way, or they might try to educate their parents on the matter. In doing so they might decide to change the form to a poem or a play. They might use the knowledge they have to analyze the production and management of energy or garbage in their school. In putting the knowledge to use, they will reveal the nature of their knowledge.

The particularly satisfying part of these transformations is that they not only reveal what we know and what we still need to find out, but the act of reconstructing helps the learners to know what they know more flexibly. Teachers, too, will find this principle operating when they have to move from checklist to narrative and from parent to colleague in their presentation of their knowledge of students.

DECONSTRUCTING

The form of a text or an argument does not lead us directly to meaning or intention. A simple list is a set of AND statements. But that does not give the meaning of the list. The meaning lies in the function of the list. There is a difference between the list of ingredients on an ice cream carton and the list of phone numbers in a teenager's notebook, and between those and a list of menu items (I concede that in certain circumstances any of these may become similar). Although a text may not be presented as persuasive, in that it does not use formal argument to persuade as expected in a writing test, it may nonetheless persuade. One can persuade by simply telling a story without overtly alluding to what one wishes to persuade the reader of. Many television advertisements use simple juxtaposition of images to persuade. Similarly, the form of a textbook may appear to be intended to convey knowledge of particular facts and relationships, but the function may well be to control knowledge and teachers and students. In the same way, a poem may just as easily serve a political function as an aesthetic one. To be able to read and write critically, then, will require students to be aware of the kinds of functions that can be served by constructions, and how they serve those functions.

We are interested, then, in how our students make texts problematic, how they unravel the strands of texts, and how they situate texts. For example, when I was in Australia a couple of summers ago, I picked up a copy of the Sydney newspaper. On the front cover was a story about Mike Tyson's fight with Michael Spinks.[33] The beginning of the story went like this:

> The Heavyweight Pay Cheque Championship of the world will be slugged out today when Mike Tyson and Michael Spinks engage in the richest-ever boxing spat.
>
> At stake: the undisputed world heavyweight crown and $38 million.
>
> Tyson will earn a record $22 million—about $612,000 a minute if they go the 12 rounds. Spinks will make do with a flat fee of $16.62 million.
>
> To get that into perspective, Greg Norman, Australia's wealthiest sportsman, has grossed $10 million from golf in the past eight years.
>
> The fight is being staged by billionaire property developer Mr Donald Trump at his Trump Plaza Casino complex. He has paid $11 million for the privilege, although that is hardly likely to worry him.
>
> Mr Trump, whose empire includes the New York Plaza Hotel and a $30 million yacht that used to belong to arms dealer Mr Adnan Kashoggi, expects to take $20 million on his gambling tables.

As you read this, you constructed your own meaning. In my case, I started to distance myself from the article as I read. The article became framed as part of the front page of a newspaper. The associated picture covered about eight inches by ten inches. The composer of the front page had pushed aside all the events of the world to foreground how much money Mike Tyson would make each minute in a boxing ring on the other side of the world. I skipped to the next few pages and scanned them to see what had been pushed aside. The deaths of hundreds of people in an earthquake two days before and ongoing rescue efforts were relegated to page seven. In these terms, what does this article mean?

The connections I made, hence the meaning I constructed from this article, had to do with statements of social values and the nature of a society, the control held by the media, and the like. But what was the *intended* main idea? The placement of the article and what is *not* said is just as important as what *is* said. Did I fail to comprehend? What of the student who reads his social studies book as a reflection of social values that he rejects? Has he misunderstood? Missed the point? Tom Newkirk quotes a fourth grader commenting on a text in his basal reader, saying, "I bet they write these things just so they can ask us questions about them?"[34] I believe that is an insightful understanding of the text. On the other hand, it may not be functional. That is, there will be consequences to the understanding that he constructs.

We will be concerned about the basis upon which readers and writers assert the authority of their statements of relationships. Readers and writers should ask each other, "Do you have evidence for that statement?" Teachers should ask it of each other about their statements about students' development, and of their students about their own statements of development in their portfolios. Indeed, I view a reading–writing portfolio as a piece of research upon one's own literacy, and learners have to attend to the support of their statements just as they would in other forms of research.

Evaluation, too, involves composing a characterization of whatever is being evaluated. That is what we do with language: we name or identify things, which is classifying things. We represent what we are evaluating to ourselves and others in various forms, and those forms serve particular functions. Very often a sensible way to construct a meaning from a text is to deconstruct it and view it as an artifact. Certain language and conventions have been used, and the ways in which they have been used in the construction say something about the likely functions of the text. Consider the following excerpt from a report which accompanied a young child to our reading lab.

**Boston Child Psychology
and Language Clinic**[35]

Client: Melissa Smith Date: 2/12/88
Parents: Arthur and Mary Smith   Birthdate: 1/26/81
Psychologist: Dr. Wilbur Wright.   Age: 7 yrs 1 month

. . . She has no dysmorphic features. Examination of her ears reveals bilateral serous effusions. Other physical findings do not appear to be of any significance. Neurologic examination shows minor difficulties with motor coordination, mirror movements and motor spread. No hard neurologic abnormalities are present.

Her major difficulty continues to be in the area of language function and semantic understanding. She continues to have significant difficulties with higher level language function with language confusion, and difficulty in higher level semantics. Given her age level, she consistently falls considerably behind expectation in those receptive areas of function that generally predict reasonable reading acquisition.

The root of Melissa's academic difficulties appears to be a developmental language disorder of a mixed semantic pragmatic/phonologic syntactic deficits.[sic] These have been translated into more academic difficulties as it relates to the pragmatic use of language in the verbal setting that academics generally require. . . .

Mr. and Mrs. Smith were probably taught in school to read this to remember it, or to find the main idea. When they received the report, they read it to receive the privileged knowledge placed in it by this person of very high social status and expertise (medical director of a large facility). Having done so they were terrified.[36] They assumed that the function of the report was to help them understand Melissa's academic difficulties. Based on the form, however, I would say that the function was more likely self-aggrandizement and the assertion of power. We could read it as persuasion—the intent being to persuade the Smiths of their powerlessness and the writer's power. This can be read from the use of language and the structure of the little details. "This is no *story*. This is exposition—science—truth," it shouts. The report wears a white coat. Though they are not present in this segment of the report, the subheadings also assert this function.

Students are capable of this sort of reading, of advertisements, for example, in the first and second grade. Teachers must become capable of this type of reading of reports which they receive, of the curricula which they are handed, and of their own teaching. Until they can read and respond to such reports critically, with an understanding of how writers exercise control over readers, they will continue to be subjected to them and the children to their consequences.

DEVELOPMENT IN CONSTRUCTION

In construction, whether reading, writing, or teaching (and children do teach one another), children are learning ways of structuring knowledge and connecting it together for particular audiences and in particular forms, to accomplish particular purposes. Students can show change in several kinds of knowledge:

knowledge of the topic and an eye for detail
knowledge of the functions of writing

knowledge of the means of achieving particular rhetorical intentions

knowledge of the conventions of writing for particular purposes and audiences, and when they can be violated with what consequences

knowledge of the characteristics and needs of particular audiences

We can really learn about these developments only by encouraging and providing a context for a diversity of writing in our classes, along with plenty of opportunity for responses from different audiences.

Children's written construction often begins with labels. The label is an answer to the implicit question, "What's that?" It is usually a picture and a verbal classification of the picture: a verbal and graphic equivalence statement. Commonly the picture identifies the topic and the word(s) restate it. One shift that takes place is the shift to the words establishing the topic and the picture moving to the status of *illustrating* the topic that the words establish. Another development of the label is to qualify the label with an attribute. For example we might have the label, "This is my hmstr. my hmstr is bran." We might interpret this more broadly as a topic with comment or elaboration.

Another type of construction that begins early is the list. The list also has a topic, which may or may not be stated, and contains elements. It may be a shopping list, a list of books read, items owned, items wished for, people in the family, and so forth. There may be organization within lists. For example, they may be ordered chronologically, causally, categorically, or associatively. These organized lists may be the entire piece of writing, or they may occur in planning a larger piece of writing. On the other hand, complicated exposition can often be reduced to an elaborated list—a series of categories or topics with relationships. Thus, selection and elaboration are as much a part of the reading process as of the writing process. We select from what we are reading given our particular purposes. When we are faced with a car repair manual and we need to replace the water pump on the car, we do not need to read the whole manual. However, we do need to know how to find exactly the parts that will help us install the water pump. If we are reading to briefly summarize an argument, we do not necessarily need to read an entire article, especially if we can see how the argument is arranged, and recognize it as one of the kinds of argument with which we are familiar.

A further development is the attribute inventory in which children tell all they know about a particular topic, like whales.[37] One of the topics children often choose is themselves and their own activity. For example, they may tell all they remember about a day—the "bed-to-bed" story. This "tell all" type of construction begins to be displaced as children learn to *select* and *expand* specific elements with particular audiences and intentions in mind. They may even begin to state their intentions in writing, thus beginning the development of the "opening paragraph." The development of thoughtful selection in the writing construction process is certainly worth celebrating. However, it is hard for a young writer to select parts of his writing to keep, marking others to eliminate, until he has sufficient to select from.

Many of the developments in composition are social. Consider the change that has occurred in these pen pal letters, written one year apart by Teresa.

> Dear Tammy
> How are you doing?
> I am doing good.
> I like playing baseball
> It is fun. you Have to hit the ball
> You Have 11 playors on you Tema.
> you have to run around the bases.
>
>   by
>   Teresa
>   Lynn
>   Wilson

>   Box 23
>   Stephensville
>   N.Y. 10025
>   2/24/90
>
> Dear Caroline,
>   Hi! my name is Teresa Wilson. I am 9 in a ½ years. I am going to turn ten on March 21. I am in thrid grade. My teachers name is Mrs. Mossman. She is nice some times but she is mean. I have blue eyes, brown hair. I am four foot eight inch. My mom's name is Sally and my dad's name is Jim sr. I have 1 brother Jim Jr. My sisters name's are Nan, Lilly, and Sarah but we call her Toots. I will send you a picture of me when I get them. I will be going to move when every we sell our house and I will give you the address so you can keep write back soon. I will write back as soon as I can. I would like to meet you some day.
>
>   Your Pen Pal
>   Teresa Wilson

There are certainly changes in the use of conventions, and in the sheer quantity of writing. However, the central change has come in the understanding of what this particular kind of audience would require—the social knowledge involved. Social knowledge influences almost any literate act; and the more complex the literate act is seen to be, the more social knowledge plays a part in it. This is one of the reasons why standardized tests of reading and writing are generally biased against minority cultures that do not share the same social knowledge as the culture of power that is responsible for setting the test, the criteria for success, and, generally, marking the test. This matter will be taken up again in Chapter 26.

CHAPTER 21

Concepts about Print

When a child first begins to write, it may not look much like writing. It may be distinguishable only by the expressed intention. It will, nonetheless, be the child's estimation of what adults or older siblings do, and hence what he must do in order to be human. However, quite quickly he notices that writing is different from drawing. Figure 21.1 shows two pieces done within five minutes of one another, one of which is a drawing and the other is a letter to a friend. Not shown in the figure is the fact that the illustration is in several colors and the letter is only in black. At some point the child understands that marks made on paper can represent speech, and he is likely to show his marks to an adult and ask, "What does this say?" Later, the writing may develop into that shown in Figure 21.2 as the child becomes aware of more of the details of the specific shapes of the symbols, and the common locations of print with respect to illustrations.

In this chapter I will describe children's development of this knowledge about the distinctive features of print, and how to notice and keep track of it.

LESS-THAN-OBVIOUS CONVENTIONS

Children construct and test all sorts of hypotheses about language structure and use as they become increasingly sophisticated in their literate knowledge. If children are given the opportunity to write, their hypotheses about language are reflected in their writing. Marie Clay has noted, for example, that children often hypothesize that there are repeating patterns in print, and so they busily go about repeating strings of the same letter or the same word which they already know.[38] They are thus able to produce a piece of writing of satisfying length. Over time, children become aware of exactly what kinds of patterns do recur. In the process of exploring these patterns, children often explore the properties of the letter combinations. For example, they may change a single letter on a word or write some or all of the word in uppercase, or write some parts in reverse. Starting from a mere handful of known letters, a child can create all sorts of patterns that look more or less like conventional words, especially if spaces are used.

But learning about letters, and patterns of letters and spaces, is only a small part of the development that is taking place. Writing in English requires, for no obvious reason to the child (or most of the rest of us for that matter), that the writer starts to make marks in the top left-hand corner (except when the picture

Figure 21.1(a). The result of a young child "drawing a picture."

comes first), proceeds from left to right across the top, returns to the left just underneath the first line before continuing to proceed to the right-hand side of the page. This pattern is repeated down to the bottom of the page (or as far as the lines go), and always proceeds from the left page to the right page (unless there is no print on the left page), beginning with the spine on the left-hand side and ending with it on the right. And there are other complexities such as:

☐ Letters are made up of repeating patterns of lines and circles (except when they are in cursive). This will show in the structure of the writing or scribbling being done.
☐ It is the black (usually) shapes which are important rather than the white spaces in between.
☐ Spatial orientation is important with letters and words.
☐ There are generally fifty-four distinct letter shapes (including upper and lower case and the two forms of g and a), plus eleven punctuation marks, and that does not include cursive writing. Letters may be identified by name, by a related sound, or by a word beginning with it. Appendix C is a form for recording children's identification of letters. Letters can be put together to form words (though some letters can be words). When a child looks at a word and says, "Oh, that starts with Peter," words and letters are being confused. A child who can take two

Figure 21.1(b). The result of the same young child "Writing a letter." This figure was produced within five minutes of Figure 21.1(a). The contrast between the two figures shows the emergent knowledge of print conventions.

index cards and mask all but one letter in a sentence or all but one word on request, can distinguish between words and letters.

☐ Some letters go together and others don't. Letter patterns in writing cease to include long strings of the same letter, and are less likely to place letters together that do not occur together in English.

☐ The message is constructed from the print more than the pictures. Children who are aware of this concept will point to the print rather than the picture when asked where to start reading, or when "pretend reading" with a book (telling a story to the book and pointing at pages).

☐ In general, words are spelled the same each time, and the words in print relate to the same words in speech every time they are read. Children knowing this latter point will correct the teacher's misreading of a story when it is being reread.

☐ Written language frequently has a different structure from spoken language. Knowing this, a child reading from a book reads in literate language rather than just telling a story in her own language, or the child's writing reflects literate language structure rather than normal speech.

☐ Certain letters are used to represent certain sounds (though the rela-

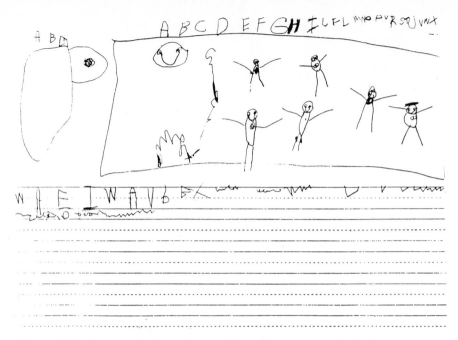

Figure 21.2. A young child's writing and illustrating, showing the further emergence of the conventions of print in relationship to illustration.

tionship rarely is one to one and sometimes you have to say a word differently in order for there to be any relationship at all). Invented spelling begins. There is usually some relationship between the initial sound in the word and the letter written.

☐ The relative length (temporal) of the spoken word is vaguely related to the length (spatial) of the written word.

☐ Print can be turned into speech and vice versa. This shows up, for example, when a child writes "BTPEEL" and says, "This says home," or asks, "What does this say?"

☐ One spoken word equals one written word. This can be seen when the child "reads with her finger" every word, or reads in a staccato manner, separating each word clearly (this is called "voice pointing").

☐ Reading something through once does not guarantee perfect memory of it.

Many of the concepts children must learn are ones adults take for granted. In school, teachers refer to these various concepts using words. If the child does not have the concept which goes with a particular word, it makes some of the language of school confusing. When the teacher keeps using the term *sound* but the student does not differentiate *sound* from *word,* instruction can be a little confusing. The following is a list of *some* of the concepts about spoken and written language that children must learn to become fully literate: word (both written and spoken), sound, story, letter, front and back (with respect to books), next (with respect to left to right spatial progression as well as with respect to time), after, before, capital letter, upper and lower case, sentence, author, read, write, draft, edit, revise, share, conference, publish, file, date.

CHECKING UP ON CONCEPTS

Children are not born with knowledge of concepts such as "letter," "word," "sentence," "story," and the like. The child's growing understanding of these concepts is very important to monitor, particularly as confusions will affect the way the child understands instruction. Marie Clay devised a test called the *Concepts about Print Test* (CAP) to check up on some of these critical concepts.[39] It is the best test available for this purpose. It is based on a book that evaluator and student cooperate in reading together. They sit alongside each other involved in the same activity rather than sitting opposite each other in a confrontational way. The concepts tested are: front of book; right way up for the book; beginning of book; print rather than pictures carries the message; directional rules of left to right through the book, across the page and back to the left moving down the page; matching spoken words with written words; first and last (with respect to story and letters in words); letter order; punctuation; letter; word; capital (uppercase) letter.

To test some of the concepts, the book has some strange features in that a picture is upside down on one page, the words are in the wrong order or reversed (was for saw) in another place, and some lines are in the wrong order. The idea is that the child notices the inappropriate aspects of the book, and in doing so demonstrates a knowledge of the concept. The major limitation of this test is that it is based on an error-detection task, which requires the child to tell you that your book is a bit weird. A child's ability to do this will depend substantially on her relationship and experience with the evaluator and other adults in a similar role. Nonetheless, this test has an excellent record as part of an early screening procedure to locate children who are having difficulty learning these rather arbitrary concepts.

The reason for the special book in the CAP test is that it is a standardized test and requires such a constraint so that norms can be generated and comparisons made. I believe that a teacher can use a regular book to evaluate most of these concepts without a formal assessment situation and a strange book. Such a procedure, being unstandardized, will not yield norm-referenced scores that may be important for some situations.[40] But many of these concepts can be evaluated in the course of normal classroom interaction, or through an individualized interaction, using a simple checklist such as that in Figure 21.3, or a more elaborate one such as that in Figure 21.4. Although it will not produce a norm-

Figure 21.3. Concepts about Print

Name: _____   Date: _____

Right way up   _____

Front of book   _____

First page   _____

Story/picture   _____

Left-right through book   _____

L/R across page & return   _____

Word-word match   _____

Sentence   _____

Word   _____

First/last word   _____

Letter   _____

First/last letter   _____

Reading makes sense   _____

Letter/sound cross-check   _____

Title   _____

Author   _____

COMMENTS   _____

_____

_____

_____

_____

_____

referenced score, it will yield a bunch of useful data and a criterion-referenced score if that is desired.

Perhaps I can demonstrate. As I describe such an interaction, I will number what I learn (and can check on my list) and explain the numbers at the end of the description. I suggested that Dane and I read together, an opportunity he jumped at (1). I asked him to bring a favorite book, and I had on hand some simple predictable books (2). I asked him if he would like to read it to me, which he also happily agreed to, though he said, ''I can't really read it properly''(3). He turned the book the right way up (4), opened it at the beginning page (5),

Figure 21.4. Book and Print Awareness

Name _____

Concept	Date	Comment
Interest/Language		
Chooses to read		
Has favorite books		
Uses "book language"		
Recalls phrases verbatim		
Terminology		
Front/back of book		
Beginning/end of book		
Title (can point to)		
Author (can point to)		
Page		
Top/bottom of page		
First/last page		
Word		
Letter		
First/last letter		
Upper/lower case		
Sound (in spoken word)		
First/last sound		
Period		
Comma		
Question Mark		
Quotation Mark		
Sentence		
Directionality		
Book right way up		
Left page first		
Left-right through book		

(continued)

Figure 21.4. Continued

Concept	Date	Comment
Directionality (cont.)		
Left-right across page	_____	_____
Left-right across page	_____	_____
Top to bottom of page	_____	_____
Left-right across word	_____	_____
Speech-Print Match		
Words = print not picture	_____	_____
Story/picture match	_____	_____
Word/word match	_____	_____
Initial sound/letter	_____	_____
Initial letter/sound	_____	_____

COMMENTS: _____

_____

_____

_____

and told me the story of *The Boy Who Was Followed Home.*[41] He matched what he said to the pictures (6) and part of his reading went, ''Robert was surprised and pleased,'' and ''He was delighted to think he was the kind of boy that hippopotomi follow home,'' which was not his normal language but ''book'' language (7). His telling of the story was extensive and detailed (8). On one occasion his story got out of step with the pictures, so he corrected himself from the pictures (9). When he had finished, I asked him how he knew where to start reading, and he told me that the pictures had to be up the right way and ''You always start at this end'' (10).

Next I asked him if he knew the books that I had. I chose to read to him *The Fat Cat,* which was one that he did not know.[42] I asked him if he knew where to find the author and the title, which he did (11). I read them to him and opened the book to the first page. I asked him where I should start reading and he pointed to the top left of the print on the left page (12), so I read it. I asked him where to go next and he turned the page since the second page had no print on it (13). I already knew from his writing that he knew to go left to right and back to the beginning of the next line (14). I had watched him write his letters, unrelated to the sounds, and with no spaces between, but from left to right and again on a second line (15), and he had then told me an extensive story about what he had written (16). I continued to read the book, pausing sufficiently to invite him to predict the ends of predictable sentences, which, by the end of the book, he was able to do (17). He wanted the book read again (18), so we read it to the class in the same way.

A week later I had a few moments with Dane, and I had two index cards. On a book that had a single line of print on the page, I asked him to use the cards as curtains to show me one word, then to show me two words.[43] On both occasions he showed me letters (19). I could have asked him also to show me one and two letters, but he clearly confused words and letters, so that I already knew to attend to that confusion.

1. This shows that he enjoys stories and books and seeks book experiences.
2. Since he did have a favorite book, and could talk about others, I have learned more about his enjoyment, and some about his repertoire of favorite books. I could explore this further with him.
3. He understands that there is more to reading than just telling a story, but he is undaunted by his partial version of mature reading. I might have asked him, later, to expand this distinction. For example, I might have said "Dane, when we started, you said that you can't really read properly. What would you do if you were reading properly?" If he had chosen to participate but not to read, I would hesitate regularly to invite him to complete lines or pages of the book. I would listen for his use of language to see whether he uses "book language" (i.e., words and sentences unlike his normal spoken language, and like the language in the book).
4. Dane knows how to orient the book. This will help a lot when he tries to learn about words. If he only orients the book correctly sometimes, it will be substantially harder for him to discover the regularities in print.
5. He knows where to start reading.
6. He has good memory for text and knows about the relationship between text and illustration. He also knows that you read left to right through the book.
7. He has begun to develop the separate register of "book language" as distinct from his normal spoken register. This will help him predict well when he reads. He is also expanding his vocabulary through his book experiences.
8. Again, his memory for text is excellent.
9. He has begun to match multiple sources of information, and look for mismatches. He is able to self-correct on the basis of a mismatch.
10. His book orientation is based on illustrations rather than text, but he does know to go left to right through the book.

11. He knows about authors and titles and that they are found on the front cover.
12. He knows that print begins at the top left of the page (in this case). Had he just shown me the left page and not the top left of the print, I would have asked him where on this page he thought I should start reading.
13. He knows that print, not the illustration, is what is read.
14. He knows left-to-right and top-to-bottom arrangement of print. Had I not known this, I could have asked him to point with his finger to show me where I should go after I started in the top left corner, and where after that, but that was not necessary.
15. He probably does not know the difference between letters and words, and he does not have any notion that letters can be used to represent sounds.
16. He has a healthy concept of himself as an author.
17. He quickly learns a new pattern of syntax and can predict based on rhyme. This also means that he is attending to the vowel sounds in the language, and can use that, along with meaning and syntax, to predict which words will come up.
18. This is more evidence of his seeking book experience.
19. This confirmed the earlier observation from his writing that he confuses words and letters.

The general form of this procedure could be used to produce a standard-operating-procedure as a regular check on the development of concepts about print and about literacy. Some parts of this type of interaction may be used to clear up the odds and ends which you haven't noticed, or when you need information on a new student (after she has settled in a bit). Many of the questions can be followed if necessary with "How did you know?" or "How could you tell?" Asking new students the author and title questions will often be revealing of the kind of instructional environment they have left.

There may be many more of these concepts such as *alphabet, vowel, consonant,* and *long vowel,* depending on a teacher's approach to instruction.[44] Indeed, what with substitute teachers, remedial classes, and the like, children often must get used to a variety of different instructional languages. Unfortunately, it is often the most vulnerable and confused children who must get used to more than one different instructional language. It is helpful to tape record yourself teaching occasionally and listen for the use of these terms that we often take for granted. Talking with colleagues about teaching, listening to and observing children, and watching each other teach can help reduce this problem.

EDDIES AND CONFUSIONS

Some of these concepts are, however, particularly difficult for many children, and for good reasons. For example, until a child begins to deal with print, she learns that a cup is a cup whether it is lying down, standing up, or upside down. With print, it is as if the cup is only a cup when it is standing up with the handle on the right hand side. A *b* is a *b* only when the round bit faces in one direction, any other direction and it is a *d* or a *p* or a *q*. For a child who has not yet developed an awareness of one side of the body being consistently different from the other, this is a difficult thing to grasp. The spatial orientation has to be *in relation* to something else that is constant. For example, it can face away from the right hand or towards it, but if you don't consistently differentiate one hand from the other, something else must remain stable, like a red margin on the writing paper (which, paradoxically, primary writing paper often lacks). This is complex because of the development of the child's awareness of his own body, and of himself in relationship to the rest of the world, not because of neurological complications. Neither is it a matter of knowing left from right, but rather developing a consistent eccentric frame of reference. It is a *con*ceptual confusion not a *per*ceptual confusion.[45]

Many children take a while to get a grasp of these concepts, and thus reverse letters, words, and even whole pages and books. For example, in kindergarten Emily made a book (kids love using staplers), which she then proceeded to write in (Figure 21.5). She began with the cover, which she wrote exactly as it should be—in invented spelling and with unconventional lowercase *d*'s. But the cover was done with the spine at the top rather than on the left. She then made a critical decision. She had to turn the book to the left or to the right in order for the pages to open properly. She made the wrong decision and turned the book so that the spine was to the right. Thus she began to write her story at the end of the book rather than at the beginning. She started at the outside edge of the (right-hand) page and went across the page, then to the next page (the left-hand

Figure 21.5. The Backwards Book

	Conventional Version	Emily's Version
COVER:	Em (*Emily)	Em
	Dedicated to Dad Mom	dAdaKAdED To DAD MOM
	Things I Hate	FEV I hD
PAGE 1:	I hate	I hD
PAGE 2:	Writing.	RAETEN
	Nick. Nick hates	NiCK NiCK hAS
	writing.	rAETIEN
PAGE 3:	(New topic)	
	Things th-	FEN D . . .
PAGE 4:		
	at grow.	AT Gro

One of the more amusing aspects of this piece is that, during free choice time, during which she could do anything she wanted, she sat at the writing table to make and write this book.

(continued)

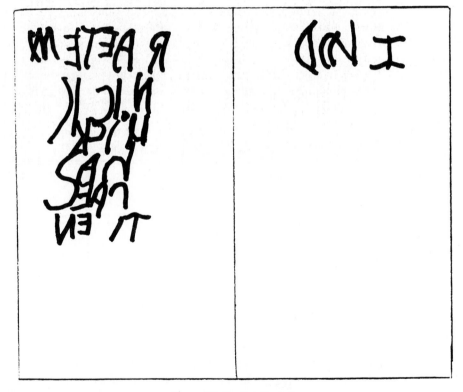

Figure 21.5. Continued

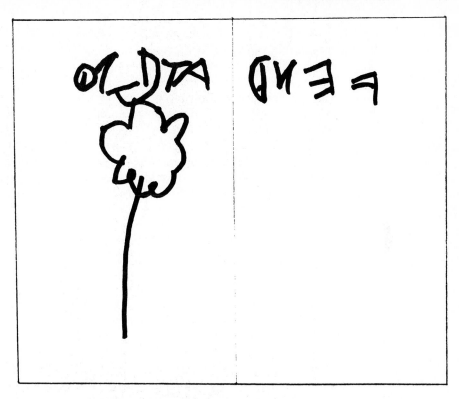

Figure 21.5. Continued

page) and so forth. Having made a single incorrect decision, everything else is exactly as it should be, if held up to a mirror.

The concept of a convention is usually indicated before the detail. For example, apostrophes at first appear in lots of places, like before every final *s*, or in words that look like those that have apostrophes such as *wan't,* which looks like *can't.* This visual similarity is idiosyncratic. Some children see likeness where we might see none. However, they are often able to describe the reason for the presence of the apostrophe. Some conventions are learned very early by some children, and some are learned much later. There is no set order of acquisition. A two-year-old will often use different words and sentence structure when telling a story from a book than when telling a story without a book in hand. The same child may not learn the difference between the concepts of *sound* and *word* until he is six. Another child might understand the separate sounds in words at two, and only later begin to "talk like a book."

Children slowly gain control over these rather arbitrary concepts and they will often appear to forget them. For example, it is common for children to exercise control over conventions when they do not have to compose, merely represent. One seven-year-old in our lab who was having difficulty with reversals in his writing had that trouble only when he was composing. He explained this in terms of his just being too busy with writing, and he could easily correct them after he was finished. Another child could read a sentence cut up and arranged in one line, but could not read it when it was arranged in two lines. There is no steady mastery of first this concept, then that concept.

The child's developing understanding, in both spoken and oral language, of the concepts of *word, sound,* and *letter* are reflected in a variety of different ways. When a child has learned a nursery rhyme, you can bring out the written version and read it to him, pointing with your finger, and then ask if he can point to the words while you read it, or if he can read it pointing to the words.[46] You might also ask if he can find particular words on a line. Watching him do this will tell you, for example, whether he uses initial sound-symbol relationships or goes back and recites until he comes to that word. Later, in reading, simply asking the child to "read it with your finger" will tell a great deal. Children will be tripped up or confused by syllabic divisions, which they will distinguish before they distinguish separate sounds, and by compound words like *today* for quite a long time. Such confusions last through high school for many students in words like *forinstance* and *alot.* The technique developed by Marie Clay for evaluating children's understanding of the concept of word is to give the child two index cards and ask him to use them as curtains to show you only one word (on a sentence presented to him). Then show you two words. What about a letter? What about an uppercase letter? And so forth.[47]

Persistent confusion over some of these concepts can produce devastating effects. Don Holdaway reports a case in which a child in remedial reading instruction broke down in tears because he could not make sense of "all the white rivers" (the patterns of white spaces between the words). Another example is the child who comes to believe that reading has to do with memorizing.[48] Small conceptual confusions used as the basis for hypotheses can produce a web of incorrect hypotheses which can entangle and eventually strangle young literants in certain conditions. The worst part is that each new hypothesis is likely to work part of the time and hence be rewarded intermittently. Such rewards are the most difficult to undo. Fortunately, confusions such as these tend to persist only under particular circumstances. For example, when children cannot experiment with and explore print, when they only read and do not write, and when they do not talk with each other about their reading and writing, they cannot consider other hypotheses about how print works so that they can build new hypotheses and get feedback about them. Such situations tend to occur in highly teacher-directed, competitive, and anxiety-producing classrooms in which either there is no time for such exploration or the risks of exploration are too great.

CHAPTER 22

The Sound, the Look, and the Feel of Words

At the same time as the concepts about print are developing, children are becoming aware of aspects of *spoken* language of which they had previously been unaware. A large proportion of children coming to school do not know the difference between a sound and a spoken word (many don't know what a word is either, even though they use them). Why should they be able to segment a word into its phonemes (speech sounds)? Such a distinction has no use in spoken English. The only reason for it is that written English happens to be somewhat alphabetic. In other words, there *is* a relationship between the patterns of letters in print, and the sounds in speech, and children must gain a flexible knowledge of these relationships, in particular so that they will be able to freely express themselves in writing. They will also find this knowledge very helpful in their reading.

PRINT AND SPEECH

Just like children in our culture, in cultures whose written languages are not alphabetic, most adults cannot segment words into sounds either. Learning about this requires learning to pay attention to and distinguish the sensations made in the mouth when making speech. This requires becoming consciously aware of a skill, saying words, that children have learned to do automatically, without awareness. However, they begin to hear that words are made up of sounds: that *MMM* is the beginning *sound* of Mary (which also has an *eee* sound in it). This little piece of information is critical when learning to write an alphabetic language, and the evidence to date suggests that more children get hung up in their development on this particular point than any other.[49]

We can tell when children are getting the hang of this concept by asking them to "Get your mouth ready to say . . . " or by seeing whether they can articulate the words slowly. I choose words like *am, man, run,* and *so,* which have sounds that can be extended, unlike *cat* for example (try saying the *c* and *t* parts of *cat* slowly). Asking children to say words slowly not only finds out whether or not they can do it; but if they cannot, that act of attempting slow articulation helps them to attend to the sensations in their mouths. This helps them pay attention to how the word is put together and hence makes them more likely to be able to do it the next time you ask. Marie Clay describes an instructional technique that involves making boxes for the number of sounds in a word, saying the word slowly, and having the child move a penny or counter into each box as he hears each separate phoneme in the word. This is an excellent assessment device. It requires the child to hear (or feel in her mouth) the sounds *and* to represent them without having to know relationships between letters and sounds. A simpler way to do this same thing is to ask the child to hold his fingers off the table and put one down for each sound he hears in a word.[50] Children's invented spelling will be revealing too, but it involves not only being aware of the phonemes, but also representing them with specific letters. If a child is not sensitive to the production of the sounds in words, then attempting to intensively teach the relationship between letters and sounds is likely to be very frustrating. If a child is sensitive to the sounds, then teaching her to represent them, in order to record important messages, is likely to be much more manageable.

As children become aware that there is a relationship between sounds and letters, they begin to build knowledge of these relationships and this knowledge is represented in their writing. Initially words will often be represented by initial (or final) letters only. For example, *cat* will be written *K* (or *T*). Before long, initial and final sounds are represented and the sounds in the middle of the word are increasingly represented, particularly beginning with tense vowels (as in *came, ice, feet, hope, cue*),[51] but quickly including blends such as *bl* and digraphs such as *sh*. This trend can be seen by watching young children write. Over this period they twist their mouths into all sorts of shapes as they emphasize the feel of the various sounds in their mouth. At this point it is mostly the feeling in their mouths that directs their representation. Indeed, if you get them to hold their tongue between their teeth, preventing them from feeling the words, their invented spelling will fall apart. It is not really that they hear the difference between two words, but that they feel the difference in the production of the words. That is why getting them to listen to you saying it slowly is less helpful than getting them to say it slowly. However, partly because they are articulating the words more slowly, they become aware of the different sounds within spoken words. This is when it becomes fall-on-the-floor funny for children to switch around the sounds in words to make nonsense.[52] This play with language is not only enormously instructional, but since it has to be done out loud, it gives the teacher an indication of when students can do it.

There is a general pattern of development for the representation of particular sounds in children's print. In general, children have much less trouble in English with representing the consonant sounds in print. Consonants are more predictable and limited in the sounds they represent.[53] However, the number of sounds that can represent particular letters is much more complex. For example, the letter *t* in different contexts can be associated with several different sounds as in: *to, ratio, there, with, trap,* and *fillet. E* is ridiculous: *read, dead, idea, live, weigh, weird, knew, they, eye, fern, oven, leotard, leopard*. This is why, provided invented spelling is accepted, the relationships are more easily learned initially in writing. Understanding the sight and feel of the word first by writing down speech allows the child to use the known (spoken language) to learn about the unknown (written language).

Again, the pattern of development of word representations relates to the distinctiveness of the production of sounds in the mouth. For example, *m* and *n* are represented easily in the beginning and ending of words, but not when part of a consonant blend such as *mp, nd, nt, nk,* or *ng* because the mouth is in the same position for the nasal (*m* or *n*) as it is for the final consonant. After some of the consonants are distinguished, tense vowels start to appear. They are tense vowels because the muscles in the mouth are tensed in order to make the sounds. The lax vowel sounds, like those in *get, bat, sit, but,* and *hot,* tend to come later because it is harder to feel the difference between how the mouth makes those sounds. Try it for yourself. You will also notice that in the tense vowels, in some words in some dialects, it is difficult to distinguish between the mouth feel of the *a* in *aim* and the *I* in *I'm.*[54] This is why they are often interchanged in children's writing for some time after the tense vowels *o* (*boat*) and *e* (*feet*) are consistently represented.

As children become able to separate the sounds of the words and represent them, their efforts often include aspects of the letter name. The fact that the names of the letters *a, e, i, o,* and *u* are associated with the tense vowel sounds makes it even easier for children to learn the relationships between tense vowels and their representation. Both mouth feel and letter name are distinctive. Other features of the letter name enter into development too. For example, *c* can represent the whole word *see,* and *Katy* can be written KT. On the other hand, *H* ("ay-ch") is often used to represent the sound normally associated with the digraph /ch/; hence, *chip* may be written HP. This makes it complicated to read the word *tree* which the child may pronounce "chree" and write HRE or simply HE.

The writing will be a representation of the child's articulation, even his slow articulation. Since children's pronunciation is not as clear as that of literate adults, they will represent words in characteristic ways. For example, *drive* might be written jv or jiv, and *three* written as fre. Actually, many children do not acquire the sound /th/ as in *this* (voiced) or *thing* (unvoiced) until ages eight or nine. Thus we get *dis* or *vis* and *fing* (or some variation on those themes). Lisps, dialects, and other variations will show up in written representations. They merely produce different regularities. Think about the place in the mouth in which the dialectical versions of words are spoken and that will help you to read students' invented spellings and to understand where help is needed and where it is not. Actually, it is the child's developing reading which influences his understanding of the standard pronunciation of words. This influence may well affect his pronunciation of those words over time, particularly in a formal context.

VISUAL ANALYSIS

Parallel to these developments in the child's ability to distinguish and represent sounds, is the child's memory for the visual form of words. A child might learn to spell her name based entirely on the visual form. For example, *EMILY* might be written as a unit before much is understood about sounds or even letters. Indeed, she might consider Emily to be incorrect because it is not recognizable in that form. Emily might also be written as ELY, EMY, EMLIY, or ELMY. The right letters are there, but the letters and the order are not as they might occur in invented spelling. Some of these look like phonetic representations since many of the appropriate sound representations are there. However, the influence of visual memory can be seen in several ways. In the first place, the *Y* is not the most obvious form for representing the /e/ sound. Indeed, MLE would be a more predictable invented spelling. A second way to see the influence of the visual memory is in the speed with which the word is written. Invented spellings are often slow and accompanied by much facial movement as the feeling of the sounds in the mouth is emphasized. Amidst a series of words labored over in such a fashion, when children suddenly write a word quickly and without facial distortion, it is very likely written from visual memory.

This visual memory is a very positive development coming in large part from the child's reading. Its timing and rate of development depend somewhat on the nature of the child's reading instruction, and the extent of reading that the child does, along with whatever predisposition the child has for attention to visual detail. The more reading, in general, the more rapidly these "sight words" tend to develop. On the other hand, some children come to rely on this sight word strategy in their writing rather than inventing the spellings of words. Occasionally this can be problematic. Every time a child invents the spelling of a word, he practices the representation process, analyzes the word, and becomes more expert and flexible in thinking about the relationships between sound and print, and secondarily, print and sound. When he uses only a sight word representation method, this development is slower and often it becomes even more difficult to read the writing back later because it is written unconventionally with little relationship between print and sound.

Lots of confusions arise over why children write words in particular ways. However, if you watch them writing, and perhaps interview them about their efforts, there will be fewer confusions. For example, as children slow down word and start to listen to what they have slowed down, their attention is taken up by the representation process and they lose perspective on the whole word. In this case they will sometimes add an unstressed vowel as in *beluw* (*blue*). The *e* represents the unstressed vowel which the child pronounced as she tried to slow down and isolate the sound commonly associated with the letter *b*. Because *b* cannot be pronounced in isolation without attaching a vowel sound to it, the child listens to the sound and represents it in print before taking a second run at the words to hear the next sound. Similarly, the *w* at the end of the word is a result of analysis of all of the mouth positions in the slowed down word. To decide why the student put the particular vowels in particular places you really have to be there to watch. Children often place letters out of sequence in the early stages because they combine different strategies for writing the word. For example, knowing that his name is Nick, a child might write NCI. Watching him write it, it becomes clear that the *I* is an afterthought. The *N* and *C* are representations of the initial and final sounds, but having written NC, visual memory tells him that something is missing. Knowing that there should be an *I* in there somewhere, it is added in as seems appropriate to the child. It is unlikely to result from sound analysis at this stage since the lax or unstressed vowels are very difficult for children to distinguish and appear rather late in their invented spelling.

Traces of visual analysis will increasingly appear with invented spellings. For example, *Won day* has *day* spelled from visual memory (as opposed to *da* or *dae*) and *Won* is invented from auditory analysis. They will even appear within the same word—for example, when human is written HYOUMIN. In this instance, in analyzing the sounds, /u/ was reached and the visual representation of the word *you* was used. Other instances will include spelling, for example, cold as *coled,* showing the realization of the common *ed* pattern on the end of words, a visual analysis. Children will also begin to become aware of other regularities in the representation system such as markers (like the "silent" *e* in same). For example, the word LIKE might be written LIEK for several different reasons. It could be a slightly inaccurate visual analysis, or it could be an over-analyzed sound analysis, or it could show a beginning awareness of the use of the *e* marker to make the tense vowel sound. We would know only by watching it being produced and by asking something like "How did you know to spell *like* like that?" or "How did you know to put the *e* in *like*?" The recognition of these common letter patterns as important indicators of development is critical. The process through which unconventional spellings are arrived at has important implications for teaching. There is certainly no point in trying to help sort out a sound analysis problem if an unconventional ordering of letters was produced by a sight word strategy relying on visual memory.

READING AND WRITING, SIGHT AND SOUND

Both visual analysis and sound analysis strategies are valuable, especially if they are used as a check against one another. Most adults run into trouble with spelling at some point and resort to such strategies as writing down a set of possible ways to spell a word and then using the visual analysis strategy to choose the correct option. In the long run we want children to write words and recognize them as individual conventional units. That saves a lot of time and intellectual energy. Visual analysis will increasingly produce conventionally spelled words. As an odd switch, in visual analysis, lax vowels like the *o* in *pot* are conventionally represented before tense vowels. They are the last to be accurately represented in sound analysis. The reason for this lies in the more complex and numerous ways of representing spoken tense vowels. For example, the tense *a* as in *hate,* can be written as in *hate, bait, say, fillet.* The lax vowels on the other hand are more limited. For example the lax *a,* as in *hat,* is represented one way.

But as this ability to represent sounds develops, word recognition also develops in reading. Readers also use auditory and visual analysis in reading. The auditory analysis being the "sounding out" of words and the visual strategies being "sight word" recognition. The visual analysis represents the development of the mature pattern recognition that drives adults' reading. These words will be the ''high frequency words'' (which really do occur with higher frequency than other words). Because of their higher frequency in print, we would expect the development of sight words to be related to the amount of reading being done. Along with the recognition of specific words, recognition of common suffixes develops, particularly; *s, es, ing, ed,* and *er.* Again, both auditory and visual analyses are helpful, especially when used to cross-check.

Data on the sight recognition of high frequency words can easily be gathered from children's oral reading, as I have pointed out. However, high frequency word lists can also be helpful if some more specific information is required. Also, Marie Clay's technique of asking the child to write down all the words he knows (allowing ten minutes and prompts if necessary) can also be revealing about the words which children know well (better than sight recognition). Generally, some confusions, often reversals, occur between some of these high frequency words. However, these confusions and reversals reflect a shift to the mature word recognition strategy without a concomitant attention to meaning and self-monitoring from print. While reading, it is very rare indeed for children to reverse words that cannot be written backwards. In other words, expect reversals of *was/saw,* and *no/on,* but do not expect reversals of *the/eht* or *going/gniog.* Furthermore, reversals of words such as *was* and *saw* are less likely to occur when there is sufficient preceding context to disambiguate them. If reversals do occur equally in these contexts, then it suggests that the reader is not attending adequately to meaning. Notice how the reasons for these patterns suggest relevant instructional strategies. Notice also that often the strategy that makes most sense is increased amounts of actual reading (particularly of relatively easy material) and writing.

Marie Clay has suggested the use of two different assessment tools that look at different aspects of children's representation strategies.[55] To evaluate the child's visual analysis, she uses a writing vocabulary test in which the child is given ten minutes to write down all the words he or she knows. Only conventionally spelled words are scored correct according to the visual analysis. To evaluate the children's sound analysis skill, she has suggested a dictation test. The scoring of the test (if scoring is required) reflects reasonable representation of each sound, regardless of whether or not it is conventionally spelled. To construct your own dictation test, just construct a brief sentence or two containing a selection of words which are unlikely to be ''sight words'' and which contain varying numbers of phonemes. It would be helpful if the words include a diversity of sounds to be represented including tense and lax vowels and consonant blends. For example, the following sentences could be used:

> My friend and I like to go and see the big sail boat. It has a blue flag.

If a child wrote, ''mi frend and i lyc tu go and ce ta big sal bot it has u blu flag,'' then she would have a perfect score on this test since all 47 phonemes are represented, albeit unconventionally. Such a test could be given again several months later to provide a reasonable measure of growth in ability to represent speech in print. Equivalent forms of such a test can easily be constructed, but are not generally necessary as the same test will do just fine with a reasonable time between uses. Ideally, the student's pronunciation should be taken into account when interpreting the performance. For example, a child who pronounces "school" as "schoo" cannot arrive at the *l* in school by auditory analysis, and must arrive at it through visual analysis. However, such accommodations make relatively small differences to scores and are not particularly relevant when you are only interested in comparing an individual's performance over time and not comparing individuals with one another.

Both visual and sound information are regularly available from students' writing. However, they are confounded by such things as the use of environmental print and support from other students. Also some young writers will copy their own invented spelling incorrectly, thus making it look more problematic than it is. Thus, dictation tests can be useful for informing decisions which must be based on the *individual's* development of translation skill. Dictation can actually be done as a natural part of literate activity. People do dictate to other people, and this has the interesting property of separating composition from representation. When a child dictates a story to you, you will learn about his knowledge of what is required in writing. A child who knows to dictate slowly enough for you to write has more sophisticated knowledge than a child who does not.

But analyzing the sounds and the feel of words does not begin and end with spelling and figuring out words when reading. Indeed, the first aspect of spoken language to which children attend as babies, is the pattern of intonation. This feature of speech, which they easily master as infants, is the basis of punctuation, which many will struggle to master when they are older and in school; yet awareness of this relationship is rarely evaluated. Interest in the sounds and feel of language and children's understanding of them continues right through school. Consider, for example, the following writing by Margaret Mahy in her book *The Man Whose Mother Was a Pirate:*

> The little man could only stare. He hadn't dreamed of the BIGNESS of the sea. He hadn't dreamed of the blueness of it. He hadn't thought it would roll like kettledrums, and swish itself on to the beach. He opened his mouth, and the drift and the dream of it, the weave and the wave of it, the fume and the foam of it never left him again. At his feet the sea stroked the sand with soft little paws. Farther out, the great, graceful breakers moved like Kings into court, trailing the peacock-patterned sea behind them.[56]

Although the use (and the recognition of others' use) of the way words sound together and the way they sound like the thing they are being used to describe are usually left for the study of alliteration and assonance in high school, young children can appreciate, talk about, and use such language. When they do, it bears documentation.

CHAPTER 23

Being Strategic

A child reading a book comes across a word he doesn't recognize. Reading suddenly shifts from recognition to reasoning. Some strategy needs to be used to render the word recognizable. Perhaps he will relate it to a different word he does know, or use some of his knowledge of the relationships between letters and sounds. Perhaps he will read on and come back to figure it out, or ask a neighbor. When you learned to take running records, you learned to record these strategies. Similar use of strategies occurs when a reader can no longer make sense of what she is reading. Though she recognizes the words, perhaps she cannot construct sufficient contact with her experience to render the text sensible. At times like these we try to find a way to make the piece recognizable. We might reread a portion of the text, or we might decide to skim ahead to see where this writer is trying to take us, or we might decide to leave the book until we have done some background reading, or we might decide to ask someone to explain it, or ditch the whole thing entirely.

The more strategies a reader has, the more options are available for solving problems. The more flexibly the strategies are used, the more likely the reader is to solve problems. The more insightfully strategies are selected, the quicker problems are solved. That is why it is useful to record the ways students go about figuring things out. Suppose that a child needs a word while writing. She might:

- ☐ find the word on classroom wall
- ☐ or in a book she knows
- ☐ or ask a neighbor
- ☐ ask the teacher
- ☐ approximate the word
- ☐ choose another word which is easier
- ☐ use a thesaurus (book or computer)
- ☐ leave a space and go on

Or, suppose she doesn't recognize a word while reading. She might:

- ☐ predict a word that would fit there and check to see if the letters could make that word
- ☐ read to the end of the sentence and come back to check the word
- ☐ use letter/sound regularities to figure out what the word might be, then try it in the sentence

    ☐ ask a friend or the teacher
    ☐ see if you know a word like that and see if it gives a clue

If she tries one of these strategies and it doesn't work, she might:

    ☐ repeat the same strategy over again
    ☐ quit
    ☐ try a different strategy
    ☐ ask for help

A student who uses only one strategy today will show growth by using more strategies next week or next month, or by using them more flexibly, or more persistently.

CONSTRAINTS ON STRATEGY USE

The strategies used in the pursuit of literate activity are constrained by:

1. The strategies they have available.
2. The knowledge they have relevant to the topic.
3. The goals they are trying to accomplish (which may change at any point along the way).
4. The situational constraints such as deadlines, having an audience, having a dictionary handy, and so forth.
5. The person's perceptions of the cause of a problem.

If a child has the wrong goal, that is a serious problem since he will not attend to the useful strategies of others, and will develop inappropriate ones himself. For example, we can tell from the strategies evident on a child's running record whether or not his goal is to make sense. Uncorrected nonsense is a bad omen. But the situation has an impact both on the goals and on the means of achieving those goals. For example, a competitive context can change the goal of writing; but even if a sensible goal is left intact, the means of achieving it may no longer involve peer assistance. If my goal is to remember what was said by a speaker, I am likely to take notes. If I do not have paper and pencil, I might use a rehearsal strategy instead. I can do the same if I wish to remember what an author said in a book; however, I also have the option of highlighting or underlining. If my intention is to subsequently use scintillating quotes, my notes will be different than if my intention is to be able to talk sensibly about the gist.

    Observing a student's reading or writing will generally provide good information on strategy use; however, if we don't know why the child used the strategy, we can misconstrue its appropriateness. For example, asking a child how he managed to figure out a word, or how he knew to spell it that way, will often yield good information on spelling strategies.[57] When these descriptions are shared with others, either by telling them or by posting them on the wall, then others add those strategies to the ones they will consider using in the future. Thus evaluation feeds back into learning. Simply asking students how they did something will provide a great deal of information for both teacher and students; but featuring this kind of question encourages children to become conscious of their strategies, to know that they are valued, and hence to become strategic, which is much better than having strategies. We can find out whether other options were available by asking, "How else could you have done that?" which also encourages flexibility in the use of strategies.

PROBLEMS WITH STRATEGIES

Availability

Obviously, not having the relevant strategies available can be a serious problem. Unless we watch people work, we are often unaware of strategies they do and do not have. And some strategies are not immediately obvious. For example, it helps to know that it is easier to compose a mystery story backwards, starting with the solution and the motive, rather than forward. Other strategies seem so obvious that we do not think to check for them. This will sound bizarre, but it was only when my master's degree thesis was being typed for me (I could not type at that time) that I learned about cutting and pasting. Mina Crooks was typing part of it for me and was surprised that it had not been cut up. This is a strategy which someone might have noticed that I lacked in elementary school. It would have saved me some pain and possibly changed my undergraduate grades. But no one noticed. I don't think anyone saw me writing. Now, of course, cutting and pasting for me involves electricity and magnetism rather than scissors and tape. The problem I have now is that I often cut and paste when I should just cut, which leads us to a second problem of strategies.

Knowing When and Where to Use Strategies

Strategies all have their prices. Going to a dictionary is time-consuming; so usually is going to an adult. There are also trade-offs in independence and ownership. How children make these trade-offs tells a lot about their idea of what it is they are engaged in.

For example, "skip it and go on" is one way to manage a difficult word when reading, but not necessarily the most efficient or most effective. It takes little time but risks loss of meaning. It may not be appropriate when reading a manual of instructions for putting together some complex piece of machinery. One adult with whom I worked, would avoid using a "sound-it-out" strategy (even though it was available to him) in favor of "skip it and go on" and reread. The problem lay in the trade-off. In order to maintain meaning, he would end up reading increasingly larger chunks of text. This took longer than if he had used his "sound it out" strategy, which he avoided because he found it difficult and slow. Of course in avoiding it, he ensured that it would continue to be difficult and slow.

Sometimes strategies are simply overused. For example, self-correction is an excellent strategy. However, if a reader corrects every single mispronunciation, then the strategy is dysfunctional. Planning, too, can be a very helpful strategy. The best writers often spend time planning, and planning certainly helps when doing research. But planning is not always helpful. For example, planning is not always what you want to do when you read or write. As Ann Berthoff points out:

> If you commit yourself to one scheme, one definite plan, then anything unexpected can only cause trouble. "Staying on the track" becomes a virtue in itself, despite the fact that that track might be leading into a swamp of the self-evident.[58]

The same is true for teaching. Having labored over plans, we are often loath to part with them when the children's responses suggest that we should. It may be worth distinguishing between planning and preparation as strategies. Planning is for reducing possibilities, whereas preparation is in order to manage diverse possibilities.

Determining the Nature of the Problem to Be Solved

If the text appears to state "The edible part of the banana is usually blue," you are likely to balk at that if you have been attending to the text and your knowledge at all. What we decide is the source of the discrepancy and what we do when we discover such a discrepancy are very important. I could, for example, attribute the discrepancy to any of the following:

inaccuracies in the author's knowledge
inaccuracies in my knowledge base
inadequate copyediting
my stupidity
my lack of effort in my reading
my failure to use appropriate strategies
author's attempt at humor

Having decided on the source of the mismatch, I would then be inclined to decide what to do about it. For example, I might decide that it was not important and continue reading the piece. I might decide that I had missed something, some piece of context perhaps, and go back and reread a section of the text. I might decide that since the author now had little credibility because of this gross error, I would just skim the rest of the book and not take it seriously. I might decide that this was simply another example of my stupidity and I should expect such conflicts to occur because almost everything is more likely to be right than I am. We discussed children's development of these attributions and criteria for self-evaluation in Chapters 5 and 6. Accurate analysis of the problem facilitates productive choice of action.

These same factors influence the methods teachers use to solve problems. Sometimes a student does not appear to be developing as a reader or writer as quickly as we might like. We set out to figure out what the problem is, and at some point we start making decisions about what is *causing* the problem. These are critical decisions as they speak directly to the kind of instructional strategy that appears appropriate. The most dedicated teacher having done his best, with all the other children developing just fine, is likely to find that the odd student out probably has some sort of learning problem. The other popular culprit is some aspect of home background, be it familial or cultural. The higher the accountability pressure, the more likely it is that the problem to be solved will be seen this way, and the less common it will be for a teacher to locate the problem in his instruction, or for an administrator to locate the problem in the organization of the school. The goal will change from problem solving to help the student, to self-defense. Parents, on the other hand, are just as likely to see the school as the problem as they are to see the student as the problem. They are less inclined to see the home setting as the problem.

There are many ways in which students can be seen as the source of the problem. They can be seen as "not very bright," learning disabled, unready, lazy, dyslexic, unmotivated, and a host of other terms. Some of these presumed causes, like *dyslexia,* carry a connotation of permanence and of being not under the student's control. Thus they invoke feelings of pity. Others, like laziness, have a tone of permanence but also a connotation of control. Thus they invoke feelings of anger or annoyance. Each of these sets of attributions invokes different instructional strategies. The causal assumptions we make have serious consequences. For the children's sake it is very important that teachers keep an open mind on the matter, and that schools are organized so that teachers can afford to seek the problem in their own practice.

The Conditions of Strategy Use

The context in which a strategy occurs or does not occur is very important. Self-corrections in reading, for example, will often not occur when the text is too difficult. This is also true in our thinking about writing. For example, we might decide that developing the ability to revise is an important step forward. We might even include it on a checklist or on a report card list of items to grade. However, a child's decision to revise depends on a number of conditions. A child is likely to revise only if the effort involved in revision is balanced by the rewards of the outcome, the social context encourages personal response to drafts, or the writer has a personal commitment to the piece she is writing. Consider students' willingness to revise in the context of how much writing they do. If there is relatively little writing produced, the writer is unlikely to decide to cut anything out of it. In fact, if he does, there is a decent chance that he will end up with writer's block from trying to get everything exactly as he wants it from the start. On the other hand, in order to want to add information, a writer must have more to say, and feel that others will think it worth hearing. Time is also a significant factor in revision; and if the time allowed for writing is limited, revision is likely to be scarce. Thus, when a child does not revise, it is not simply a comment on the child's development, but also on the goal and the context of that development.

This is why as teachers we must think through our own views of the goals of particular literate activities. Because of our own schooling, we often think of revising as fixing up something we have written. But "revising" means "seeing again," not "fixing the bad bits." In other words, the goal of fixing up is not the same goal as revising, and they are likely to produce different strategies. We can revise our reading and our teaching just as much as we can revise our writing. We can revise our evaluation of particular students too. Seeing again from another perspective can help us find things that we did not see the first time. We learn through experiencing the responses of numerous different audiences to predict how they will hear something, and what kind of response they will have. Even editing is, in many ways, like this. You have to be able to read as if you were someone else, perhaps a newscast reader, in order to imagine what your piece might sound like to a person whose language is prototypical of the culture of power.

Not All Strategies Are Productive

As another example of problematic strategies, I make a distinction between coping strategies and literate strategies. Literate strategies help you solve the reading or writing problem you have encountered, the kind of strategies we have just reviewed. Coping strategies, on the other hand, help you manage the situation you are in, given the difficulties you have encountered with literate activity. As an example of a coping problem, an adult student of mine made an inappropriate strategy choice when he was quite young. As a young student, he found that he was not doing as well as his peers in reading. His analysis of the problem was that he was retarded and thus had little hope of being successful. Thus the strategy he chose was to avoid print. This did indeed relieve his frustration initially, but over the long run it also ensured that he would not learn to read. Having chosen this strategy on many occasions, very soon it became automatic. Not only would he physically try not to be caught in a situation in which he might be expected to read print, but when print was about he averted his attention. Once this strategy was automatic, all of this was done essentially without his having to consciously make a choice. It was also quite difficult to stop.

Eliminating these automatic unhelpful strategies often involves raising them to the level of consciousness and then consciously overriding them. For example, in my adolescence I taught myself to play the guitar from books with the little black dots on the lines showing where to put my fingers. In the process, I learned some strange fingerings for certain chords. After playing in a band for a couple of years, I quit, sold my guitar, and did not play for over fourteen years. When I once again picked up the guitar I began to learn a different fingering for one chord in particular, but I had difficulty getting rid of the one I had learned so long ago. Several things helped me to get rid of it. One was by consciously, and clumsily, overruling the old pattern and placing my fingers in the new pattern. However, if I played with an audience of any sort (such as my children), I found that I slipped right back to the old automatic routine. When I began to take lessons, I was taught many different ways to play the same chord. The flexibility I gained eliminated the problem of the automatic and incorrect fingering. I have seen an analogous pattern in children's reading.

A CAUTIONARY TALE

Most of the research over the past few years has stressed the strategic nature of literate activity and the importance of strategies. This technical view has its advantages, but I would like to end this chapter with a cautionary tale. Although most people do not know this, those who know me well know that I am disabled. I am swimming disabled. If you are a swimmer, you probably think this is silly, but I come from a country where it is hard to be more than a few miles from water. I managed perfectly well to conceal my shameful disability by staying well clear of water or forgetting my swimming trunks and the like. But when I came to the States and met my wife, Tina, who comes from a long line of swimmers (eleven children in the family—all swimmers), things became more difficult. Early in our relationship, at the extremely ego-involving stage, a family picnic brought us to the shores of a lake. The family immediately swam to the other side to play. Fortunately, an inner tube allowed me to paddle across while casually appearing to sunbathe. Unfortunately, Tina's youngest sister brought the tube back.

Fortified by the fact that I had learned to teach swimming at teachers' college and indeed had taught a good number of children to swim, I decided to swim back. About halfway across the lake I realized that I was going to drown. My first thought was to attract attention by waving and asking for help, but my already established reputation as a joker precluded that strategy. My antics would simply have brought them to the ground with laughter. I decided to swim on my back, which worked fine except that I am right-handed. The youngest in the family swam alongside me and asked "Why are you swimming in circles?" By careful compensation for this tendency I made it to shore completely exhausted—but alive. I had to fess up.

"No problem," they said. "We'll teach you to swim." So after lunch, they got me in the water to teach me to float. They formed a circle around me treading water and gave me instructions and watched me sink. My Sicilian father-in-law explained, ''Feed him more pasta.'' But I was, and still am, a sinker. They misconstrued the problem to be solved. I *know* how to swim. I can swim the length of a pool very well and very fast—but no farther. It is fear that stops me from swimming. I am afraid to let go of my first breath in case I drown. To me the goal of swimming is staying alive in the water. More strategies are not what I need. You might say I have a kind of swimmer's block, like writer's block. What I need is swimmer's compulsion.[59] Many aspects of this metaphor relate rather well to the difficulties that some people develop with reading and writing. Strategies are fine, but not out of the context of affect and goals. The last thing we need is a country full of people who have had all the strategies checked off on their checklist but who never pick up a book.

CHAPTER 24

Putting It Together: The Patterns of Development

In Chapter 18 I described some conceptual issues in the development of what it means to be literate, and how people think this development takes place. In this chapter I shall discuss further issues of development, describing some dimensions of literacy development, and some of the difficulties involved in keeping track of literate activity. First, let me address some of the difficulties and misconceptions involved.

DIFFICULTIES AND MISCONCEPTIONS IN UNDERSTANDING LITERATE ACTIVITY

The Nature of Growth

As I described in Chapter 18, literacy development is not the product of sudden insight or neurological maturation, as has been believed by those who produce ''reading readiness'' tests. Many of the concepts and strategies are learned by children younger than two, and a surprising number of children read and write before entering school.[60] The average two-year-old in the United States can read (make sense of) a McDonald's or Burger King sign from a moving car at 400 paces (600 paces when hungry). But the various pieces of knowledge and patterns of response do not develop in linear, "mastered" sequences. While there are some general developmental trends, they develop in complex integrated ways, somewhat differently for different children. I would say that the major developmental trend *in a literate environment* is understanding the *role* of a literate person (what literate people do), followed by understanding the *function* of literate activity (why they do it), followed by the details of the *form* of printed language. The parallel with the learning of oral language is quite strong.

Neither does literacy develop evenly on some simple linear scale as current assessment procedures, such as reading tests and reading rate, would lead us to expect.[61] These indicators are based on averages across students and samples taken at least a year apart. Individual students do not grow in this steady manner. Nor do they all grow on the same dimension at once. Not even trees do. We should *expect* irregular, nonlinear patterns of literacy development. I do not mean to imply that increases in rate of reading, for example, are not a useful indicator of development, or that extended stability of reading rate might not be a possible sign of lack of progress. Actually, reading rate is easily measured and interesting enough; but out of the context of the kinds of words, familiarity of the material, and kind of reading being done, it is difficult to know what it means. Indeed, William James refers to a study by George Romanes in which he had people

> read a paragraph as fast as they could take it in, and then immediately write down all they could reproduce of its contents. He found astonishing differences in the rapidity, some taking four times as long as others to absorb the paragraph, and the swiftest readers being, as a rule, the best immediate recollectors, too. But not,—and this is my point,—*not* the most *intellectually capable subjects,* as tested by the results of what Mr. Romanes rightly names "genuine" intellectual work; for he tried the experiment with several highly distinguished men in science and literature, and most of them turned out to be slow readers.[62]

It is much more productive if we emphasize the complexity of development rather than reducing it to simplistic scales. Literacy development is not a simple journey along a straight and narrow path. The roads are bumpy and slippery, and the many crossroads are not well marked.

The print conventions, for example, are not mastered in any particular order. Indeed, children will appear to have mastered some and then appear to have "slipped back." Usually these apparent regressions are caused by the child grappling with awareness of another concept or a new aspect of the activity either not encountered before or not attended to before. Marie Clay calls this the "pebble in the pond" effect because the new addition can draw attention from other aspects that are not fully automatic, and can also cause a reorganization of the knowledge developed to date.[63]

In other words, development often comes in bits and pieces. Punctuation marks, for example, can come quite early though not necessarily accurately. For example, Figure 24.1 shows a student who uses periods after each word. The period is, after all, a terminal punctuation mark. A number of other concepts may develop before the period concept is straightened out. Similarly, the *concept* of vowel markers develops before it is regularized as, for example, in the spellings: *caek* (*cake*) and *yere* (*year*) which show development over the earlier versions of *kak* and *yer*. But how shall we describe this development, or what shall we code it as on a checklist? Should we wait until all regularization has taken place? Conventional use of upper- and lower-case letters also commonly develops over a period of time, and is more or less evident depending on the extent to which it is the focus of attention when the child is writing. We

Figure 24.1. A piece of writing in which the author has used periods after every word.

might consider a checklist that has different columns for "appears in first draft" and "appears in editing."

Divided Attention

Another reason why keeping track of development is complex is that the child's attention can be split between many different demands, making for somewhat erratic productions. For example, a child for whom analyzing speech and representing it is still very difficult will tend to make trade-offs between composing and representing when she writes a story. In order to work on representing a word in the most accurate way she can, the child's attention becomes completely taken up with the word or part of the word, so that the composition takes second place. On the other hand, another child, faced with the same dilemma, will opt to focus on the composition, with common deterioration in spelling and certain other conventions. For example, the composition in Figure 24.2 (pages 232–233) entitled *The Mud* was written by my daughter Emily. This book reads:

> Em (Emily) 1990 28, Feb.
> THE MUD
> To Tina and Peter
> It was Sunday and me and my brother and my friend were riding bikes when we went through some grass and we found some mud and I almost lost my boot in it.
> My boot was full with mud. Ew!
> Actually I like it! That oozy mud, so good against the feet. I can't stand without it.
> Then I went back to the mud and a man came along with a big dog. We ran.
> That is the end until I go back again.

The Mud is interesting to me because Emily wrote it, of course, but also because of the following features:

- ☐ It was written in a situation in which the author could have chosen other things to do and in which the noise level and possible distractions were numerous.
- ☐ The words have been chosen based on criteria other than ability to spell them accurately.
- ☐ The words are expressive, and include the use of onomatopoeia (*ooze*).
- ☐ The writing includes a poetic turn of phrase "so good against the feet," which is not normal spoken language.
- ☐ The story has a climax, a temporal sequence, a surprise at the end and in the middle, and has two episodes. It is also set up for a sequel (of which there turned out to be two).
- ☐ The writing has voice.

- ☐ Illustrations are used to support the text rather than the other way around.
- ☐ The organization of the book shows knowledge of title, dedication, authorship, and date.
- ☐ The knowledge of print conventions of right to left across the word, the page, and through the book.
- ☐ In the invented spelling, almost all phonemes are represented, including lax vowels.
- ☐ The invented spelling suggests that the author is aware of the use of *e* as a marker (*amoste, rideing*), though it is used inconsistently, and is overgeneralized.
- ☐ The invented spelling suggests an awareness of some common spelling patterns with double letters (*grass, boot, fownd*).
- ☐ Some words are spelled conventionally rather than phonetically (e.g., *with, was, my, along*).
- ☐ The exclamation mark has been used appropriately, as has the period to abbreviate Feb., and the hyphen has been used almost appropriately in splitting "druthe-r."
- ☐ Spatial orientation of letters is mostly, but not entirely, accurate.
- ☐ Upper- and lowercase letters often are used conventionally.

There is significance in the order of these observations. It is easy for us to get caught up in the print detail of children's accomplishments in writing and forget the reflections of the principal characteristics of individuals who view themselves as writers and readers.

We should not infer from these observations that what is lacking in convention is because of a lack of knowledge or skill. For example, what can we infer about Emily's spelling? To find out, the next day I asked her if she could help me edit her paper. She did not yet know the term "edit," but understood what I meant when I described it. That task, she explained, was the role of the teacher's aide in the class. In a flat voice which pointed to each word, she began reading aloud her story, looking for problems, and she found a couple near the beginning: *wr* (*were*) and *throo* (*through*), which she proceeded to try to correct. However, after that, her reading became more fluent and expressive, and she detected no more errors. Her involvement in the story made her forget about editing again until the end when she repeated *agen* and commented, "Perfect," referring to the spelling. The next morning I asked if she would do some spelling for me and, one at a time, I asked her to spell the words which I had collected from her misspellings in the story. The words and their spellings in her composition and as a spelling list, are shown in Table 24.1.

In the spelling, as opposed to the composition, upper- and lowercase letters were not mixed. Except for the *K*, all were used appropriately. As a further shift in context, the next day I asked her to spell my name and she spelled it *Peter*.

EM ιρρ. 2ı,Fed.

The mud

IT WAS SUN DAY
AND ME AND MY dfUtk
r AND My frind
TO TINO A Nd PITR   wr rideINP diks
wene we weNT
thrpo sum prass
AND we fownd sum
MUD AND I
almoste lost
MY
boot in it.

Figure 24.2. Emily's ''Mud Book''

Figure 24.2. Continued

TABLE 24.1. Spelling under Different Conditions

Correct Spelling	Spelling When Composing	Spelling When Spelling
Peter	Pitr	Peater
brother	druthr	deruther
friend	frind	firend
were	wr	were
riding	rideing	riding
bikes	diks	dikes
when	wene	wene
through	throo	throur
some	sum	some
found	fownd	found
full	ful	foll
actually	aktuleye	ackcholly
liked	like	liked
almost	amoste	almost
against	agenst	agenst
can't	cant	can't
without	withot	withont
back	bak	dack
came	cam	came
that	tat	that
until	intil	antill
again	agen	agen

The trade-offs have to do with the time-consuming and laborious nature of the translation process, the motor movements required, the complex decisions about which words to use, and the constant need to maintain the construction of the story. These also lead to word omissions and the like as children reread only one word back to remind themselves where they are, or do not even spare the time for that. The trade-offs do not stop as we get older. Grown-ups hastily writing a letter will often hesitate to write the word they would like to use because they are unsure of the conventional spelling. Not wishing to appear uneducated, yet not wishing to take time to consult the dictionary or spelling guide, they choose a word or phrase of whose spelling they are confident. Children frequently use this strategy. These trade-offs are a reason why, in order to get a good sample of the student's ability to represent speech in print (*if* you have a particular need to do this), it is often better to use a dictation exercise rather than the student's normal writing in which composition and convention both compete for attention. The trade-off *dilemma* for the children can be reduced by making a very clear split between the responsibilities of editors and the responsibilities of authors. However, many trade-offs remain unavoidable.

These trade-offs are not confined to trade-offs between transcription and composition. For example, in children's fiction the actors are initially there simply to serve the action. Their early character descriptions are like early portraits. They are all face. Just as children's artwork shifts from flat frontal portrayal to profile as it becomes more focused on the action of the characters, so do their characters become more rounded and more fully developed.[64] Sometimes as a child focuses on her characters she will spend less effort composing a plot; sometimes as effort is spent on the plot, the characters suffer somewhat.[65]

Problems with Keeping Track

Often we have to make do with approximate indicators of development. For example, writing is only a rough indicator of the child's visual analysis of words. At times her hands may lack the skill to accomplish what she knows should be there. Reading, too, is only a rough indicator of visual analysis. For example, I asked a third-grade student who was reading books like *Pee Wee Scouts,* but whose conventional spelling was limited, to identify a word I was making out of plastic letters. I had put together only the first three letters of *because* when he identified it. I finished the word and then asked him to study it until he could make the word himself out of the scrambled letters. He immediately said, "No problem." I scrambled the letters and he could not put it back together. We tried again and he studied the word longer before he said he was ready, and he was almost able to put it together. The third time he studied it even longer and was able to put it together. In that brief interchange there began a level of awareness of print detail that he had previously lacked as a guide to his word analysis. Without analyzing that level of detail, his reading was not having much impact on his spelling. Although this is an important aspect of development, we are unlikely to be able to describe it except as it appears through the increasing conventionality of his spelling.

If we make up checklists to keep track of development, we have to remember that some skills are forever developing so that they cannot be checked off on a list. Choosing a topic is an important skill that goes from kindergarten to doctoral level, as do the skills of providing information, writing conventionally, organizing writing, providing focus, writing leads and endings. We can't just say, "Hears the sounds in language" either. Hearing and using the sounds in language goes all the way through to high school, university, and beyond. In the early stages we might be looking for children to hear the phonemes in words in order to represent them in print. Later we are looking for writers' use of them in their choice of exactly the right word to enhance the melody or the power of the language. For example, we hear glimpses of this skill in *The Mud,* when Emily writes, "I had oozy mud, so good against the feet." At what time in our curriculum should we assert that a child should master these skills? Will anyone ever *master* them? And if we cannot put them on a checklist, will they be overlooked?

So Many Dimensions

In the early stages of writing, the illustration commonly determines the writing that goes with it ("This is a plane") and, as Ellen Blackburn observes, when the words take control over the picture, this can be an important sign of development.[66] For example, the illustration might follow from the text rather than the other way around, or the illustration might be revised on the basis of development of the text. At some points in a child's writing development, simply an increase in the *amount* of information in the writing is an advance. At other points, it is how parts of the information are linked, or how details are added for elaboration, or how focus is maintained and detail is controlled to do so. Is development on one of these fronts equivalent to, or more important than, development on another, such as increased experimentation with new forms and language, or increased involvement in reading, or selection of more challenging reading?

I hope you can see that there are so many possible aspects of development to describe that any simple test will provide a limited reflection at best. Furthermore, placing everything on a checklist is going to make for a very complex list, and selecting the most important aspects of development to write on a list will represent a statement of personal values. As I have pointed out elsewhere in this book, the most important point in putting together a checklist is the negotiation among those deciding what should and should not be included to make for a balanced and manageable checklist.

In order to expand on this issue, let me describe some of the many kinds of development we might look for.

ASPECTS OF DEVELOPMENT

Much of the present section of the book has been devoted to describing how literate activity occurs and what development looks like. The following simply highlights, for the sake of order, some of the dimensions on which development takes place.

Quantity, Rate, and Fluency

Sheer quantity of reading and writing is possibly the easiest and most important area to look for development. Amount of time spent reading, or pages read, and time spent writing, or words or pages written are important indicators of how a student is developing in a classroom. A consistent change of five minutes a day of voluntary reading is far from trivial. A young reader reading sixty words per minute would be reading an extra 300 words in those five minutes. Over the course of the school year this is about 60,000 extra words. If the five minutes occur outside of school, it can represent a shift of enormous importance.[67] Apart from anything else, it would not stop for school vacations, adding almost an extra 50,000 words.

As children spend more and more time reading and writing, many routines and common patterns become automatic. When they become automatic, they are faster and they actually go through a different part of the brain and no longer involve conscious effort.[68] Mature word recognition takes about 200 milliseconds, and it gets that way with sheer frequency of use. The whole thing is cyclical. The faster you read, the more times you recognize words. So, if the reader who increased his reading by five minutes a day ends up increasing his rate of reading from sixty words a minute to eighty words a minute, he will read yet another 20,000 words over the course of the school year. This will probably make him an even faster reader. Similarly, the more children write (or type), the faster they get at it.

However, lack of fluency is not always a sign of lack of progress. The fluency which young readers have, based on their memory of the text, often goes away as they devote greater attention to print detail. Conversely, accuracy is often reduced with increased attention to fluency. These trade-offs have to be taken into account whenever we talk about development.

Independence, Involvement, and Persistence

Indicators of quantity are somewhat related to involvement, or resistance to distraction. In Ann Berthoff's terms, this might be termed ''writers' (or readers') compulsion'' (as opposed to writer's block). It can take the form of a writer persisting extensively with a single piece of writing until she gets it right. It can take the form of blocking out all other experience while reading a book. This might be measured by the number of decibels of sudden noise (doorbells, door slams, screams) required to extricate a person from a good book. On two occasions I have encountered children who have been referred for evaluation of their suspected deafness because of this level of involvement. It is also related to what Don Graves calls ''bingeing,'' in which a child, for example, reads everything available by a particular author, or spends a month reading and writing about one particular topic. Persistence is a reflection of a number of things such as commitment to a goal, to literateness, or to the topic. Or perhaps simply to a belief that problems can be solved, and that you can solve them.

Central to independence is the ability to detect and solve your own errors.

At all stages, increased ability to self-correct is an important indication of development, as is the ability to choose materials and activities that are close to the edge of one's learning.

Conceptual and Strategic Knowledge

In the earlier chapters of Part III, I have described many of the concepts and strategies that children develop. I need not repeat the fact that documenting their development is important.

Complexity

Many strategies that children use will start to become more complex in different ways. For example, they begin to use more complex and more numerous cues as the basis for predictions and self-corrections. Their explanations of characters' motives may become more sophisticated, taking into account a greater number of different contingencies. The complexity of the connections that students make with what they read will also develop.

The complexity of compositions develops in numerous ways. For example, of children's fiction we might ask, "How many characters with dimension are there, and do they interact in meaningful ways?" Composing a new character rather than using one directly from a TV series represents development. It represents the composition of smaller parts into a unique construction rather than the reuse of another's construction.

Flexibility and Diversity

Diversity is as important as quantity of reading and writing. If a child reaches fourth grade and has never read any nonfiction, then he will find his lack of experience a considerable disadvantage. If a child has written only personal narratives, then writing letters and research reports will be a problem. If he has written only letters to friends, writing a persuasive letter to the principal may be hard work. We are interested in children's trying out the range of nonfiction genres including essays, letters, satire, directions, travelogue, reportage, editorial, satire, and various types of argument.

However, listing the possible kinds of literature and writing, and requiring all students to do one essay on Tuesday and Wednesday, one letter of request on Thursday and Friday, for example, will defeat the purpose. Students will have attempted a range of genres and have a dislike for writing each. When only children who are interested set out on a particular genre, they can be given support, and their enthusiasm will bring some converts. Their sharing of the process of their efforts will provide help in advance for those yet to try. The other side of this is that there needs to be a way of keeping track of what they are doing; otherwise some students will fall through the cracks and their lack of diversity will not be noticed. Diversity can be documented from writing folders, cumulative folders, portfolios, and processes like Nancie Atwell's "status of the class" report that was described in Chapter 15.

Flexibility comes from having, and exercising, options. For example, when one strategy doesn't work, try another. We might see the ability to adopt a variety of different genres to address the same issue, or the flexibility to shift from one voice to another or one audience to another. Another kind of flexibility might be seen in the ability to make a variety of different kinds of connections with particular books, or to apply different metaphors to books.

Expectation, Recognition, and Memory

Prediction is central to literate, indeed intelligent, activity and it should become evident in a variety of ways and at a variety of levels. For example, the child can anticipate with increasing accuracy the kinds of things that will happen next in a story, or the kinds of feelings that a character might have, and will be able to fill in words omitted in sentences (or words anticipated as likely to come next). Patterned language in many early texts will begin to be anticipated too. This is the early form of attention to language structure that is evident in mature readers. Children will also develop in their ability to recognize violations of these expectations, sometimes being amused by them, and in their ability to savor surprise more than the predictability that younger children tend to favor.

Knowledge of stories begins to be built up. Initially children ask to have the same story over and over until they have considerable control over the expectation of what will happen next. As more and more stories are introduced, fewer repetitions become necessary (except with long, complicated texts) and the knowledge of story structures begins to generalize and become more flexible. Memory for stories and the components of stories will increase as the children build up a general schema for that genre of text. Memory for stories will be evident in story retellings too. This increased memory is a reflection of pattern recognition and the expectation of meaning from reading. It develops with lots of experience of successful understanding of stories to the point where no less is expected. This expectation is what allows self-correction. The increased memory is what carries the child over the decreased fluency which comes with increased attention to print detail as word-by-word reading develops and new words are analyzed in greater detail.

The predictability of how stories work will include increased ability to tell and retell culturally appropriate stories. Awareness of various genres of text such as lists, instructions, letters, cards, signs, invitations, and advertisements may be shown in the children's writing. It surfaces too in their pretend reading in role-play situations such as the situational use of "book language" and different context-appropriate structures like starting pretend letters with "dear . . ." and ending "love from. . . ."

Awareness and Reflection

More able readers tend to be more able to talk about how they do things and why they do them that way—the consequence of their learning how to do things and then reflecting on what they are doing. Thus, children's increasing awareness of the whys and wherefores of their literate activity is generally a sign of development. One of the principal causes of this development is their development of prediction or expectation. It is when expectation is violated, and they are surprised, that learners become newly aware of what they are doing, and contemplate the differences that produced the surprise.

It is also a healthy sign of the classroom environment in that somewhere in the class reflection is being encouraged, possibly along with an interest in the language as an object of study. Consequently, a good sign of healthy development of literacy and a healthy literate environment is children's language play. For example, when children make up rhymes, particularly nonsensical ones, they are demonstrating the use of the language as an end in itself. In order to do this, they must separate the language from its contextual supports and not use it as a means to an end but as an object of study. When we use language simply as a means to an end, we do not attend to the details of the language. As Daniil Elkonin pointed out, it is rather like the window that we look through to see the world.[69] When we stop and look at the window itself (language), we have a way of studying the language as an end in itself. When we see children doing such things then, we should understand that it is an important sign, and that, since it is voluntary, it also reflects the child's interest in the language. When children laugh at the nonsense that they create, it suggests that they understand the conflict inherent in the use of a sense-making tool to produce nonsense.

Language Use and Imagination

Several aspects of oral language development are closely linked to becoming literate. First, there is the growth in vocabulary, much of which comes from books. When we hear a child using words or phrases out of a story that are not common in everyday dialogue, such as "unhand her, you varlet" or "as I live and breathe, you are insufferable" or "your words show true generosity," we are seeing an important side of literacy development. The ability to imagine the language a particular character might use is very important both to the composition of believable stories and to the ability to address a variety of audiences.

Imaginative storytelling and role-playing are important signs of the development of the ability to create alternative realities, separate from the here and now, that is central to both reading and writing. In this type of activity children develop and exhibit their ability to identify with various characters, and their awareness of behavioral evidence of affect and motive. However, imagination is not only related to narrative. It is imagination that allows us to propose and test hypotheses in our heads, to imagine the consequences of particular actions.

TAKING STOCK

The simple fact that keeping track of development can be messy and involves many consequential decisions, should not stop us from doing so. We must, and we must avoid the temptation to reduce it to a simple number here and there. Regular recordkeeping and productive classroom procedures are important. However, it is also important to set aside times and means for taking stock. For example, Marie Clay suggests that after a year in school, children should be quite thoroughly evaluated in terms of their reading and writing so that children developing difficulties might be helped before they develop a history of failure. To accomplish this, she provides a Diagnostic Survey, which is a set of individual evaluation procedures including running records, dictation, letter identification, writing vocabulary, word recognition, and the *Concepts About Print Test*. While it does not pretend to cover all areas, such as children's concepts about literacy, this Diagnostic Survey presents a detailed description of an individual's conceptual and strategic development in literacy learning.[70]

Report cards (or reporting time) and individual conference times with students provide such opportunities for stocktaking too, and we should be certain to build them into our school and classroom planning. Two children considered in detail each day is a useful practice. Similarly, we must set aside times to take stock of our own teaching practice.

Notes and References for Part III

1. Nancie Atwell (1987). *In the middle: Writing, reading, and learning with adolescents.* Portsmouth, NH: Heinemann-Boynton/Cook.
    Go directly to this book and study it at length. For this particular aspect see pages 270–272.

2. These are not all from her survey, and she has many more than I have noted here.

3. Elizabeth Bondy (1985, April). Children's definitions of reading: Products of an interactive process. Paper presented at the annual meeting of the American Educational Research Association, Chicago, IL.

4. Rhoda Spiro and Peter Johnston (1989). Children's choices of, and placement in, books. Paper presented at the annual meeting of the National Reading Conference, Austin, TX.

5. Thomas Newkirk (1986). Young writers as critical readers. In Thomas Newkirk and Nancie Atwell (Eds.), *Understanding writing: Ways of observing, learning and teaching K-8.* Portsmouth, NH: Heinemann, pp. 106–113. (p. 113)

6. This example was contributed by Ellen Adams.

7. Donald Graves (1987) describes this in his book *Experiment with fiction* in the series *The reading/writing teacher's companion.* Portsmouth, NH: Heinemann/Boynton-Cook.

8. To learn more about this perspective, read:

David Bartholomae and Anthony Petrosky (Eds.), Facts, artifacts and counterfacts: Theory and method for a reading and writing course. Upper Montclair, NJ: Boynton/Cook, 1986, p. 24.

9. Dennis P. Wolf and Martha Perry (1988). Becoming literate: Beyond scribes and clerks. *Theory Into Practice 27*(1): 44–52. (p. 49)

10. See note 9 above.

11. Mabel Morphett and Carleton Washburne (1931). When should children begin to read? *Elementary School Journal 31*: 496–503.

12. This historical argument was presented by Dolores Durkin (1978), *Teaching them to read*. 3rd ed. Boston, MA: Allyn and Bacon.
It has also been presented by:
William Teale and Elizabeth Sulzby (1986). (Eds.), *Emergent literacy: Writing and reading*. Norwood, NJ: Ablex.

13. Penelope Peterson and Michelle Comeaux (1987). Teachers' schemata for classroom events: The mental scaffolding of teachers' thinking during classroom instruction. *Teaching and Teacher Education 3*(4): 319–332.
These writers found that expert teachers recognized and remembered substantially more episodes from a videotape of classroom activity than did novice teachers.

14. Alexander Luria (1970). The functional organization of the brain. *Scientific American 222*(3): 66–79.

15. Indeed, some more proficient readers' word recognition is actually *slower* when the word is in context. See Tom Nicholson, Christine Lillas, and M. Anne Rzoska (1988). Have we been misled by miscues? *The Reading Teacher 42*(1): 6–10.

16. Georgia Green (1981). Competence for implicit text analysis: Literary style discrimination in five-year-olds. In Deborah Tannen (Ed.), *Analyzing discourse: Text and talk*. Washington: Georgetown University Press.

17. Connie Juel (1988). Learning to read and write: A longitudinal study of 54 children from first through fourth grades. *Journal of Educational Psychology 80*: 437–447.

18. Linda Fielding (1988). The role of discussion questions in children's story composition. Unpublished doctoral dissertation, University of Illinois at Champaign-Urbana.
Actually, teaching children to predict is something of a misnomer. Children predict very well in most aspects of their lives. They probably would not learn language unless they were quite good at it. It is more a matter of helping children realize that prediction is also appropriate in reading, or preventing them from developing the idea that it is not.

19. Sylvia Ashton Warner (1963). *Teacher*. New York: Simon & Schuster.

20. Thus, as Donald Schon puts it, the reflective practitioner's "ability to construct and manipulate virtual worlds is a crucial component of his ability not only to perform artistically but to experiment rigorously." (p. 157)
Donald Schon (1983). *The reflective practitioner: How professionals think in action*. New York: Basic Books.

21. The following books are a sample of useful ones to read on this matter:
Donald Graves (1983). *Writing: Teachers and children at work*. Portsmouth, NH: Heinemann.
Lucy Calkins (1986). *The art of teaching writing*. Portsmouth, NH: Heinemann.
Lucy Calkins (1983). *Lessons from a child*. Portsmouth, NH: Heinemann.
Tom Romano (1987). *Clearing the way: Working with teenage writers*. Portsmouth, NH: Heinemann-Boynton/Cook.
Thomas Newkirk and Nancie Atwell (1988) (Eds), *Understanding writing: Ways of observing, learning, and teaching*. 2nd ed. Portsmouth, NH: Heinemann-Boynton/Cook.

Donald Murray (1990). *Shoptalk: Learning to write with writers.* Portsmouth, NH: Heinemann-Boynton/Cook.

22. This is a useful exercise to try with a group of your colleagues. You will not get perfect agreement, but you will have an interesting and informative discussion, and new grounds for observation.

23. A very fine way to learn about these things is:
Ken Macrorie (1980). *Telling writing.* Rochelle Park, NJ: Hayden Book Company. Nancie Atwell's book *In the middle* is another good resource.
Another very good way to learn is, when you have read a book, to sit down with it and another book, and compare the way the two authors wrote. Better yet, take three books by different authors (or three by the same author) and see how many different ways you can classify the three books into two categories. If you can do this with a friend, or a group of friends on a regular basis, so much the better. This is the kind of thing to see in the classroom.

24. Note 1. Nida, 1954, p. 223. Cited in:
Naomi S. Baron (1981). *Speech, writing, and sign: A functional view of linguistic representation.* Bloomington, IN: Indiana University Press.

25. *Nasty* is, of course, now passé, as would be any example I used by the time the book came to print, although this use of *nasty* began in the 1930s.

26. Mary Belenky, Blythe Clinchy, Nancy Goldberger, and Jill Tarule (1986). *Women's ways of knowing: The development of self, voice, and mind.* New York: Basic Books.

27. Gordon Bower (1978). Experiments on story comprehension and recall. *Discourse Processes 1*: 211–231.
Norman Holland (1976). *Five readers reading.* New Haven, CT: Yale University Press.

28. Lev Vygotsky's research on children's inner speech shows this appreciation of audience in very young children. As they talk to themselves, their speech becomes very abbreviated to accommodate the fact that both speaker and listener (in both cases themselves) share an enormous body of information.

29. This list is largely adapted from Bonnie Meyer's work and that of Walter Kintsch and Teun van Dijk. For example, see:
Walter Kintsch and G. Elizabeth Yarbrough (1982). Role of rhetorical structure in text comprehension. *Journal of Educational Psychology 74*: 828–834.
Bonnie Meyer and G. Rice. (1984). The structure of text. In P.D. Pearson, R. Barr, M. L. Kamil, and P. Mosenthal (Eds.), *Handbook of Reading Research,* Vol. 1. White Plains, N.Y.: Longman.

30. Thomas Newkirk (1989). *More than stories: The range of children's writing.* Portsmouth, NH: Heinemann, p. 86.

31. Jerome Bruner (1986). *Actual minds, possible worlds.* Cambridge, MA: Harvard University Press.

32. Anne DiPardo (1990). Narrative knowers, expository knowledge: Discourse as a dialectic. *Written Communication 7*: 59–95.

33. "Heavies square up for knock-out $38m." This headline was in the center of the front page of *The Australian* newspaper, June 28th, 1988, no. 7417. The article was assembled from material provided by staff writers in Atlantic City.

34. Newkirk. *More than stories,* p. 86.

35. All names have been changed to protect even those not so innocent—but only the names.

36. Parents are not always terrified by such reports. For some it is very satisfying as, for example, if they felt it would be socially helpful to have a medical explanation

for their daughter's lack of success in so intellectual a task as reading. We have encountered this on many occasions.

37. Although I take this from Tom Newkirk, he attributes it to:
Susan Sowers (1985). The story and the all-about book. In Jane Hansen, Thomas Newkirk, and Donald Graves (Eds.), *Breaking ground: Teachers relate reading and writing in the elementary school.* Portsmouth, NH: Heinemann.

38. Marie Clay (1975). *What did I write?* Portsmouth, NH: Heinemann-Boynton/Cook.

39. The *Concepts About Print Test* is described in detail in:
Marie Clay (1985). *The early detection of reading difficulties.* 3rd ed. Portsmouth, NH: Heinemann-Boynton/Cook.
The test is part of a detailed *Diagnostic Survey* which is used to select the group of children who are having the most difficulty as they begin their second year of school, to provide intensive one-to-one instruction (The Reading Recovery Program).

40. For example, the norm-referencing of this test is used as part of the selection process in the Reading Recovery program so that the lowest group of students receive the available support.

41. Margaret Mahy (1975). *The boy who was followed home.* Illus. Steven Kellogg. New York: Dial Books.

42. Jack Kent (1971). *The fat cat: A Danish folktale.* Harmondsworth, Eng.: Picture Puffins.

43. This is the procedure used in the *Concepts About Print* test.

44. I do not find the use of the terms *long vowel* and *short vowel* very helpful. Indeed, they are often confusing since the child's normal concept of long and short does not help, even though teachers often refer to it. The /a/ in *cat* can be just as long (temporally) as the /a/ in *hate*.

45. To read more about this, I suggest:
Marie Clay (1972). *Reading: The patterning of complex behavior.* Portsmouth, NH: Heinemann-Boynton/Cook.

46. Darrel Morris has written about this technique in:
Darrel Morris (1980). Beginning readers' concept of word. In Edmund Henderson and James Beers (Eds.), *Developmental and cognitive aspects of learning to spell: A reflection of word knowledge.* Newark, DE: International Reading Association.

47. See Clay's book *The Early Detection of Reading Difficulties.*

48. An example of this is reported in:
Peter Johnston (1985). Understanding Reading Disability, *Harvard Educational Review 55:* 153–177.

49. Jose Morais, Luz Cary, Jesus Alegria, and Paul Burdelson (1979). *Cognition 7:* 323–331. Does awareness of speech as a sequence of phonemes arise spontaneously?

50. The boxes have an instructional advantage for conveying the concept that a sound can be represented by more than one letter.

51. Some people call "tense" vowels "long" vowels, which is a bit misleading because the "short" vowel in *hat* can be just as long as the "long" vowel in *hate*.

52. Some great books that get children involved in this sort of play are:
Jan Slepian and Ann Seidler (1967) *The hungry thing.* New York: Scholastic.
Jan Slepian and Ann Seidler (1967) *The cat who wore a pot on her head.* New York: Scholastic.
Also useful are songs like "Apples and Bananas," a good source for which is

Nancy and John Cassidy (1986). *The book of kids' songs: A holler-along handbook.* Palo Alto, CA: Klutz Press.

53. However, this is not to suggest that it is simple. For example, the sounds of the phoneme /t/ in three different words *sat, stand,* and *top,* are quite different from one another, which can readily be seen in a spectral analysis of speech. To get at the invariant aspects of those sounds requires complex analysis and synthesis.

54. Evaluation based on this knowledge would show the absurdity of basing initial reading instruction on all "short" (or lax) vowel sounds as in the "Dan can fan the man" type of book. Such reading programs based on "phonics first" take the part of the spoken language that is hardest for children to distinguish—the lax vowels—and attempt to teach them first on the grounds that the written words look simpler. But the *representation* of those words is harder. The tense vowels which are easier to distinguish are taught later in these programs.

55. Clay. *The early detection of reading difficulties.*

56. Margaret Mahy (1985). *The man whose mother was a pirate.* Illus. Margaret Chamberlain. New York: Viking Kestrel.
    Margaret Mahy is one of the most distinguished and versatile authors of books for children and young adults.

57. Asking, "How did you decide to spell it that way?" is quite different from "Why did you spell it that way?" More good spelling strategy questions can be found in Sandra Wilde's chapter in:
    Kenneth Goodman, Yetta Goodman, and Wendy Hood (Eds.) (1988). *The whole language evaluation book.* Portsmouth, NH: Heinemann, p. 229.
    If you have forgotten about asking questions like this, you might review Chapters 12 and 13.

58. Ann Berthoff (1978). *Forming thinking writing: The composing imagination.* Rochelle Park, NJ: Hayden Book Co. (p. 65)

59. See note 58 above.

60. Studies of the early development of reading include:
    Dolores Durkin (1978). *Teaching them to read.* 3rd ed. Boston, MA: Allyn and Bacon.
    Margaret Clark (1976). *Young fluent readers: What can they teach us?* London: Heinemann.
    Arthur Gates (1937). The necessary mental age for beginning reading. *The Elementary School Journal 37*: 497–508.

61. Ron Carver. (1989). Silent reading rates in grade equivalents. *Journal of Reading Behavior 21*(2): 155–166.
    As a brief aside, reading rate is probably highly correlated with sheer number of words read; thus it may be just as useful to keep track of words read as of reading rate. Since these words appear in books, the additional exposure to diverse vocabulary and concepts would mean that reading rate would only be a small part of the actual development taking place.

62. William James (1899). *Talks to teachers on psychology.* New York: Henry Holt and Co., p. 136.

63. Marie Clay (1979). *Reading: The patterning of complex behavior.* Portsmouth, NH: Heinemann-Boynton/Cook.

64. I believe Tom Newkirk drew this to my attention.

65. Jane Hansen (1988). I wonder what kind of person he'll be. Paper presented at the annual meeting of the National Reading Conference, Tucson, AZ.

66. Ellen Blackburn (1988). The rhythm of writing development. In Tom Newkirk and

Nancie Atwell (Eds.), *Understanding Writing: Ways of observing, learning and teaching.* Portsmouth, NH: Heinemann-Boynton/Cook.

67. Richard Anderson, Paul Wilson, and Linda Fielding (1988). Growth in reading and how children spend their time outside of school. *Reading Research Quarterly 23*: 285–303.
    Fewer than 70 percent of fifth graders read books for more than ten minutes a day outside of school. As Keith Stanovich points out, based on Anderson, Wilson, and Fielding's data, the child who is at the 80th percentile in amount of book reading reads twenty times as much as the child reading at the 20th percentile.
    Keith Stanovich (in press). Are we overselling literacy? In Charles Temple and Patrick Collins (Eds.), Stories and readers: New perspectives in literature in the elementary classroom. Norwood, MA: Christopher Gordon Publishers.

68. Alexander Luria (1970). The functional organization of the brain. *Scientific American 222*(3): 66–79.

69. Daniil Elkonin (1971). Development of Speech. In A.V. Zaporozhets and D.B. Elkonin (Eds.), *The Psychology of Preschool Children.* Translated by J. Schybut and S. Simon. Cambridge, MA: MIT Press.

70. Clay. *The early detection of reading difficulties.*

PART IV

WHAT WE VALUE IN EVALUATION

This section of the book really focuses on issues of interpretation and their consequences. I begin by addressing the conflicts between beliefs about objectivity and the interpretive and personal nature of evaluation and instruction. I try to convince you that traditional beliefs about objectivity are not only untenable, but counterproductive. Fairness and bias, two closely related domains, are dealt with in the second chapter. Then, in Chapters 27 and 28, I describe the various frameworks through which we can make sense of the data we gather. Some of these frameworks are more constructive than others. For example, I make it clear that I find little use for normative interpretations, favoring instead interpretations that place present performance in the context of past performance.

Traditionally, the field of measurement has attempted to produce generalized, context-free statements of how much ability a student has. I argue that more specific, contextualized statements about exactly what a student did under which conditions tend to be the most instructionally useful. This tension between the need to generalize and to specify is taken up in Chapter 29. Readers who have read "educational measurement" textbooks and who are puzzled by the absence of a chapter on "reliability" will find much of that discussion in this chapter. Chapters 30 to 33 all address specific aspects of validity, although readers who have been schooled in educational measurement will notice that many traditional validity issues appear in chapters throughout this section of the book. For example, the issues of objectivity and fairness and bias are not commonly given their own chapters, but are dealt with under the heading of validity. I finish the section with two chapters on the writing of reports about literate activity.

CHAPTER 25

Autonomy and Objectivity: Some Differences between Rocks and People and Men and Women

> . . . the language of education, if it is to be an invitation to reflection and culture creating, cannot be the so-called uncontaminated language of fact and "objectivity." It must express stance and must invite counter-stance and in the process leave place for reflection
>
> Jerome Bruner

The public has always been a bit skeptical of psychologists and educators. They had certainly not considered the study of human behavior to be a science until psychologists devised "objective" tests. Objective tests were devised to be scored by a machine and thus mimicked the measuring devices of the "hard" sciences like physics and chemistry. An extensive industry has been based on these tests and their assumed objectivity. Teacher judgment, on the other hand, is generally regarded as being *subjective*. Subjective judgments are believed to be unscientific, found more in the "soft" sciences than in the "hard" sciences, and more characteristic of women than of men. The gender issue is not trivial, particularly since the vast majority of elementary school teachers in this country are women. I shall return to gender issues later in the book.

But first, what does the term objective mean? According to my Webster's, objective means:

> 1. existing as an object or fact, independent of the mind; real 2. concerned with the realities of the thing dealt with rather than the thoughts of the artist, writer etc. 3. without bias or prejudice.[1]

In other words, the argument being made by those involved with "objective measurement" is that the tests which they construct produce facts, untouched by human minds.[2] Tests are assumed to be products of, and tools for use in, "the scientific method" which has been reified in Western societies, and particularly in educational measurement. Psychometricians wear white coats.

INTERPRETATION, LANGUAGE, AND THE MYTH OF OBJECTIVITY

We in education and other social sciences, have been a little slow to see the inadequacy of the objectivity premise. We borrowed the idea from the physical sciences, and it would be nice if we could give it back, but I doubt if they would want it. Quantum physicists realized some time ago that their "hard" science lacked objectivity. In 1958 Werner Heisenberg noted that the object of observation and the act of observing it are inseparable. The measuring instrument has been constructed by the observer, and the particles to be seen must be seen through photons, the units of energy that constitute light. Heisenberg commented that

> in science we are not dealing with nature itself but with the science of nature—that is, with nature which has been thought through and described by man. . . . Modern physics, in the final analysis, has already discredited the concept of the truly real.[3]

In other words, what we already think we know, and how we talk about it, constrain the kinds of questions we ask about the world, and the kinds of data we attempt to gather. Even when we collect data we do it with instruments or procedures that we have constructed from what we already understand, and then we describe what we see with the language we have available.[4]

Despite this recognition that the observer and observed are inseparable, we still have a large number of educators and social scientists who refer to "objective tests" of children's reading and writing as if the tests were not composed by human beings with particular ways of viewing reading and writing, and as if any data produced by these instruments did not have to be interpreted by people with different ways of viewing reading and writing. We cannot "see" mental activity, or even children's overt behavior, without interpreting it. There is no way to avoid this state of affairs, and we may as well drop any pretense that it is possible lest we delude ourselves into thinking it true. Every act of perception is an act of interpretation. If you doubt this, consider the following two sentences:[5]

Jack and Jill went up the hill.
The high jump was the next event.

Even though the words *went* and *event* are written identically, you read them as quite different without any confusion or hesitation. You imposed meaning on them just as you do on everything else. We look with our eyes, but we *choose* what to look at, and we *see* with our minds.

There is no way to avoid the fact that no matter how we go about evaluation, it involves interpretation. Human symbol systems are involved, and thus there is no "objective" measurement. Tests are constructed by people with their particular frame of reality, responded to by people within their different view of reality, and responses are analyzed by people within their version of reality which is different again. Computer analysis does not avoid this. People write computer analytic programs based on various human cultural assumptions; and whatever score the machine produces, it must be interpreted, or made sense of, before it can be used. We are stuck with the fact of interpretation, so we had better get used to it and make the most of it. Furthermore, unlike measurement and description in the physical sciences, when we are assessing literacy, we are engaged in examining something which is personal and cultural in nature, using tools similarly of cultural origin. In doing so we engage in a social interaction with the individual being evaluated, and thus influence in powerful ways the nature of the understanding constructed.

Evaluation of literacy development is thus in some ways fundamentally "subjective." The Russian linguist and literary critic Mikhail Bakhtin noted that

> The exact sciences are a monological form of knowledge: the intellect contemplates a thing and speaks of it. Here, there is only one subject, the subject that knows (contemplates) and speaks (utters). In front of him there is only a voiceless thing. But the subject as such cannot be perceived or studied as if it were a thing, since it cannot remain a subject if it is voiceless; consequently, there is no knowledge of the subject but dialogical.[6]

To make matters even less objective, in that sense, the performance of the subject about which we wish to make a statement involves his interaction with a text. The text, of course, was written by another subject in a particular time and context and had particular symbolic meaning that cannot be known to us. Furthermore, these interactions take place in social contexts that are different from one another. In other words, evaluating someone's "comprehension" involves a social interaction between two subjects, one of whom is interpreting the interpretive interaction between the other subject and a text produced by yet another subject within a quite different social and historical context. Objective? Hardly. Hard science? You bet it's hard—very difficult indeed.

REJECTING THE SUBJECTIVE/OBJECTIVE DICHOTOMY

I do not want you to think that the alternative to "objective" is "mushy" or "limp," or that assessment of literacy development is unscientific or unsystematic. Rather, I want to suggest that the subjective/objective distinction may not be as simple an evaluative criterion as we think. Rather than seeking to make evaluations objective, we must seek ways to make observations by a single, personally involved individual as clear, insightful, and fair as possible. Some of the confusion about objectivity and subjectivity might be reduced if we make some additional distinctions. Let us call the belief that we can understand children (or anything else) better by treating them as if they were rocks "objectivism."[7] Objectivism is concerned with placing distance between self and other, and the intentional avoidance of involvement. This we can do without. Involvement is what generates caring, motivation, and insight, which distancing reduces.

Since objectivism in applied human science is not very helpful, we need to look at other criteria for quality in our evaluations. I propose that we consider criteria for evaluating the quality of the evaluation process, as much as its outcomes. We need to see that the process produces reflective action on the part of the individual or program being evaluated. This implies commitment on their part. Berk and Rossi suggest that evaluation data's effectiveness can often be increased when those to be evaluated are encouraged to participate in the design of the evaluation procedure.[8] Indeed, I have stressed self-evaluation throughout this book. At the very least, students should participate in decisions about what goes into their folders or portfolios. The idea is to maximize personal responsibility for the improvement of teaching and learning, to set up rather than break down feedback loops, and so to motivate the use of whatever information is gathered.

However, since there will be varying degrees of diversity of interpretation of the outcomes of evaluations, the process must be reflective. That is, it must be continually examining itself in terms of internal coherence, the consequences of the evaluation, and the values underlying the teaching–learning activity. Furthermore, it must be open to dialogue with individuals and communities from outside the interpretive community in order to maintain a reflective stance. A good evaluator internalizes such dialogues. By knowing other evaluators who have somewhat different perspectives and by engaging in dialogue frequently, she is able to view the situation from their eyes, and contrast perspectives against one another. We should always be on the lookout for ways to get a second opinion or another frame of reference. Independent opinions are commonly used for important decisions in the medical field. It doesn't eliminate difficulties, but it does present a greater likelihood that a useful description is made. We could go one step better, however. If egos and expense were not involved, we might get the two physicians together after their independent examinations, so that they might engage in dialogue to consider one view in the context of the other. This dialogue might accomplish the development of a response which neither participant alone could have reached. At the same time it might encourage the development of knowledge in both parties and increase the shared language and the possibility of communication. The possibility of teachers discussing students' reading/writing portfolios with the students and other teachers raises the possibility of coherent, and somewhat self-regulating interpretive communities.

Ultimately, there is a responsibility on the part of teachers to practice what Erik Erikson calls "disciplined subjectivity."[9] That is, we are responsible for examining ourselves as evaluation instruments, and describing the factors that influence our own interpretation. We try to describe our practice to ourselves in a social, personal, and historical way. This requires us to consider such influences as the training we had, the friends and colleagues we socialize with, the professional environment we live in, the teaching situations we have been in, our political and social backgrounds, and our own experiences as literate people and as learners. Probably the most helpful tool for doing this is our own journal writing. The "double-entry notebook" which Ann Berthoff describes is most helpful.[10] Simply writing on one side of the page leaves the other side of the page for comment when we go back to reflect. It helps us put ourselves and our praxis in perspective, and if we write about an experience or even talk about it with others, it can help us as a community to accomplish a balance that would elude us as individuals. Indeed, unless we can see our own practice from another's point of view, it is difficult for us to know our own point of view—our own subjectivity.

DYNAMIC OBJECTIVITY AND THE CONTEXT OF TEACHING

Ultimately, it is not the elimination of either subjectivity or objectivity that we are after. Rather it is in being so aware of one's *self* that we can reflect on both the subjective or phenomenological reality (that which is unique to us), and the objective reality (more properly, that reality which we share with others). This is not something we can ever fully attain, but rather something toward which we should continue to strive. Evelyn Fox Keller calls this *dynamic objectivity,* which she says

> is not unlike empathy, a form of knowledge of other persons that draws explicitly on the commonality of feelings and experience in order to enrich one's understanding of another in his or her own right. By contrast, I call static objectivity the pursuit of knowledge that begins with the severance of subject from object rather than aiming at the disentanglement of one from the other.[11]

Currently, this is not encouraged in teachers. Such an awareness requires a confidence in self-knowledge. It requires awareness that we each construct our own worlds and our own knowledge. With the current view of science as something that people in white coats in universities do and then pass on in the form of "findings" to the nonscientists in the world, teachers are not encouraged to think of themselves as researchers or constructors of "real" knowledge. Standardized tests are a major tool for holding this perspective in place. Tests are seen as scientifically producing real knowledge, and they do not value the kind of knowledge which allows a kindergarten teacher to read her student's writing: it is not "objective" knowledge. At the same time, the insecurity bred of not being confident that one's own knowledge is "real," prevents teachers from asserting their own views and seeking other divergent views. *Self-knowledge is real knowledge.* It is no more nor less scientific than *objective* knowledge. It is not by distancing ourselves from our students that we will see them better or teach them better. Insight comes from being inside things, not outside at a distance. The trick is to maintain an awareness of ourselves while maintaining involvement. The more clearly we know ourselves, the more clearly we can see those aspects of our observations that are due to the uniqueness of our individual perception.

The capacity for dynamic objectivity evolves along with the development of self-knowledge and autonomy.[12] The development of autonomy is essentially a developmental task of childhood, although many do not complete a healthy development in their lifetime. It is certainly not a goal we have set for schooling, and it does not appear in "scope and sequence charts" as part of becoming literate. What Evelyn Fox Keller calls Dynamic Autonomy refers to a sense of self as clearly delineated from, but connected to, others. It is rooted in both the awareness of the ability to affect others and one's environment in satisfying ways, and the awareness of the continuity with and similarity of self and others.

One of the major problems with testing, particularly as it is currently used, is that it systematically works against teachers developing this dynamic autonomy. In the first place it enforces an objectivism in which children and teachers are seen as objects—converted to numbers and averages. This objectivism is rationalized on the grounds that administrators need that type of information in order to make decisions. However administrators make different kinds of decisions based on that type of information than they do on the basis of personal knowledge. But tests devalue personal knowledge. Indeed, a second way in which testing prevents the development of dynamic autonomy is by devaluing the kind of knowing of others that depends more on connectedness than on separateness.

A third way in which tests prevent this development is through collaboration with their siblings, the basal readers. Teachers are expected to produce regular gains on standardized tests, but if there is a general trend for improved performance, the tests are seen as inadequate. At the same time, along with the constant threat of standardized tests, the basal reader materials control so strongly what teachers can do in classrooms, that teachers are constrained to instructional practice which prevents their being effective; and even if they were, credit is given to the basal reader—the technology. Meanwhile, the basal reader structures classroom time to reduce choice and dialogue, and the adversarial nature of the social interaction prevents teachers from knowing their children in a detailed and personal manner. All of which leads to a reduced sense of agency, and hence autonomy, on the part of the teacher.

Patricia Ashton and Rodman Webb in their studies of teachers' sense of efficacy, or agency, found that:

☐ All teachers who had a low sense of self-efficacy defined their classrooms in terms of conflict.
☐ Teachers with a low sense of self-efficacy relied on positional authority, the authority conferred by virtue of being the teacher, whereas

those with a greater sense of self-efficacy tended to establish personal authority, the kind that is earned rather than conferred.

☐ Teachers with a high sense of efficacy were more likely to show students that they cared about them and their problems and were interested in their progress. Teachers with a low sense of self-efficacy felt that such relationships undermined their authority.[13]

Self-efficacy has to do with being able to see the consequences of one's efforts, and having one's efforts valued by others, neither of which is fostered by standardized tests.

I believe that it would be more sensible for us to seek conditions that will help teachers become more self-aware (as opposed to self-conscious) and more involved with their students, rather than less. It will involve their gaining greater knowledge of how children develop, in order to see the consequences of their teaching, and it will involve them in reflective activity such as journal writing. I will take up the description of these conditions in the last section of this book.

CHAPTER 26

Fairness and Bias

Bias has been an issue in the field of assessment for a long time. Tests were used in ancient China as a means to avoid bias in job selection. Before these tests, influential folk appointed relatives to lucrative government jobs and those without connections remained without jobs. People have greater rights these days in this country, and many are aware of and exercise these rights. If a school simply selected a group of children and gave them privileges such as special "enrichment" instruction, personal computers, and so forth, some parents would become quite rightly upset and create a scene—possibly in court. Schools use tests to avoid such messy and potentially expensive scenes. If a group of children is selected for a "gifted and talented" program on the basis of their test scores, there are likely to be fewer protests even if the selected group contains no minorities. The test is seen as "scientific" and hence "fair" even though there might be a demonstrable bias in the group selected.[14] If blame is to be placed, it must be placed on the child or the scientific test, the former being easier than the latter.

A major argument that has always been used to support tests is that they are not supposed to be influenced by "subjective judgment." I have already spent some time on the issue of subjectivity and objectivity and the trade-offs involved, but I must still address the following question about making instructional decisions about students. If we could construct an unbiased test, would it be better to use such a test, or would we prefer to risk the vagaries of teacher judgment? This is not a simple question and I shall take it apart into its component pieces as a way of answering it. But first, I hope that I have already convinced you that even if we had an unbiased test available, its results must always be interpreted and acted upon. Thus human judgment with its potential biases cannot be avoided. Indeed, James Ysseldyke's studies have shown that one of the most serious placement decisions, who is classified as learning disabled, has relatively little to do with the actual test scores and a great deal to do with teacher judgment.[15] We might interpret this as being problematic as far as trusting teachers is concerned, and redouble our efforts to produce and enforce better tests; or we might interpret it as suggesting that teachers need a greater understanding of children's development and of their own teaching practice so that their interpretation is better. Indeed, that seems like a substantially more efficient, indeed easier task than attempting to fix up the assessment of learning disability.[16]

WHAT IS BIAS?

When there is a systematic difference in the outcome of a decision procedure across different groups in the population, then the procedure is biased. This is the most common view of bias. For example, black students might, on average, score higher than Hispanic students on a test, or boys might score higher than girls. But suppose we have a reading test on which boys consistently score higher than girls. Does that mean that the test is biased or that the boys can read better than the girls?[17] Suppose that the testing company removes the items that produce the score difference and in the new test boys and girls score equally. Does that mean that the test is now unbiased? Alas, the Hispanic students still score lower than the white students. Again, is the problem in the test or are there real differences? Well, the Hispanic lobby is nearly as strong as the women's lobby, so the testing company replaces the items that produce the discrepancy. This results in equal proportions of students being placed in the gifted and talented program. It also results in the elimination of support instruction for some of the students who were previously eligible because of their low scores on the test.

Now the testing company has a test that produces equal scores among the subgroups male/female, and white/black/ Hispanic. The test constructors are happy because they have produced an unbiased test. They have used the "golden rule" and selected items from the same domain that do not discriminate between population groups. They are legally safe. However, it turns out that Navajo students do not score nearly as well as the other subgroups on the test. Fortunately for everyone, except the Navajo, nobody notices the discrepancy, and even if they did this particular subgroup does not have a strong enough lobby to be heard. In any case, we are still not sure whether the test is biased or whether it actually does measure reading and there really is a difference in learning.

Suppose the test is actually biased. What might have caused the bias? One major factor is simply the amount of relevant background knowledge. For example, if we have a text about baseball, boys are more likely to answer questions about it accurately than girls because of the likely extent of their relevant knowledge. If we have a text about hunting, certain groups are likely to know more about it than others, making it easier to read, more interesting, and easier to answer the questions. Actually, whatever topic we choose, people of equal "reading ability" (whatever that might be) will differ in their relevant knowledge base and in their consequent performance. Bias really operates at the individual level.

What can we do about that? We can choose texts that no one would know anything about, but that would mean we would not be examining reading because without any knowledge of the topic, a reader cannot make appropriate inferences, has no way of predicting, and his ability to self-correct is hampered. Alternatively, we could choose a sufficient variety of topics so that everyone finds a text they know something about, and so that each major minority group is represented. Indeed, this is one of the major techniques used by test manufacturers. Unfortunately, the elimination of this type of bias produces a different type of bias. Students who score well on intelligence tests also happen to know more about more different things. Vocabulary tests are the most consistent subtests on IQ tests. The result then is a reading test biased toward students with greater intelligence test scores, and we have to wonder to what extent we are measuring reading ability and to what extent intelligence (whatever that turns out to be).

But subtle differences in language can make a difference too. Indeed, small differences are possibly the worst. My wife is from Chicago. I am from New Zealand. In the early stages of our relationship we would sometimes find that, though we thought we were carrying on a conversation, without our awareness the dialogue had gradually diverged until we suddenly reached a point at which we were clearly not even within the same galactic space. Differences can be as subtle as the associations different people make with words. For example, Anglo-American students associate the word *environment* with words like *air, clean,* and *earth.* African-American students, on the other hand, associate *environment* with words like *home* and *people.*[18] These subtle differences are the reason why we can never have an unbiased test. One of the unfortunate characteristics of standardized tests is that the evaluator is not able to interact with students while they do the test. If she does, then she ruins the standardization and thus invalidates the use of the norms, which are based on a lack of interaction. But without the interaction we cannot understand why children made the errors they made. Indeed, test manufacturers concede this point. For example, the manual for the *Degrees of Reading Power* suggests that to make the test diagnostic we should go back over the test with the student and question him about why he selected a particular answer. They do not, however, suggest that we should change his score if we then understand his logic.

But there are other ways of biasing testing. For example, when an unfamiliar person administers a test (common in accountability testing), scores for lower income and black students are reduced but the scores of the upper income students are not affected.[19] Interestingly, the most intensive use of the tests is in districts with larger proportions of low-income and minority students, principally in the southern states and in large urban areas. Furthermore, the tests, couched as they are in an elaborated and stylized English, are most biased against these very groups.[20] Standardized tests of reading tend to be biased against minorities also because of item selection criteria. In order to obtain high internal consistency, test makers select items that perform similarly to the whole test. Minorities are, unfortunately overrepresented in the lower end of the test performance, and thus items on which they do not do well fit well with the overall test performance. In addition, minorities are, of course, in a minority, and hence their performance on the item is less consequential for item selection. The bias turns out to be cyclically reinforced by tracking which is based on test scores. These students are placed in courses with lower expectations and more limited content.[21] These self-fulfilling consequences begin early too. For example, in 1984 in South Carolina standardized tests resulted in 40% of the black five-year-olds being classified as not ready for kindergarten.[22]

There are many other types of bias in evaluation and I shall return to these presently. For the moment, let us consider test bias, which has received the bulk of the attention to date.

SHOULD TEST BIAS BE A PRIORITY?

Most of the work on bias has been devoted to making unbiased tests based on the definition of group membership: male-female, black-white, and so forth. Minority groups who have attained recognizable power status in this way earn the right to argue that tests should not discriminate between them and others. There are many issues which are problematic. Which groups are allowed such status, for example? Do we do the same for American Indians? By tribe? Jewish American versus Other American? Asian American versus Other American? What about those subgroups who score higher than the others? Should we worry about that too? Whenever we use tests we are faced with these issues. To be fair, we do not want to be biased in favor of one group or another.

In the chapter on objectivity, I described the costs and benefits associated with objectivity, and I explained that neutrality comes at the cost of reduced investment. I also explained that motive and investment often come with the cost of some sort of bias. Now it is very important that we consider this in instructional terms, such as what kinds of decisions must be made for what purpose and how bias might influence them. The major decisions that concern me are those made by teachers about how to interact with students and what kinds of activities to involve them in. These decisions have the greatest influence on students' lives. If we consider these issues first, the major point becomes not so much eliminating test bias, but eliminating negative instructional bias. This is part of the same business of eliminating interpretive bias. I believe that we know enough about the effects of teacher expectations to know that it would be better if we could arrange a positive bias for all students. When teachers see a student through her strengths, the interactions are different. Teachers tend to treat differently children they view as being not very able readers. They interrupt them more, they allow themselves to be interrupted more when teaching them, they do not allow such children time to figure out words for themselves, they focus feedback on print detail and phonic analysis rather than on meaning, and so forth.[23] Even if the tests that placed the children in these reading groups were unbiased, the consequence of their use is considerable instructional bias.

I find it much more important, then, that we face the issue of how to set up a positive instructional bias towards each child. We do have some research on how to do this, though it was never suggested quite for this purpose. One method that Marie Clay has suggested is what she calls "roaming the known."[24] In her suggestions to teachers for tutoring individual children, she suggests that the first few sessions be spent doing no teaching. The importance of this for the child has to do with becoming fluent in the strategies and knowledge already possessed before others are introduced. However, for the teacher it requires finding out what it will take to set conditions that will allow the student to be independently literate. At least as important as this, however, is that the teacher gets to see the student being independently literate, demonstrating strengths more prominently than his weaknesses. This contrasts strongly with reading tests that force children to fail consistently before testing is stopped (in order to make more reliable classifications), leaving the last image of the child as a negative one.

A second study that relates to this issue was done by Victor Delclos and his colleagues.[25] They trained people to evaluate children using "dynamic assessment" methods. The idea behind this approach to assessment is that the normal "level" provided by a test does not give as much information as might be obtained if the evaluator finds out what kinds of assistance will help the student perform at a higher level, and how far the student will go with some form of assistance. This higher level is seen as a more accurate reflection of *real* or impending ability than the level derived from the more "static" approach to assessment. For me, the important point is that Delclos and his colleagues found that other teachers watching children tested in this way had their expectations for those children's achievement raised. In other words, the procedure introduced what amounts to a positive bias by showing the consequences of supportive intervention.

I want to argue that it is also important to introduce this sort of bias into self-evaluations too. When a student examines his learning, it is critical that he emphasize the positive aspects before turning attention to areas in need of improvement. If this does not happen, then attempts at self-improvement will be sabotaged by a shift in goals from self-improvement to avoidance of failure, along with denial, blame, or possibly self-recrimination. Negative self-talk (e.g., "I knew it—I'm stupid," "I'll never figure it out") is the kind of activity engaged in by ineffective learners. The same, of course, will happen with teachers. Our self-evaluations are influenced by our history of evaluative interactions with others. Indeed, whether we self-evaluate at all is influenced by the extent to which we have learned to take responsibility for doing so in the past.

The importance of a positive bias in the instructional interaction is clearly stated by the United States Commission on Civil Rights, which noted that:

> The heart of the educational process is in the interaction between teacher and student. It is through this interaction that a school system makes its major impact upon the child. The way the teacher interacts with the student is a major determinant of the quality of education that the child receives.[26]

I have described the nature and effects of these evaluative interactions in an earlier chapter.

James Ysseldyke and his colleagues have shown that children's classification as learning disabled is more a consequence of teachers' judgments than of the children's performance on tests,[27] and that professionals are biased in these judgments.[28] If the teachers are biased (with respect to race, gender, looks, etc.), and it is they who teach the children, simply shifting to tests to make apparently less biased classifications is not an adequate solution. The teachers' interactions with the children will still be biased. Removal of this bias cannot be done by test or mandate, as Donna Kerr points out:

> Rules and regulations, the common form of distal directives, cannot themselves educate. A state might order desegregation, but it cannot itself effect integration. Moral indignation regarding racial discrimination cannot spring from state directives, but is uniquely the task of education that "liberates the mind from dogma, bias, and conformity."[29]

The fact of the matter is, even if it were possible to remove test bias, and it is not, if we have biased teachers, the central problem remains. I do not believe that the majority of teachers are consciously prejudiced. Many are, however, unconsciously creating situations in their classrooms that are racist and sexist. If told that they were racist or sexist, these teachers would deny it vehemently. Most have philosophies that would make such accusations offensive. Confronting such teachers with differential test scores, particularly in a high-profile testing situation, will only force them to blame either the students or their home life in order to protect their beliefs in their own unprejudiced status. Only through arranging situations of reflection on data that illuminate their differential interactions can they confront the problem. In such situations, where the only major threat is to their internal harmony between their beliefs and actions is serious change likely to occur.

DIFFERENT TYPES OF BIASES

But I have dwelt on the simple valence of bias too long. It is important, to be sure, but there are other forms of bias that are similarly important, but more subtle. Evaluation focuses children's attention on particular aspects of literate activity and in doing so produces consequences of which we are often unaware. For example, Ralph Reynolds and his colleagues have shown that the way readers read can be altered by the kinds of questions asked of them along the way. Their studies of college students show that without prompting they figure out the pattern of questions that have been interspersed in a textbook chapter. Having figured out the pattern, they increase the time they spend on segments containing information relevant to the category of question and less time on segments that do not contain such information.[30] In other words, the pattern of evaluative interactions we have with readers can substantially influence the way they read. Similarly, reading tests used for accountability purposes can focus teachers' attention on particular domains. For example, if a test is heavily loaded with phonic analysis, that can shift a teacher's attention toward greater amounts of phonic analysis in his instruction.

A larger scale version of this problem is also relevant. A test can be considered biased toward one curriculum or another. A reading test with a strong phonic analysis component is likely to produce higher scores for children in programs where phonic analysis is emphasized. This type of bias is problematic in program evaluation since people are likely to decide that certain children are not doing as well as certain others, and to attribute the disparity to something like poor teaching or poor learning rather than to a test biased toward a particular curriculum. The discovery of this "curricular bias" has, interestingly, led to more change in the curriculum than in the tests. Most of the major testing companies also own basal reading series, a principal selling feature of which is their curricular match with the test. This has been referred to as the *real test bias* by Norman Frederickson, who points out the consequent trivialization of curriculum.[31]

Another major curricular bias in current evaluation is toward the outcome or product of literate activities. This makes literate activity less exploratory and more directed to a particular end. It also tends to move the satisfactions associated with literate activity to the end of the activity, dissociating them from the activity itself. For example, children can come to gauge their success in reading from their success in answering the questions at the end of the basal story, detracting from the feelings of success associated with involvement in the activity. In addition, the pattern of these outcome questions appears to be important. If children can figure out a pattern, it is likely to influence their reading of other stories.

A further type of bias that often goes unnoticed is the strong favoring of external evaluation. Students and teachers are evaluated by others; and even though the others might encourage self-evaluation, the external evaluation is always what counts most heavily if not solely. The more strongly the individual comes to depend on the external evaluation, the more the structure of that evaluation is likely to make a difference to the actual process of his reading.

In line with the currently popular (but waning) view of science, there is a bias toward the countable. What we can count is what counts. It is popular to believe that if it can't be counted, it is probably "fuzzy," "vague," and "subjective." But this view seriously restricts the aspects of literacy to which we attend. For example, we cannot readily quantify such things as "involvement," so instead we talk about "time on task," which is countable but quite different. You can buy time on task, but you can't buy involvement.

Along the same lines, and for similar reasons, there is a bias toward the standardized, or the directly comparable. This means that the kind of information to which teachers' and parents' attention is drawn is that which is collected under particular, sterilized conditions. Information gathered in the grime and from the sticky fingers of classrooms is not valued by this view. This severely restricts what teachers see as useful and how they value their own intuitive knowledge. Standardized situations are solely for comparison purposes, and comparative contexts produce particular beliefs and behaviors among children. As comparative information becomes valued, we have competitive contexts where children see information about their own prior performance as irrelevant.[32] Thus children who consistently perform less well relative to others are deprived of the experience of success and the experience of self-evaluation on the basis of their own development.

A further type of bias to be reckoned with is the bias in interpretive frameworks and hypothetical constructs. Currently evaluations are largely done within a comparative framework, and interpreted in terms of constructs such as "reading ability." These two biases actually go hand in hand and have several consequences. First, students also interpret them in terms of a construct called "ability" that is differentiated in such a way that it places effort and ability in opposition.[33] Once children have developed this evaluative framework, they often adopt the goal of ego-defense in academic situations and supply little effort so that they cannot be accused of having low ability. Alternatively, if they come to believe that they have low ability, a relatively stable trait, then they are also robbed of motivation, since effort is seen as not being able to change ability.

Another type of evaluative bias results from the stereotypical biases in interpretation typified by the analyses of sports performance. When two basketball players have the same number of steals or interceptions, the white basketball player often is credited by announcers as having great insight, whereas the black player is credited with having great speed.[34] These stereotypes and expectations influence the way teachers respond to their students. Carol Dweck and Carol Diener found that teachers' evaluative feedback to girls about their academic performance tends to be different from this feedback to boys in ways that reflect social stereotypes. Girls receive much less negative feedback than boys, but a greater proportion of it is directed at the intellectual quality of their work. A greater proportion of the positive feedback they receive is directed at nonintellectual characteristics of their work. A consequence is that, on average, girls, while achieving higher scores on tests than boys, paradoxically feel less confident academically, and are less likely to continue in school.[35] Evaluative biases can be subtle, pervasive, and powerful.

Many biases are not so readily classified as positive or negative. Rather, their valence depends on one's value structure. For example, a bias toward dependency in evaluation is seen as positive by many people because it is seen as maintaining more control over standards of quality and of values. Similarly, a tendency toward "factual" or "literal" questions is seen as positive, for example, by some religious groups who feel that the Bible should be read "literally." Indeed, the structuring of questions that follow the reading of a story can be considered a powerful instructional technique or somewhat destructive, depending on how the questions are structured and one's point of view. Questions based on a story grammar are seen by some as a powerful instructional technique and by others, concerned about the culturally limited nature of the questions, as obstructive.[36]

Explanations of biases are critical. For example, the simple explanation ordinarily given for the high correlation between class status and reading test scores is that children of the lower classes have less experience with books and have impoverished language. Pierre Bourdieu describes this kind of experiential difference, instead, as a difference in *cultural capital.* This difference is not to say that children from lower classes are lacking in experiences or language. It is not that their background is less rich, but rather that their cultural capital is not in the coin of the realm. Couched this way, cultural bias is seen as a form of technological oppression. Carolyn Marvin describes tests as an instance of mass communication. She highlights the fact that they are an unusual form of mass communication in that, unlike other forms, they require a response from the audience. The response is not the usual response, allowing for individual and cultural diversity, but one that must be highly constrained and performed in a routinized manner. What will count as correct literate performance, then, arises from a contest for social power and dominance. Most of what is evaluated in tests of reading and writing are values which are presented as conventions.

High-profile testing also exacerbates these differences in other ways. When test scores are reported in many states, realtors carry them around to help in selling higher priced houses. This, of course, produces a self-fulfilling prophesy. Those children who are most culturally prepared for the tests are those whose parents are attracted to such schools. Thus we get "preferred school districts." Districts where test scores are high are desirable places for those who can choose where to live. These are people with cultural capital. Consequently, housing prices in these areas are high, ensuring that those without cultural capital shall not enter, and test scores will remain high. Again, the most intensive, and highest profile, use of the tests is in districts with larger proportions of low-income and minority students. These districts have lower scores on the tests and they tend to enforce highly structured teaching focused on the tests in order to address this most visible problem. But the bias extends further. What teacher who is going to be judged on the basis of her students' test scores is going to view students with less cultural capital as assets? Worse, the high-profile accountability testing produces very unhappy teachers who are biased towards placing blame on the student and the home, and towards teaching a very limited form of literacy. In addition, when asked to describe a student's literacy development, teachers in these test-beleaguered districts are more likely to begin with statements like ''He's a 3.2 . . . '' and to give a much more limited description than teachers in less oppressive situations.[37]

FAIRNESS

The issue of fairness is not the same as that of bias, but it is at least as problematic. The two are often equated, and it is assumed that the best course of action is neutrality and the same for all. However, a teacher who is very negative to all children can be unbiased by being equally unfair to all. Taxes are demonstrably and deliberately biased in that there are different rates of taxation for different subgroups of the population. The question of their fairness depends on which subgroup you are in and is likely to be judged on quite different grounds by each subgroup, depending on their own interests and values. However, after negotiation, an elected group of officials feels that overall they are fair.

Teachers, schools, students, and parents also have their own criteria for fairness. Some teachers feel that all children should have equal time; some feel that all children should be given the same opportunity (defined variously); some feel that all children's needs are different and that each has the right to the most appropriate (but different) instructional exposure and feedback.

My own view is that each child is different, and each deserves the most appropriate instructional situation. You may immediately protest that it is impossible for a teacher to constantly monitor each child and set optimal conditions for each, even in a class of ten, much less a class of twenty-five or thirty. Indeed, if the teacher is responsible for arranging this for each child all day every day, he will be unsuccessful and possibly go mad. Children must become capable of assisting in the process. If this arrangement is dependent on placement tests, children will spend a large proportion of their time taking such tests, and this will clearly color their view of what literacy is all about.

I have my own predilections about allocation of resources in response to evaluation too. For example, if on the basis of performance on an apparently unbiased test, some children are assigned to ''gifted'' status and given additional resources such as student mentors, and other children are denied them, I find that unfair. Such an arrangement would benefit all students. On the other hand, I am less inclined to claim unfairness when children who are seen as having difficulties in a particular area are given additional support in order to get them over their difficulties. It would seem to me that requiring such support for all children would be tantamount to arguing for hospitalization for all, whether or not in need. This is clearly a value-laden issue and others will differ, but my position colors my writing and you may as well be aware of it.

CHAPTER 27

Common Frames of Reference

To evaluate students' development in literacy, we collect data through observation and systematic recordkeeping. This in itself is a selective, interpretive, and intructional activity. But before we make use of any data we have collected we must interpret them further—translate them into what we think they mean. This interpretation is done by viewing the data through one or more frames of reference. Unfortunately, the most common of these frames of reference at present is the normative frame in which a student's performance is compared with that of a particular peer group. I say "unfortunately" because this is the least useful and most problematic frame of reference. Indeed, it should take the smallest amount of space in this book of all the frames but actually takes the largest because researchers, educators, and the general public have invested most heavily in it, and because it requires the greatest number of cautions. I shall first address this and other common but less helpful frames of reference in this chapter and then describe more constructive frames in the next chapter.

CRITERION-REFERENCED EVALUATION

One way of viewing performance is in relation to predetermined criteria. The simplest example to illustrate this is statewide minimum competency testing. A criterion level of performance is set and those performing above that level pass and those below it fail. On a smaller scale, the placement tests in basal reading series have fixed pass/fail criteria. A slightly different example might be informal reading inventories and standardized oral reading tests. These have categories of performance often called independent (or easy) reading, instructional level, and frustration level (or hard reading). These are defined by error rates. For example, an oral reading accuracy rate of between 90 and 95 percent is often considered to be learning level material. Let us suppose we have taken a running record of Jenny reading her classroom textbook. It meets these criteria, and her performance did not lead us to believe that she was encountering additional barriers to her development. Her reading thus might be considered to have reached the criterion for learning level reading, in that textbook.

There are many ways in which criteria are generated. In fact there is a whole branch of educational measurement devoted entirely to the mathematics of setting these criteria.[38] These mathematical exercises are based on several faulty premises and ultimately the criteria are largely arbitrary except in the most trivial of cases. For example, it is assumed that the mathematics of the issue are content free—that criteria for reading literature can be derived from the same formulae as criteria for writing letters or doing long division. In reading, there has been an ongoing argument over the appropriate error rates to indicate independent, instructional, and frustration reading levels. Some of the disagreements are shown in Table 27.1 and their history can be found in the paper by Richard Allington from which this table is reproduced.[39] In fact, these criteria are very situation dependent and take little account of the nature of the errors, the purpose for reading, or the propensities of the individual child. For example, some children read with a ponderous concern for word identification accuracy, making few oral reading errors but are nonetheless under considerable stress. Others are more concerned about understanding with some speed the nature of the ideas and have little regard for word identification accuracy. Some children cease to predict, monitor, and self-correct with an error rate of one in every twenty words, whereas others do so only when the error rate reaches one in eight. In other words, what is frustrating for one child is not for another, what a child finds frustrating in one book at one time he may not at another, and all errors are certainly not equal. The use of criterion-referenced evaluation depends on the clear specification of the domain of the "test" that is supposed to include these factors.

The development of criteria for success or failure has implications for the individual's development of criteria for self-evaluation. In particular, what

TABLE 27.1. Proportion Word Recognition Accuracy Necessary for Instructional Level Designation for Various Authors

Grade	Gray (1915)	Durrell (1937)	Betts (1946)	Gilmore (1951)	Spache (1963)	Powell (1971)
1	86%	67%	95%	67%	67–75%	85%
2	91%	92%	95%	88%	90%	91%
3	91%	94%	95%	92%	94%	91%

Note: These data are not necessarily comparable in a straightforward manner, since not all authors consider the same behaviors as "errors." However, given the degree of congruence among authors on what constitutes error behaviors these data may, in fact, be quite comparable.
Source: This table is from Richard Allington (1984). Oral Reading. In P. David Pearson (Ed.), Handbook of reading research. White Plains, NY: Longman, p. 838. Reprinted by permission.

counts as successful reading of a book can have a variety of different criteria. Unfortunately, such criteria as *involvement* are not easily specified and hence do not figure large in criterion referencing, although Frank Hodge has suggested one such criterion in his scale of one to ten handkerchief books (indicative of the emotional involvement).[40] Another such criterion might be a decibel scale, constructed in terms of the number of decibels of sudden noise (doorbells, telephones, etc.) required to interrupt the reader.[41]

Many have argued for the use of criterion-referenced testing in schools, particularly because it avoids the problems with norm-referenced testing that I shall describe presently. Basal reader programs have batteries of criterion-referenced "mastery" (you got it or you ain't got it) tests. Magically they have a cutoff of eight out of ten as evidence of mastery. However, let us think where these criteria came from. When the tests were being put together, they were field-tested (at least they should have been). If only 40 percent of the students passed the test, then some items would be changed until a more reasonable proportion of students passed. In other words, criterion-referenced tests often boil down to norm-referenced tests, which we shall consider presently.

DOMAIN-REFERENCED EVALUATION

Domain-referenced evaluation refers to evaluating performance on activities that are tied to a particular theoretical model of reading or writing. It is often seen as little different from criterion referencing, but domain referencing depends to a greater degree on the clear theoretical description of the dimensions of the "items" in a "test." An item is essentially any describable situation which evokes a describable human response. The domain of items refers to the set of items that have explicitly defined, fundamental properties in common. So, for example, we might define a domain of writing activity in terms of the dimensions:

1. The context of the activity: for example, it may be to be completed in class in the space of one hour, independently, and without revision (context specifications could end up being *very* lengthy).
2. The audience for the writing, such as *the manager of a store.*
3. The response expected of the audience, such as *being persuaded.*
4. The source of the information used: for example, it may be supplied in a description of a scenario, or it may be personal experience.
5. The relationship of the writer to the audience.

You can see that, depending on your theory of writing and writers, specifying the dimensions of the activity might differ markedly, especially in terms of the priorities. In any case, the idea in domain-referenced evaluation is that each dimension can be independently manipulated so that a set of tasks can be set that differ in theoretically relevant ways from one another. The object then is to describe the specific dimensions of the domain in which the learner might be having difficulty.

The specification of domains can reach quite outrageous proportions, making the practical value of the approach in serious doubt. For example, one multiple-choice, domain-referenced test was developed to assess the domain of *pronoun usage*. The original test, developed to represent the entire domain, had 92 items, and that included only two parallel items on each practical combination of five factors: pronoun rule, pronoun form, pronoun number, pronoun person, and cognitive complexity.[42] Consider the possibilities of breaking *literacy* into dimensions of this proportion! A similar experiment was done on a domain of reading called "finding the main point" in which texts were written and rewritten to independently change the following factors: text difficulty (high, medium, and low), statement of the main idea (direct, indirect), frequency of statement of the main idea (low, high), ideas nonsupportive of the main point (many, few), and the fit of the text structure to the reading strategy found to be common among able college students (good, poor).[43] This resulted in sixteen different texts (one for each practical combination of variables). Again, you can see that dimensions such as "difficulty" might be expanded to more detail, and other dimensions might be added. This is all assuming that we can agree on what is a reasonable domain and what its dimensions might be. (As you will have noticed, I for one do not like the idea of *the* main idea.)

However, if we take the essence of this concept, that we have a theory about the domain and its dimensions, and teachers must, then there is something useful here. As contexts shift in the classroom, and as children take on different literate activities, teachers can become aware of how particular children perform differently in different kinds of activities and contexts. These patterns may become apparent through their writing folders, through their running records, through anecdotal records, or reports from other teachers in conjunction with classroom observations. Once a hypothesis is formed about a pattern it might be sensibly tested. Sometimes this may involve focused observation under particular circumstances, and sometimes it may simply involve asking the student about it.

NORM-REFERENCED EVALUATION

Let us return for a moment to Jenny's reading. We shall see in the next chapter that with respect to our theory of reading, her reading looks healthy, and with respect to her performance two months ago, her reading has shown improvement. However, Jenny is a second grader and *all* her classmates can read the book she is reading faster and with fewer errors while still understanding it. Viewed in this way, Jenny's performance looks problematic. In other words, viewed through another frame of reference, the peer group, our interpretation of Jenny's performance is different.

Since there are several ways of defining Jenny's peer group, there are several possible outcomes of such a comparison. For example, Table 27.2 provides some of the more common peer reference groups, and how these might vary across children and across schools.

Given these possible comparisons, we can report the comparison in different ways. In the table we have reported Jane's standing with respect to one hundred of her peers. This comparison is called a *percentile rank*. She scored better than 60 percent of her peers in a national sample, giving her a national percentile rank of 60. Thus, the percentile rank of a student's score refers to the percentage of students whose scores fell below that score.[44]

How can there be so much variability between the rankings of these two girls? Let us consider Jenny to begin with. Nationally in her age group she is in the lower quartile (the bottom 25 percent of students). However, in her own school, which serves mainly a very low socioeconomic neighborhood, she performed better than 40 percent of the other students. Compare this with Jane, whose performance is better than that of 60 percent of the national sample of students. In her own school, which is in the same district as Jenny's but which serves a predominantly upper middle-class neighborhood, she performed better than only 50 percent of her age group.

It happens that because of the birthdates (September and December) of these two eight-year-olds, they are in different grades in school. Jenny is in second grade and Jane is in third. Thus, although Jane might be classified as a good reader by comparison with her national age peers, in her grade level at school, she is considered a below average reader (percentile rank of 40). Jenny, on the other hand, is a poor reader compared with her national age peers, but in her own grade at school she is an average reader. The district-wide grade peer group comparison shows the girls' schools to be near the extremes of the district. The district-wide grade peer group is more competent than the average student in Jenny's school but less competent than the average student in Jane's school, as reflected in their rankings.

On the face of it, percentile ranks appear to provide a very clear way to report student's performance. However, there are some catches which make them less helpful than they appear. The major problem is that the scale of one to one hundred is not an equal interval scale like a tape measure. The interval between individuals in the middle of the distribution is smaller than the in-

TABLE 27.2. Ranking of the Student with Respect to 100 of Her Peers

	Jenny (Rosebud School)	Jane (Hawthorn School)
National sample of eight-year-olds	20	60
Eight-year-olds in own school	40	50
Grade level peers at school (Jenny 2nd, Jane 3rd)	50	40
Student's district grade peers	30	60

terval between individuals at the ends of the distribution. This can be seen in Figure 27.1. Among other things, this means that you can't add or divide them, which means that you can't average them.

A second, increasingly common norm referenced metric is the *Normal Curve Equivalent* (NCE) score. This is like the percentile rank in that it places a student on a scale of one to one hundred, but its calculation includes standardization, which makes it an equal interval scale like a one hundred unit tape measure. The comparison between NCEs and percentiles can also be seen in Figure 27.1.

For most purposes a detailed one hundred unit scale is quite unnecessary, and usually suggests a level of accuracy which is quite illusory. It is like suggesting that brain surgery can be done with a carving knife. A less pretentious metric that can be used to report the peer comparison is the *stanine*. The stanine (*standard nine*) is a standardized score, which ranges from one to nine in equal intervals, each half a standard deviation wide[45] (except for the extreme points). Thus it can be treated as a nine-point equal interval scale, as can be seen in Figure 27.1. Teachers and administrators can explain to parents the meaning of

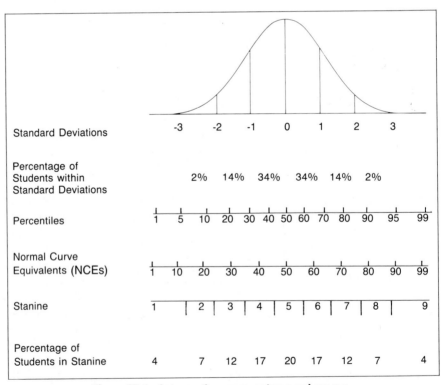

Figure 27.1. Interpreting norm-referenced scores.

a stanine score without much difficulty, and it does not pretend to offer fine gradations of measurement. It is like having a nine-unit measuring stick with no parts of units marked on the measuring stick. The stanine provides about as much detail as is usually required, and is less pretentious. Indeed, sometimes even the stanines are grouped into 1–3, 4–6, and 7–9, representing below average, average, and above average.

Another metric that is frequently used for peer group comparisons is the *grade (or age) equivalent score.* For example, having taken the reading comprehension subtest of the *Stanford Diagnostic Reading Test* (Harcourt Brace Jovanovich, 1976), red level, form B, John achieved a raw score of 48. The norm tables in the test manual tell us that this score converts to a grade equivalent of 4.6. In other words such a score would be expected of the average (median) student in the sixth month of fourth grade. Since John is in the second month of second grade, the grade equivalent score appears to tell us that John is reading two years and four months above grade level. It also seems to tell us that John can read material that the average fourth grader can read. Sounds clear and straightforward doesn't it? It sounds as if we could simply place John halfway through the fourth-grade basal for reading instruction. However, none of this is true.

First, no fourth-grade student took the test when it was normed. The test company simply estimates that if an average fourth grader had taken the test, that is what he would have scored. Second, the test contained very little material used in the fourth grade because the test is designed for second and third graders. Third, the test was given only once to the norming population and that was in September, not in November which is when John took it.[46] This seems to take the gloss off an apparently desirable measure.

However, measurement specialists have very sophisticated statistical techniques for accomplishing the apparent sleight of hand, which is necessary to present us with the finely graduated scale. Unfortunately, even this is not enough to make it a desirable score. Interpretation, which is the reason for transforming scores in the first place, is still complicated by the fact that grade equivalent scores do not give an equal interval scale. From the example of grade equivalents given in Table 27.3 you can see that the inequalities in the scale are not even symmetrical, and differ from grade level to grade level.[47]

Grade equivalents are probably the most commonly used, and certainly the most commonly misused, test scores provided by testing companies. However, there are sufficient problems with this type of transformed score that the International Reading Association has asked test publishers not to provide such scores. The scores are simply too deceptive. However, test publishing is a commercial enterprise; and since so many consumers feel it is important to use these scores, the request has had no effect.[48]

If you are going to use a norm-referenced procedure, you will want to check where the norms came from. For example, suppose you are wanting to assign a child to a percentile rank among her national age peers. You will look

TABLE 27.3. Number of months below or above grade level in comprehension and word analysis for the 33rd and 67th percentile students on the California Achievement Tests (Forms E and F)

Grade Level	33rd percentile	67th percentile
	Comprehension	
1.6	0 months below	7 months above
5.6	6 months below	12 months above
8.6	10 months below	33 months above
	Word Analysis	
1.6	0 months below	6 months above
5.6	13 months below	15 months above

Source: These data are taken from the California Achievement Tests Forms E and F Norms Book, March through June. Monterey CA: CTBS/McGraw-Hill. (1986).

in the test manual to check the representativeness of the sample used to derive the norms. Perhaps the manual says that the publishers gave their test to a sample of 1,000 children from a range of socioeconomic groups in Nashville, Tennessee, including 10 percent minorities and 40 percent females. This could hardly be called nationally representative. The sample is small and in several ways biased. Even if the sample were perfectly balanced with respect to gender and race, there is a considerable lack of national representativeness in terms of language and knowledge base.

Always consider carefully the information about the norm group before using norm-referenced interpretation of any kind. Unfortunately, it is not uncommon for test publishers to forget to describe the norm group adequately or even at all. If someone reports to you that on a given test a student has a percentile rank of 40, you must ask with respect to which peer group, and there are all sorts of peer groups. For example, one might be less interested in comparisons with the group of all first graders than in those first graders involved in "whole language" programs, since in many forms of evaluation their performance will differ in substantial ways from those involved in intensive decoding programs.

In order to make comparisons among individuals, there is a requirement that the task and situation be comparable. Thus most norm-referenced comparisons involve tests with standardized instructions that are read to the students by the evaluator. However, multiple-choice tests are not the only way to make normative comparisons. In evaluating writing, it is not uncommon to train examiners using samples of writing so that they get the "feel" of what an average performance is like. Teachers get a feel for this within their classes, but it would not be difficult to help teachers get a broader perspective on writing quality within the school or district through teachers discussing and examining representative types of writing or by visiting each other's classes, or even by having their students write letters to one another. Decisions about what aspects of the task and situation need to be controlled, to what degree, and what constitutes a reasonable norm, are all professional decisions to be made in the context of the purpose for which you are evaluating, given that the overriding goal is optimal instruction for all children. In general, this goal will actually move us away from focusing on normativeness, and toward concentrating on understanding the diversity of writing.

Some federal and state regulations require the use of norm-referenced evaluation procedures. Perhaps a more useful course would be for schools to form coalitions to generate their own norms. For example, a group of schools across the country might get in touch with one another (it would not take many to match the efforts of current published tests) and norm their own procedures. A simple dictation test might easily be normed, or writing samples. All that is needed would be for teachers in each school to take dictation samples from their students, record the data collected by age and grade, and have someone coordinate the effort and do some simple calculations. Schools could thus cut out the testing companies and save substantial amounts of money. Ultimately, these efforts could change the face of evaluation over time.

A great deal more might be said about the many different norm-referenced scores and how to calculate them. However, I believe that what I have described so far is sufficient knowledge for the classroom teacher and the reading, writing, or language arts specialist, and already the size of this section drastically overrepresents its importance. Actually, the whole principle of normative comparisons has unfortunate consequences for literacy development and should be avoided as much as possible (see Part I of this book).

Nonetheless, teachers are often faced with parents whose sole interest is in the normative comparison. They ask questions like "Why is Steven not in the top reading group?" or "How does Alison compare with the other kids in the class?" It is important to counsel these parents about what you are trying to do for their child and how you are going about it. But it is also very important to educate the parents about their child's development by showing them and explaining to them samples of the child's work (running records, writing samples, etc.) and how you respond to the child's work in class. If parents' only way of knowing children's development is through test scores, then that is what they will focus on.

PROFILE REFERENCING

Jenny's brother Billy poses a different interpretation issue to us. His pattern of reading processes looks like good reading should look: it shows good progress relative to earlier performance, it is in the instructional range, and even falls on the 50th percentile for his age group. However, Billy's "intelligence" test score is in the "superior" range, so many people expect him to have a similarly high performance on the reading test. We might call this frame of reference *profile referencing* since it is usually associated with a pattern of scores on a battery of tests or a pattern of subtest scores. The expectation argument is based on the premise that individuals differ mainly in their overall ability, and should thus perform most intellectual tasks with a similar level of competence. The assumption is particularly strong with tasks assumed to involve similar cognitive activity, like listening and reading, or assumed to be part of the same task, in the way that decoding nonsense words (e.g., *wug, stip,* and *baugh*) and filling in cloze blanks are assumed by many to be part of reading. For example, George Spache uses a listening comprehension test to determine "reading potential."[49] The comparisons made in profile referencing produce such terms as "underachiever" or "gifted learning disabled." These terms or analyses are not useful in any way as they fail to say anything about instruction.

Nonetheless, profile referencing is institutionalized in Public Law 94-142, which provides for the disability classification of those with significant discrepancies between skill domains. However, recently Jeanne Steele and Kurt Meredith found that states varied in their requirements of a discrepancy for special education placement. Some left it to the examiner's judgment, others specified discrepancies between "expected achievement," based on "intellectual ability" and "achievement," ranging from 0.5 standard deviations to 2 standard deviations, some states varying the discrepancy by grade level. The point is that these criteria are fundamentally arbitrary.[50] We would be better off using students' actual reading and writing performance as a guide for instructional programs.

CHAPTER 28

Constructive Frames of Reference

Although the frames of reference described in the last chapter currently are the most common, they offer very little to those who wish to improve children's literacy learning. Fortunately, they are not the only frameworks available for interpretation. Throughout the book so far I have used a theory of how people read and learn as the interpretive touchstone. We have looked for patterns of behavior and described them in terms of a theory of what constitutes a healthy pattern of development. I shall call this *theory-referenced interpretation*.

THEORY-REFERENCED EVALUATION

Suppose Jenny reads the passage from *Encyclopedia Brown Takes the Cake*[51] as shown in the running record (Figure 28.1). What does it mean? From your reading so far (and from my analysis in the figure), you will see that Jenny predicts, that she self-corrects for meaning, and from print, which also implies that she monitors her reading. From the meaning-based strategies she used in her reading, and from a subsequent discussion, we can infer that Jenny also understood what she read. Thus, within our frame of what we consider to be healthy reading processes, Jenny's reading is healthy. That is to say, Jenny read this text in the manner I would expect a good reader to read.

I call this *theory-referenced* evaluation since I am using a theory of the reading process to understand what the performance means. It is the theory that tells us whether the performance involves something to worry about or not. Indeed, different people with different theories will worry about quite different things. From the theoretical perspective presented in this book, we are concerned if the child is not predicting, and if no self-correction is taking place, or if there is evidence that meaning construction is not the central goal. Thus, Brian's running record (Figure 28.2) appears to be problematic. It shows a reader who is strongly concerned about print detail and substantially less concerned about meaning. Stephen's record, on the other hand, shows prediction, self-correction, and the preservation of meaning. It looks very encouraging to me. An evaluator with an entirely different reference theory might see Brian's careful concern for print detail first and foremost, to be extremely encouraging. Stephen's running record, on the other hand, might be considered distressing to

TEXT

page 18

Chester Jenkins was impatient. "Let's get started cooking the food for our party," he urged.

    "Golly," Sally said. "I almost forgot."

    "I never forgot for a minute!" Chester said.

    Chester took his appetite straight to the Brown
kitchen. Encyclopedia, Sally, and the friends they had
invited for the Fourth of July party had trouble keeping
up with him.

    Mrs. Brown settled Chester down. She assured him
that she would help with the cooking. All the food would
turn out just right.

    With that, Chester became her number one assistant.
He followed instructions faithfully and never stole a taste
ahead of time.

RUNNING RECORD

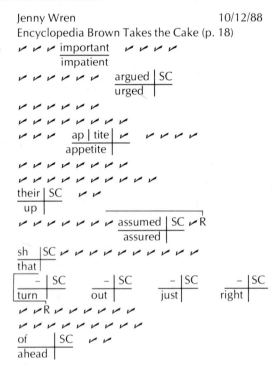

Jenny Wren   10/12/88
Encyclopedia Brown Takes the Cake (p. 18)

(continued)

Figure 28.1. Running record of Jenny reading from *Encyclopedia Brown Takes the Cake*. (*Source for text excerpt:* Donald Sobel (1982). *Encyclopedia Brown Takes the Cake.* New York: Scholastic. Chapter 4, The Fourth of July Party.)

ANALYSIS
Words = 101
Errors = 1
Accuracy* = 99%
SC = 9
SC rate* = 1:1

* These figures are rounded to the nearest whole number.

Strategies Used
Predictions:
their/up, sh/that, of/ahead.
Self-corrections from print:
argued/urged, their/up, sh;/that, of/ahead.
Self-corrections for meaning:
assumed/assured, all the food would [omitted line] with that.
Repetition:
3 words to sentence beginning and 6 words to the beginning of the omitted line.

Figure 28.1. Continued

someone whose theory requires accurate decoding as the first and most critical aspect of learning to read. Such an evaluator might worry if the child is showing evidence of predicting (''guessing'') and hence not attending primarily to the print detail. Our view of how readers read and learn actually determines what we see, and what we say it means.

Theory-referenced evaluation is a form of what has been called ''construct-referenced'' evaluation. Several writers have suggested that all educational and psychological measurement is construct referenced,[52] and we shall discuss constructs more in the chapters on validity. The things we study in educational evaluation are mostly mental processes that we cannot see, and must imagine. Rather than calling them figments of imagination, which is not very flattering or scientific sounding, measurement specialists call them *hypothetical constructs*. We infer them from children's behavior. We cannot see prediction or monitoring or comprehending but we can talk about them. I can say that Jenny is predicting and justify the inferred construct from her reading behavior, and I may say that, from the standpoint of my theory, predicting is generally a good thing. Another evaluator might have inferred the same construct but from his theoretical frame of reference think that it is a bad thing. Thus I have chosen to call this tying of constructs to their theoretical networks, theory referencing. These constructs and theories are at the heart of evaluation and are the source of instructional implications. This is the reason it is important for teachers regularly to articulate their understandings of the data available and to engage in dialogue with others about the data, particularly those who do not share the same perspectives and assumptions. These colleagues are likely to question the

---

TEXT

page 13

He opened his eyes,
and saw two little squirrels.
"Play with us," they said.

"No time," said Little Bear.
"I have to go home for lunch."

RUNNING RECORDS

Brian

13

✔ ✔ ✔ ✔

✔ ✔ ✔ ✔ s |sprs | skrs
           squirre | s

✔ ✔ ✔ ✔ ✔

✔ ✔ ✔ ✔ ✔

✔ ✔ ✔ ✔ ✔ ✔ l |oo |ch | looch
              lunch |

Stephen

13

✔ ✔ ✔ ✔

✔ ✔ ✔ ✔ chipmunks
         Squirrels

✔ ✔ ✔   said | SC   ✔
        they |

✔ thanks   ✔ ✔ ✔
  time

✔ ✔ ✔ ✔ ✔ ✔

Figure 28.2. Running records of two readers reading from *Little Bear's Friend. (Source for text excerpt:* Else Holmelund Minarik [1960]. *Little bear's friend.* New York: Harper & Row.)

parts of our theories that we leave unquestioned, and thus help us to develop and rethink our interpretive frameworks.

SELF-REFERENCED EVALUATION

Self-referenced evaluation refers to the use of other performances by the same individual as criteria for comparison. For students' development, this framing is particularly important. As an example, I might take the writing samples in Figure 28.3 and note that there is a shift from prephonetic writing to phonetic writing over the time period. I will need to feel confident that the situations were similar on the two occasions in terms of the nature and extent of teacher assis-

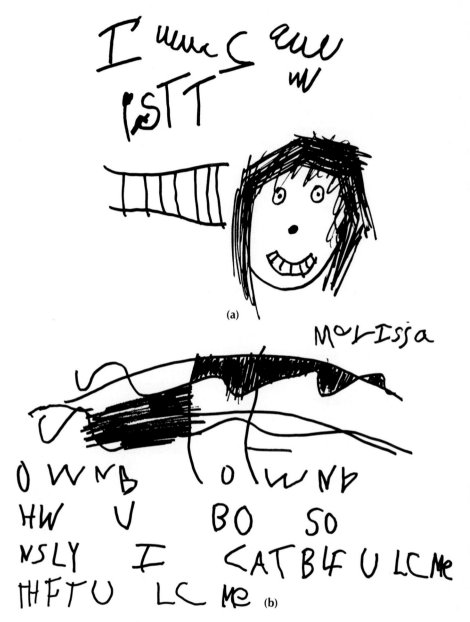

Figure 28.3. Examples of the change in Melissa's writing from prephonetic (a) to phonetic (b) representation.

tance, but the argument will be reasonably clear. As a second example, let us return to Jenny's performance in Figure 28.1. With respect to my view of reading, I reasoned that the performance showed healthy reading processes. With respect to criteria, her reading showed that her classroom text was in her instructional range. However, I can also consider this performance in relation to her performance six weeks ago when she was not self-correcting at all in her classroom text. Relative to the earlier performance, this performance is positive in that it shows development. I shall call this form of referencing *self-referenced evaluation* since the learner's performance is interpreted by comparison with her own earlier performance.

There are several ways in which to make arguments for development. In Jenny's case, I am arguing that over time, an aspect of the reading process, self-correction, had shown change. In order to make such an argument, the different pattern of the reading process must be in a comparable context. For example, to show that self-correction is a new development, it must be shown on material of similar difficulty to the reader. If the earlier reading had been on very hard text, let's say with an error rate of 15 percent, we would not be surprised if Jenny were not self-correcting at that time. She was deprived of meaning, which is an important tool for self-correction. Now, on text of an appropriate difficulty, she is self-correcting. This is also not surprising. The only change that we could argue for is that she is now reading material of a more appropriate level of difficulty. However, if both readings involved a similar error rate and both were first-time readings, but the later reading showed that Jenny had begun to self-correct, then we can argue that there has been a change in her reading process.

There are many different types of change that can be documented in this way. In each case we must show that something has changed, but that the relevant context is comparable. In the self-correction example, it can be argued that the relevant context is the error rate, which is a modest indicator of individual difficulty. Suppose instead we wanted to argue that the student can now read harder text than before. Consider Terry's reading. On 2/10/87 Terry read *The Small Potatoes Club* with 90 percent accuracy, and on 3/12/87, one month later, he read *The Small Potatoes and the Birthday Party* with 100 percent accuracy. I would argue that because these books were written by the same author for the same audience with similar language, they are very roughly comparable in absolute difficulty level for any given child. If we demonstrate differential performance over time, then we have an argument for the reader's development. Several series of books by the same author(s) are good for making this kind of argument. Some examples are:

Donald Sobol's *Encyclopedia Brown* series. New York: Bantam Books.
Arnold Lobel's *Frog and Toad* series. New York: Harper and Row.
Peggy Parish's *Amelia Bedelia* series. New York: Avon Books.

Tony Johnston's *Mole and Troll* series. New York: Dell Publishing.

Else Holmelund Minarik's *Little Bear* books. New York: Harper and Row.

Marjorie Sharmat's *Nate the Great* series. New York: Coward, McCann & Geoghegan.

Harriet and Jon Ziefert's *Small Potatoes* series. Pine Brook, NJ: Dell Publishing.

Stepping Stone series. New York: Random House.

Elizabeth Levy's *Something Queer* series. New York: Dell Publishing.

This type of argument is obviously based on the assumption that books in a series by the same author, for the same audience, are of comparable difficulty. It is not a perfect assumption, but it is no worse than readability formulae or the inconvenience, limitations, and assumptions that underlie standardized reading tests. Similarly, a book that had to be set aside because it was too difficult, might be returned to at a later date, and the running records would provide evidence of change.

In a similar way we might use a consistent readability formula to contend that a book read in the instructional range six months ago had a readability of 3.2 grade level and a book read also within the instructional range yesterday had a readability of approximately 5.1 grade level. The readability procedure is fraught with more problems than the same series/author procedure since across books the authors tend to maintain similar assumptions about such factors as readers' prior knowledge. This is not taken into account in readability formulae. In addition, there is a marketing incentive to have the books in a series be of comparable difficulty for a given individual so that readers will "get hooked" and proceed through the whole series. The readability formula argument can be strengthened by having multiple examples. If three instructional range books read at the beginning of the year had readabilities of 1.2, 1.4, and 1.4, and three books read six months later had readabilities of 2.2, 2.8, and 2.6, then the developmental argument is more convincing to certain audiences.

Whichever procedure is used, the larger the differences (within reason), the more credible the argument. A change of 3 percent error rate is not very convincing, nor is a change from 4.1 grade level to 4.2. The argument for growth is also stronger with both forms of evidence and perhaps more than one example of each. I mention this approach to demonstrating development not because I think it is a great idea, but because it has considerable advantage over using the same test twice or a parallel form of the test. First, it can be done without taking time out of learning for testing. Second, it can be done without anxiety. Third, it can be done using real literature, and fourth, we are not restricted to the number of available parallel forms of the test. This form of referencing also works particularly well with writing. Portfolios are, obviously, a sensible vehicle for this form of evaluation referencing.

CONTEXT REFERENCING

Another reference frame for interpretation is the context in which the student is operating. From your reading so far in this book you will realize that this is one of the most important frames of reference. For example, let us go back to Stephen's and Brian's reading of *Little Bear's Friend*. Recall that Brian does not predict, monitor, or self-correct, but he does make very systematic use of phonic analysis, sometimes producing nonsense words, a written representation of which would look similar to the word being attempted. In a classroom in which children read natural language texts, Brian's approach will not work well and may set him up for failure. On the other hand, in a class with an instructional diet of linguistic readers of the "Dan can fan a tan man" variety, Brian's performance may be superior, putting him in no risk of at least normative failure. The reverse might be true for Stephen. I view this type of framing as *context referencing,* by which I mean interpreting performance and differences in performance in relation to the context in which they occurred. Context referencing will be important, for example, in situations where one considers whether a child in a remedial program is ready to function adequately in the regular classroom, or when a child comes from a different school. It will also be critical in explaining why his performance is the way it is.

Consideration of the context helps to clarify instructional interactions too. For example, the metaphor of whole language suggests that we should not fragment literacy instruction. Occasionally this has been taken to mean that we should not discuss small pieces of language. In my opinion, it is fine to analyze language into pieces in certain contexts. For example, when I am learning a song, I find it helpful to focus my attention on how particular transitions are accomplished on the guitar, or to take a phrase with difficult intervals and practice singing it without singing the whole song. What is important is that the phrase or interval or whatever be returned to the song. The stronger my understanding of the song, and of what musicians do, and the stronger my commitment to being a musician and being able to sing the particular song, the more I can tolerate splitting a piece off and studying it in detail without loss of the overall purpose of the music. Taking things apart is also least problematic if the initiation of the analysis is mine, or if the problem to be solved by the analysis is one that I understand will help me solve a problem I have identified.

A second context that justifies breaking language into parts is when it is part of play. Language play often involves breaking language apart, frequently producing nonsense. Nonsense is often frowned upon with good reason. When children's everyday reading consists of "Dan can fan the man. Dan has a fat cat. The cat can fan Dan. The cat sat on the can," and similar texts based on phonetic regularity rather than on meaningfulness and interest, we can rightly be concerned. They will learn a completely inappropriate view of what it is that authors and readers do.[53] Any other learning will be situated within that view and will be in many ways dysfunctional. However, Dr. Seuss has done very nicely, thank you, from books like *Hop on Pop* that have stressed similar aspects of the language in the context of silliness and having fun, and out of direct instruction. The non-sense helps to clarify sense; indeed, without it, sense is meaningless. In the context of a knowledge of the functionality of language, freeing language from its shackles of meaning allows exploration of the limits of generalizations.

The context of a performance is the first place to look for explanations. The way children define literate activity has a lot to do with the kinds of literate activity in which they are engaged. Children who are engaged in different activities learn different things. As a classic example of this, consider the two pieces of writing in Figure 28.4. These were written by two children in the same class. The two pieces could not be more different from one another. One child clearly rejoices in writing. He has voice, and your response may have been to laugh or shudder, but the response was certainly to the content. The second piece has no voice. These are not this writer's words. The goal of this piece of writing is nothing to do with meaning. He believes that the point of writing is to get the words right. But an examination of the context explains the difference. Nate is in a reading group that reads stories whose words are selected to tell an interesting story. Charlie reads stories like *The mud is up in a cup.* Reason enough for the difference in their views of writing. However, the teacher's responses to the reading and writing are different. Just as you responded to the content of Nate's writing by laughing or shuddering, so does the teacher. The response is to the content. On the other hand, it is hard to respond to the content of Charlie's writing. Instead the teacher has responded to the conventions of writing. You can see the little marks indicating what was left out of his story. The same kind of response focus can be expected in Charlie's reading. The context provides a very instructive frame of reference.[54]

MULTIPLE FRAMES

I have described these frames of reference as if they are quite distinct, whereas they actually overlap with one another in various ways. For example, the use of the readability formulae in self-referenced evaluation might be conceptualized as criterion-referenced if turned around so that a goal is consistent independent level reading of material classified as in the fourth grade range. Similarly, theory referencing may be viewed as another form of expectancy referencing with the expectation driven by the theory. Profile referencing is clearly another form of expectancy referencing. Of greater importance than this lack of distinctness, is the need to view children's performance through multiple frames. When a child is going into third grade, it can be important to know that while his reading is healthy with respect to a theory, his profile, and his earlier performance, it is not the level of reading that the third-grade teacher expects of third graders. This does not locate the problem in the student, but clearly identifies a problem.

We have been inclined in the past to be rather restricted in the use of these different frames and the respectability which each is granted. Norm-referenced

284

I have a tranchala
A tranchala is dageris
A tranchala is an cold Bkdid
An amol. he livs in rock e hells.
I cep the theng in the Box
I cech Fliys far it to iet

Figure 28.4(a). Average group member (Nate).

John | The bug
The bug is in The mud.
The bug in The sun.
The bug in The rain.

Figure 28.4(b). Bottom group member (Charlie). Figures 28.4(a) and (b) are from ''The Gridlock of Low Achievement: Perspectives on Practice and Policy'' by Anne McGill Franzen, 1991, *Remedial and Special Education,* in press. Copyright 1991 by Pro-Ed, Inc. Reprinted by permission.

interpretation has probably seemed most respectable for the worst reasons. Teachers need to be most concerned about theory-referenced performance since it is that which directs their activity; about context-referenced performance, since the major part of their teaching is arranging the context; and about self-referenced performance as that speaks to the issue of development.

Although I recommend using multiple frames of reference, different types of data are more amenable to different frames. For example, in order to make a norm-referenced interpretation, it is critical to have a task that will produce a great deal of variability so that different children's performances will be quite different from one another along some continuum.[55] However, this is not the type of data needed for criterion referencing or theory referencing. For both norm and criterion referencing it will be helpful to have some end product that can be compared. However, for theory referencing it will be of more use to have process information (usually derived from by-products such as drafts, revisions, running records, observations, etc.). Again, let me stress that these and other considerations need to be made in the context of the reason for evaluation.

SELF-RECALIBRATION

I have emphasized that teachers are the essence of evaluation expertise, and that they should reference their notion of how a child is performing to some theory of how children learn and what it means to be literate. However, some might protest that we do have to help the children set ever greater goals. We do not want them to be satisfied with less than they are capable of. How do we maintain some idea of their capabilities?

First, we should be looking at development, checking that progress is being made. Second, we need to take a look at the context we are providing to see if we can improve it. However, there is the chance that our standards for ourselves and our students might become lower than they should be. How can we check ourselves on this? One way to prevent a parochial attitude from developing is for teachers frequently to observe each other's teaching and each other's students learning. Especially teachers who are in schools in which children are "tracked" in ability groups (in which I include remedial reading classes, resource rooms, and gifted and talented programs), there is a need to get a perspective broader than one's own classroom. Observing someone else teach also helps us to see ourselves through a different lens.

It is especially helpful for us to observe in different contexts our own students who are not doing well. Particularly we need to see them in contexts where they are doing quite well. Dialogue with the student's teacher from this other context can be helpful simply because it can help us think of the difficulties that a student might experience. This helps us to not get locked in to lower expectations for those students. We might think of these activities as standardizing our observation lens—a recalibration activity.

FINAL COMMENT

The choice of frame is not without consequence. For example, if I examine my professional efforts in the light of different frames, I can feel depressed or elated, fulfilled or frustrated. I can evaluate by comparing my "accomplishments" with various groups such as people roughly my age who teach at universities or with other fathers of three young children. I can evaluate with respect to my view of how I think I should spend my time, or with respect to the model provided by a valued colleague. I can evaluate my efforts with respect to how many papers and books I have published, how much satisfaction I get from my work or from my family, how thoughtful or detailed my writing is compared with three years ago. I could evaluate my efforts on the basis of the expressed satisfaction of my students or on the quality of their written products. There are numerous ways to frame my efforts, and it matters for the quality of my life and work which ones I choose, and possibly when I choose them.

The teachers I encounter also are busy evaluating themselves. There are consequences for them and for their students in the frames they choose to see themselves through. If they frame the valuing of their teaching activity through their students' performance on standardized tests, they will be in a precarious position, and so will their students, unless that particular frame is balanced by alternative frames that are given at least as much credibility as the normative frame. When we try to force frames on people, we should be aware of the consequences of doing so. In my opinion, ranking a child's performance against others serves no useful purpose *for that child*. Indeed, when we encourage a competitive frame, the consequence is active discouragement of a balancing self-referenced frame. Children watch very carefully to see how we view them, and they will generally tend to adopt the predominant frame of reference through which they are viewed.

CHAPTER 29

Being Specifically General or Generally Being Specific

Deciding on the degree of generality is central to the composing process. The more details you develop, the more particular the form becomes; the fewer the details, the more general. That trade-off is the dialectic in operation.

Ann Berthoff

When will we find it necessary and possible to make a statement about a student's overall ability as a writer or reader? "This student is very bright" is not particularly helpful instructionally, neither is "this student is a good writer." Quite specific evaluations are mostly called for in instructional settings. "When Stephen writes fiction, the rich descriptions which he gives in personal narrative are not present" is a much more instructionally useful statement. Certainly the evaluations that take place in day-to-day teaching are most helpful when they are very specific. Nonetheless, it is common to hear teachers and parents make statements like "Sandy is a B student." This type of comment refers to a quite stable, general aspect of Sandy, something that does not change over time or context. Indeed, the stability of reading groups helps children to make such judgments about themselves.

For a teacher to help Sandy improve her reading or writing, it would be more helpful to know that "Today Sandy corrected most of her own punctuation when she was writing her final draft. Her first draft had no punctuation." Indeed, it would be more helpful for Sandy to know that too. It would be instructionally helpful to know that "Today Richard chose a very difficult book to read. It was *Danny the Champion of the World*. His word-level accuracy was about 85 percent, but he continued to read it to himself, was able to talk with me about it, and clearly enjoyed it." Certainly for a student, it is more helpful to know that his strategy of comparing the word he is trying to figure out with a word he already knows is sometimes an effective one, than to know that he did a good job or that he is reading at the 23rd percentile for his age group.

Teachers, too, will find it more useful to have specific information about their own practice. Suppose you are a first-year teacher and in your school it is the principal's job to evaluate your teaching. He comes in for half an hour, sits at the back making notes, and the next day presents to you a statement concerning your teaching ability. He does this twice over the course of the year. How representative are those observations of your overall teaching? What if you were only seen teaching math? Or reading? Or it was just before lunch or just after lunch on Friday both times? What should the principal be allowed to say after these observations? Can he say that you are an incompetent teacher (teaching disabled)? What can he say? What do his observations represent? What if he simply described in detail what you said and did? Or what if he described very specifically what you wore, what was on the walls of the classroom, and so forth? There is always a balance to be struck between the need to be general and the need to be specific, when to be general or specific, how specific, and what to be general or specific about.

In planning our evaluations we need to consider exactly what we will want to be able to say to whom about what. How representative is the performance, and of what is it representative? Does the inelegant, poorly constructed, less-than-persuasive letter in front of us represent the current state of Mark's writing ability? Does it represent his current performance level in the domain of writing that requires the establishment of authority and construction of a coherent argument? Does it represent his current ability to write persuasive letters? Does it represent simply his performance of that activity at that time, on that day, given that particular situation? Does it represent simply our analysis of what he did under a particular set of circumstances? Clearly the more examples of his writing we have, the more comfortable we are going to be making more general statements.[56]

Reading-test manufacturers set out to make instruments from which they presume to make statements such as "Jane has more reading ability than 38 percent of the children in the country in her age group." From a child's performance on a few brief texts followed by a selection of odd questions, answered in a strange set of circumstances, we make a statement about a child's reading ability that generalizes to all types of texts, on all topics, in all contexts read for all purposes. I believe this to be an interesting but futile enterprise, like trying to strike a match on Jell-O. For example, it is easily demonstrated that, on average, a child who lives in the inner city will find it easier reading about inner city things than will a country child who has limited experience of the city.[57] This difference will occur even though both might use a very healthy set of reading strategies in the process. Similarly, a child with extensive experience of being read to or told stories will find it easier to understand stories than will a child who lacks that experience, or whose experience has been restricted to expository reading or dialogue.[58] Indeed, Karen Wixson, Marge Lipson, and their colleagues have shown that this kind of within-reader variability exists.[59] The pattern of children's oral reading errors also varies with certain characteristics of the text-reader relationship, including overall relative difficulty.[60]

The problematic thing is deciding what a particular behavior represents. A frequent trap we fall into is assuming that a particular activity will be the same in different contexts. Observation of a bird in its flock through field glasses provides a certain type of information, much of which cannot be obtained any other way. A quite different type of information is obtained by containing the bird in a cage by itself and observing more closely how it eats its food and preens itself. Different information again is obtained when the bird is placed in a very small cage and required to perform different activities in order to eat. Obviously trade-offs are made in each case in terms of what we can say after we have made our observations, about what the behavior represents.

Understanding children's reading and writing development is very similar. We can observe a child for a considerable period of time in a classroom and the child never performs the behavior we are looking for. On the other hand, we might force the performance of the behavior by arranging a test. In a test we may be able to get the child to perform in a particular way, but that may not be representative of how he would normally do it. The more substantial the intervention required to produce the activity, the less we are able to generalize the behavior to other, independent situations. The best we are likely to be able to say is that under certain specified conditions the person did certain things.

Current testing practices involve manipulations of both the task and the context with consequent effects on motives and strategies. Consequently they represent an extreme form of intervention, like the small cage with a lever to press for food, that thus is much less likely to generalize to normal reading activity. For example, in order to find out whether children can "decode," or translate print into sound, it is still common practice to give a nonsense word test in which children "read" *buc, nad, sentle,* and so forth. However, whether they can do this or not does not mean that is the way they go about figuring out words when they are reading. As Carole Edelsky and Kelly Draper have pointed out, there is a difference between reading and "reading."[61]

CONTEXTS, TASKS, AND GENERALIZATIONS

There have been two major schools of thought on evaluation. The currently dominant approach, which is evident in the ubiquitous testing that goes on in schools, is rationalistic. The aim is to describe an essentially context-free (universally generalizable) set of truth statements, which has directed us toward examining the average performance of large numbers of individuals within highly controlled contexts.[62] The second major approach to evaluation is more naturalistic. The aim of naturalistic inquiry is to describe the individual case in terms of a series of working hypotheses. This focuses the evaluator's attention on the individual student and changes in his or her behavior in different contexts.[63] The naturalistic approach has stressed the lack of manipulation of the child's behavior. The argument is that the more one intervenes, the less one can generalize the findings to real situations. The rationalists, on the other hand, argue that it is simply inefficient to wait around expecting things to happen. A busy teacher simply does not have time for that. It is much more sensible to go after the information you need directly with a test. Besides, you can control the context so that you can compare students one with another, and look at smaller parts of reading in order to be diagnostic. The naturalistic supporters respond that you may get information quickly that way, but it bears so little relationship to normal reading behavior as to be worthless.

Nonetheless, we have been inclined to cooperate with the test makers in making even very general statements about children's reading on the basis of their participation in activities that bear little relationship to reading. Rather than saying that "William has in the past had some difficulty comprehending his science textbook," we are likely to say that "William is a poor reader." Notice that this statement "poor reader" (or worse, "disabled reader") implies the most extreme generality. Not only has William not read well in the past, in all domains, but he is unlikely to read well in the future. We must constantly consider the extent to which we need to generalize statements about a child's performance, and the extent to which performance can reasonably be generalized. When someone asks, "How well is Lucy writing?" it is reasonable then to answer, "Writing what for what purpose in which situation?" or to ask, "Which aspects of her writing?" Marty may compose well-rounded stories, and may revise the content of his work extensively and thoughtfully, but he may represent the phonetic aspect of the language with only initial and final letters. We should not necessarily expect Lucy to write as persuasive an essay, or as innovative a research report as her personal narrative is exciting. It rather depends, among other things, on her background and on the writing activities in her class. Similarly, if we are asked the same general question about Lucy's reading it would not be unreasonable to respond, "Reading what for what purpose in which context?"

Research has shown that characteristics of texts, tasks, readers, and situations influence reading performance, and many of these characteristics were described in Chapter 8. For example, performance can differ between familiar versus unfamiliar texts, expository versus narrative texts, interesting versus uninteresting texts,—and when the reader is required to summarize the text versus answer questions about it or complete cloze items. Evaluations of a reader's performance may also vary between different occasions and between different evaluators. Traditionally, and unfortunately currently, measurement experts and test makers have accepted that some of this variability does exist but have classified it as "error." In other words, they have believed that children have a single "true" reading ability that is measured by the test and that any variability in the performance of a given reader on the test is simply "noise" or testing error. Indeed, test makers have tried to ensure that there is a diversity in the topics and text types within a given test so that they will feel confident in making generalizations across these factors, and that the variability of any given reader on the test or between tests is simply "noise." An analogy might be that it is like trying to measure the depth of water near the seashore with a measuring stick (in millimeters) when the sea is rough and then reporting an average depth of two or three observations, ignoring the ten-foot waves and the ten-foot tidal fluctuation. However, if we take several observations over a period of time and record also the timing and conditions of the observations, we would be more likely to understand what was going on.

Suggesting more samples implies that the more literate activity students are engaged in, the more samples will be available. However, it does not mean that all samples of everything must be studied. Suppose my intention was to make some statement about the kinds of writing done by fifth graders in a large school district that offered a great deal of teacher autonomy, and many teachers offered students a great deal of autonomy in their choice of writing. I could simply go through all the students' writing folders and describe what I saw. On the other hand, I could select, say, every fifth student from an alphabetical listing in each school and examine their folders. I would then make an argument that my selection was representative of the overall group. The smaller my sample, the more likely it is not to be representative in some way. I might use this same sort of procedure to examine the general nature of composing, revising, and editing in the school district, or in a given grade level or school. I might use this type of sampling to report to the parents in a district, and even make available for inspection a fairly substantial sample of work.

SUMMARY

Whenever we attempt to generalize, it would be wise to remember that:

1. There are different domains of literate activity and performance in one is not necessarily representative of performance in another domain.

and:

2. There is likely to be some variation in each student's performance in different situations and over time. These different facets of our evaluation are all important for us to know about. If there is a substantial discrepancy between a student's performance in two different domains, then it *may* be instructionally useful.

and:

3. It is not necessary to have several samples of every literate act or every person in order to make a general statement. From a selected sample of students' work we may be able to make a reasonably general statement about how students in a particular school or class are reading.

But:

4. The more time students spend engaged in literate activity, the larger will be the samples of their literate behavior available for us to generalize from when we need to do so.

and:

5. The more specific the information, the more instructionally useful it is, and the less likely it is to be misinterpreted.

Novice teachers make general stereotypical evaluations such as "he doesn't know his phonics" or "he can't make inferences," even though a person who could not make inferences would never have learned to talk and would certainly not be able survive very long. Only when teachers begin to view the work from the child's point of view will these unhelpful and dependency-producing categories begin to loose their grip on instruction. But teachers will be restricted in attempting to reexamine these general categories as they try to deal with what they see as poor performance and the consequent shame and vulnerability. For the reflective practitioner, generalizing has less to do with producing general principles than with contributing new metaphors through which to examine subsequent cases of teaching and learning as possible variants.

Specificity is critical in our reporting for several reasons. First, authority, involvement, and voice are three critical factors of writing, whether it is reportage, fiction, or a report card, and they come from the *particulars*. (Essay test prompts, by encouraging overgeneralizing, tend to set conditions in which writers will lack these qualities.) Second, only personal, specific knowledge can produce the vignettes necessary for involvement. Third, it is the specificity of examples that allows the reflective reformulation of theories of what is going on. Generalizations discourage such reformulations.

CHAPTER 30

Validity and Values

Evaluation is a decision-making process, and validity is a statement of the worth or value of that process. It is not incidental that "evaluation," "validity," and "value" all stem from the same Latin root *valere* meaning strength or worth. Validity is a judgment of the overall appropriateness and adequacy of the inferences *and consequent actions* stemming from an evaluation procedure.[64] In other words, whenever we decide to use an evaluation procedure we need to be certain that it is the right one for our purposes. We need to be sure that the procedure provides the kind of information we need for the purpose we have in mind, and we need to weigh the costs and benefits of its use. Some of the costs and benefits are financial, some are in available student learning time, some are in teacher learning time, some in social consequences, sense of self-worth, motivation, and many other areas.[65] The most important thing to remember is that the validity of any evaluation procedure cannot be described separately from its consequences and its interpretation, and each of these is value-laden. Thus, the burden of validity ultimately rests on the person or people who interpret and use the procedure and the information, and the burden includes the responsibility for social, personal, and academic consequences.

Suppose we were interested in using the widely employed *Metropolitan Readiness Test* to decide whether or not a child should be promoted to first grade: we must consider the validity of the whole procedure including (indeed, especially) its consequences for that child and those involved with her as well as any other considerations of the quality of the instrument itself.[66] This will include such things as the characteristics of the teacher to whom she will be assigned, proximity to siblings, the nature of the program in the school, the child's personal development, and evidence of the consequences of promotion or nonpromotion on other such students (the latter being overwhelmingly negative).[67] And when we discuss these issues we must be aware that different people considering the issue are likely to have legitimately different views.

In the past we have tended to avoid this responsibility because tests have been at the center of evaluation. Test makers either made pronouncements of the validity of their instrument in their test manuals and other forms of advertising, or neglected the issue almost entirely. For example, in a large and detailed ten-page flyer advertising the *Metropolitan Achievement Tests* (1986), the term validity, or anything vaguely like it, does not occur once. However, manuals are generally careful to note that validity is dependent on use. For example, the Teacher's Manual of the Metropolitan Achievement Test has in its single paragraph on validity, the following to say:

> The validity of an achievement test is defined primarily in terms of content validity. . . . Since each school's curriculum differs from that of other schools, the content validity of the *Metropolitan Achievement Tests* must be estimated by each school. It cannot be claimed that the tests are universally valid.[68]

But test users have generally ignored these cautions and acted as if validity is the responsibility of the test maker. After all, if an expert test developer can't make a valid test, who can? How could a person who is not a measurement specialist know all about that complicated statistical stuff? Unfortunately, as educators our responsibility is to ensure optimal instruction for all our clients, and evaluation cannot be taken out of its role in serving that end. We cannot give away this responsibility whether we would like to or not. This means that teachers, specialists, and others involved in evaluations must understand the nature of the responsibility they are taking on. While the process of making judgments of validity is unavoidably complex, we can separate out some of the issues for discussion, provided we do not forget to put them back together.

Samuel Messick has described quite clearly the nature of the decisions involved in the evaluation of validity.[69] He suggests that before we use evaluation procedures, we need to have evidence to suggest that the procedure is better than other procedures or even no procedure at all. We also need to be sure that our interpretation of the data holds up against counterevidence or evidence supporting alternative interpretations. We must seriously consider the educational and social consequences of our using the procedure for the purpose we intend to use it, and how these consequences affect the short- and long-term goals which the evaluation is meant to serve.

If a test were proposed to sort people into certain genetic subpools so that people with a particular genetic makeup could be denied access to state and federal jobs, there would be considerable protest in this country. The *first* thing protested would be the legitimacy of denying them the jobs. Only after that had been decided might we start to worry about whether the genetic test was adequate, but only if the issue were relevant *after* the decision about the social consequences of the testing program. This is the heart of the matter of validity. If the use of a test has so many benefits for the individual and society that its shortcomings are relatively unimportant, then we can talk about a test being reasonably valid. But even if the genetic test mentioned at the outset were extremely accurate, the evaluation would still be invalid. Thus, even if a test were able to discern a child's reading difficulties with the accuracy of laser surgery, and do so time and time again with nanosecond speed, if it were used to assign children to a resource room from which they never returned, and their reading never improved, the test would be invalid. Thus, contrary to popular belief, the *first* thing to consider is the value-laden consequences of the use of a procedure. This assertion has some important consequences. For example, because of the mountain of evidence showing that ability grouping and tracking is fundamentally destructive,[70] I can assert that *all testing used for tracking students in school is invalid.*

VALIDITY AND THE CONSEQUENCES OF EVALUATION

Often educators have been led, along with the public into thinking that evaluation instruments are "scientific," "technical" instruments that are value-free. Nothing could be further from the truth. Tests often determine curricula and placement and access; and when a child is classified in one way or another, it is rarely without consequence for the child's social situation and instructional curriculum. Consider the following questions and responses. You probably have your own responses, and I would encourage you to think about the values underlying them.

Why do we need to evaluate the second-graders' reading achievement?
A1: So that we can make sure that the teachers are doing a good job.
A2: So that we can prevent some of the children from slipping through the cracks in our instruction.

A3: So that we can help the teachers provide the best instructional conditions.

What test shall we use?

A1: No test.

A2: The *Stanford Diagnostic*

A3: A reading/writing portfolio

Why can't we use the teacher's judgment and records of the child's performance?

A1: Teachers' judgments are merely subjective and quite biased. They may even fudge the data in order to look good.

A2: Records of children's reading performance are unreliable. Besides, we can't tell the circumstances under which the records were taken.

A3: That's a good idea. It would be a whole lot cheaper.

A4: Great idea, then the teachers would be more involved in the evaluation process.

As you can see, different values produce different problems and different solutions and the expected consequences of one approach or another are particularly value-laden.

The examination of consequences can be far-reaching and complex, and involves extensive prediction. For example, a procedure that results in a child's being classified as learning (or reading or writing) disabled is likely to have her placed into a special program. We will not know in advance whether the advantages of the special program outweigh the personal and social costs of the labeling procedure and the loss of the regular instruction that has been displaced.[71] We can never be sure about how one thing will influence another, but I shall give some descriptions of conflicting evaluation practices and the conflicts in values and consequences they represent. Two extremely different views of how we might ensure optimal instruction for all children might be represented by the use of objective tests to hold teachers and students accountable for performance, versus the use of teachers as expert evaluators engaging in ongoing evaluations. Some may feel that these are perfectly compatible approaches providing two sides of the same coin, perhaps representing summative and formative evaluation. However, I hope it will become clear that many of the consequences of each approach are likely to be incompatible.

Let us consider some of the possible consequences of using standardized tests to hold teachers accountable for the achievement of their students. This is currently a common practice and so we do have an idea of some of the likely consequences, although we are woefully short of detailed data. First, we have reasonable evidence that where a test is used to evaluate instruction, the nature of the test comes to be reflected in the curriculum.[72] Indeed, some political leaders have referred rather proudly to this as an asset.[73] It is likely that the more teachers and the public define the quality of instruction in terms of the students' performance on these tests, the greater will be the effect on instruction. A consequence of this will be that the instruction will be defined in terms of what is easily measurable in a controlled, timed, standardized setting, which will exclude such things as enjoyment of reading, diversity of reading, use of alternative information sources for research, use of study techniques, participation in discussions of literary works, construction of alternative realities, and so forth. I need hardly mention the parallel trivialization of the evaluation of writers. In other words, a change will come about in the goal of instruction. Teachers will optimize instruction with respect to the new goal which may or may not relate well to the original goal however it was conceived.

If teachers and possibly students come to view their success in terms of performance on the test, then there are motivational consequences. Teaching may become a less continuously rewarding activity since the emphasis is placed on the product rather than the process. Reading and writing, too, may become less rewarding through the redirection of the teacher's (and hence the children's) attention primarily to the product rather than the process. Teachers and students may come to think in terms of success and failure rather than process and progress. *Success* tends to invoke feelings associated with winning and losing, whereas *progress* is more likely to invoke feelings associated with the activity itself.[74] Evidence suggests that an emphasis on the process is likely to produce more active learners. Carole Diener and Carol Dweck describe "helpless" students as being poor at self-evaluation, largely unaware of their own use of strategies, and oriented toward failure. They describe "mastery" students as being very strategy-oriented, making strong connections between strategies and outcomes, and engaging in strategic self-instruction.[75] These patterns have important affective and behavioral correlates in teachers and learners.[76]

Aesthetic reading is likely to be minimized or eliminated in the press for the efferent reading that must be stressed in the tests.[77] Self-evaluation will be minimized because the locus of evaluation is external for both teachers and students. These consequences may lead to affective changes on the part of both teachers and students. There may be greater anxiety about reading and writing performance. Coupled with the reduction in the self-reinforcing nature of the teaching activity, this may produce greater teacher burnout.[78] The competitive situation set up between teachers as to who is doing well and who is not, may increase teacher isolation and job dissatisfaction, and decrease teachers' sharing of information and ideas with one another—all of which is likely to be reflected in teachers' behavior and attitudes in the classroom.

The nature of the evaluation procedure may also induce a redefinition of what it means to *be* a teacher and a learner since there are implicit roles in an accountability system. The external locus of the evaluation suggests that the teacher is not responsible—not to be trusted—and therefore must be *held* accountable. This is likely to reduce the teachers' desire to be responsible. Teachers are likely, for example, to adhere more closely to a basal reading system so that if the students do not score well at the end of the year, the responsibility can be attributed to the basal rather than to the teacher.[79] Similarly, the students who are not doing well will be unwelcome additions to the classroom in the first place and are likely to be dealt with as if the responsibility for their failure lies not in instruction, but in the students' intellectual or neurological characteristics or home backgrounds, thus setting up a self-perpetuating situation.[80] Teachers and students may even resort to cheating in one way or another, coaching for specific known test items, pretending certain children were not present when the testing was done, providing hints during the testing and so forth.[81]

A situation may be set up in which the teacher, knowing the curriculum implicit in the test, has all the answers. He may become unable to accept multiple responses as being useful contributions. The role of teacher and learner may become one in which the teacher has the information that the student is to "get" and then be evaluated on to determine the extent to which it was "got." Thus the learner becomes not responsible for his own learning—a passive learner. Students, losing control of their own learning may also reflect many of the thoughts, feelings, and actions of the teachers. Classroom climate may change. There may no longer be any place for digression or fun.

On the other hand, teachers who were previously indolent *may,* when held accountable, begin to apply themselves and actually teach the children who were previously neglected. They *may* be motivated to work more diligently on areas the test showed to be weak. The competitiveness between teachers *may* elevate all the teachers' teaching such that the average performance of the school increases to a level above which no further increments might be expected. Any of these outcomes is possible. The point is that we have to think through them carefully in order to make a judgment on the validity of our procedures.

Suppose we decide to adopt a responsibility approach to evaluation, oriented toward processes and self-evaluation. Again, the possible consequences are many and various. It is possible that more teachers will become lazy or delinquent, that a certain smugness might take over and that the teachers, as a body and individually, will not act responsibly, failing to be reflective and not working to improve their practice. Students too, expected and encouraged to self-evaluate, may fail to do so and become slothful and develop poor reading, writing, and learning habits if not motivated by an external test.

On the other hand, there is also the possibility that teachers and students will take control of their teaching and learning. It is possible that through their process-oriented self-evaluation, they will become active, self-motivated, persistent learners and teachers. The process orientation may reduce the comparisons between students and hence, along with it, the unmotivating perception of failure by some students. Perhaps this will be mirrored in the relationships between teachers, and they will be more inclined to share their knowledge. They may engage in cooperative activities, including more detailed but less ego-threatening self-evaluation, through observing one another teach in the manner in which they observe their students' learning. Cooperative, supportive colleagues coupled with the ongoing feedback provided through their process evaluation might increase teacher satisfaction and reduce teacher burnout.

Perhaps the curriculum, no longer held in place by force, will become less rigid and more learner-directed, and learners will respond to the increased ownership with greater enthusiasm. Since the focus on processes reduces the emphasis on responses being right or wrong, perhaps students will become more respectful of each other's work, and teachers, too, will become more respectful of the activity of even the least able students, no longer treating them as failures. Perhaps there will be room for response diversity and even humor. This may change the roles of teacher and learner, allowing some reciprocity in their roles so that the teacher can allow the student to be the expert, and trust that the student will continue to define and develop that role through self-evaluation. The emphasis on self-evaluation is likely to be reflected in instructional practice and in the metacognitive awareness of the children and the reflectiveness of the teachers.

In both these examples, I have described some of the possible consequences; however, this is not enough. Ultimately in order to make our judgment call on the validity of our evaluation, we must deal with the probabilities of these outcomes actually occurring to varying degrees, and how wonderful or terrible those outcomes would be. We have so little data on which to base probability decisions that in many ways the whole procedure at present comes down to professional and personal judgment. It is clear from the above descriptions where my values and suspected probabilities lie. I make no apology for this. It reinforces the overall point that judgments of the validity of evaluations are fundamentally political. They are based on assumptions about and models of teachers and learners and on decisions about what it means to be literate—the goal of literacy instruction.

CHAPTER 31

Validity and Interpretation

In education, whenever we interpret a learner's performance, we interpret it in terms of hypothetical constructs. In other words, we have hypotheses about why a student performed the way she did. When we take running records of children's oral reading, we interpret them in terms of prediction, monitoring, self-correction from print, self-correction for meaning, and so forth, all of which are hypothetical constructs since we cannot actually see the mental processes as they happen. If we interpret reading test performance, it is in terms of "comprehension ability," or "ability to infer cause and effect," and so forth. We cannot actually see these processes, so we infer them from what we can see. We do not know for sure that these constructs exist—they are hypothetical constructs—yet it is on these that we base our instructional decisions.

Since we are inferring these mental processes, there is obviously a possibility that we are mistaken, and that someone else could infer completely different constructs from the same data (and be equally mistaken). Consequently, the burden is on us to provide evidence that our interpretation is the most plausible one. This evidence consists of the data and the argumentation needed to make a case for our interpretation. For example, in Chapter 28, we argued that Jenny was predicting (Figure 28.1). The justification might lie in the following arguments. Jenny made several sense-preserving substitutions and false starts in situations where the text provided strong contextual information. They occurred particularly at the beginning of lines. In addition, later Jenny groaned in anticipation of an ironic but predictable turn of events in the story. We might also have noticed that Jenny does less of all these things on material that is less familiar or substantially more difficult. Each of these indicators points to our conclusion that Jenny was predicting.

Suppose David performs badly on the reading test at the end of the year. We may wish to explain this performance in terms of the construct "reading ability (or disability)." However, we must reckon with other plausible interpretations too. Could the performance be more adequately interpreted in terms of the construct "anxiety" or "misinterpretation of instructions" or "inadequate background knowledge"? We will never know. We can only build a plausible argument. Even though Shirley answered accurately all the comprehension questions the teacher asked about the story, there is no guarantee that she even read it. She may have been able to answer or guess, based on what she already knew or on subtle signals from the teacher, or she may have previously been read a version of the story by someone else.

Every important aspect of evaluation involves inferring mental activity (hypothetical constructs). Statements about behavior alone are not usually sufficient for instructional purposes. Even when we want to make the statement that Jennifer is an avid reader, we will be making an inference based on limited samples of data and perhaps verbal reports, which some researchers and educators reject as inadmissible evidence. We can say that in school Jennifer reads a great deal. But that does not tell us enough. She may read only because she feels pressure to do so. If we add that she reads a lot when she has free time, it only clarifies the issue further because of the inference about Jennifer's motives that the information invites.

EVIDENCE FOR INTERPRETATIONS

I will turn my attention briefly to the kinds of data and argument commonly used at present. Most official evaluation is currently done using tests. Test makers provide evidence of validity in the manuals that accompany these tests, but the evidence is never strong. Consider, for example, the *Stanford Diagnostic Reading Test,* possibly the most carefully developed of the group diagnostic reading tests. The validity arguments in the manual consist of:

1. Students' scores on this test are closely related to their performance on the *Stanford Test of Academic Skills,* which also purports to test reading and is published by the same company.
2. Experts (working for the testing company) can certify that the test is a good one. As this manual states:

That the test covers the area of reading can, of course, be ascertained by inspecting the items. In the judgment of the authors, the items in SDRT III are representative of the important aspects of reading. (p. 32)

3. Students' performance on a given subtest is more consistent than is their performance across different subtests.
4. Subtest items tend to discriminate well between children who perform well overall on the subtest and those who perform poorly.[82]
5. One way to validate a diagnostic test is to use the diagnosis as the basis for differential instruction and see whether it is more effective than other instruction. The manual notes that:

Some positive clinical evidence has been collected about this type of validity, and experimentation with the diagnostic reliability of the SDRT II has been sufficiently positive to warrant encouraging the use of SDRT III as a diagnostic test. (p. 33) [No references are supplied].

This is about as detailed as the arguments go in any published test. They are less detailed for nondiagnostic achievement tests, which usually simply add data on how well the test predicts later achievement. Probably the most powerful evidence to be used in the argument is the effectiveness of instruction based on the test information (number 5 above). However, I have yet to see such evidence presented in a test manual. It does not seem unreasonable to ask for a description of the conditions under which, and purposes for which, a good argument can be made for the validity of a test.

In every argument there is bound to be a hole or two, but the most important thing is that we try to use several relatively independent sources of information, logically connected, to show that our interpretation is plausible enough for the purpose at hand. It can also be helpful to make counterarguments and try to pit them against other arguments and data. For example, an adult who is reading a book makes many substitutions that make sense in the context, like *motor* for *engine* and *ran* for *raced* or *cab* for *taxi,* even when the context preceding the word does not allow prediction. We hypothesize that either (a) he is a *deep dyslexic* and that somewhere in his neurological equipment there is a glitch that prevents him from locating the exact word but allows the maintenance of meaning, or (b) while orally reading, he is scanning ahead to gain more context and then guessing the word from context. In order to make a supporting argument for the latter construct, the following pieces of evidence are put together.

1. Reading becomes more hesitant for some distance before Bill reaches a word that gives him trouble.
2. Bill reports looking ahead to words that he thinks will give him trouble.
3. When asked to read using a masking card to expose one word at a time, his error rate decreases markedly, self-corrections increase, and both return to former levels when the masking card is not used (see Figure 31.1).

These separate pieces of data strongly suggest that as Bill begins to read he begins to scan ahead to look for words that might give him trouble. As he approaches one of these words, he begins to devote part of his attention to figuring out the word before he actually arrives at it. This divided attention produces the hesitant reading. Such a strategy cannot be used with the masking card, and indeed, the strategy appears to be blocked by the use of the masking card.

This argument for the validity of the construct is quite different from the arguments presented by testing companies for the constructs they claim to measure with their reading tests. The inclusion of intervention data is of critical importance in making the argument more convincing. It should not be unreasonable to expect such data from testing companies. However, many people, mesmerized by the scientific appearance of tests, remain convinced by the scant logic of the arguments provided in test manuals. What is considered convincing has to do with the values and beliefs of the people to be convinced.

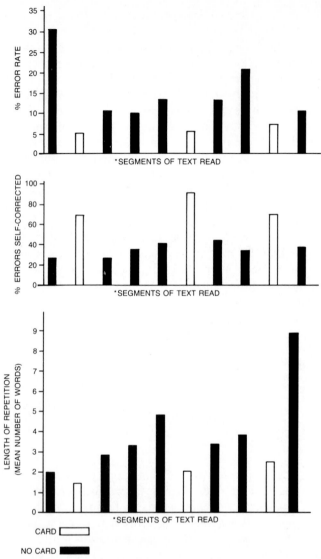

Figure 31.1. The effects of a self-controlled masking card on oral reading behaviors. Segments of text were read with and without the use of a card masking all but the word being read. These text segments were not identical in length. Longer segments were broken into smaller units of similar length. The average number of words per segment was 134. (From Peter H. Johnston, "Understanding Reading Disability: A Case Study Approach," *Harvard Educational Review,* 55:2, pp. 153–177. Copyright © by the President and Fellows of Harvard College. All rights reserved.)

THE FORM OF EVALUATION AND THE INTERPRETATION

The constructs we end up with can be highly constrained by the format of an evaluation procedure. For example, consider the *Diagnostic Reading Scales* (Spache, 1981). This is an individually administered diagnostic reading test that the publishers say tests oral (instructional) and silent (independent) reading comprehension, reading potential (listening comprehension), and decoding ability (through twelve different decoding subtests). Of the time spent testing, at least 60 percent will be spent testing at the word level or below, which presumably reflects the author's theoretical orientation to reading. Similarly, the test presents an "independent level" of reading that must be at least as high as the "instructional level," since it is sought only on passages that are more difficult than the already failed "instructional" passage. Other tests such as the *Analytic Reading Inventory* (*ARI*) provide "independent level" reading scores that are as low as or lower than the "instructional level." These notions of what constitutes "independent reading" are both plausible and yet quite different. The *DRS* assumes that independent reading is silent and that it is unnecessary to be able to say or even understand all the words, so long as the reader generally understands the story. The *ARI,* on the other hand, assumes that independent and instructional reading are similar, except that in independent reading the reader will be unable to obtain help to figure out problems. The use of nonsense syllables as a means of testing decoding is a procedure not accepted by all reading researchers. Similarly, the choice of the term "reading potential" for listening test performance also reflects a different orientation.

You may say that an evaluator may choose and highlight the information that she presents. That is true. However, when faced with thirteen scores relating to decoding and word recognition, and two scores relating to comprehension, some explaining has to be done, and a more difficult argument must be made on the part of an evaluator who does not share the test author's theoretical orientation toward the nature of reading.

This situation is worse in the case of group tests like the *California Test of Basic Skills* when they are used to hold teachers and/or students accountable. In that case the theoretical orientation of the test maker is transferred to the classroom by administrators selecting basal reading programs to match the test and by teachers who are anxious to help their students do the best they can on that test. A first-grade teacher whose approach to instruction deemphasizes phonic analysis is in a difficult position. The simple fact that standardized tests of reading almost without exception have a single right answer, reflects another value that is certainly not universally held, but that is strongly reflected in school activities.

In the case of teachers' direct observations and records, these value judgments are certainly not avoided. Indeed, the staunch supporters of testing, denying the problem in testing, attack teacher observation most strongly on this issue. The old adage that "if I hadn't believed it I never would have seen it" is certainly true for teachers' observations, as I have already noted, but it is also true for test driven evaluation. The difference is that the test producer prescribes the lens.

THE CONSEQUENCES OF INTERPRETATIONS

Both direct and indirect evaluation procedures produce information that is interpreted and reported to an audience. The reporting provides another window on the value/theory side of things. Suppose a child reads a text as follows:

> **TEXT**   "Do you think they will come
> to our party?" asked Janet.
> "I do not think so."
>
> **RUNNING**
> **RECORD**   yes | SC ✓ ✓ ✓ ✓
>   ✓
>   ✓ ✓ ✓ ✓ ✓
>   ✓ ✓ ✓ ✓ ✓

One teacher will report this recorded observation as "John predicts while he is reading." A second teacher will report that "John is inclined to guess at words." Both teachers may further reveal their values by adding modifiers to their description such as "actively predicts" or "guesses roughly." Everyone knows that it is good to be an active reader, and who needs rough guessing! Notice how each of these interpretations implies certain hypothetical constructs. We see (interpret) with these constructs, and we communicate through them too; thus they have consequences for students' literacy learning.

Remedial reading efforts are based on our interpretations of students' reading and writing. Anna Gillingham, for example, originator of the Orton-Gillingham remedial reading technique, interpreted children's reading difficulties in terms of neurological problems, the permanence and severity of which required special procedures:

> . . . words are to be sounded out and blended from phonetic units, increase in speed coming from greater and greater facility in blending, not from wider and wider recognition. Sentences thus slowly and painfully worked out, must be reread so as to give the thought "to sound like real talking."[83]

Words which had not yet been covered in the child's "drill" are to be "pronounced quietly by [the teacher] before he has looked at them at all." In spite of this intensive one-to-one, specially designed instruction, she believed that:

> . . . four years is the minimum [of this remedial instruction] but that really the child who has specific language disability should be taught by special techniques of this kind throughout his entire life.[84]

Almost invariably, however, the pupil who as a little child has had trouble in acquiring mastery of the reading technique will all his life be a very slow reader; for example, he will find courses in history which require a large amount of supplementary reading extremely laborious. Sometimes it will even be necessary to have some of the mass of subject matter read aloud to him.[85]

Committed to her interpretation, she was unable to consider the possibility that the laborious decoding emphasis she recommended may actually have been the cause of the continuing slow reading, or that the extreme displeasure in reading caused by this particularly dreary instructional technique may have virtually eliminated most of the child's reading, and hence the automation of word recognition. Neither was she able to consider the possibility that the continued dependence of her clients on her instruction might be a function of the instruction itself. Our interpretations have considerable consequences, and we must continually reflect on the patterns of responses, the nature of instruction, and their possible meanings. This reflection can take place in many ways—within our journals, in our heads, and in our conversations with colleagues and other professionals; but we must set aside time for it and enter it without ego involvement.

CHAPTER 32

Validity and the Uses of Evaluation

As I described at the outset, one cannot make a judgment about the validity of an evaluation procedure out of the context of the use to which it is put. Let us consider then, the kinds of uses to which evaluation procedures are put. The following are some common uses:

☐ Placing students in:
　　tracks
　　classes
　　books
☐ Diagnosing students' instructional needs (within a given instructional program)

☐ Screening students so that those seen as not yet ready for a program are kept out of it
☐ Procurement of state or federal funding (e.g., Chapter I)
☐ Classification of students (for example as Learning Disabled)
☐ Holding teachers and schools accountable
☐ Providing motivation for students
☐ Finding out whether instruction (or a change in it) was effective

Not everyone would agree on the appropriateness of all of these uses and, again, they all have implicit values. Some of these uses would not likely be stated overtly. For instance, the procurement of state or federal funding would generally not be stated as a reason for an evaluation procedure, but it can be inferred, for example, from the rate of classification of children as learning disabled in a context in which funding formulas provide incentives for classification. This rate increased over 100 percent in New York State once funding became contingent on the classification of learning disability.[86] This suggests that the procedure for classifying children took on a new instrumental value.

VALUES AND CONSEQUENCES OF EVALUATION

Some of the uses listed above are probably seen by most readers as being obviously necessary and not open to debate. However, I would hasten to say that each and every one is open to debate as to the need for its existence. For example, someone might argue that it is critical to identify reading disabled students so that they can be placed in the remedial reading program. Another might counter that the remedial program is ineffective, or disruptive, and therefore the classification is unhelpful. I might argue that there is a central need for self-evaluation, both of teachers and students. Someone might counter that we have managed so far without much of either so it is not a real need, and I would counter that for the kind of schooling that I think is needed in a democratic multicultural society, self-evaluation is critical. Again, we have a question of values.

In a similar vein, many feel that an accountability system is critical for maintaining public faith in the schools. "Taxpayers need hard data to show that they are getting their money's worth." Again, this depends on how you see the problem. If the issue is one of whether the public trusts the schools to do the best possible job, then perhaps a better way is for the school community to be very open about what it does, making sure that it is responsible and dedicated and that the public sees this to be so. Actually, this may be seen as a form of evaluation in which the school supplies the public with information so that the public's judgment of the school's activity is well informed. Under such circumstances, the roles of the school and the public are like those of teacher and student in a process approach to evaluation in the classroom. It rather depends on both parties being trusting and open to dialogue.

When we have decided on a need for evaluation, and laid out the options and their expected consequences, we must decide on an appropriate procedure or set of procedures. We need to decide which procedures would provide the most relevant information in the most timely and useable fashion for the decisions we or others need to make. At the same time we will be concerned about the resources needed such as money, expertise, and time. In other words, we will be concerned about how to find out exactly what we want to know most efficiently and effectively. If we had decided that the consequences of using a standardized test would, on balance, warrant its use, this would be the time to read test manuals written by responsible test manufacturers. Although these are written in such a way that virtually nobody actually reads them, doing so is important if you are going to use the test. This can be an amusing or distressing exercise, depending on how you look at it. However, tests will rarely be called for.

Suppose we need to find out why Rachel never reads when the class has "free reading" time. It would not serve our purpose well to have her take a standardized test to find out where she is having trouble. It would take unnecessary time and money, and at the same time probably limit our progress toward optimal instruction by making her less happy with reading than before. A better technique might involve altering the context somewhat to see whether some change could be induced. Perhaps the teacher might begin reading aloud to the class a book that Rachel would be able to read and that happened to be on a topic of importance to Rachel. After getting the class hooked, the teacher allows Rachel to borrow the book and moves on to start another book. Further exploration could occur in a subsequent individual reading interview, whether or not she began to read the book independently.

POSING USEFUL PROBLEMS AND COLLECTING USEFUL DATA

Possibly the biggest obstacle to development in evaluation practices has been the rather restricted view of what constitute appropriate data. Our own histories have been filled with so much testing, and virtually all the writing about related theory (such as reliability and validity) has been based on tests as the sole source of legitimate data. There is an enormous variety of sources of data and ways of recording it. I have presented a number of these in the earlier sections of the book, but the selection is by no means exhaustive. Remember that the most instructionally useful information is that which tells us *how,* and *under what conditions* a student performs an activity rather than *how well* it was performed relative to some standard. However, the most important part of the evaluation is not the quality of information it provides, but the effect it has on the learner. If the learner has no answer, but has his curiosity piqued, then the focus of the question may be attended to subsequently. A reflective question can have the effect of making a person reflective. The initial question itself may yield little evaluation information, but the *consequences* of the evaluation procedure may be great.

We will be concerned that the information provided is what we need and that our interpretation of it is reasonable. Some forms of data are more widely acceptable than others and, in general, multiple data sources are even more helpful since they provide convergent evidence for construct validity. Thus, we need not think in terms of a single procedure as being optimal. Sometimes two rather simple sources that are quite different from one another may be more useful than a single more elaborate procedure. For example, the information provided by a sample of oral reading, together with a sample of writing or a brief dictation test, can provide more useful information than can an entire battery of phonics tests. In the first place, together they provide information about the relationship between speech and print *in use*. Second, they focus the teacher's attention on helping students learn how to learn about patterns and relationships rather than on discrete pieces of information about phonic regularities. This difference in focus is one of the critical distinguishing features between more and less successful teachers of young children with reading difficulties.[87]

The utility of an evaluation procedure must also take into account human factors such as the likelihood that the information will be used at all. For example, the technology is now available to actually have microcomputers listen to a child read out loud, record and analyze the performance, and provide a written analysis of the strategies and cues the child used. This could provide an enormous amount of detailed data with minimal teacher involvement. Very efficient, perhaps. However, only if the teacher actually uses this information will it be of any value, and there is no way that the teacher is going to be able to carry all this information around in his head since he does not own the information. Though it takes more time for the teacher to collect the information himself, it is worth the effort because when we see a child actually perform an activity, it sticks in our mind. When we are simply provided with a variety of decontextualized data about a child, such as the previous year's subtest scores, it is usually quite abstract and rather difficult to recall. It is manageable with one or two children, but not with a whole class. Thus, what looks like an efficient procedure may well be extraordinarily inefficient when we take into account the information actually used. This same argument can be made with respect to timing. If a standardized test is used at the beginning of the year and the teachers do not receive the information from the testing company scoring the tests for another month, then even if the information is detailed and accurate, time will have passed, the information will be out of date, the teacher will already have had to make important instructional decisions, and the procedure becomes inefficient.

Any decision on an evaluation procedure has to involve not only our immediate goal, but also the long-term goal of optimal literacy instruction for all children. Thus, when we look at efficiency and effectiveness, we must not fall into the trap of focusing on the evaluation of minute details of a child's performance in order to, say, pass an end-of-unit test in a basal, at the cost of the longer term goals and the larger picture. Another trap involves our definition of what it means to be literate. It is easy to become myopic about the particular grade level where we are teaching, and to define activities in terms of the performance on the end-of-level basal test. Even the notion that being literate is somehow a unidimensional (''measurable'') construct is problematic. Not everything of importance is measurable, or even definable. Sometimes in the measuring and defining (necessary for measuring) we trivialize the construct. Try measuring or even defining love, for example. Literacy is similarly complex.

CHAPTER 33

Alternative Approaches to Validity

I have described validity so far in terms of construct validity. At the center of construct validity is the value-laden interpretation and use of behavioral data in terms of hypothetical constructs. Although many have argued that virtually all validity involves construct validity,[88] most practitioners of educational measurement, including the testing industry, and popular textbooks on educational measurement tend to stress a less unified view of validity. The language of the more traditional approach is still common, so I will describe it here and relate it to construct validity and the generalizability that we have already discussed. The major difference is that validity has generally been described in terms of a wide variety of different types of validity.

Construct validity has been described in terms of *convergent validity* and *discriminant validity*. These refer to types of evidence that are presented to show that the construct is plausible. Convergent evidence is evidence from alternate sources such as direct observation and interview, which suggest the existence of the same construct. Discriminant evidence is evidence that indicates the uniqueness of the construct by showing that it is unrelated to other constructs it theoretically should not be related to, such as evidence which shows that Matt's reversal of certain words is related to the use of particular word identification strategies rather than to the structure of his brain. The use of clearly described criterion variables has been referred to as *criterion-related validity* and is essentially convergent evidence for the construct. For example, we might argue that a sample of dictation taken at the end of kindergarten is a good and very quick indicator of reading ability. In order to demonstrate this, we might relate it to running record performance or to standardized reading test scores, depending on whom we wanted to convince of our interpretation. Often standardized tests use teacher judgment as a criterion variable. This is a very interesting argument. If teacher's judgment is a good criterion for how well a test measures reading ability, then surely it obviates the need for the test.

Several other forms of validity have less to do with the construct per se than with the generalizability or relevance of the interpretation. *Ecological validity,* for example, refers to the extent to which a construct described in an artificial setting, such as a multiple choice test, can be generalized to what happens under normal conditions. For example, does Mary's failure to figure out nonsense words on a test have anything to do with her reading when she reads books at home? For our purposes, it is the transfer of assessment to the individual that ultimately develops ecological validity. If we can develop self-evaluation, then ecologically valid observations occur because students and teachers will observe themselves engaged in the activity in the context in which it naturally occurs, and the observation will also be part of their natural behavior. What will have developed is what Donald Schon calls "reflection in action."

Population validity, task validity, and temporal validity would better be termed population generalizability, task generalizability, and temporal generalizability since they refer to the extent to which the interpretation will hold up across different samples within these variables. For example, is the performance of this group of students generalizable to another group of students (population generalizability)? Is this student's behavior today representative of his behavior at other times (temporal generalizability)? *External validity* refers to the whole set of these facets of generalizability.

Predictive validity is frequently used as a selling point by test manufacturers, showing that performance on their test in kindergarten, for example, predicts performance in third grade on a different test. This is better referred to as predictive utility.[89] The validity of a construct is not necessarily involved. For example, a math test in kindergarten may well be a good predictor of reading test performance in grade two, and if that information were useful, the test would have predictive utility. However, the traditional application of this concept has ignored the consequences of use. Earlier this century it was found that cultural background predicted performance on "intelligence tests." However, the reliability of the relationship had nothing to do with the validity of the construct. It was simply not the case that the majority of Italians, for example, were intellectually incompetent. Rather, they spoke a different language and had different cultural experiences from the folk who constructed the test. Prediction is one thing, but we can only understand the nature of the prediction and what causes it, in terms of constructs shared by the predictor and criterion variables. Without knowing why it predicts (the underlying constructs), and without considering the consequences of the use of the predictive information, we are likely to make some bad decisions. Thus predictive validity is better seen in terms of constructs and the consequences of use.

Face validity has been used to refer to the extent to which the evaluation procedure appears to be a reasonable procedure to those involved in being evaluated (a threat to construct validity) and to those who use the data from the evaluation (a problem in making a coherent argument for a specific audience).

The major area of concern in the past few years has been *content validity,* which refers to the extent to which an evaluation procedure represents a clearly specified content domain. Tests and basals readers are keyed together for this purpose with tests of main idea, details, and so forth. Samuel Messick of ETS notes that in its traditional form this is actually not a matter of validity at all but one of describing procedures for test construction.[90] In addition, it is limited to describing them in purely behavioral terms; otherwise it once again becomes construct validity. A purely behavioral description is inadequate for instructional purposes. The critical domain to be specified is the intellectual process used by the individual to produce the behavior. Once again we are in the area of construct validity.

SUMMARY COMMENT

All evaluation is value-laden and is based on *inferences* made by individuals. These inferences form the basis of the second most important aspect of validity: construct validity (the most important being the consequences of the evaluation). Constructs are socially negotiated constructions of reality that are subject to change in interpretation. Many students who were once called *remedial readers* are now called *learning disabled* as a result of Public Law 94-142, which provides funding for students who are considered to have a neurological handicap. The constructs change, but so do people's values. The funds currently devoted to students classified as handicapped may disappear at any time, depending on the decisions of legislators who represent the adult population of the country. Thus, validity is neither fixed nor antiseptic. As Samuel Messick points out, both the evaluator's interpretation and the consequences of interpretation are important for judgments of validity. Thus, as he puts it, "validity judgments are value judgments."[91]

At the heart of the judgments of validity lies the teacher's (and others') ability to imagine what thought processes on the part of the child could have lead to her performance, to research and rule out various hypotheses, and to imagine the consequences of the evaluation for the child. These interpretations are value laden from the start.

CHAPTER 34

Reporting to Others

A person does not have to be a professional writer to tell a case-history with authority and power. He has only to know his journey intimately and carry some attitude toward it which enables something more than a bad list of names and dates.

Ken Macrorie

I have stressed the fact that the student is a teacher's client first and foremost. Consequently, some of what a teacher learns is privileged information given by the student with the understanding that it remain confidential. However, teachers have responsibilities to others as well. Parents of the student are interested in his progress. Every year teachers write millions of report cards to expectant parents (and their children). Others in the school system such as specialist teachers, next year's teacher, and administrators are also interested in the student's progress. This means that part of the responsibility of an evaluator is clear communication of useful information to the appropriate audience. Part of this responsibility is not merely passing on information but, rather, educating the other party. For example, parents and many administrators currently are most persuaded by test scores. They were not born with this interest in test scores; and if they are ever to become interested in more important and relevant information, they will need to learn the alternatives. Writing about students' literacy development should not be taken lightly.

LANGUAGE

When you write a report, you are trying to communicate to another person a clear, accurate picture of a student's literacy development as you see it. It should be as unambiguous as possible and should contain the level of detail necessary for someone to make instructional decisions. Descriptions that resemble Rorschach designs or Cubist paintings are of little value. Clear language and examples are essential. People writing about children commonly use abstract words. For example, a teacher might say, "Jack has an improved attention span," instead of saying that he attends to his work for longer periods of time, or even "Yesterday, Jack wrote for an hour without leaving his chair or even talking to anyone." More abstract words have two distinct disadvantages. In the first place they do not invoke memorable mental images. Second, they tend to carry an implicit permanence. Being "learning disabled" is not seen as something that will go away in a hurry.

Most professions have their own specialized language that allows them to talk with others in the profession in such a way that those outside the profession feel unable to participate. This makes the client feel helpless and the professional feel indispensable. Medical doctors speak of hemorrhaging or exsanguinating rather than simply bleeding. School psychologists, speech therapists, and others all have developed these languages. Such languages are, in part, a sign of a lack of confidence that respect can be earned any other way, and in part a lack of consideration for their audience. All educators must avoid this trap. Some specialized terms may be unavoidable, when they refer to a completely new phenomenon, but we should aim for no jargon. Even terms such as "syntax" can be replaced by "sentence structure." "Semantics" is probably better spelled m-e-a-n-i-n-g or called "sense." Consider the difference between the following two versions of the same report:

> Lucy's text processing skills are very weak in the decoding area, particularly in decoding polysyllabic words. She decodes accurately the initial and terminal elements of monosyllabic and bisyllabic words but cannot adequately process the medial elements, particularly diphthongs, and does not integrate syntactic and semantic contextual information with the graphic cues. Whereas processing textual information is weak, auditory comprehension is strong.

> versus

> Lucy understands stories very well when they are read to her. However, when she reads them for herself she sometimes has trouble, particularly in figuring out longer words. She generally figures out how the beginning and the end of the word might sound, but is often confused by the middle of the word, particularly when there are two vowels together. She has not yet learned to use the meaning of the other words to help her to figure out confusing words.

In other words, try to use plain English as much as possible. Pretentious, thoughtless language, though it is usually used to establish a power difference, has more consequences than people think. Melissa, a seven-year-old, came to our reading lab with a report from the director of a medical center. The report contained the following segment (more of which is presented in Chapter 21):

> . . . The root of Melissa's academic difficulties appears to be a developmental language disorder of a mixed semantic pragmatic/phonologic syntactic deficits.[sic] These have been translated into more academic difficulties as it relates to the pragmatic use of language in the verbal setting that academics generally require. . . .

Never, never do this. It may inflate your ego (errors notwithstanding) but to parents who care deeply about their child's welfare, this is devastating. One way or another this is passed on to the child. Physicians are the worst at mystifying and terrifying their patients with abstract technical terms. But this behavior has its consequences. The field of iatrogenics is the study of, as Neil Postman puts it, "how doctor-talk can intensify and even induce illness."[92] As you can see from the above report, children's literacy development might well produce a similar field of study.

FRAMING

It is common practice to present background information at the beginning of a report to provide the reader with a context within which to interpret the evaluation information. This is a recognition that the child's reading and writing activity is influenced by the current and historical context. Sometimes, however, we inadvertently present contexts that are less than helpful for one reason or another. Consider the following beginning of a report we received.

> Bruce is a nine year old fourth grader who is about to enter the Maplehill School remedial reading program. He has a central auditory processing deficit, significant language, reading and writing deficits, and visual perceptual difficulty. The City Hospital has determined that Bruce has moderately low receptive and expressive language skills, moderately severe delays in syntax development, decreased language processing abilities and pragmatic skills (ability to label categories, sequence, follow more than a 3-step directive, continue a conversation, and think imaginatively), and a moderate articulation disorder. He has been referred to the school speech therapist but the parents have refused this help.

There are several instructive points in this report. First, the choice of words is critical. For example, it would be better to say "his parents have declined this help" or "have decided against this course of action" than to say "refused this help." Refused has a negative valence which is unnecessary and biases interpretation. Second, no matter what information is presented after this introduction, it is likely to be interpreted as "Well—this is only to be expected given the student's disabilities." One way of preventing this problem is to avoid attributing to the student such stable traits as "central auditory processing deficits" and to save any such relevant information until somewhere near the end filed under "instructional history," which emphasizes what the child *does* and his instructional environment, and takes the blame away from the child. At least the example might be rewritten as follows:

> Bruce is a nine year old fourth grader at Maplehill school who is about to enter the reading support program. He receives speech/language therapy at Hillside Hospital three times per week. The school has offered the services of the school speech therapist. However, Mr and Mrs. Green have declined this service as they feel that with his reading support program as well, Bruce would be away from his regular class too much and would fall behind in other areas.

There is some discrepancy between the evaluations of his reading performance made by the school and by the hospital.

Filed under "Additional Information" at the end you might write:

David's speech therapist, John Morton, reports that David has been later than most children in developing mature speech patterns. In test situations he appears not to speak or listen as well as his peers. Sometimes Bruce's speech is not easy to understand as he does not articulate Ls and Rs very clearly. In a test situation he does not participate well in discussions with adults, and he has trouble repeating exactly sentences of more than four words which are read to him. He tends to alter them to his own language patterns. Greater detail on this aspect of David's development can be found in the hospital's report. However, it is not yet clear that this is the source of any difficulties with David's reading or writing.

There are other framing problems too. Children who are least able are most likely to be described in negative terms because:

1. Schools are structured normatively, and those below the norm are generally seen through what they do not know and can't do, rather than through what they know and can do.
2. Tests (and I include basal readers in this) enforce and make consequential a normative view of children, particularly when the tests are used for teacher accountability.
3. Less-able children are most likely to be placed in material that is too difficult for them, so they show more negative behaviors.

Thus when evaluators observe a child's performance, particularly if the child has already been determined to "have a problem," they tend to see and report a lot of negative information. In the same way, readers who assume at the outset that the child has a problem (otherwise why would there be a report and why would I have to read it?), tend to scan, looking for the problems. In my experience with teachers, if the student's activity is analyzed into "strengths" and "weaknesses," these readers will often bypass the strengths and go directly to read the weaknesses, especially if they are short of time. One way around this is to format the report in a manner which will not facilitate this abuse. A second way is to ensure that the recipients of the report are not novices. The latter method is most feasible within a school district, and is probably not adequate by itself. Nonetheless, whatever ways can be found to educate other relevant people should be taken. For example, send home regular explanations of what is being done in school and why, what changes parents should expect to see, why invented spelling is important, give examples in newsletters, parent nights, and on local TV channels.

Sheer weight of information can present a serious framing problem too. Take, for example, a test like the *Diagnostic Reading Scales* (Spache, 1981).

This test essentially provides three text level scores—an instructional reading level, an independent reading level, and a potential reading level—and twelve test scores below the word level. Once all that lower level detail information has been reported, it is hard to write instructional suggestions that focus on the less easily counted and less frequently mentioned aspects such as enjoyment and frequency of reading. Unfortunately, the resulting instructional suggestions are often antithetical to one another. Close attention to a child's spelling or decoding is likely to make writing or reading even less enjoyable by distracting her from the meaningfulness of the activity.

VOICE AND STYLE

Throughout this book I have tried to make it clear that we are people describing the activity of people. We cannot avoid being involved in interpretation. Thus it is proper for us to write reports that sound as if an involved person wrote them. In an earlier chapter I discussed the issue of "objectivity" in evaluation. I described how educational assessment has been dominated by a positivistic philosophy in which SCIENTIFIC ASSESSMENT is seen as able to produce statements of FACT that are independent of human judgment. Hopefully I convinced you that this is not the case, and that pretending so is dishonest. It is easier for people to take this perspective using group tests that depersonalize the situation and make it seem as though the group is not made up of individuals, but reports are usually written about individuals in the same way. Reports are frequently written as if the writers were simply passive recorders of TRUTH. People fear that if there is a strong, active voice in the writing, then the subjectivity of the process will become obvious.

This is an unfortunate practice that I would like to see discontinued for several reasons. First, the practice is dishonest in that it pretends to an unquestionable status that is not possible. Second, such writing is done in the passive voice, which is boring and eminently forgettable. Third, the style of writing depersonalizes the person being written about and discourages the reader from attempting to know the person whose activity is being described. Indeed, such writing is an attempt to disguise the fact that there is a person to know. Mikhail Bakhtin has called this type of activity *thingification* as opposed to *personification*.[93]

Writers favoring the "objective" approach to report writing avoid narrative writing in favor of more expository styles. Such writers feel that narrative style is indicative of "stories" with their implicit subjectivity. After all, stories are based on motives and goals and feelings and other such "soft" stuff and they are associated with fiction. But from my perspective, when I have read a report of a child's writing and reading development, I like to have the feeling that I know the student and will remember her. It is not enough for me to have lots of bits of information, no matter how good the information is. I must relate to the person who was responsible for the activity, not to the behaviors per se.

Although reports are functional (and often legal) documents, they need not be boring and unreadable.

There is bound to be a tension between brevity and the concreteness and narrativity, which I mentioned earlier. I think this is a fine balance that is gained only by practice and sharing with colleagues. Part of your practice might include:

1. Take five minutes in class and choose a student you don't know very well, and write continuously about what you observe about him and what he is doing.
2. Take five minutes and write continuously about what is going on in the classroom. Do not be afraid to record questions and other responses to what is going on.

Do this on different occasions at different times of the day.[94] These practices should help you to become familiar with what you are writing about, with noticing details, and with being aware of the context. Such observations help flesh out other data you already have about students. In combination with the interview and other one-to-one observations, they give a good balance between the distance and personalization needed in the writing.

Always remember in writing about students that the child is your client and there should be nothing in the report that you would not be able to say in front of him. Indeed, normally it makes considerable sense to go over the report with the student before sending it anywhere. This does not mean that you should expect a six-year-old to be able to understand all you might have written, but you should weigh carefully the consequences of what you have to say. Do not send a report such as that suggested in the manual for the *Degrees of Reading Power* test.[95] The writers of this manual suggest a form letter to parents:

> This test score indicates that (David) cannot read many of the books commonly used in school, and that (he) is not reading as well as most other third grade students.
>
> In order to help (David) improve (his) reading ability, we are placing (him) in a special reading program called _____. A description of the program is enclosed with this letter.

Please!

CHAPTER 35

What Goes in a Report

Reports on students' literate development are written for a variety of different purposes. For example. there is the standard end-of-quarter (or whatever the year is broken into) report card to parents, the report written for a Committee on Special Education meeting, and the report to an outside agency. Different audiences and different purposes will present different challenges. In this chapter I will give some guidelines for putting reports together.

IMPORTANT INFORMATION

When I read a report I want to learn how the student goes about literate activity and in what context he normally does so. I want to know what aspects of literate activity the student controls, and I want useful information about the instructional conditions. Probably the most important item to report about the student's literate activity is whether or not she actually engages in it and becomes involved. If a student does not read or write independently and is very reluctant to do so even with support, this is the most important piece of information. Second, I want to know about self-directed activity in a supportive situation. Does self-monitoring and self-correction occur in reading and writing? Are different sources of information integrated in the process (self-correction from print cues and from grammatical and meaning cues)? Does the student predict at the sentence *and* text levels? Does the student's activity show that she is reading to construct a meaning? Does the student use a variety of strategies to solve problems with the text? Are the strategies used flexibly? If the student is stalled when figuring out a word, what kinds of support will restart a healthy reading process? Does the student ask critical questions of authors when reading?

The Context

I find it helpful to have some contextual information about the nature of the relevant school curriculum and organization. For example, if Jennifer is out of her classroom for reading and for speech, it is helpful to report this and comment on what is missed in the regular program. If a child has been retained, or changed schools recently (or frequently), then this should be mentioned. It is not, however, helpful to know that Sarah is a "cute little girl with sparkling green eyes."

For those who are writing reports from outside the classroom, describing the classroom context can be quite tricky. It is easy to offend by reporting the context in a manner that is seen as inappropriate or inaccurate. It would be tacky to describe a classroom as being "drab and uninteresting." However, to say that the walls displayed the following items: a clock, two pictures of birds, and a Santa Claus—raises this as an issue for reflection for the teacher. An instructional context defined as "whole language" or "direct instruction" is likely to be less than helpful. More detail is required lest people's assumptions take over. "I observed Michael during his language arts period. He spent a total of 2:36 reading. The story was *My Dog Al* in his reading book, and his accuracy rate was 85%. This reading was done orally for the teacher. He spent a total of one minute and twenty seconds composing a piece of writing. He completed four worksheets that required filling in the blanks in sentences and drawing lines between words and pictures. Of the 31 items on the worksheets he completed seven accurately. These seven involved matching a word with a picture. Michael participated in one whole class lesson on the subject of capitalization. In an interview he had the following responses:

> Q: What does a good reader do?
> A: Says all the words right.
> Q: I have a friend who will probably be in this class next year. Do you have any advice for him about how to do well in reading?
> A: Sit quietly and have a sharp pencil.

The order in which observations are addressed in a report, and the emphasis given to them will determine to some extent how the reader of the report addresses the student's needs. The effectiveness will also be influenced by the extent to which the information is memorable. Clear, concrete examples or brief anecdotes help people to know the students better and to remember and use the information during instruction. Annotated, dated photocopies of samples of a student's writing make a large difference to the comprehensibility of a student's report.

Instructional Suggestions

In most reports there should be clear instructional or support suggestions. This is usually the least well handled by school psychologists and others who lack experience in teaching reading and writing. For the teacher, however, this is the bottom line. Consequently, if the suggestions are confusing, unclear, conflicting, or otherwise unhelpful, then don't write any.

For the parent, too, this should be an important part of a report. Often the parents of children who are failing to become literate feel powerless in the face of a severe threat to their child. This feeling of helplessness is terrible and can lead to emotional complications of the child's problem. Children read faces and actions better than words and, unwittingly, parents can pass serious messages about failure to their children (just as teachers do). Often, parents can be helped as much as children by helping them to develop a supportive role at home. Some of the possibilities are such things as:

☐ Reading to the child
☐ Providing study space and study time, free of television and other distractions
☐ Spending time discussing world events in the newspaper or on television
☐ Recommending local parent training or involvement programs
☐ Describing the nature of the activities a child brings home to do, such as the repeated readings from a tape

When making suggestions be sure to make them practical and clear. The following actual example would not be accepted well by a parent or teacher looking for help.

William needs to develop print skill strategies. He has a limited sight vocabulary that needs to be addressed. In addition, William needs to progress beyond blending of initial consonant sounds. He would improve his reading fluency and accuracy if he understood variations made by vowels including the r-controlled vowel. William's word analysis and phonics test showed a weakness in identifying common consonant digraphs such as ch and th. Include in the lessons writing samples using sight words and other phonetic skills. Once William has mastered some of these print skill strategies, comprehension based on visual modes of instruction will reflect an understanding of the author's intended meaning.

A more helpful response to this same student would be:

William's reading program should focus on two areas. First, he needs to read a great deal of easy material in order to develop his fluency. Many books could be reread, and some books could be made easy enough for him to read by first reading them to him. I have added to this report a list of books that will be appropriate and match some of his interests.

In order to help William figure out words using the letter–sound relationships, involve him in writing. Also find opportunities in his writing to highlight words containing th, ch, sh, since these are particularly difficult for him. Since he already is comfortable with the words "the" and "she" in both reading and writing, I would use these as keys to help him work out related words. His use of vowels will be helped by attention to rhyming, particularly in his writing, and to the feelings in his mouth when he says them.

Some parents will still see standardized test scores as a central part of a report. I believe this is because of a lack of understanding of the limitations of such scores and of the possible alternatives. It would be helpful if test scores were reported only as the range within which they fall rather than as a single score. It seems reasonable that we report only the range within which we are 95 percent confident that a student's score lies. On the auditory discrimination subtest of the *Stanford Diagnostic Reading Test* (red level, form B, 1976) a second grader with a raw test score of 32 would have his percentile rank reported as somewhere between the 25th and the 93rd percentiles. Not exactly laser precision.

REPORTING CONVENTIONS

Whenever you report particular types of information about a student, you should explain briefly, but clearly, the date and source of the information. If you used a test, you should report which one in full, including the name of the publisher, copyright date, form (A, B, C, etc.), and any deviations from the standardized procedure. For example, you might report:

Sonja's (date) performance on the *Stanford Diagnostic Reading Test* (Harcourt Brace Jovanovich, 1976) Red level, form A, was as follows:

	Raw Score	Stanine
Auditory Vocabulary:	20	2
Auditory Discrimination:	30	3
Phonetic Analysis:	19	2
Word reading:	36	4
Reading Comprehension:	45	5

Running record of *There's a nightmare in my closet* (M. Mayer, 1968). Record taken on 4/3/85. This book has been read to the class twice in the two weeks preceding this running record. However, Tony has never read it himself before.

Any writing samples will require comments about the context in which they were produced along with the dates and any other relevant contextualizing information. For example, a writing sample might have the following information appended:

This is the first draft of a story by Paul Simpson written on 2/24/90 during a free choice period. He chose the topic himself and the piece was completed in less than thirty minutes. He did not return to it.

It makes a considerable difference if a piece of writing is an example of reflex writing in a five-minute period, or the result of four drafts and three hours work. It makes a difference if the piece was copied, or if the topic or activity was selected by the author.

STRUCTURING A REPORT

In part the content of your report will determine the structure. That is, if you are reporting on someone whose development is limited, you might structure the report differently than if you were reporting about a student who could manage eighth-grade work. Depending on the type of report, some of the detail might be abridged at the outset in a form that is easily accessed. For example:

NAME:	PARENT(S):
AGE:	TELEPHONE:
DATE OF BIRTH:	ADDRESS:
SCHOOL:	EVALUATOR:
GRADE:	DATE OF REPORT:

However, such headings are not necessary for most reports, and have some side effects. They are reminiscent of a hospital chart. Mostly the student's name and the date are best displayed clearly at the outset.

People who read reports are usually busy people, and they need good information in a reasonably short time. A sure way to have information ignored is to bury it in lengthy discourse. In general, then, provide good detail (but not so much as will turn the reader's eyeballs upward), structure the report clearly, and write with an engaging style so that the reader will spend more time reading about the student. One way is to write quite brief reports and to highlight information so that different readers can find what they need without difficulty. Subheadings and indenting can be very helpful and can allow you to include more information than, say, a classroom teacher, might want, without making it so that he simply feels its weight and puts it back down on principle. You may find some of the following subheadings useful to think about, though many others are possible, perhaps even better:

Background
General observations
Evaluation procedures
Concepts about print
Reading
   text level
   word level
Understanding

Studying
Writing
  text level
  word level
Summary evaluation
Summary test information
Teaching suggestions

On the other hand, you could use headings like:

Classroom situation
Composing
  reading
  writing
Revising
  reading
  writing
Editing
  reading
  writing
Reading for enjoyment
Reading for remembering

On the other hand, you could use the chapter titles from Part III of this book.

The three reports shown in Appendix D are ones that have some very good features. These reports are for different audiences, and provide varying degrees of information detail. They are also structured differently. There are advantages to each style and I do not suggest that one is better than the others. Each has its advantages for particular purposes. There is, however, some advantage to consistency of style within communities. Within a given school or school district, it makes sense for teachers to arrive at a form that is quick and provides information in consistent ways. Once teachers are used to the form, it helps them both in preparing and in using the reports. On the other hand, people will tend to squeeze children into the form rather than try to start with the child and find a structure or form to help represent the child.

Regardless of the structure chosen, we must consider the effects of framing and style on our audience. For example, the styles of listing critical information versus a narrative report are shown in Appendix D. The major differences between these brief styles are that the listing has more information that is easily taken out of its context, whereas the narrative is more memorable and contextualized but must be read through. Thus, with the narrative, you have more control over how someone reads the report. With the list format, when someone is in a hurry, he is likely to go straight to such things as the list of "weaknesses," a practice which almost ensures a negative view of the child.

REPORT CARDS

Recently I have spent considerable time with people who can no longer tolerate the report cards they have been using, and are struggling to create new ones. Rather than thinking through the problem from scratch, often a committee tries to come up with a new way of dividing up the old report card. The outcome is a report card that looks very much like the old one but with some different labels. In order to make progress, I think it is important to consider what we do report cards for, and what the possible ways of serving those functions are.

It seems to me that report cards function to inform parents and students of the progress that the students are making in school. For many parents they are the principal source of information on their child's development. However, report cards also provide a time for the teacher to take stock of each child's progress, so that no one falls through the cracks. These two functions can be served in many different ways. But habits and unexamined assumptions frequently limit us unnecessarily. It seems to me that:

1. The report does *not* have to be on a single side of a sheet of paper. It could be a whole book with a page for each domain. It could be a portfolio, as discussed in Chapter 15. It could include a videotape or audiotape. The form and medium can be whatever we want provided people understand it. When we make serious changes, we have to spend time educating parents and teachers to understand them in the same way so that we have a reasonably coherent interpretive community.

2. The form that we choose this year (or for this school, grade, or teacher) does not have to be the same for the next ten years, or even for the next year. We really should view report cards as drafts. Microcomputers have made it possible to change formats at will. The major drawback is that each change requires renewed education of the parties involved.

3. Reports of a student's progress do *not* have to be written entirely by the teacher. The more we can involve students in the reporting of their own development, the more reflective and involved they will become in their literacy learning. Indeed, the less they are involved, the more they come to believe that evaluation is something that is done to them, rather than something for which they are responsible. Involving parents in the evaluation process also has its benefits. If parent comments on portfolios, for example, also go on permanent file, they will very likely respond and consider their comments very carefully before

doing so. Like teachers, parents may well need some help in learning how to respond to children's work.

4. The reporting does *not* have to include grades or ratings of any kind. Grades do not serve children well, and would best be replaced by descriptive details of the child's development. Grading is fundamentally problematic. As Nel Noddings puts it:

> The teacher does not grade to inform the student. She has far better, more personal ways to do this. She grades to inform others about the student's progress. Others establish standards, explicitly or implicitly, and they charge her to report faithfully in observance of these standards. Now the teacher is torn between obligation to the employing community and faithfulness to the student.[96]

After a relationship with the student as a subject, grading requires us to treat the student as an object. Focusing on some objective body of knowledge or performance standard and allowing students to repeat attempts at tests or projects to attain those standards helps deflect some of this problem, and helps students learn about themselves, about persistence, and about the extent that they are prepared to strive. At the same time, it constrains the nature of the learning to that which can be measured in such a way. Arranging contracts of so much for an A, so much for a B, and so forth also reduces this conflict, but as Noddings points out, places the emphasis almost entirely on quantity rather than quality. Standardized tests and external exams get teacher and student out of this bind, by placing them together against the test constructors. However, they do so at a high price, especially when the stakes are high.

As long as we fail to help parents think through the costs and benefits and the alternatives, we will be stuck with grading. Even if we continue to grade, educating parents is a must. Parents will continue to think of things in their own terms. For example, even if we use a scale of 1 = *almost always,* 2 = *mostly,* 3 = *sometimes,* 4 = *never,* many parents, because of their own schooling, will immediately convert these numbers into A, B, and C as they knew them. But they mean different things to everybody. In our studies of teachers writing report cards, teachers themselves differ in their assignment of grades. Some give weight to effort, some to normative achievement, some to amount of improvement, and some take into account probable parental response (for example fearing consequent physical damage to the child). Others balance these and other factors differently for each child, and most find it stressful.[97]

If you are grading for a report card, the students should know where they stand, what the grade means, and what produced it, well before the report card comes out with the grade.

5. The form does *not* have to be divided up into categories that are the

same for each child. Although it can be useful to refer to a checklist to make sure that we do not leave important aspects of particular children's development unexamined, I would just as soon see a report card that was essentially a blank page. Such a report card demands of a teacher a great deal of knowledge. A teacher who cannot write such a report needs help with organizing his classroom, or methods of keeping track, or the kinds of patterns of development that can be seen. Such reporting also demands a fair amount of time.

6. All reports do *not* have to go out on the same day. Once we get rid of this habit, we can consider quite different possibilities. For example, if teachers are given a month within which to send out reports, they can identify a child or two each day to meet with and work through their reading and writing with them to take stock, and then write up the narrative at the end of the day and send it out. Procedures like this would ensure an up-to-date concrete description of the child's development. It might also prevent such problems as all of the children on the school bus opening their report cards, showing them around and making destructive comparisons.

7. The report does *not* have to carry the entire burden of informing students or parents of the student's progress. The more we can shift this burden from the report card, the better. For example, reports could be timed to coincide with parent-teacher conferences. The teacher's understanding of the student would be at its freshest, and potential misunderstandings could be dealt with. Parent conferences offer the possibility of attending to parents' particular concerns, especially if the conference focuses on parents' concerns. To facilitate this, a letter could be sent to parents in advance of the conference asking if they have any specific concerns which they would like addressed in the conference. In addition, the first thing a teacher must do in the conference is *listen* to the parent's concerns in a nondefensive manner. If a parent has a particular concern, it is often hard to listen to someone else spouting until your concern has been addressed.

Some of the burden of communication can be spread out over time. For example, we might send home an envelope of children's work with a letter attached to it explaining what changes parents should look for in the work. The letter might be a short version selected from a longer letter on word processor so that the specific part of the letter that relates to a particular student's development might be easily provided and read with limited time.

In general, it is *the act of writing* a report that is important in coming to grips with, or pulling together, what you know about a child and applying that to your instruction.

Notes and References for Part IV

1. Webster's Unabridged Dictionary (1979).

2. Unfortunately, classical measurement has enshrined some of these concepts in terms like "objective tests" and in distinctions such as that between a "true score" (the absolute reality) and "actual score" (the sample of reality).

3. This quote is from:
   Werner Heisenberg (1966). Planck's discovery and the philosophical problems in nuclear physics. In A. Vavoulis and A. Colver (Eds.), *Science and society: Selected essays,* San Francisco: Holden-Day, p. 112. Reprinted from the *Atlantic Monthly 204:* (November 1959).
   This line of argument was brought home to me most clearly by Cy Knoblauch and Lil Brannon in a paper. See note 4 below.

4. As Cy Knoblauch and Lil Brannon, put it:
   "Human beings are not privileged observers outside of phenomenal reality but rather participants within it: they share its physicality and to that extent are constituted by it: they also act upon it through symbols, hence constituting it in human terms." (p. 2)
   Cy Knoblauch and Lil Brannon (1988). Knowing our knowledge: A phenomenological basis for teacher research. In Louise Z. Smith (Ed.), *Audits of meaning: A festschrift in honor of Ann E. Berthoff.* Portsmouth, NH: Heinemann-Boynton/Cook.
   They also point out that these observations about science have not been restricted to the field of physics. Anthropology, psychology, chemistry, history, linguistics, sociology, and literary theory have all been made aware of this issue. Closer to home, see Steven Gould (1981). *The mismeasure of man.* New York: Norton.

5. The motive and model for this example came from Bonnie Nash-Webber (1975). The role of semantics in automatic speech understanding. In Daniel Bobrow and Allan Collins (Eds.), *Representation and understanding: Studies in cognitive science.* New York: Academic Press.

6. Tzvetan Todorov (1984). *Mikhail Bakhtin: The dialogical principle.* (Trans.) Wlad Godzich. Minneapolis: University of Minnesota Press, p. 18.

7. These distinctions are taken from the work of Evelyn Fox Keller (1985). *Reflections on Gender and Science.* New Haven, CT: Yale University Press.

8. Richard Berk and Peter Rossi (1976). Doing good or worse—evaluation research politically reexamined. *Social Problems 23:* 337–349.

9. Erik Erikson (1964). The nature of clinical evidence. In Erik Erikson, *Insight and responsibility; lectures on the ethical implications of psychoanalytic insight.* New York: Norton, pp. 47–80.

10. Ann Berthoff (1978). *Forming thinking writing: The composing imagination.* Rochelle Park, NJ: Hayden Book Co.

11. Keller. *Reflections on Gender and Science,* p. 117.

12. For a discussion of this see note 11 above.

13. Patricia Ashton and Rodman Webb (1986). *Making a difference: teachers' sense of efficacy and student achievement.* White Plains, NY: Longman.

14. The lack of protest in such situations, which are far from uncommon, is due at least in part to the minority groups being less aware of their rights and feeling less powerful or less able to change such situations, and having less time to do so in any case.

15. James Ysseldyke, B. Algozzine, and S. Epps (1983). A local and empirical analysis of current practice in classifying students as handicapped. *Exceptional Children 50*: 160–166.

16. For an illuminating analysis of the learning disabilities assessment see:
Gerald Coles (1978). The learning disabilities test battery: Empirical and social issues. *Harvard Educational Review 48:* 313–40.
Gerald Coles (1987). *The learning mystique: A critical look at learning disabilities.* New York: Pantheon.

17. Recently, a judge ruled that New York state's use of the SAT exam to award scholarships was biased because more young men than young women were awarded scholarships on the basis of their test scores. The state was ordered to cease using the test for that purpose because the consequence of its use made it invalid.

18. This example is from James Loewen, Possible causes of lower Black scores on aptitude tests, an unpublished paper from the University of Vermont, 1980. It is cited by D. Monty Neill and Noe J. Medina (1989). Standardized testing: Harmful to educational health. *Phi Delta Kappan 70*(9): 688–697.

19. Douglas Fuchs and Lynn Fuchs (1986). Test procedure bias: A meta-analysis of examiner familiarity effects. *Review of Educational Research* Summer: 243–262.

20. Mary Hoover, Robert Politzer, and Orlando Taylor (1987). Bias in reading tests for Black language speakers: A sociolinguistic perspective. *Negro Educational Review* April-July: 81–98.

21. Jeanne Oakes (1987). *Keeping track: How schools structure inequality.* New Haven, CT: Yale University Press.

22. Report on the implementation of the Basic Skills Assessment Program, 1984–1985 (1985). Columbia: South Carolina Department of Education.

23. Richard Allington (1983). The reading instruction provided readers of differing reading ability. *Elementary School Journal 83:* 548–559.
Elfrieda Heibert (1983). An examination of ability grouping for reading instruction. *Reading Research Quarterly 18*: 231–255.

24. Marie Clay (1985). *The early detection of reading difficulties.* 3rd. ed. Portsmouth, NH: Heinemann.

25. Victor Delclos, Susan Burns, and Stanley Kulewicz (1987). Effects of dynamic assessment on teachers' expectations of handicapped children. *American Educational Research Journal 24*: 325–336.

26. This was brought to my attention by an excellent paper by Robert Carrasco (1973), that describes an example of "ethnographic monitoring in a bilingual classroom." The paper also provides a good illustration of the effects of teacher expectation and changes therein.
Robert Carrasco (1973). Ethnographic monitoring in a bilingual classroom. In Henry Trueba, Grace Guthrie, and Kathryn Au (Eds.), *Culture and the bilingual classroom: Studies in classroom ethnography.* Rowley, MA: Newbury House, p. 7.

27. James Ysseldyke, B. Algozzine, and S. Epps (1983). A local and empirical analysis of current practice in classifying students as handicapped. *Exceptional Children 50:* 160–166.

28. James Ysseldyke and B. Algozzine (1982). Bias among professionals who erroneously declare students eligible for special services. *Journal of Experimental Education 50:* 223–228.

29. Donna Kerr (1987). Authority and responsibility in public schooling. In John Goodlad (Ed.), *The ecology of school renewal. Eighty-sixth yearbook of the National Society for the Study of Education, Part I.* Chicago: University of Chicago Press, p. 31.

30. Ralph Reynolds, Sally Standiford, and Richard Anderson (1978). *Distribution of reading time when questions are asked about a restricted category of text.* (Tech. Rep. No. 83). Urbana: University of Illinois, Center for the Study of Reading. (ED 153 206).

31. Norman Frederickson (1984). The real test bias. *American Psychologist 39:* 193–202.

32. Carole and Russel Ames (1984). Goal structures and motivation. *Elementary School Journal 85:* 39–52.

33. John Nicholls (1984). Achievement motivation: Conceptions of ability, subjective experience, task choice, and performance. *Psychological Review 91:* 328–346.

34. These issues were brought to public awareness recently when Jimmy the Greek, the sports commentator, was publicly hauled over the coals for making statements which were seen as racial slurs.

35. Carol Diener and Carol Dweck (1980). An analysis of learned helplessness: II. The processing of success. *Journal of Personality and Social Psychology 39:* 940–952.

36. A story grammar is a framework that attempts to describe the typical elements found in narratives, and the relationships among them. Proposals to use these grammars as the basis for generating questions about stories have been made by:
    P. David Pearson (1982). Asking questions about stories. In Albert Harris and Edward Sipay (Eds.), *Readings on reading instruction.* (3rd ed.). New York: Longman.
    Marilyn Sadow (1982). The use of story grammar in the design of questions. *The Reading Teacher 35:* 518–522.

37. Peter Johnston, Peter Afflerbach, and Paula Weiss (1990). *Teachers' evaluations of the teaching and learning of literacy and literature.* Technical Report, the Center for the Teaching and Learning of Literature. Albany, NY: The University at Albany.

38. Huynh Huynh (1976). Statistical consideration of mastery scores. *Psychometrica 41:* 65–78.

39. Richard Allington (1984). Oral reading. In P. David Pearson (Ed.), *The handbook of reading research.* White Plains, NY.: Longman, pp. 829–864.

40. Frank Hodge is owner of Hodge Podge Books, Lark Street, Albany, NY, and adjunct professor of children's literature at the State University of New York at Albany.

41. These *are* tongue-in-cheek, but I hope you get the point.

42. Joan Herman, Noreen Webb, and Beverly Cabello (1985). A domain-referenced approach to diagnostic testing. Paper presented at the annual meeting of the American Educational Research Association, Chicago, IL.

43. Thomas Anderson, James Wardrop, Wells Hively, K. Muller, Richard Anderson, Nicholas Hastings, and John Fredericksen (1978). *Development and trial of a model for developing domain referenced tests of reading comprehension* (Tech. Rep. No. 86). Urbana: University of Illinois, Center for the Study of Reading. (ED 157 036).

44. Some authors say percentiles refer to the number of students "at or below" the student's score.

45. A standard deviation is an index of how spread out a set of numbers (such as test

scores) are. It uses the variability of the entire set of scores to produce a single unit of variability which has predictable, linear, equal interval properties.

46. Testing companies sometimes supply test norms for two different administration times like September and May.

47. A good reference for grade equivalent scores is:
Donald Horst (1976). *What's bad about grade equivalent scores.* ESEA Title I Evaluation and Reporting System (Technical Report No. 1). Mountain View, CA: RMC Research Corporation.
Rumor has it that there is a companion volume called *What's good about grade equivalent scores.* It contains simply thirty blank pages.

48. One exception that I am aware of is the *Test of Written Language* (TOWL) by Donald Hammill and Stephen Larsen, published by PRO-ED. Although they publish the grade equivalent tables, they have attached a strong warning and a brief description of the problems.
Not everyone agrees that grade equivalent scores are a bad idea. For example:
H. D. Hoover (April 1983). The most appropriate scores for measuring educational development in the elementary school. Invited address to Division D of the American Educational Research Association at the annual meeting in Montreal.
I should say, however, that no one that I am aware of supports grade equivalent scores who does not work for a testing company.

49. George D. Spache (1981). *The diagnostic reading scales.* Monterey, CA: McGraw-Hill.

50. Jeanne Steele and Kurt Meredith. (1989). Standardized measures of reading achievement for placement of students in chapter 1 and learning disability programs: A nationwide survey of assessment practices. Paper presented at the National Reading Conference, Austin TX, November.

51. Donald Sobol (1982). *Encyclopedia Brown takes the cake.* New York: Scholastic. Chapter 4, The Fourth of July Party.

52. See for example:
Samuel Messick (1981). Evidence and ethics in the evaluation of tests. *Educational Researcher 10*(9): 9–20.
Samuel Messick (1980). Test validity and the ethics of measurement. *American Psychologist 35:* 1012–1027.
Samuel Messick (1984). Assessment in context: Appraising student performance in relation to instructional quality. *Educational Researcher 13:* 3–8.

53. The same can happen when children are restricted to books designed solely for their predictability.

54. One of these pieces is from:
Ann McGill-Franzen (in press). The gridlock of low achievement: Perspectives on practice and policy. *Remedial and Special Education.*

55. In order to be able to report high reliabilities on their tests, test makers specifically select test items that will spread the distribution as far apart as possible.

56. We could always have him write more such letters. On the other hand, every time we get him to write another one of these pieces in order to get another sample, there are consequences. For example, we stop him doing other things. Of course, he may get better at that kind of writing because of the practice, and our estimates of his ability will keep changing, or we may simply make him less interested in writing generally because of the repetition.

57. Peter Johnston (1984). Prior knowledge and reading comprehension test bias. *Reading Research Quarterly 19:* 219–239.

58. Although this is just the tip of the iceberg, see for example:

Shirley Brice Heath (1983). What no bedtime story means: Narrative skills at home and school. *Language in Society 11:* 49–76.

59. Kathleen Hric, Karen Wixson, Margaret Kunji, and Anita Bosky (1988). Individual variability among less able readers. *Reading, Writing, and Learning Disabilities 4*: 49–67.
Margory Lipson and Karen Wixson (1986). Reading disability research: an interactionist perspective. *Review of Educational Research 56*(1): 111–36.

60. Herbert Simons and Donald Leu (1987). The use of contextual and graphic information in word recognition by second-, fourth-, and sixth-grade readers. *Journal of Reading Behavior 19*(1): 33–47.
Mary Taft and Lauren Leslie (1985). The effects of prior knowledge and oral reading accuracy on miscues and comprehension. *Journal of Reading Behavior 17*(2): 163–180.

61. Carole Edelsky and Kelly Draper (1989). Reading/"reading," writing/"writing," text/"text." *Reading-Canada-Lecture 7:* 201–216.

62. Nel Noddings in her book *Caring* notes that generalization is a characteristic that is more common of men than of women. The science which produced standardized reading tests is also aligned with men. Good reading on this topic can be found in: Keller. *Reflections on Gender and Science.*

63. This approach has been described as "kidwatching" by Yetta Goodman (1978), as "sensitive observation" by Marie Clay (1985), and as "diagnosis by observation" by Pat Cunningham (1982).
Marie Clay (1985). *The early detection of reading difficulties.* 3rd ed. Portsmouth, NH: Heinemann.
Pat Cunningham (1982). Diagnosis by observation. In Jack Pikulski and Timothy Shanahan (Eds.), *Approaches to the informal evaluation of reading.* Newark, DE: International Reading Association.
Yetta Goodman (1978). Kidwatching: An alternative to testing. *The National Elementary Principal 57:* 41–45.

64. According to Samuel Messick, all measurement should be construct-referenced. Messick. Evidence and ethics in the evaluation of tests.

65. For analyses of these costs and benefits see:
Peter Johnston and Peter Winograd (1985). Passive failure in reading. *Journal of Reading Behavior 17:* 279–301.

66. *Metropolitan Readiness Test.* Harcourt Brace Jovanovich.

67. To study this matter, an excellent resource is:
Lorrie Shephard and Mary Lee Smith's book *Flunking grades: Research and policies on retention.*

68. *Metropolitan Achievement Tests* (1978). Intermediate Forms JS and KS. Psychological Corporation, New York: Harcourt Brace Jovanovich, p. 68.

69. Messick. Evidence and ethics in the evaluation of tests.

70. For a good read and an excellent summary of this research, see:
Jeannie Oakes (1985). *Keeping track: How schools structure inequality.* New Haven, CT: Yale University Press.

71. Evidence on this matter is presented by:
Richard Allington and Anne McGill-Franzen (1989). Different programs, indifferent instruction. In A. Gartner and D. Lipsky (Eds.), *Beyond separate education.* Baltimore, MD: Brookes, pp. 75–98.

72. Norman Fredericksen (1984). The real test bias: Influences of testing on teaching and learning. *American Psychologist 39:* 193–202.

73. Gerald Tirozzi, Joan Baron, Pascal Forgione, and Douglas Rindone (1985). How testing is changing education in Connecticut. *Educational Measurement: Issues and Practice 4:* 12–16.

74. Evidence on this issue comes from:
    Mihalyi Csikszentmihalyi (1975). *Beyond boredom and anxiety.* San Francisco: Jossey-Bass.

75. Carole Diener and Carole Dweck (1980). An analysis of learned helplessness: II. The processing of success. *Journal of Personality and Social Psychology 39:* 940–952.
    Further reading on these issues may be found in:
    Margaret Clifford (1986). The comparative effects of strategy and effort attributions. *British Journal of Educational Psychology 56:* 75–83.
    Peter Johnston and Peter Winograd. (1985). Passive failure in reading. *Journal of Reading Behavior 17:* 279–302.
    Bernard Weiner. (1983). Speculations regarding the role of affect in achievement change programs guided by attributional principles. In James M. Levine and Margaret C. Wang (Eds.), *Teacher and student perceptions: Implications for learning.* Hillsdale, NJ: Erlbaum, pp. 57–74.
    Peter Winograd and Lynne Smith (1987). Improving the climate for reading comprehension instruction. *The Reading Teacher,* December: 304–310.

76. W. I. Thomas (1928) has said, "If men define situations as real, they are real in their consequences." Cited in Jill S. Bartoli (1986). Is it really English for everyone? *Language Arts 63*(1): 12–22.

77. The distinction between efferent and aesthetic reading was made by:
    Louise Rosenblatt (1978). *The Reader, the text, the poem: The transactional theory of the literary work.* Carbondale, IL: Southern Illinois University Press.
    Aesthetic reading is reading done for what it does to you as you read. Efferent reading, on the other hand, is done in order to remember what is read. The derivation of efferent is from the Latin *effere,* meaning *to carry away from.*

78. Sara Freeman, Jane Jackson, and Katherine Boles (1983). The other end of the corridor: The effects of teaching on teachers. *Radical Teacher 23:* 2–23.

79. This is suggested by the work of Patrick Shannon:
    Patrick Shannon (1989). *Broken promises: Reading instruction in twentieth century America.* Granby, MA: Bergin Garvey Publishers.

80. James Ysseldyke, Bob Algozzine, and S. Epps (1983). A local and empirical analysis of current practice in classifying students as handicapped. *Exceptional Children 50:* 160–166.

81. This type of consequence of high-profile testing has been suggested by:
    John Cannell (1987). *Nationally normed elementary achievement testing in America's public schools: How all fifty states are above the national average.* Daniels, WV: Friends for Educations.
    Robert Linn, M. Elizabeth Graue, and Nancy Sanders (1990). Comparing state and district results to national norms: The validity of the claims that "Everyone is above average." *Educational Measurement: Issues and Practice 9*(3): 5–14.

82. Actually this merely shows that the test maker selected items that distinguished high-scoring students from low-scoring students. We do not yet know why.

83. Anna Gillingham (1932). Detailed description of remedial work for reading, spelling and penmanship. In Susan Childs (Ed.), *Education and specific language disability: The papers of Anna Gillingham.* Pomfret, CT: Orton Society, p. 124.

84. Anna Gillingham (1956). The prevention of scholastic failure due to specific language disability. In Childs (Ed.), *Education and specific language disability,* p. 89.

85. Anna Gillingham and Bessie Stillman (1936). Remedial work for spelling and pen-manship. In Childs (Ed.), *Education and specific language disability,* p. 170.

86. Anne McGill-Franzen (1987). Failure to learn to read: Formulating a policy prob-lem. *Reading Research Quarterly 22:* 475–490.

87. Carol Lyons and Nora White (1989). Characteristics of the most successful and least successful teachers trained in reading recovery. Paper presented at the annual meeting of the national reading conference, Austin TX.

88. Messick. Evidence and ethics in the evaluation of tests.

89. Messick. Test validity and the ethics of measurement.

90. See note 89 above.

91. Samuel Messick (1989). Meaning and values in test validation: The science and eth-ics of assessment. *Educational Researcher 18*(2): 5–11. (p. 10)

92. Neil Postman (1976). *Crazy Talk, Stupid Talk.* New York: Delacorte Press, p. 228. Postman does not waste the opportunity to take a jab at the term *iatrogenics* itself as an example of mystification. He adds that if educators came up with such a field they would probably call it something equally mystifying like *pedagantics.*

93. Tzvetan Todorov (1984). *Mikhail Bakhtin: The dialogical principle.* Trans. Wlad Godzich. Minneapolis: University of Minnesota Press, p. 18.

94. On other days, you might choose other things to write about. For example, you might describe the inside of your classroom without the children in it, or the inside of another teacher's classroom, or a piece of a child's writing, or a folder of a child's writing. Watch yourself read for ten minutes and write about what you saw.

95. New York State Education Department (1986). *Reading test in New York state el-ementary schools: Manual for administrators and teachers.* Albany, NY: The Uni-versity of the State of New York, p. 35.

96. Nel Noddings (1984). *Caring: A feminine approach to ethics and moral education.* Berkeley: University of California Press, p. 194.

97. Peter Afflerbach and Peter Johnston (1989). Making the grade: The construction of the report card. Paper presented at the annual meeting of the National Reading Conference, Austin, TX.

PART V

TOWARDS MORE SANITY IN LITERACY EVALUATION

This section of the book is a bit different from the earlier sections. You will notice a change in tone as I deal with topics I find somewhat frustrating. In the first chapter, I point out why we should be more critical of tests and testing, and why we cannot simply blame testing on someone else. This first chapter also explores some of the mythology that surrounds testing, in a deliberate attempt to undermine the unquestioned scientific status of tests. However, merely reducing the credibility of tests may loosen their stranglehold a little, but it will not break it. In the second chapter, I propose some positive ways of reducing the extent of testing in schools. In the long run, more permanent change will require us to completely rethink the purpose and ground rules for evaluation. Thus, the third chapter in the section is an attempt to think through the beliefs and language that hold current evaluation practices in place, and to propose some ways of reframing the enterprise more constructively. I focus particularly on the importance of examining our assumptions and the consequences of the language we use in evaluation.

CHAPTER 36

Evaluation Mythology: A Critical Look at Tests and Testing

You probably have noticed by now that I find little use for tests, particularly standardized, norm-referenced ones, in improving children's learning. Indeed, even as a way of documenting children's learning they have little to offer. But complaints about tests and testing are not new. In 1899 William James described the problem as follows:

> Many of the enthusiasts for scientific or brass-instrument child-study are taking accurate measurements of children's elementary faculties . . . Now I can only repeat here what I said to you when treating of attention: man is too complex a being for light to be thrown on his real efficiency by measuring any one mental faculty taken apart from its consensus in the working whole. Such an exercise as this, dealing with incoherent and insipid objects, with no logical connection with each other, or practical significance outside of the 'test,' is an exercise the like of which in real life we are hardly ever called upon to perform. In real life, our memory is always used in the service of some interest: . . . This preponderance of interest, of passion, in determining the results of a human being's working life, obtains throughout. No elementary measurement, capable of being performed in a laboratory, can throw any light on the actual efficiency of the subject; for the vital thing about him, his emotional and moral energy and doggedness, can be measured by no single experiment, and becomes known only by the total results in the long run.[1]

Alas, James's concerns fell on deaf ears, and tests continue to hold a seemingly impenetrable scientific mystique.

I began this book with some bizarre stories about current evaluation practice that I expected would shock you a little in order to pique your interest. In this chapter I would like to defuse some of the currently held beliefs about assessment and to tell some silly stories that are, nonetheless, true. The purpose of the chapter is not simply to mock. When I began to get serious about writing this book, I felt obliged to study the available tests in the area of literacy, but I ran into a problem. Our university test library contains no recent literacy tests. I like to think of the test library as having historical importance. In order to get copies of test manuals to study, I called around and visited local schools to see if I could borrow them. Of five schools in three school districts, not one could find a technical manual describing the characteristics of the test that they routinely administer to their students.

"Educational" testing has become a technology used so commonly and with such unquestioning resignation, that only a shrill alarm is likely to awaken us. So let me use a blunt metaphor—intended to shock—to point out an ethical dilemma. The following quote is from Albert Speer's memoirs. Speer was Hitler's Reichminster and architect of the death camps:

> Basically, I exploited the phenomenon of the technician's often blind devotion to his task. Because of what seems to be the moral neutrality of technology, these people were without any scruples about their activities. The more technical the world imposed on us by the war, the more dangerous was this indifference of the technician to the direct consequences of his anonymous activities.[2]

I do not wish to imply that people who use tests or related technology are on a par with the people who constructed and operated the death camps, nor even that people who make tests are similarly heinous. However, I do wish to point out that just because someone else makes an instrument and another person or group requires its use, that does not absolve the person who actually uses the instrument from responsibility for its consequences. I also wish to point out that tests provide a technology that depersonalizes education and risks changing the apparent ethicality of the decisions people make. I do not wish to suggest that test makers have no responsibility in the matter. They charge more for these manuals than for almost anything else, and the manuals are generally written so they will not be read. And make no mistake, test publishers, just like weapons manufacturers, are careful to argue that the user is responsible for the consequences of use. But since the makers refuse responsibility, *somebody* has to act responsibly and with an understanding that our approaches to evaluation have a substantial effect on the course of many people's lives.

HOW WE GOT HERE

Standardized testing has been with us for a long time, so long that we generally take it for granted. The rise of norm-referenced testing began in the 1920s, and by the 1930s 1.5 million copies of the Stanford Achievement Test alone were sold annually. The move to these tests from oral and written criterion-related performance assessment, which was more common last century, came about because of the increasing numbers of students in the public schools, and the discovery of the unreliability of (untrained) teacher judgment. In the fifties and sixties further increases in testing came about through federal legislation such as the National Defense Education Act of 1958. In the 1980s the calls for reform have virtually all included calls for even more testing. Walt Haney and George Madaus estimate that there has been a 10 to 20 percent increase in standardized testing in schools per year for the last forty years.[3]

The public's faith in tests is extraordinary. When the general public was at school, they hated tests with a vengeance but, like cod liver oil, they believe them to be good for the health and thus to be taken regularly. At the same time the public continues its considerable disrespect for educators. The public's distrust of educators has increased since the press gleefully reported the findings of an informal survey by John Cannell that all states claim their students to be performing above the 50th percentile in national norms. This finding was essentially verified and extended to a representative sample of school districts by Bob Linn and his colleagues.[4] The causes of this seemingly remarkable statistical feat are many and are still being debated. However, several are prominent:

1. Teachers cheat by teaching to the test, both specifically and generally, and by helping students.
2. Test makers cheat and try to make everyone look good so schools will still buy their tests.
3. Schools exclude, retain, and transition children to provide extra schooling prior to important tests (state competency tests, etc.).
4. Schools classify children as handicapped and exempt them from the testing (or simply encourage certain children not to come to school on testing days).
5. Schools use old test norms that are no longer seen as appropriate because students, on average, are now doing better on the tests than they used to.[5]

There is evidence that all these strategies occur.[6] The general public is incensed by them and blames teachers and (for a change) test manufacturers. But it seems to me that we should ask why such defensive strategies occur and what they mean. My belief is that the social context produces a goal of avoidance of failure, rather than one of optimal instruction, and educators adopt the strategies necessary to attain that goal. The most intriguing point to me is that the public, at this point, would refuse to accept positive information about teaching and teachers. Improved performance is not the possibility focused on by the press. Furthermore, using old norms is seen as inappropriate because students are now generally doing better than before, and to show them as doing so is somehow cheating. At the same time, without a shred of evidence to suggest that mass testing is in any way beneficial, we assume that it must be.

"WE HAVE TO TEST AND THAT WON'T CHANGE"

Because of an enormous parochialism in the United States, we tend to forget that testing is a cultural activity, and a particularly common one in this society. Children in the United States are tested more than children in any other country.[7] In other countries they test substantially less or very little and manage to get by very nicely. Mentioning this probably raises visions of Third World countries and "commies" for some, but New Zealand has been the source of curiosity for many American educators because of the extent and quality of literacy among its people. New Zealanders read more than do people in other countries (not that it's a competition).[8] However, the first external test taken by New Zealand children is at what would be tenth grade, and it is a set of achievement tests based on a defined curriculum rather than an aptitude test based on a notion of "scholastic aptitude."

Although many admit to the frailties of tests, many argue that "Tests are always going to be here. The best we can do is try to make them as good as we can." This is accompanied by a belief that if we just work hard enough we can make a really good reading test that will be a good measure of real reading—a more valid test.[9] This is what has motivated recent Illinois and Michigan revisions of their state reading tests, involving some of the most thoughtful people in the field. These efforts depend on the fallacy that the principal aspect of validity is in the test construction. In fact, the Michigan test, for example, is invalid and will continue to be, because of its *use*. It is used as an accountability measure, and average test scores in some states can be presented to the public classroom by classroom in the newspaper. Given this use—or abuse—the evaluation was invalid before the test was constructed because of the undesirable side effects. The uses of testing are also cultural peculiarities.

I am less negative about the possibility of overthrowing the testing industry. The changes in Eastern Europe in 1989–1990 were a great encouragement to me in that regard. There must have been a large number of citizens in those countries who had been saying, "We will never have democracy, so we might as well try to do the best we can with the system we have." Of course, it is easy to see that even though these changes were massive, they did not immediately produce utopian communities. Eliminating standardized tests would not immediately (or necessarily) produce sane, fair, high quality education or evaluation either. A great deal of work and rethinking would still be necessary.

"TESTS ARE SCIENTIFIC AND NO-NONSENSE"

One of the reasons why tests remain so powerful is that they remain unexamined. The work of teachers has been intensified by the addition of more topics and detail to be taught and tested, so that few have the time to study tests and test manuals in any detail, even if they were available and readable. I would like to take the liberty of looking at the logic of a couple of tests. These two tests were not singled out because they are especially inferior. Indeed, the *Degrees of Reading Power* may be one of the least offensive of standardized reading tests. A critical reading of *any* test will produce the same results.

Reading Styles Inventory[10]

I am quite convinced that children have different ways of going about learning, and learning to read is no exception.[11] There is ample evidence to attest to cultural differences in social interactions, ways of viewing the world, and foci of attention.[12] Part of growing up in a culture is the socialization of attention patterns and patterns of interaction with others and with the world. I also believe that failure to deal with this fact will cause difficulty for some students. That said, I do not think it appropriate to test for learning styles. Such testing has reached epidemic proportions, and I am sure that the people making substantial sums of money from it have the best of intentions of helping children. School administrators and many teachers have been caught up in this apparent solution to a problem they were astute enough to recognize.

The popular test in this area, possibly the only one, the *Reading Styles Inventory,* also has capitalized in a primitive way on the technology of microcomputers, giving it a further air of technical efficiency and scientific validity. It gives a printout on every child's learning style with associated teaching suggestions (see Table 36.1 for an example). Aside from the fact that a number of these teaching suggestions are antithetical to one another, an average teacher has twenty-five or so of these printouts in which students can differ on all of the dimensions shown in the table. She has ten who prefer bright lights and no music, some of these prefer hard seats rather than soft, and some of those who prefer no music prefer direct instruction. On the other hand, ten students prefer music while they read, some of them prefer bright lights and some of them prefer warm temperatures. And then of course there are the chairs. A teacher taking this advice seriously would either go mad or at least constantly feel guilty that she had not managed to accommodate particular children's learning styles.

Again, I want to point out that children in healthy environments are quite good at seeking situations in which they feel more comfortable. In other words, money spent on tests would be better spent on more books and more flexible reading situations for children to choose. As described earlier in the book, teacher–student interactions can be more accommodating to learning style differences as well. At the same time, some students are prescribed no instruction in phonic analysis. Even aside from reading, this will effectively cut some students off from writing since invented spelling depends on analysis of the sounds in speech. It is recommended that some students not self-evaluate! I find this whole matter distressing.

TABLE 36.1. Sections of an Individual Reading Style Profile from the *Reading Styles Inventory* for a Fourth Grader

DIAGNOSIS	RECOMMENDED STRATEGIES FOR TEACHG READG[a]
Perceptual Strengths/Prfrnces	
good auditory strengths	use listng actvties; use decodg as needed
good visual strengths	use visual aids (word cards, board word)
moderate tactual prefrnces	use tactual actvties (writing, typing)
moderate kinesth prefrnces	combine readg w/bldg/doing/floor games
Preferred Reading Environment	
quiet (no music)	prvide quiet areas, stdy carrels, headsets
quiet (no talking)	prvide quiet areas, stdy carrels, headsets
cool temperatures	allow stdnt read coolest area of room
formal & informal design	hav hard chairs & soft chairs available
Emotional Profile	
This student is:	
not self-motivated	prvide material based on stdnt's intrsts
fairly persistent	prvide short & longer-term assgments
This student prefers:	
some choices	prvide some choice hi-intrst materials
much direction	give few options, set time limits
Physical Preferences	
intake while readg	prmit stdnt to eat/drink while readg
not to read in the morning	dont schedule readg in morning often
not to read early noon	dont schdule readg in early noon often

[a]Each strategy has a page reference for the location of the relevant strategy in the RSI manual. The truncated spelling is presumably to allow a single line format for each entry.
Source: Excerpted from a student profile printout from the RSI Individual Profile Diskette, published by National Reading Styles Institute, Inc., Roslyn Heights, NY.

The Degrees of Reading Power

The Degrees of Reading Power is a test used as a statewide testing device in New York, and widely used elsewhere. What does it measure? On page 8 of the manual, *Alternative Testing Techniques for Students with Handicapping Conditions,* we find the guidelines and restrictions for alternative administration of the state reading tests for grades five, eight–nine, and eleven–twelve. The instructions read:

> Test can be read or signed to only those students whose handicapping condition impairs ability to gain meaning from printed materials.

In other words, if a student has been determined to have difficulty in reading, the test may be read to her. There is humor in the fact that this is still considered a reading test.

Isolated example? Consider what psychometricians think it measures.[13] The manual states that:

All of the information that is needed to select the correct response is provided in the text of the passages; there is no need to supply information concerning each passage's content from memory or past experience. This means that the DRP should be culturally fair. Knowing a great deal about the content of any passage should not bias a student's ability to respond. Only the ability to process sentences for meaning is required for success on the DRP.[14]

Let me paraphrase that. "In order to read, you do not have to use previous knowledge and experience." What, then, is reading? Apparently what they call reading has nothing to do with what research has been describing for at least the last twenty years.

Nonetheless, after years of research and annual expenditures of considerable public money, the test must be useful for something. The manual asserts that it:

is especially designed to aid in the management of instruction. It provides the diagnostic information needed to match student ability to instructional materials, a feature which is considered by many psycholinguists to be the most important diagnostic capability of a test. Matching allows a teacher to control the amount of challenge in various reading situations. A teacher may desire challenge in materials supplemented by instruction but may prefer materials that students can comprehend without help for independent reading. Students who might become bored or frustrated with the usual instructional materials can be *identified immediately* with the test, and their reading assignments changed accordingly.[15] [emphasis mine]

Identified immediately! Apparently the designers are unaware of the mechanics of test scoring and the changes that students undergo in their literate activity. Also, apparently they did not notice that children, in sensible situations, will actually cease doing boring things or things that are frustratingly difficult, without adults having to waste money and valuable instructional time trying to do so for them. Perhaps the other diagnostic benefits are worthy?

Reading specialists can also use the test diagnostically to identify problems individual students have with the comprehension of prose. A student's test responses can be studied and the student questioned concerning why a particular incorrect answer was selected.[16]

If teachers must interview students about their test responses in order to find out what they mean, then why not simply interview them about the books they are reading and how they are doing research? Where is the advantage of the test? Most of these statements simply reflect psychometricians' lack of experience with teaching and learning in classrooms.

Again, I want to remind you that these tests are not isolated examples. A critical reading of *any* test will produce the same results.

THE MYTHOLOGY OF INTERPRETATION AND REPORTING

If we are to believe the advertising claims of testing companies, their tests can split hairs at fifty paces. But consider the *Stanford Achievement Test Intermediate Level II.*[17] Nancy and Jean were identical twins who took the test at the same time. Nancy scored 43 on the vocabulary test, whereas Jean scored only 41 because she became flustered when her pencil lead broke. When we refer to the norms for this test we find that Jean has a vocabulary grade equivalent of 9.5, compared with Nancy's grade equivalent of 10.4. A difference of two items in 45 makes a difference of a grade level. Jean's friend Milly scored two less than she did, which earned her a grade equivalent of 8.8. This is not an isolated example either. It would be more honest if testing companies refused to report single scores and only reported the score bands within which they were at least 90 percent confident the student's "true score" lay.

But testing companies are making some efforts (to keep up with the market). For example, the *Comprehensive Test of Basic Skills,*[18] in recognition of the call for narrative description of children's development, provides a "narrative report" on its "Student Profile Report." The example provided in their documentation reads:

> This student's test performance may be compared with that of the national norm group at the same grade level by referring to the national percentile scores above. Achievement in basic skills is best summarized by the "total" scores. The student's total score is above the national average (the 50th percentile). In total reading, the student's achievement is better than approximately 87 percent of the national norm group; in total language, the student's achievement is better than approximately 58 percent of the national norm group; in total mathematics, the student's achievement is better than approximately 38 percent of the national norm group. (p. 7)[19]

A few words thrown in to augment scores does not seem to me to make a narrative. Bending over backwards to undo their impersonal image, they note of their "Parent Report" that we should:

> Note that the information is stated in terms of "your daughter" or "your son" to make the report as personal as possible. (p. 4)[20]

Full marks for trying.

Educators and the general public also hold some serious misconceptions about grade levels, norms, and expectations. It is very common to hear people in influential positions making such statements as "60 percent of children in this country are reading below grade level," and from a principal of a school cited by the federal Office of Educational Research and Improvement as being outstanding, "We do not allow students in our school to read material which is below grade level." This misconception appears to have been spawned by grade equivalent scores. The feeling is that there is a definable and defensible ''grade level performance'' at or above which all children in the grade *should* be reading. Since grade level performance is defined by the median student (half the students fall above and half below her score) a large number of children are guaranteed the experience of constant failure. At the same time, educators and the general public are guaranteed a considerable amount of anxiety and a certain amount of defensive stone throwing. Performance on norm-referenced reading tests produces a normal distribution of performance. This is not because of any inherent distribution properties, but rather because these tests are *specifically designed* to produce such a distribution. If they did not, test manufacturers would select different items so that they did.

The prevalence of misconceptions about the meaning of tests is particularly serious. In 1988 I read a newspaper headline, ''Education gets a 'C' from Bennett.'' Under this heading the then Education Secretary was quoted as making several distressing statements:

> The news is not what it should be. Test scores are in a dead stall.
> We're paying top dollar to educate our children, but we're not getting top return.[21]

When asked whether citizens should use the statistics as ammunition to vote down school levies, he was quoted as saying, ''That depends on how well the schools perform.'' The beliefs that ''the more you pay, the higher the test scores you get,'' and ''if you punish schools who are not doing well on the tests by reducing their funds, their children will get better literacy instruction'' are depressingly simplistic. With norm-referenced tests the former produces a no-win situation because if the majority of students score above average, the public cries ''Foul!'' The latter is demonstrably foolish as it simply shifts the goal of schooling to the avoidance of test failure, which increases retentions, disability classifications, and ''transition room'' placements. These misconceptions are even minor compared with the notion that the public pays top dollar for education. Out of every tax dollar, three cents goes to education whereas fifty cents goes to the military.[22]

Many misconceptions are promoted by influential people who should know better. The U.S. Department of Education, in a booklet designed to help parents understand testing, has this to say:

> Test. It's a loaded word. Important . . . something to care about . . . something that can mean so much we get apprehensive thinking about it.
> WHY TEST?
> Tests are a yardstick. Schools use them to measure, and then improve, education. Some tell schools that they need to strengthen courses or change teaching techniques. Other tests compare students by schools, school districts, or cities. All tests determine how well **your child** is doing. And that's important.

. . . some schools give students practice in taking tests. . . . Find out whether your child's school gives ''test-taking practice'' on a regular basis or will provide such practice if your child needs it.[23]

I cannot imagine any psychometrician who would argue that ''All tests determine how well your child is doing.'' I am also surprised that the Department of Education actually encourages schools to allocate substantial amounts of time for practicing doing the tests. Is this time allocation:

1. so that children will become more literate?
2. so that children's test scores will improve?

MYTHS ABOUT COST AND EFFICIENCY

It is part of a common mythology that a standardized machine-scored test is both cheaper and more efficient than an individualized evaluation procedure. This notion derives from the mass production metaphor and maintains its credibility even though the standardized test:

a) produces virtually no instructionally helpful information,
b) produces information which is unmemorable for the teacher and hence not likely to be used,
c) produces data that arrives at a time when, even if the information were good, it would no longer be instructionally relevant,
d) has a negative impact on both the student's view of himself and literacy, and on the relationship between student and teacher,
e) is, in practice, expensive because of administration and scoring. Walt Haney and George Madaus estimate that the time involvement of administering the tests is four to five times the original purchase price.[24]

The problem here lies in the limited view of efficiency that is adopted. The testing companies view efficiency as the most rapid collection of data. It seems to me that the efficiency of evaluation should include the entire cycle from the gathering of information to the use and consequences of the collection of the information, *and* the cleaning up of the side effects (a similar definition would help us deal more sensibly with plastics). From this perspective, commercial standardized tests are outrageously inefficient.

MYTHS ABOUT TEST CHARACTERISTICS AND CAPABILITIES

Consider the following advertising Material for the Stanford 7 Plus tests:

Stanford 7 Plus meets the needs of students, teachers, administrators, and parents alike.

Stanford 7 Plus results can be used to determine instructional priorities, group students for instruction, describe overall trends in achievement, measure growth in learning, evaluate program effectiveness, screen students for inclusion in special programs, communicate levels of achievement to parents, the board, and the community, and make school district policy decisions. (p. 2) [25]

And probably wash the dishes too.

Some members of the measurement community apparently believe that all these functions can be performed by the same test. On the other hand, a sizeable segment of the measurement community asserts the incompatibility of some of the characteristics required to serve these functions, particularly those that involve accountability as opposed to instructional guidance.[26] The view is summed up by Lorrie Shepard, who writes:

Large-scale assessments must be formal, objective, time-efficient, cost-efficient, widely applicable, and centrally processed. Most important, results must be in a form useful to policymakers, which usually means reducing complexity to a single score. In contrast, assessments designed to support instruction are informal, teacher-mandated, adapted to local context, locally scored, sensitive to short-term change in students' knowledge, and meaningful to students. They provide immediate, detailed and complex feedback; and they incorporate tasks that have instructional value in themselves. . . . Classroom tests and observations do not have to meet the same standards of accuracy.[27]

Shepard is one of the most thoughtful researchers in the measurement community—I hold her work in the highest esteem and refer to her work often. However, I believe that operating these systems on different principles has some serious problems. The first of these is that the one with the higher stakes will dominate. In high stakes testing, which is almost universal in the United States, whatever is tested takes up the lion's share of class time. It is taught in the most narrow manner possible to be certain that children will "get it," including teaching it in the format in which it is likely to appear on the test.[28] Classroom evaluation will be separate from large scale evaluation only if it is not accountability evaluation. Second, classroom evaluation must be *more* accurate. There is no hope for children if classroom evaluation is as inaccurate and uninformative as standardized multiple-choice tests.

The reason these measurement specialists would like a split between the two types of evaluation is that they realize the inadequacy of standardized tests in the classroom but are unwilling to similarly deny their value outside the classroom. Possibly they have not realized the inadequacy of the standardized tests outside the classroom or they feel there is little hope of changing things outside the classroom, or they have some ego involvement in the tests. Let us, for argument's sake, apply the same set of criteria to the two types of evaluation, but operate from the central premise that the whole point of the assessment is to educate, or inform in an involving sort of way, the stakeholders. The following assessment characteristics would make sense:

1. Adapted to the local context
2. Locally analyzed
3. Sensitive to short-term changes in learning
4. Meaningful to learners
5. Provides detailed and complex feedback
6. Incorporates tasks that have instructional value in themselves

I do not believe that administrators and policymakers are incapable of learning. Just because many policymakers assert that policy decisions require complex information to be reduced to a simplistic number does not mean that they are correct in their assertion. Indeed, if we supply them with information that, although more complicated, has the effect of educating them about the concrete situations, then perhaps fewer simplistic decisions will be made.

Proponents of the use of tests for accountability, such as the National Institute for Education, always concede that they are not particularly good measures. For example, in the widely read book which they sponsored, *Becoming a Nation of Readers,* the authors comment:

> The strength of a standardized test is not that it can provide a deep assessment of reading proficiency, but rather that it can provide a fairly reliable partial assessment cheaply and quickly.[29]

Having made these cautions, they are then quick to insist that teachers adopt practices drawn from research based on such measures.

This use of tests reminds me of a story I heard as an adolescent. There was a drunk under a street light looking around as if he had lost something. A teacher happened by and asked him the matter. He said he had lost a quarter, so the teacher set about helping him to find it. After a considerable period of searching the teacher said, "Are you sure you lost it here?" The drunk responded immediately, "No, I lost it over there, but the light is much better over here."

CHAPTER 37

Low-Test Solutions to High-Test Problems

"This is all fine and dandy, Johnston," you might say, "but I have to deal with Chapter I evaluations, state-mandated testing, and a whole host of folks who want to see test scores. Do you think I can just tell them to go away?" A point well taken. P. David Pearson once made the excellent suggestion that perhaps we could get students to "Just say no" to tests. I have a lot of sympathy with this proposal. The analogy to drugs is closer than might appear at first glance, and it certainly would be interesting to see the effects of students exerting political action of this sort. I imagine such insurgence would promptly be crushed. Indeed, a similar type of resistance was recently tried by a group of California students at West High School in Torrance. They vented their anger at administrators' emphasis on the tests, and teachers' interruption of classes to practice for the test, by deliberately performing badly. They managed to reduce the average test score in reading from the 85th percentile to the 51st. They were so systematic in their efforts that some students managed to have raw scores of zero, which, on a multiple-choice test, takes a considerable amount of skill to accomplish.[30]

Other university types have suggested that teachers could take a similar stand. But teachers, alas, cannot take this stand without its being seen by an untrusting public as simply another predictable attempt to avoid being held accountable. I believe it would be more powerful if parents took the stand instead. It would take only, say, 15 percent of the parents to forbid the testing of their children (possibly on religious grounds) for the realtors to find it difficult to ensure the representative sample necessary to use test scores as a marketing tool.[31] But even if concerned parents rallied and successfully ousted standardized testing, unless something better was already available to serve the desirable functions the public believes tests perform, or unless the public had been educated to understand teaching, learning, and literacy differently, the tests would return in two or three years with increased virulence. American education is rife with examples of such massive pendulum swings. Changes in people's views on such matters as education and human nature do not occur overnight.[32]

I believe that the best option we have is to seek low-test solutions to as many of the problems of schooling as we can, and thus to render most testing blatantly wasteful if not obviously destructive. At the same time, we must set the conditions for the community to begin to see the limitations, and the unfortunate consequences, of testing. Schools and school districts are often faced with problems that seem to require tests. For example, school personnel often feel obliged to demonstrate accountability, or to classify children as disabled or gifted, or to decide who should receive remedial services. The default solution is to test: "Test first and ask questions later." There are usually many more options open to us if we stop to think. I have often wondered what would happen if the default option were to not test. For example, what if children were only tested at the end of the school year if a parent required it—other children being allowed to carry on with their regular instruction. I suspect that many testing companies would go out of business and start buying up children's book publishing companies where the real money would be.

So let us give some thought to what we can do to solve some of the problems in schools without using tests. To begin with, we need to strip down the testing to the absolute minimum. See which tests are required by whom, and why. For example, the state may require reading tests at sixth and ninth grades and writing tests at fifth and tenth grade. The federal government may require standardized tests both fore and aft of instruction supported by federal dollars. The school district may require standardized tests at all grade levels. Let us see which procedures and functions are redundant with each other and eliminate those first. For example, in New York students are required to take the state *Degrees of Reading Power* test in third grade, and many school districts also administer the *California Achievement Test* or some other such test, though the one test would serve the purposes of the school district, and state and federal agencies, just as well.

CLASSIFICATION AND SELECTION

The actual act of classifying children is fundamentally problematic and should be prevented as much as possible. A good rule of thumb is to "label jars, not children."[33] Instead of changing the method of assessment used for classifying children, we might change the need for classification. For example, in one local district, the gifted and talented program was altered from a pullout program to a program to help teachers work with students with special abilities, and to include all students as much as possible. This change in focus essentially eliminated the need for the classification and selection function. In school districts that emphasize the "least restrictive environment" aspect of the law on the education of handicapped students, there is less emphasis on classification and more emphasis on adapting classroom instruction to individual needs.

Much of the classification that takes place can be prevented if steps are taken early enough. Marleen Pugach and Lawrence Johnson have met with considerable success using what they call "prereferral intervention."[34] The idea is that as soon as a teacher detects a problem, he writes a brief but clear description of the problem and meets with his partner (a colleague). These teachers have been trained in how to help each other work out problems. In the meeting, they propose a strategy to address the problem and set a follow-up meeting. Since the meeting occurs early, the problem does not have time to escalate, and it is easier for teachers to locate the problem in the relationship between teacher and student, or in the teacher's practice rather than in the student. Since support is sought from a colleague and not a supervisor, teachers are more likely to confront problems, especially in a noncompetitive context. As both teachers work through the problem, both learn from it. The technique reduces the referral rate, and hence the classification rate, by a substantial margin.

Consider another situation. When Lucy arrived at Picker Elementary School, she came with a file that said she had been in a self-contained resource room for two years prior to arriving at the school. In another state she had been in an abusive family situation which had ended in divorce with mother and children moving out of town. Other than that, the file contained little information of any use. Sheila, the principal, had to make some important decisions. In the first place, she had to decide what to do immediately. Next, the school psychologist was asked to evaluate Lucy so that she could convene the Committee on Special Education and decide on the best course of action for Lucy. Sheila first placed Lucy with a secure and open teacher. Lucy became part of the class and by the time the psychologist had time to schedule Lucy for evaluation, the most important piece of data available was that Lucy had been working in a regular third-grade classroom and to outside observers, she was indistinguishable from the other students. She read when the other students read. She wrote when the other students wrote. She was able to fit into the classroom community. The psychologist faced Sheila with the problem that to have Lucy do a lot of tests would single her out and make her feel different, possibly at the risk of undoing the excellent adjustment she had made to the new school. But she was already classified as learning disabled. What if a court were to view Sheila's school as not supplying the appropriate instruction? As the psychologist pointed out, even if Lucy were handicapped, it was still very clear that she was in the least restrictive environment. In any case, a sixty-day diagnostic placement is allowed under the law; and if her reading and writing and math showed reasonable progress over that time, while maintaining her personal stability, what could be a more valid diagnosis than that? It is also noteworthy that "declassification" is now funded too.

The basis on which most students are diagnosed as learning disabled has come under serious scrutiny over the last ten years. Gerald Coles has written two thorough critiques of learning disabilities and their evaluation, the most recent of which, *The Learning Mystique* leaves little to be respected in the classification of children as learning disabled.[35] Whatever we can do to prevent the need for this label, let us do it.

Most schools in the United States are supplied with funds to provide remedial assistance to students who are not doing well in reading and/or writing. Schools may even be required by state law to provide remedial assistance. Who should receive these extra resources? Several questions need to be answered. Do we have a set criterion below which we consider there is a need for support? Or will our resources allow effective support for so many students and not any more? Do we have a certain amount of support to give, and if there are many more students who need it will we just spread ourselves thinner? What is our goal with remedial instruction? Decisions about who shall get remedial services are usually made by having all the students take a standardized reading (or, less frequently, writing) test. However, there are other ways to view the problem to be solved.

In Bedford School, they were using a standardized reading test to test students at the end of kindergarten to see who would get remedial help in first grade.[36] The overall cost to the district for purchase and scoring of these tests was around $2,000. Administration of the tests took approximately two days out of the time for teaching and learning and terrified some of the students. It happened that some of the teachers were trying to obtain more instructionally useful information about students' reading development. They were using a variety of different individual evaluation devices including a word recognition list, a dictation test, and a sample of writing. One of the teachers decided to look at how much these evaluation procedures were overlapping each other. She calculated the simple correlation between each of these assessment methods and found that the correlations were actually quite high. In other words, when they listed the students from highest score to lowest score on each different test, roughly the same order occurred each time. The principal of the school was reluctant to give up the standardized test but quickly realized that the dictation test alone (a measure of phonemic awareness and the ability to represent the phonemes alphabetically) was so highly related to the reading test that the children were ranked almost identically by the two methods. Indeed, given how upset the students were by the standardized test, it seemed likely that the dictation test was actually the more valid measure for the purpose. After making some calculations, he found that the additional tests added nothing to the prediction of the standardized test score.[37] Since they were not required by the state to test for these purposes, they stopped using the test and spent the money on books, using the alternative data for making decisions instead.

But how to decide which students needed remedial support? The first year they simply decided which dictation score was most closely related to the cutoff percentile they had used on the standardized test, and used that as their criterion. The second year they went about things somewhat differently. They first decided how many students could receive optimal help, given the resources available. Optimal help was based that year on calculations negotiated among the teachers about how best to handle the students in an in-class support program. The following year, "optimal help" was based on their employment of a Reading Recovery teacher[38] who worked with students individually each day for half an hour and thus eliminated their need for support within a period of about 15 to 20 weeks. In line with the requirements of that program, the *Diagnostic Survey* was used.[39] This procedure extends further the information which they were gathering, to describe the children's concepts about print, and alphabet knowledge, although not all of the procedure was used with all the children.

Only the less experienced half of the readers and writers, as established through an oral reading sample and the dictation exercise, were evaluated with the remainder of the survey.

That same year, it was found that the scoring procedure used on the dictation sample could easily be applied to the students' writing in their journals. A representative sample of writing taken from the last three weeks in May was selected for each student, and teachers in two adjacent schools switched samples and scored the students' writing for proportion of phonemes represented and message quality. They found that the scoring was highly reliable and that with that information plus a recent running record, they could readily select a group of students for remedial support based on the rank ordering thus produced, which would be virtually the same group of students. Nonetheless, they were reluctant to rely on teacher judgment even though it saved time and money and appeared comparable to other approaches. Interestingly, too, the teachers were just as nervous about this as were the administrators.

TRANSITIONS

One of the commonly stated purposes of evaluation is to facilitate transitions between grades (and, hence, teachers) and between schools. But there are better ways to smooth transitions. A student taking a portfolio of work on to his next class to discuss in his first conference with his new teacher would seem at once to provide more detailed, more concrete, more personal, and more memorable data on which to base instruction than would any test scores, particularly if accompanied by a narrative description from the teacher.

If the purpose of the evaluation has to do with the transition between two schools such as elementary and middle school, or an alternative school and a public school, then the purpose normally served by tests might better be served by getting the teachers together and getting expectations out in the open. Discussion of sample portfolios and related data again would be particularly helpful in making the discussions concrete. When the samples are provided by both sides of the transition, it will help to keep the discussion balanced. Copies of the books students will be expected to read might be used for assessment, and for discussion of their appropriateness. As another possibility, we might have teachers teach students for two years spanning the transition between the schools, or collapse schools into clusters of small 5-year-old to 17-year-old gradeless schools with cooperative teaching, thus removing the transitions. Whichever way, increased focused contact between faculties would be helpful. However, preparing students for the next grade should not be the constant concern of teachers. If it is, the elementary school curriculum and teachers will end up being subordinated to the high school curriculum, which is the worst possible situation.

Often when two teachers work with the same student, they do not capitalize on each other's experience, and the student has to manage the transition between them. We have found that such situations often leave the child to try to make sense out of instructional situations that are like oil and water. One technique we have used when a second teacher comes into the classroom to provide additional instruction for certain students is to have a spiral-bound notebook divided into sections, one section for each child and one at the beginning for overall planning. Each teacher is to work with the group or with each individual student each day, and both teachers write observations about each student in dated entries as a dialogue journal. Running records are also done in this journal, providing a dated history of the child's development, informed by both teachers, the shared observations providing a depth of perspective otherwise unavailable to either teacher. This provides a forum for constantly sharing information and instructional suggestions. It also helps develop a common language and a shared perspective.

The most important point for dealing with transitions is to consider the need for the transitions just as seriously as the need for information to bridge the transition, and to arrange for grounded, balanced dialogue between the parties involved.

IMPROVING TEACHING THROUGH TEACHER LEARNING

Improving teaching means helping teachers learn how to become better teachers. The focus must be on helping teachers become better learners so that they will improve their practice. Even if tests were useful for detecting problems that teachers were having in their teaching, they do not solve the problem of helping teachers learn to improve. Indeed, they set a context in which it is difficult and particularly threatening for teachers to admit to, and confront, difficulties. There are three parts to the improvement of teaching, and each depends on teacher learning. The first part is knowing more about children and their development. The second is knowing more about literate activity. The third is knowing more about one's own teaching practice and its consequences for the children's learning.

There is a lot to learn. How can teachers be helped to become better learners? To answer this, we might look at the conditions that we know foster learning in classrooms. Some of these conditions are as follows:

1. *Self-evaluation.* This is central. Unless we have control of our own evaluation, we have no control of, and hence no direction in, our learning. It would not be very efficient if we had to wait until the end of the year to see whether we had learned anything or needed to know something else. External evaluation can produce rejection of the evaluation, resentment, and entrenchment, particularly under certain conditions.

2. *Noncompetitive contexts.* These are more conducive to learning than are competitive ones.[40] In competitive contexts learners do not ask

each other for help as it will be taken as a sign of their lower ability.[41] They also are less likely to share knowledge for which they are differentially rewarded. Standardized tests are very good at setting up competitive situations, though there are other ways to produce such inclement circumstances.

3. *Ownership and involvement.* Students write better when it is their story than when they are assigned a story to write. They work harder and enjoy it more. When they are involved in a book, they become lost in it and do not become tired but drawn on. Teaching is rather like writing, and reading children can be just as absorbing as reading a book. Standardized tests used for accountability frequently invoke lack of ownership of any problem raised by the tests. The tests in that context are used to seek a place to lay blame rather than to help find a way to solve problems.

4. *Having a community of learners.* When a community of learners exists, there is greater knowledge in the community than can ever exist in the individual. There is also greater strength and support. Standardized tests have ways of breaking up community, the main one being the arranging of comparative contexts and the undervaluing of teachers' knowledge of their students and their practice. Without having their knowledge valued, teachers are perpetually insecure in the nature of their expertise.

5. *Trusting, respectful relationships between learners and between teachers and learners.* These relationships allow individuals to ask each other for advice, and to recognize different kinds of expertise without suspicion and threat. Testing, when there are consequences attached to it, can hardly be seen as respectful or trusting.

6. *Arranging for teachers to regularly observe one another and talk about their practice.* Just as one way to develop a person's writing is for them to observe another person writing and to talk about how and why she wrote that way. The same is true of a teacher observing another teacher and talking about how and why he did things that way. Currently it is common, in my area of the country, for teachers to have built into their teaching contract, several days a year in which they can go and observe other teachers. It is quite rare that they do so. In part this is because of teachers' insecurities, which are aggravated by high-profile testing and the technological view of teaching which the tests enforce. I shall discuss this further in Chapter 38.

As you can see, I argue that these conditions for learning are just as appropriate for teachers as they are for other learners. The question is how to foster these conditions for teachers so that they will optimize their learning.

Setting these conditions is critical. If teachers cannot become learners and improve their practice, then other developments are also cut off. For example, having teachers stay with their students for more than one year can reduce problems with promotion and competitive contexts at the same time as allowing teachers to develop greater knowledge of, and involvement with, their students. However, the common objection to this is, "What if the child gets a bad teacher—for two or three years?" We have been working on a scheme of damage control. We are arguing that maybe it won't be so bad if students get a bad teacher for a year. As Nel Noddings points out, a bad teacher for one year is unsatisfactory. Perhaps if students were to be faced with an unsatisfactory teacher for two years, we would take the issue of the teacher's unsatisfactory status seriously and work hard at helping him to learn. In addition, perhaps the public would take more seriously the matter of hiring the best of teachers. At the least they might, as some schools do, observe them teaching a class, or have them talk through a videotape of themselves teaching, perhaps as part of a personal teaching portfolio. Indeed, the same principle could be used for regular teaching evaluations. Apart from anything else, the effort to produce a videotape which the teacher was happy to talk through with others would have the effect of developing his teaching practice through reflection.

Another approach that encourages teacher learning is a procedure described by Dennis P. Wolf:

> At least once a year, a letter arrives in the mail asking teachers to select three to five folders that illustrate exceptional, moderate, or limited progress in writing. The letter alerts teachers that a supervisor will be coming to talk with them about writing. The conference is a time to describe how they are teaching a variety of types of writing, how they encourage students to engage in the several phases of the writing process, and how they comment on and critique student work. . . . During that half hour, teachers take active responsibility for portraying *their* work; they examine many facets of teaching; they don't use tests or first-draft writing samples, but evidence of the writing process and the back-and-forth between teacher and student.[42]

Procedures such as this not only produce a situation in which teachers learn more about their students and their practice, but also inspire greater public confidence. Part of what inspires the increased public trust is the way teachers learn to speak with authority and detail about their students.

ACCOUNTABILITY AND PUBLIC TRUST

Let's face it: the public simply doesn't trust teachers. When you ask why, they generally can't put their fingers on it, but that no more counters their concern than explaining the dark to a four-year-old makes it less fearsome. Fear of the dark is basically what we are dealing with. Switching on the light, or at least having a flashlight beside the bed, is probably the best solution. Switching on the light involves being as open as possible to the public, making sure that they see the things that are happening in the school, listening to the public, and working on problems together. For example, the use of local television stations can show the public what is going on in school (in our local area this is called "Principals' Report"). School and classroom newsletters can be very productive, as well as simply encouraging the public to visit, and participate in, classroom and school activity. Having a flashlight beside the bed is having available for audit as much information as possible. Egon Guba and Yvonna Lincoln have stressed the importance of what they call "auditability," using the accounting audit metaphor.[43] The important thing is to leave a trail documenting the methods, the interpretations, and the data, so that external auditors might evaluate them. The trail might include archives of teacher logs, student portfolios, videotapes of instruction (perhaps with accompanying comments), records of meetings, audiotapes of case studies, and whatever else might be seen as useful data. With available technology, information storage is no problem if we set our minds to it. Large samples of every student's work might be stored on disks or tape using computer scanners or microfiche.

This audit trail should be sampled by school personnel themselves, but it is also available for systematic examination by other stakeholders such as the board, and parents, or by mutually agreed-upon outside examiners. Susan Klein and her colleagues at the U.S. Department of Education report the successful use of what they call "the convening process," in which a school invites external review of its practice by a group of respected external school practitioners, and engages in dialogue with them about ways to develop their practice.[44] The dialogue should include some local board members and should result in specific recommendations being made. In my opinion, it is important that the reviewers describe the school's practice in terms of the practitioners' views of their activity rather than in terms of psychometric data, so that the participants recognize and claim ownership of the evaluation. Plausibility will be gained with all participants if the evaluation involves engagement in the school for several days. Note that such evaluations include administrators as much as teachers, and can certainly include evaluations of the public's responsibilities such as provision of adequate libraries, buildings, teacher salaries, attendance at conferences, and so forth.

Leaving the lights on is one thing, but flashlights at the side of the bed have to be pointed at something, and it is helpful if the public has a constructive idea of what to look at. Last year one of our kindergarten teachers, Aster Grimanis, used samples from one student's writing folder through second grade to explain invented spelling and the development of writing competence to her students' parents at the open house. This is exactly the same kind of activity I use to help teachers understand students' development better. As understanding increases, fear of the unknown is reduced, and parents become able to document their own child's development and to encourage her in a manner compatible with her teacher and fellow students. Even if the parent disagrees, at least the level of discussion is raised so that issues can be clarified and both parties can become better informed.

Donna Dunn, a local teacher, involved parents in her class reading program. Some of the parents questioned the children's choice of easy books, and their decision to reread books. Donna set up a tape recorder and encouraged students to read instructional level books onto the tape two or three times and to listen to themselves. With a single rereading she was recording up to a 14 percent increase in reading rate, with improvement in expression as well. She encouraged the students to take the tapes home and play them to their parents, who were suitably impressed. She does not do this often, but a simple demonstration like this can help allay parents' fears and gain their support through understanding.

Undertaking sensible dialogue from a nonadversarial position will prove very helpful. It certainly helps to increase personal contact and openness. In the Guilderland School District, at a majority of the school board meetings there is a presentation by some curriculum group (math, social studies, language arts, etc.) on one of the school's programs or curriculum projects. This keeps the board members well informed of the logic of changes that are taking place, and ensures that they understand that teachers take their curriculum seriously. It also keeps the board generally supporting expenditures on staff development since they are aware that the money is well spent.

It is important to listen to both sides and get all the cards on the table. Consider the following scenario. The teachers in the Wensleydale School District[45] had complained for two years that the testing that was being done in the district was not helpful, was expensive, and had unfortunate consequences for their teaching. The state required reading and writing assessment in three different years—fourth grade, eighth grade, and eleventh grade. However, the district required them to test every year. They could not get the board to sit down and listen to their arguments. Last year they took a different tack. They asked the board to sit down and tell them what they wanted out of the assessment system. This caused the board to do some serious thinking. They had two closed sessions before they met with the teachers, and they came up with the following reasons for their added assessment:

1. To document children's development
2. To make sure some children don't accidentally "miss the boat"
3. To keep students appraised of their progress
4. To help the teachers evaluate their own teaching effectiveness
5. To keep the public informed and
6. To make sure that the district is held to high standards

Once the rationale had been laid out in this manner, the teachers were able to sit down themselves and come up with some alternative ways of accomplishing these functions. The proposal they brought to the board was comprehensive and focused on dealing with the board's concerns within the framework of the teachers' needs and expertise. The proposal was as follows:

1. To document children's development the teachers proposed that most teachers already had in place a system of classroom writing folders and/or literature logs, journals, and portfolios. These could be used to document children's development, along with descriptions of the kinds of books children were reading. For the younger students, running records of their reading could be taken at least once a month. Twice each year, a narrative description of the child's development would be written. The writing of this summary narrative would ensure that teachers keep track of students' development, and the required running records and writing folders would ensure that there was data available to do so accurately.

2. This practice would also ensure that children did not accidentally "miss the boat." However, to make doubly sure, a special "safety net" would be set up—a simple dictation test would be given to all students at the beginning of first grade. Teachers would consider the dictation scores in the context of their classroom writing from the first two weeks of class and a running record of their reading an appropriate book. Students scoring below 15/40 on the dictation test would be considered for some intensive support instruction, as would children not showing self-correction in their running records. To make this system self-improving, a sample of ten fifth- and sixth-grade low-performing students would be identified and their archive files examined to consider ways in which their instructional histories might have been improved, in order to better manage similar, younger students' instruction.

3. The reading–writing portfolios would certainly keep the students apprised of their progress. Not only that, but it would help them to think about what to do to improve their progress, without the unmotivating effects of negative comparisons with others.

4. In addition to these activities, in order to help the teachers evaluate and develop their own teaching performance, teachers would be required to visit other teachers in the district to observe and discuss their teaching, and have other teachers return the favor. This option was already in their contract but few teachers ever took up the option.

   As a second strategy for self-evaluation and development of professional knowledge, once a month teachers would meet in groups K–2, 3–6 (others welcome though) to discuss a case study. Teachers would take turns at being responsible for providing for the discussion—a thorough case study of a child whom he found problematic. Each teacher would be responsible for one session per year.

5. To ensure high standards, at the end of each year, the board would arrange a sampling procedure to select a representative sample of portfolios that could be examined and discussed by the board, made available for public viewing and discussion, and evaluated by an outside examiner. Each portfolio would be accompanied by the end-of-year and mid-year narrative descriptions.

6. The accomplishment of public confidence was to be obtained by ensuring that regular writing samples went home and by increasing informative contact with parents. Videotapes of classroom teaching practice

would be made by teachers to describe their work to parents on parent-conference nights.

When this was presented to the board, several problems still had to be solved. In the first place, not all teachers agreed to this proposal. Some would rather have the tests which, in their view, required less work. Second, some of the board members were skeptical about the loss of objective measures. Although they liked the proposed efforts, some felt that they should have both—an opinion not well received by the teachers. However, it was agreed to have a two-year trial during which time only the state tests would be given. It was agreed that only those teachers who wished to needed to participate. Those teachers who did not participate would be required to give the tests.

In this scenario, both parties risk something. Teachers risk the possibility that their proposal will take more work and still eventually be rejected. They risk the fact that their more rigorous evaluation procedures will expose them to more critical standards than they were held to previously. Administrators stand to lose some control over teachers. They cannot hold test scores over their heads and make demands based on them. On the other hand, all parties stand to gain. Teachers stand to gain more control of their classrooms and of the curriculum. They also stand to gain more motivated and reflective students and more informed administrators. Administrators stand to gain more involved, more reflective teachers. They also stand to gain what amounts to free in-service, since the teachers self-evaluate and discuss issues among themselves. Parents stand to gain more interested and literate children, but lose the simple numbers they had used as gauges.

MAINTAINING STANDARDS

Along with the arguments for accountability come arguments for maintaining standards. In the North Scott Community District in Iowa, students write a piece (including "prewriting" and drafting) on a district-wide topic in fall and in spring. After the spring writing sample, students write evaluations of their pieces and describe their development. The samples and the comments are sent home to parents for their comments. The whole package, including parents' comments, is placed in the student's cumulative file. The writing is also scored holistically. Teachers rank-order the papers, and anchor papers are chosen to illustrate the characteristics of good writing and particular score points.[46] The useful principle in this is, I think, involving the parents and having their response as part of the student's file. A second useful point is the selection of anchor points that the parents can examine and understand in a concrete way. Having all children at all levels do a set piece of writing is the least useful feature. It is an example of the confusion between standards and standardization. We could easily come up with more interesting outcomes to look at.

Grant Wiggins argues that we should start with interesting graduation requirements, authentic tests, and then design schools backwards so that students will meet those requirements.[47] "Authentic assessment" has, alas, become something of a buzzword, almost reaching the status of "natural," as in "natural polysorbate 80." The point of the term "authentic" is to suggest some connection between the method of evaluation and the kinds of activity likely to be required of the student in the "real world." This is one of the advantages of portfolios, which, aside from avoiding the incidental traumas and instabilities of single-item tests, provide the possibility of a greater diversity of interesting ways of demonstrating the attainment of standards.

Projects, too, make a lot of sense for encouraging students to research areas of interest, and involving them in reading and writing in functional ways along with other forms of representation (visual art, dance, etc). When it comes to producing a grade or other evaluation, Howard Gardner has suggested that the following five dimensions are useful: conception, presentation, quality (including accuracy and innovation), individuality, and collaboration.[48] Each of these dimensions might be rated on a five-point scale. This has the advantage of being "true to life," in that these are dimensions on which students' efforts will be judged after they leave school. Unlike current testing practices it gives emphasis to both individuality *and* collaboration. A further advantage is that the breakdown in dimensions makes it a little harder for simplistic comparisons to be made. A similar set of dimensions has been described by Charles Cooper as: impact (interest, convincingness, completeness), inventiveness (surprising language, point of view, title, plot twist, organization), and individuality (voice, point of view, persona).[49]

Although these examples might make the standard setting of a meritocracy more sensible, there is still only a limited likelihood of their improving teaching and learning. Self-directed projects are more likely to have such an effect than standardized "authentic assessments." The latter represent the outdated "quality control" approach, which produced the demise of many industries in the United States. Quality pressure on the product does not increase productivity and quality, but personnel involvement and consultation in the process does.[50]

But in all these arguments there lurks a confusion between *standards* and *standardization*. When people lament the decline in standards, they are lamenting a perceived fall in the quality of teaching and learning. When they progress to a solution of "holding them to higher standards," particularly through a test procedure, the problem has changed to one of standardization. Holding the same "high standard" for all students will invariably result in a standard that is too low for most and too high for many, with motivational consequences for all concerned. To improve the quality of instruction, the teacher must help students have high standards relative to what they have produced. As Bob Stake puts it, rather than worry about using tests to "set high standards," educational reforms should:

demand and reinforce what good teachers have always given us, a controlling sense of what each youngster is learning, and the knowledge of how experience and study fit together and lead toward highly personalized lives in distinctive families, neighborhoods and communities.[51]

WHAT IS POSSIBLE

What is possible in terms of alternatives depends completely on the knowledge of the parties involved. A teacher who frames children's performance through tests and a basal reader will often continue to do so even though these instruments are no longer available to her. For example, a teacher's concept of her role and responsibilities can make her task more or less difficult. A teacher who feels obliged to have read all the books his students read could understandably be overwhelmed by an open approach to children's literature and the evaluation of his students' development. Similarly, a teacher who is required by administrators to adopt a method of keeping track of individual students' development through writing folders, observational checklists, and the like, but who is also required to use a basal reader in detail, might very well ask where the time is to come from. Just as it helps a teacher to know her students if she is a learner, it helps an administrator to know teachers if she is a teacher too (note the lack of past tense in this statement).

Until the public has learned a different way to know children's development, they too will expect the numbers they learned to know in school. In the early years, parents tend to have a more nurturing attitude toward their children and are more receptive to learning about the detail of their development. They are also more inclined to be involved in their schooling by turning up at parent-teacher nights and other nonroutine times. If the process of helping parents think about their children in constructive ways does not begin then, it will become increasingly difficult, as the years go by, to interest them. A parent whose principal concern is a high score on the SAT is simply not as receptive as one who has learned about the complexity of development. Tests are mainly called on by the public for force because the caring relationship has broken down and because the test scores represent a simple way for the parents to feel they have some control over monitoring their children's progress that does not depend on untrustworthy teachers. The tests would not be sought so readily by the public if reflectiveness and the caring relationship were stronger. The worst of it is that the tests ensure their own survival by their continued emphasis on the negative, particularly in those large inner-city schools where most alienation takes place, and through their objectification of both student and teacher. By consistently breaking down relationships, they ensure the need for force.

The suggestions I have provided in this chapter are merely a small sampling of what is possible. You and your colleagues can just as likely come up with better ones. In my dealings with State Education authorities to date, they have been most interested in alternative possibilities. I wonder how many imaginative proposals have been put before them in the past that directly address their concerns but from a different angle, and that clearly involve commitment from the district involved. Such proposals offer the possibility of changing regulations by influencing thinking and providing practical models.

CHAPTER 38

Reframing Evaluation: Revaluation

If the more things change, the more they remain the same, it is because our ways of looking and thinking have not changed.

Seymore Sarason

The way we frame problems has a lot to do with how we go about solving them. The frames we choose are drawn from those which we can imagine, and most prominently they reflect the values and assumptions of our culture. It is significant, for example, that the many current complaints about the quality of literacy instruction are attached to national competitive failures such as the launching of Sputnik by the Russians before we managed to accomplish a similar feat, and our failure to build television sets and cars as well or as cheaply as the Japanese. Concerns about schooling could just as easily have come from elsewhere. We could, for example, have looked at the extent of crime at all levels of society and looked to our schools for solutions. The questions we ask, and problems we define, are important indicators of our values.

Currently, everyone seems to want schools to provide higher levels of achievement. Educational psychologists produce study after study relating to achievement and achievement motivation. But most forget that what will count as achievement is an open, and politically laden, question. The causal connections that we seek are also important statements. Is it lack of academic achievement that produces our trade deficit, as newspapers assert, or is it the extreme individualism characteristic of this society[52] and the lack of a reflective and caring ethic? What if we sought, through schooling, a more caring society rather than the wealthiest and most powerful? What kinds of evaluation would we develop to serve that end?

EVALUATION AS LEARNING

I began with an intention to base this book on the metaphor of "evaluation as learning." As I progressed, however, I found that not just any learning would do. Chris Argyris and Donald Schon describe the concept of double-loop (as opposed to single-loop) learning.[53] In single-loop learning we learn to solve problems within the existing framework of "givens." For example, we might discover that our report cards are not giving parents a clear understanding of their children's literacy development. We might become convinced that report cards would be better written as extensive narrative descriptions than as grade lists. Yet, keen as we are, we might find this belief impossible to put into practice because of the increased time requirements on teachers. Consequently we might solve the problem by restructuring the report card. By contrast, in double-loop learning, we learn to change the "givens." For example, if we look carefully at the givens, we might realize that something we took as a given is actually not immutable after all. Where is it written, for example, that report cards must all be sent out on the same day? If they could be sent out over a period of a month, the enterprise might become manageable. By reconsidering our assumptions through double-loop learning, we solve the problem in an entirely different manner. Often we redefine the problem itself. It is this latter type of learning on which we must base constructive evaluation.

Double-loop learning is related to what others call "critical inquiry,"[54] and refers to the examination of underlying assumptions, metaphors, and motives. It is essentially a dialectic around generic questions such as:

- ☐ What goes on in the name of X? (Where X refers to reading instruction, individualization, writing conferences, accountability, in-service, reporting to parents, and so forth.)
- ☐ How did this come about?
- ☐ Whose interests are (and are not) being served by the way things are?
- ☐ What are the real and imagined constraints that are operating?

Critical inquiry is directed at exposing not only the assumptions, but also the political nature of situations, in order to expose oppression, be it inadvertent or otherwise.

Recently I listened to an eminent researcher talking about his research on trying to prevent children from having difficulty becoming literate. He had been impressed by the need for children to develop phonemic awareness and was, in cooperation with a testing company, using federal funds to produce a test of phonemic awareness along with an intervention program of carefully regulated exercises. I asked whether he had compared the tests with the teachers' ability to evaluate the students. He did not see the need for that because the teachers, he said, knew nothing of phonemic awareness. My objection was that it would be better to help the teachers learn than to invent the test. Indeed, unless the teachers became learned about the problem, the test itself served little purpose. I also asked how the test compared with samples of the children's writing. His puzzled response was that they do not do any writing in kindergarten. If children do no writing, it is not clear to me why they would see the need to become sensitive to the phonemes in words. In countries that do not have alphabetic languages, the *adults* are generally unaware of the phonemes in words.[55] In addition, with the object of communicating in a somewhat alphabetic language, children will explore with invented spelling the nature of the relationships between print and speech.

It is time for all the stakeholders in education to question such problematic framings as these, and to consider who benefits from them. Just as we teach children to examine advertising in terms of the potential motives for particular uses of print and other images, we need to demonstrate a similar critical literacy ourselves. For example, it may or may not be important that royalty checks or consulting fees are contingent on one particular framing of the problem and not on another.[56]

TECHNOLOGICAL THINKING

Expertise and Relationships

Schools, particularly secondary schools, are organized around a view of teaching and learning in which technical experts impart privileged knowledge in a sequential manner, and in which individual students compete to get the largest stack of knowledge. The space is divided up into cellular, age-related units, and the day is divided up into units within which the curriculum is to be dispensed to the students. The units are approximately forty minutes, and the class length is a semester. This structure, and many related phenomena such as current evaluation practices, is held together with a mortar of beliefs based on a technological view of the world. Technological beliefs emphasize winning over trying, behaving rationally and suppressing feelings, and controlling others through reward and punishment.

People who have learned to behave according to this set of beliefs tend to build relationships with others that emphasize conformity and competitiveness rather than individuality and cooperation, mistrust and covert antagonism rather than trust and helping others.[57] Central to this way of thinking is the belief that the world is basically competitive. Whether or not this is true is immaterial because when individuals act as though it were true, they induce the behavior in others. Indeed, if they believe this, then even if others behave differently, their behavior may still be interpreted as competitive. Consequently, just talking about schooling in terms of competition is problematic and has considerable consequences. Still many people assert that "kids will have to compete later," yet we find businesses looking for more team players. We could just as easily argue that "Kids will have to cooperate and negotiate later," ("It's a dog-help-dog world out there"), which would certainly put a different slant on our efforts at evaluation.

Chris Argyris and Donald Schon argue that this set of beliefs is part of a pattern that has even broader consequences. For example, current norm-referenced accountability testing tends to produce conditions of high threat and low self-esteem—exactly the conditions that tend to induce self-deception and a lack of congruence between what one believes and how one behaves and feels. Such conditions also encourage people to place blame rather than to solve problems. These conditions are most common in urban schools, and produce alienation on one side and burnout on the other, as Nel Noddings points out:

> Many urban teachers are symptoms of battle fatigue and "burn-out." No matter what they do, it seems, their efforts are not perceived as caring. They themselves are perceived, instead, as the enemy, as natural targets for resistance.[58]

Systemically, it seems to me, this constitutes an autoimmune disorder.

One of the principal obstacles to challenging assumptions lies in the common technological view of teacher expertise. Teachers are viewed, and view themselves, as technical experts. A paradox of expertise is that with experience, unless it is reflective, we can become very good at selective inattention. We conceptualize ourselves, our practice, our students, and our classrooms through particular metaphors and carefully overlook things that do not fit within those metaphors. We use wastebasket categories and we control situations in order to protect the technical knowledge we have made. Donald Schon describes the problem clearly:

> As practice becomes more repetitive and routine, and as knowing-in-practice becomes increasingly tacit and spontaneous, the practitioner may miss important opportunities to think about what he is doing. He may find that . . . he is drawn into patterns of error which he cannot correct. And if he learns, as often happens, to be selectively inattentive to phenomena that do not fit the categories of his knowing-in-action, then he may suffer from boredom or "burn-out" and afflict his clients with the consequences of his narrowness and rigidity. When this happens, the practitioner has "over-learned" what he knows.[59]

Within this trap of technical expertise, it becomes increasingly difficult to explore different metaphors. The more we see ourselves required to be this sort of expert, the more we feel discomfort when we face uncertainty. This is one of the reasons why standardized tests, particularly used for accountability purposes, are destructive. They at once apply pressure to preserve a singular view of teaching, learning, and literacy, and produce a context of insecurity in which uncertainty is even more likely to be threatening. In addition, by limiting exploration and enforcing certain metaphors, the possibilities for developing improved pattern recognition and reflection-in-action are reduced. For this very reason we must not become enamored with a view of ourselves as technical experts.

In order to reframe evaluation, we must reframe the nature of teaching expertise. Its center must lie in reflective practice and critical inquiry rather than in technical expertise. Thus, the expertise we need to value involves the ability to constantly make our own knowledge and practice problematic. When we begin a dialectic about our own knowledge and practice, and with our colleagues about our collective situation and practice (particularly those with different views), then we will begin to break the fetters of the frames to which we have become welded.

Language and Knowledge

Although I have asserted in this book that language is metaphorical, many people, perhaps the majority, disagree. They think of language as referential, as a medium that is neutral and functional, and that is used to describe the world as it exists. People with this belief are inclined to think teaching is mostly communicating knowledge to students. The positivists of the world find this perspective particularly inviting.[60] Having uncovered some of the *universal truths* of the world through application of the *neutral* scientific method to issues that are *naturally* important, they inform their unscientific subordinates of the knowledge they have discovered (as opposed to made). Their privileged access to this *real* knowledge gives them power through their possession of something that others, who lack the education or constitution to possess *the scientific method,* cannot get.

The neutral communication view of language also appeals to the formalists of the world.[61] These folks tend to believe that *literature* is a special type of text, readily identified by standard objective analysis, that speaks to universal truths. Literature, they believe, can be divorced from its context and everyday life. It is a work to be emulated and revered, a work that is above politics, an individual and psychological rather than communal work.[62] Individuals who hold this perspective believe literature to be something that few are capable of writing, thus conferring on it the economic power of scarcity and the cultural value of competition and class. This limited body of literature is also believed to have specific, unique meanings hidden from those of us who lack the keys to the codes (the literary equivalent of the scientific method), but which can be revealed by those with the keys. These are, of course, the university professors and the teachers.

These views of language and science share an implicit assertion of what will be allowed to count as knowledge, and thus who will count as a knower. Both views insist upon a dualism between subjective and objective, cognition and emotion. The scientific method involves eliminating or suppressing one's feelings and values, lest they make one feel connected to the thing that is to be understood. Nonscientists, beset with feelings and values, cannot hope to glimpse the truth. One must make oneself an object, separate and distinct from the object under study, in order to get the facts.

These dominant technological views of both science and literature—of knowing—are united through the common belief that language is referential, simply reflecting reality rather than constituting it. It is a belief that actually discourages reflection. But our naming of the world actually constitutes the world for us and we must always see reality through a veil of language. We *make* knowledge using language, but language also allows us to know the knowledge we have made. This is the nexus of evaluation, reading, writing, teaching, and literature: language and knowing our knowledge of ourselves and the world. If we accept the theoretical stance that language is neutral and referential, and that knowledge is objective and separate from the knower, then we will be denying that individuals make knowledge and that connected, personal knowledge is real knowledge. In such a world we would be unable to sustain a concept of teachers as researchers. Knowledge of the teacher's practice must then be generated by others who have no personal involvement. The teacher would be able to know her own practice only impersonally, through others, and to know herself as an object, not as a subject. Neither could her personally involving knowledge of students count as real knowledge; and when one's knowledge is not valued, it is easy to feel insecure and lacking in authority. Within the dualism of a truly objective view of science and of reading and writing, we cannot hope to know ourselves since we are inextricably caught in our own subjectivity (barring, of course, a very cleanly split personality).

Language is a form of power. Through language we name and constitute our worlds. Indeed, Northrop Frye argues that a central function of literate activity is to cultivate the imagination: to expand the sense of the possible—to multiply the metaphors we have available to render the world sensible.[63] Conferring the title of literature upon certain forms of language is a way of institutionalizing the power of particular kinds of language and particular namings of the world. At the same time, institutionalizing literature as something not functional, not political, allows this conferral of power to have extensive consequences for teaching and learning without appearing to do so. Its effects are thus moved from the external curriculum to what Eliot Eisner calls the hidden curriculum and the null curriculum.[64]

The null curriculum is those works deliberately omitted from study because there is simply not time—for example, the writing of native Americans, Hispanics, blacks, women. We do not have an accounting of the effects of the null curriculum for example on the likelihood of such groups viewing themselves as readers, authors, or active agents in a political world. However, Frantz Fanon has described the development of self-hatred in blacks who identify at once with the culture of power and with members of their own culture who are presented as victims, servants, and non-knowers.[65]

But there is also a *hidden* curriculum that emerges directly from the beliefs about literature, reading, and writing. For example, the continued presentation of text as if there were only one interpretation and the teacher owns that, produces people who are perpetually insecure in their knowledge, always fearful of interpreting incorrectly. As Norman Holland points out:

> All such discomfort proceeds from the debilitating assumption that each of us experiences something imperfectly and someone else knows just how imperfectly.[66]

This holds equally well, I might add, for writing. When we feel that our knowledge is inferior, or that our representation of it might be inferior, we are not likely to write a great deal—certainly not to produce literature. Similarly it holds for teaching. When a teacher believes that there is a single correct way to teach, verifiable by science, she is extremely likely to feel insecure about her own knowledge. Both the null curriculum and the hidden curriculum are enforced by standardized tests that, through their apparent objectivity, also appear nonpartisan.

It happens that these technological views of language and science favor particular groups. Those who determine what will count as literature, what will count as knowledge, what meanings language is allowed to make, hold a great deal of power. It is no accident that the bulk of works considered authentic literature, and studied as such in school, were written by folk who were all white and all men.[67] The perspectives and roles in these works represent the perspectives of the dominant class, white men. It is also no accident that positivistic science has been dominated by men and has never been particularly friendly to women.[68] Neither is it an accident that it is folk who hold these views of the world who make, and insist on the use of, tests. Nor is it coincidence that teachers mostly happen to be women. These issues must not be ignored as we attempt to develop a more humane approach to evaluation.

QUESTIONING ASSUMPTIONS

We suppose that we teach children to make inferences, and we test to see whether we managed to accomplish this feat. The blunt fact is that if human beings did not make inferences they wouldn't live long and they certainly wouldn't learn language. It seems to me that we should worry more about teaching children to examine the inferences they are so good at making. But the same goes for us. We are particularly good at making inferences, so good that we do not even notice that we have done so. *It is these unconscious inferences, or assumptions, that carry the political hegemony*. It is the unspoken that is most dangerous politically because it is least easy to examine.

We assume tests to be an essential key to the improvement of schooling, and continually seek to improve education by fine-tuning them. This is like trying to hone a sledgehammer to a finer point in order to nail together picture frames that should probably be jointed and glued anyway. Testing is so common and unexamined that it is now "common knowledge" that the bell curve is a natural part of achievement. But the bell curve is not a necessary feature of literate activity or knowledge. Rather, it is one of statistical convenience and a by-product of making literacy a linear, competitive commodity. If research has shown us anything in the last few years, it has shown us literacy's complexity, its relativity, and its political nature.

Sometimes we notice an assumption only when we see something working just fine without it. Many people find the use of norm-referenced tests obvious and *natural*. To those people, eliminating norm-referenced tests would seem like an extreme position. However, to people in more literate countries than this, proposing the norm-referenced testing that children face in the United States would constitute an extreme position. This suggests some ways to expose these lurking assumptions. One way is to spend time talking with and, more importantly, listening to, others who have substantially different views from our own. Another is to expose ourselves to very different circumstances than we are familiar with. A third is to play "What if?" Consider, for example, the placing of children in isolated classrooms by age. We know this is not essential. Some schools do not do it. What if we did not have grade levels? Imagine what could happen to the following:

☐ retention in grades
☐ transition rooms
☐ school readiness
☐ peer group
☐ grade equivalents

Many of our assumptions are maintained in the face of conflicting evidence. For example, we are not short of models of alternatives. "Family plan" schools and classrooms (organized across age levels and in smaller units) are to be found in places such as the Prospect School in North Bennington, Vermont, the School Without Walls in Rochester, New York, and in many parts of New Zealand. Similarly, the changing of teachers each year is not found in Waldorf Schools, the largest private school system in the world. The highly successful Central Park East school in New York City, developed and run by Deborah Meier, works on the family plan and on teachers remaining with children for more than a year. Although we assume that standardized testing is a necessary component of schooling and the improvement of schooling, we have ample examples of literate nations who engage in relatively little testing at all. Schools like Central Park East, the School Without Walls, and Prospect School were not produced or even stimulated by test scores. They are produced by a concerted and creative act of will among a group of caring individuals who have engaged in double-loop learning.

What is it, then, that holds in place the current framing of the evaluation problem? The answer is probably twofold. On the one hand, there is an integrated set of beliefs about language, science, and human activity. On the other is the fact that some people benefit from this set of beliefs.

RETHINKING OUR LANGUAGE

Many assumptions are built into the metaphors of our language and they at once come from, and maintain, the status quo. The conditions described above both produce and sustain the metaphors of being "in the trenches," or "on the front line." This is why, at the beginning of the book, I was particularly careful to define some contrasting terms such as accountability and responsibility. Once we are within a metaphor we construct and label the world from within it.[69] Consider some other common terms and their consequences. What if instead of "instructional level" we spoke of "involvement level"? The term "disability" is based on the normative notion of "ability." How about "disinvolved" as an alternative framing of the problem? This concept we could apply to all parties: teachers, parents, and administrators, as well as students. Notice also how the implicit instructional consequences differ substantially. We often talk favorably of students being "smart," "brilliant," "intelligent," and "quick." Perhaps we should talk more of students being "involved," "thoughtful," "caring," and "reflective." Being quick is not the same as being reflective, and you don't teach it the same way.

For too long now psychometric language has held the high ground in discussions of evaluation. For example, it is common practice to talk about teachers' evaluation procedures as "informal" or "more subjective" or "anecdotal." These terms are used in a derogatory fashion with standardized, "objective" tests being the basis of "scientific" evaluation. I think it more proper to talk about classroom observations as *direct* evaluation and tests as *indirect* evaluation.[70] These terms reflect in a more realistic way the more salient features of the approaches. We might also refer to tests as *invasive* evaluation and classroom evaluation as *non-invasive* evaluation. As another example, we commonly talk of *theory* as quite separate from *practice*. But theory and practice are inseparable, and best referred to in the singular as "praxis."[71] Practice always has an underlying theory to guide it. Indeed, unless the theory in one's practice is made explicit, it is often hard to change it. While theory and practice are spoken of separately, change will be slow. Indeed, a constructive approach to evaluation will not become widespread until "being philosophical is recognized as a legitimate and time-consuming part of *being practical*."[72] This applies to teachers and their students in equal measure, and to administrators and the public too.

I hope these examples give you a sense that language is not simply a neutral vehicle for conveying information. Rather, it is metaphorical, and we always get more than we bargain for when we use words. We actually use language to make our worlds. Calling someone disabled carries many connotations. It is different, for example, from calling everyone else "temporarily able."[73] Imagine a world in which parking lots had special places for the temporarily able and another unmarked set for everyone else. Part of examining the framing of problems, and reframing them, involves studying the language being used and what it implies for the way we would like the world to be.

Once we detect assumptions, we are in a position of more informed choice about where we want to put our resources. For example, do we want to invest them in efforts to detect and publicize who is making mistakes, the assumption underlying current accountability assessment, or do we want to invest them in maximizing the construction and sharing of knowledge about more and less productive practices? Challenging such simple assumptions can be no less consequential, nor less difficult, than challenging the obvious flatness of the earth among people who are afraid to explore for fear of falling off the edge.

CONSTRUCTIVE THINKING

I have tried to reframe evaluation on the basis of a constructive view of knowledge. I do not wish to pretend that there are no problems associated with my perspective. There are. To begin with, if we wish to develop a constructive approach to evaluating literate activity, we must actively change the context in which we work. We must build a relationship of trust between the stakeholders in the enterprise. We must simultaneously change some basic cultural understandings, bearing in mind that teachers, just like test makers, are ordinary people—desires, fears, defenses, and all. But when all is said and done, it is teachers who touch children's lives. The more observant and reflective, and the less fearful and defensive they are, the better will be our children's learning experiences, and the greater will be the prospects for their future. If we are to invest in evaluation, it must be an investment in teachers and in conditions that will encourage them to become more constructive.

With Mary Belenky and her colleagues in *Women's Ways of Knowing,* I believe that a constructive teacher of reading, writing, and literature realizes that people construct realities and that the teacher's job is to come to grips with her students' realities and help them come to grips with the consequences of those realities. She does not assert her own response to literature as the standard through which she has power *over* her students. Her authority is based on cooperation rather than subordination. She has power *through* community and trust. Her students are treated as independent *subjects* (not objects) whose personal, value-laden constructions in reading and writing matter. A participant observer, this teacher enriches her own understanding of literature by empathizing with her students' understandings. She practices a "disciplined subjectivity," and encourages the practice in her students so that they may know themselves as independent and interdependent knowers capable of constructing knowledge and reflecting upon it.

As Belenky and her colleagues point out, the motive to improve one's teaching lies within the constructive perspective itself:

> Once knowers assume the general relativity of knowledge, that their frame of reference matters and that they can construct and reconstruct frames of reference, they feel responsible for examining, questioning, and developing the systems that they will use for constructing knowledge.[74]

From this perspective, reflectiveness and responsibility are integral parts of teaching, learning, and literate activity. They are woven into the fabric of what it means to be a teacher. The students of such teachers are continually presented with models of reflective learning.

The theoretical consistencies between reading, writing, teaching, and evaluation are underpinned by theories of language and knowledge that are, ultimately, intensely political. How students and teachers know themselves, their world, their culture, and the culture of others is at stake. No less. And if I have to choose sides, and as a teacher I must, I will choose a constructivist perspective on knowledge and the intimate place of language and the knower in its construction. In a democratic, multicultural society it seems my only option.

Notes and References for Part V

1. James's writing, this book in particular, is well worth reading.
    William James (1899) *Talks to teachers on psychology.* New York: Henry Holt & Co., pp. 130–131.
    Ann Berthoff brought this to my attention in her book:
    Ann Berthoff (1982). *Forming/Thinking/Writing.* Portsmouth, NH: Boynton/Cook.

2. Albert Speer (1970). *Inside the Third Reich: Memoirs by Albert Speer.* Translated by Richard and Clara Winston. New York: Macmillan, p. 212.

3. This observation and much of the material surrounding it came from a paper by:
    Walt Haney and George Madaus (1989). Searching for alternatives to standardized tests: Whys, whats and whithers. *Phi Delta Kappan,* May: 683–687.
    This and other articles by this pair are recommended reading.

4. Robert Linn, M. Elizabeth Graue, and Nancy Sanders (1990). Comparing state and district results to national norms: The validity of the claims that ''Everyone is above average.'' *Educational Measurement: Issues and Practice 9*(3): 5–14.

5. Indeed, norms have changed from the 1970s to the 1980s because of improved performance on five of the six major test batteries. Linn et al. Comparing state and district test results to national norms.

6. See note 4 above.
    Richard Allington and Anne McGill-Franzen (1989). Different programs, indifferent instruction. In A. Gartner and D. Lipsky (Eds.), *Beyond separate education.* Baltimore, MD: Brookes, pp. 75–98.

7. Daniel Resnick (1982). History of educational testing. In Alexandra Wigdor and Wendell Garner (Eds.), *Ability testing: Uses, consequences, and controversies. Part II: Documentation section.* Washington: National Academy Press, pp. 173–194.

8. The following study is instructive:
   John Guthrie (1981). Reading in New Zealand: Achievement and volume. *Reading Research Quarterly 17*(1): 6–27.

9. This is the same argument used by many white-coated research folks (myself included, for a brief period), working for basal reader companies—that basals are here to stay, so it's the best we can do; and that many teachers are so hopeless as to be damaging if they didn't have basals.

10. The *Reading Style Inventory*. Roslyn Heights, NY: National Reading Styles Institute.

11. Good readings on this include:
    On reading—
    Ann Bussis, Edward Chittenden, Marianne Amarel, and E. Klausner (1985). *Inquiry into meaning: An investigation of learning to read*. Hillsdale, NJ: Erlbaum.
    On writing—
    Ruth Hubbard (1989). Inner designs. *Language Arts 66*(2): 119–136.

12. The following studies are instructive:
    Courtney Cazden (1988). *Interactions between Maori Children and Pakeha teachers*. Auckland, NZ: Auckland Reading Association.
    Courtney Cazden and E. Leggett (1981). Culturally responsive education: Recommendations for achieving Lau remedies II. In Henry Trueba, Grace Guthrie, and Kathryn Au (Eds.), *Culture and the bilingual classroom: Studies in classroom ethnography*. Rowley, MA: Newbury House, pp. 69–86.
    Susan Philips (1983). *The invisible culture: Communication in classroom and community on the Warm Springs Indian Reservation*. White Plains, NY: Longman.
    For a review of related issues see:
    Roland Tharp (1989). Psychocultural variables and constants: Effects on teaching and learning in schools. *American Psychologist 44*(2): 349–359.

13. Alternative testing techniques for students with handicapping conditions (1986). The University of the State of New York, the State Education Department, Albany, NY, p. 8.

14. Reading test for New York State Elementary schools, Manual for administrators and teachers (1986). The University of the State of New York, the State Education Department, Albany, NY, pp. 10–11.

15. See note 14 above, p. 22.

16. See note 14 above, p. 23.

17. *Stanford Achievement Test, Intermediate Level II.* (1973). New York: Harcourt Brace Jovanovich. Manual Part II, p. 18.

18. *Comprehensive Test of Basic Skills.* 4th Ed. (1988). Monterey, CA: Macmillan/McGraw-Hill School Publishing.

19. *CTBS/4: Scoring Reports* (1988). Monterey, CA: Macmillan/McGraw-Hill School Publishing.

20. See note 19 above.

21. These were reported on the front page of the *Daily Herald* of Chicago on Friday February 26, 1988, along with a listing of local suburban school districts' College entrance exam scores, state average performance, and national average performance.

22. How tax dollars are spent. *The Milwaukee Advocate,* May 1990, p. 8.

23. Office of Educational Research and Improvement, U.S. Department of Education (n.d.). Washington, DC. *Help your child improve in test-taking*.

24. Ron Brandt (1989). On misuse of testing: A conversation with George Madaus. *Educational Leadership,* April: 26–29.

25. *Stanford 7 Plus.* The Psychological Corporation, 1987, p. 2.

26. Nancy Cole (1988) A realist's appraisal of the prospects for unifying instruction and assessment. In *Assessment in the service of learning: Proceedings of the 1987 ETS invitational conference.* Princeton, NJ: Educational Testing Service.

27. Lorrie A. Shepard. (1989). Why we need better assessments. *Educational Leadership 46*(7): 4–9.

28. Good studies on this issue are:
Linda Darling-Hammond and Arthur Wise (1985). Beyond standardization: State standards and school improvement. *The Elementary School Journal 85:* 315–336.
Linda McNeil (1986). *Contradictions of control: School structure and school knowledge.* New York: Routledge and Kegan Paul.
Leslie Salmon-Cox (1981). Teachers and standardized achievement tests: What's really happening? *Phi Delta Kappan 62:* 631–634.

29. Richard C. Anderson, Elfrieda Hiebert, Judith Scott, and Ian Wilkinson (1985). *Becoming a Nation of Readers: The report of the commission on Reading.* Champaign, IL: Center for the Study of Reading, p. 98.

30. Reported in (1989) *Fair Test Examiner 3*(3): p. 6.

31. I called our state Education Department about this problem. I asked them, "What happens if a parent does not want their child to be tested?" The representative's first response was, "Why do you want to know?" However, he did say that they counsel the person that the tests are not harmful and that children have to get used to them, but they do not force compliance. I also asked the Chapter I people and their response was identical, so apparently this type of resistance is possible.

32. It has taken me years to arrive at the view I now have, and I did not begin with an investment in testing. Indeed, the writing of this book has taken me six years because I kept having to throw chapters away because they became obsolete as more and more parts of the metaphor fell into place for me.

33. I found this statement "Label jars, not children," on the desk of a feisty principal, Florence Gugino, in Buffalo, New York.

34. Marleen Pugach and Lawrence Johnson (1989). Prereferral interventions: Progress, problems, and challenges. *Exceptional Children 56*(3): 232–235.
Marleen Pugach and Lawrence Johnson (1990). Developing reflective practice through structured dialogue. In R. Clift, W. Houston, and M. Pugach (Eds.), *Encouraging reflective practice in education: An analysis of issues and programs.* New York: Teachers College Press, pp. 186–207.

35. Gerald Coles (1978). The learning disabilities test battery: Empirical and social issues. *Harvard Educational Review 48:* 313–340.
Gerald Coles (1987). *The learning mystique: A critical look at learning disabilities.* New York: Pantheon.

36. This scenario has not, to my knowledge, occurred as described. However, it has been put together from a variety of different situations I have encountered.

37. The calculations made involved a multiple regression analysis in which other tests were used to predict the standardized test score. Of course, using the standardized test as the criterion is a debatable thing to do. It is not clear at all that it is the best measure for the job. This was simply the most comprehensible way to proceed, given the background of the people to whom the problem needed to be explained.

38. Reading Recovery is the early intervention program developed by Marie Clay that has proven extremely effective in virtually eliminating reading failure through early intervention. The program involves individual one-on-one tutoring for half an hour each day. However children exit the program at the level of the average children in the classroom in 12 to 25 weeks. As each student exits the program another student can enter, so that over the course of the year a given teacher can return

about 40 students to the regular program at the level of the average student in the class.

39. This set of procedures can be found in:
Marie Clay (1985). *The early detection of reading difficulties.* 3rd ed. Portsmouth, NH: Heinemann-Boynton/Cook.

40. This statement is contrary to one made recently by President Bush to the state governors. He stated that we needed "more competition between students, between teachers, and between schools."

41. Russell Ames (1983). Help-seeking and achievement orientation: Perspectives from attribution theory. In Bella DePaulo, Arie Nadler, and Jeffrey Fisher (Eds.), *New directions in helping.* New York: Academic Press, pp. 165–188.

42. Dennis P. Wolf (1989). Portfolio assessment: Sampling student work. *Educational Leadership 46*(7): 35–40.

43. Egon Guba and Yvonna Lincoln (1983). *Effective evaluation: Improving the usefulness of evaluation results through responsible and naturalistic approaches.* San Francisco: Jossey-Bass.

44. Susan Klein, Norman Gold, and Charles Stalford, (1986). The convening process: A new technique for applying knowledge to practice. *Educational Evaluation and Policy Analysis 8*(2): 189–204.

45. This is a fictitious, but plausible, scenario.

46. This set of procedures is reported by Melva Lewis (an eighth-grade language arts teacher) and Arnold Lindaman (assistant superintendent in the North Scott Community School District, Eldridge, Iowa) in: How do we evaluate student writing? One district's ANSWER. *Educational Leadership 46*(7): 70–71.

47. Grant Wiggins (1989). Teaching to the (authentic) test. *Educational Leadership 46*(7): 41–49.

48. Howard Gardner (July 1990). Institute on New Modes of Assessment, Harvard Graduate School of Education, Cambridge, MA.

49. Charles Cooper (1977). Wholistic evaluation of writing. In Charles Cooper and Lee Odell (Eds.), *Evaluating writing: Describing, measuring and judging.* Urbana, IL: National Council of Teachers of English.

50. There is now a substantial literature on "quality circles," which are the reason "made in Japan" is now synonymous with high quality whereas 25 years ago it was synonymous with poor quality. Quality circles operate somewhat differently in the United States because of the different social context, but just as effectively. Instead of focusing directly on increased quality control and worker output, these outcomes have been achieved through quality circles' focus on participative management, job satisfaction, self-esteem, the assumption of trust, and the development of interpersonal skills—essentially the humanization of the workplace. More interesting still is the very successful application of quality circles to "service industries." If we must look to industry for metaphors, let us at least choose sensibly.
Relevant reading can be found in:
Patrick Townsend with Joan Gebhardt (1990). *Commit to quality.* New York: John Wiley.
Sud and Nima Ingle (1983). *Quality circles in service industries: Comprehensive guidelines for increased productivity and efficiency.* Englewood Cliffs, NJ: Prentice-Hall.
Olga Crocker, Johnny Sik Leung Chiu, and Cyril Charney (1984). *Quality circles: A guide to participation and productivity.* New York: Facts on File Publications.

51. Robert Stake (1987). Confusing standardization with standards: An expert on testing and evaluation questions our reliance on centrally-mandated standards. *Networker: Perspectives from the Schools 2*(3): 29.

52. Robert Bellah, Richard Madsen, William Sullivan, Ann Swidler, and Steven Tipton (1985). *Habits of the heart: Individualism and commitment in American life.* New York: Harper and Row.

53. Chris Argyris and Donald Schon (1974). *Theory in practice: Increasing professional effectiveness.* San Francisco: Jossey-Bass.

54. For example:
Kenneth Sirotnik (1987). Evaluation in the ecology of schooling: The process of school renewal. In John Goodlad (Ed.), *The ecology of school renewal: Eighty-sixth yearbook of the National Society for the Study of Education, Part I.* Chicago: University of Chicago Press.

55. Jose Morais, Luz Cary, Jesus Alegria, and Paul Burdelson (1979). Does awareness of speech as a sequence of phonemes arise spontaneously? *Cognition 7:* 323–331.

56. I do not mean to frame this in an adversarial manner. I am not suggesting that people who are involved in these activities have material gain as their primary objective. The obvious response to that would be "sour grapes"—"you're just jealous that you don't get a royalty check." Indeed, although I did not write this book for financial reasons, my personal investment of time and ego alone will make it hard to agree with a reviewer's arguments that it is destructive. But, time and ego notwithstanding, if I were to agree with such an argument, and my publisher kept sending me royalty checks, I would be certain to encounter cognitive discomfort each time I picked up subsequent checks. It would be difficult for me then to avoid self-deprecation. My argument is simply that *all* of us must recognize that it is harder to question an assumption from which we benefit materially or socially, particularly when the outcome of the questioning has apparent implications for our ethical status as well.

57. Chris Argyris (1962). *Interpersonal competence and organizational effectiveness.* Homewood, IL: Dorsey Press.
Chris Argyris (1964). *Integrating the individual and the organization.* New York: John Wiley.

58. Nel Noddings (1984). *Caring: A feminine approach to ethics and moral education.* Los Angeles: University of California Press, p. 181.

59. Donald Schon (1983). *The reflective practitioner: How professionals think in action.* New York: Basic Books, p. 61.

60. Positivists are those who believe that science consists of examining "objectively" observable "facts" and relating them to "natural laws."

61. Formalists are those in literary circles whose analyses are bound tightly to the forms and structures of text rather than to the social context of use and negotiated understanding.

62. The bulk of analyses of reading and writing also fall into this category.

63. Northrop Frye (1964), *The educated imagination.* South Bend, IN: Indiana University Press.

64. Elliot Eisner (1979). *The educational imagination: On the design and evaluation of school programs.* New York: Macmillan.

65. Frantz Fanon (1967). *Black skin, white masks.* New York: Grove Press.

66. Norman Holland (1975). *Five readers reading.* New Haven, CT: Yale University Press, p. 282.

67. They are virtually all also dead, which helps to maintain the belief in the single meanings.

68. The unfriendly nature of positivistic science toward women is documented by Evelyn Fox Keller (1985) in her book *Reflections on science and gender.* New Haven, CT: Yale University Press.

69. An important book to read on this topic is:
George Lakoff and Mark Johnson (1980). *Metaphors we live by*. Chicago: University of Chicago Press.

70. I have borrowed this distinction from Ted Chittenden of ETS.

71. The term ''praxis'' originated, I believe, with Paola Friere.

72. Kenneth Sirotnik (1987). Evaluation in the ecology of schooling: The process of school renewal. In John Goodlad (Ed.), *The ecology of school renewal: Eighty-sixth yearbook of the National Society for the Study of Education, Part I*. Chicago: University of Chicago Press. (p. 48).

73. This idea came from a contemporary folk song by Fred Small called ''The Wheelchair Talking Blues,'' recorded by Iain MacKintosh on his *Gentle Persuasion* album (1988), Greentrax Records, Edinburgh.

74. Mary Belenky, Blythe Clinchy, Nancy Goldberger, and Jill Tarule (1986). *Women's ways of knowing: The development of self, voice, and mind*. New York: Basic Books, pp. 138–139.

APPENDIXES

APPENDIX A

Practice Running Records

Appendix A contains examples of running records that appear on the audiotape accompanying this book.

OOPS!

By Fran Hunia

TAPE EXAMPLE #14

page 4
Billy wanted a biscuit . . .

page 5
but
he
couldn't
reach

page 6
He stood on a chair . . .

page 7
but
he
couldn't
reach

page 8
He put a box
on the chair . . .

page 9
but
he
couldn't
reach.

page 10
He put a bucket
on the box
on the chair . . .

page 11
but
he
couldn't
reach.

page 12
He put a book
on the bucket
on the box
on the chair
but

page 13
OOPS!

page 14
Down came the biscuits
and the book
and the bucket
and the box
and the chair . . .

page 15
and Billy.

page 16
Silly Billy!

OOPS!

4.

✓ ✓ ✓ ✓

5.

✓
✓
✓
✓

6.

✓ ✓ ✓ ✓ ✓

7.

✓
✓
✓
✓
✓

8.

✓ st | SC   ✓ ✓
  put |

✓ ✓ ✓

9.

✓
✓
✓
✓

10.

✓ ✓ ✓ box
         bucket

11.

✓
✓
✓
✓

12.

✓ ✓ ✓ box
        book

✓ ✓R ✓

an | SC ✓ ✓
on

✓ ✓ ✓
✓

13.

✓

14.

✓ ✓ ✓
✓ ✓ ✓
✓ ✓ pa | SC
     bucket

✓ ✓ ✓
✓ ✓ ✓

15.

on | on | SC   ✓
and

16.

✓ ✓

GREEDY CAT

by Joy Cowley

TAPE EXAMPLE #15

page 3

Mum went shopping
and got some sausages.
Along came Greedy Cat.
He looked in the shopping bag.
Gobble, gobble, gobble,
and that was the end of that.

page 5

Mum went shopping
and got some sticky buns.
Along came Greedy Cat.
He looked in the shopping bag.
Gobble, gobble, gobble,
and that was the end of that.

page 7

Mum went shopping
and got some potato chips.
Along came Greedy Cat.
He looked in the shopping bag.
Gobble, gobble, gobble,
and that was the end of that.

page 8

Mum went shopping
and got some bananas.

page 9

Along came Greedy Cat.
He looked in the shopping bag.
Gobble, gobble, gobble,
and that was the end of that.

page 10

Mum went shopping
and got some chocolate.

page 11

Along came Greedy Cat.
He looked in the shopping bag.
Gobble, gobble, gobble,
and that was the end of that.

page 13

Mum went shopping
and got a pot of pepper.

page 14

Along came Greedy Cat.
He looked in the shopping bag.
Gobble, gobble—

page 15

YOW!

page 16

and that was the end of that!

GREEDY CAT

3.

✔ ✔ ✔
✔ ✔ ✔ ✔
✔ ✔ ✔ ✔
✔ ✔ ✔ ✔ ____–____ ✔
            shopping

and   he   ____–____
———   ———   gobble | T   ✔ ✔
 –   –

✔ ✔ ✔ ✔ ✔ ✔ ✔
_____

5.

Momma ✔ ✔
—————
Mum

✔ ✔ ✔ ✔ biscuits
               buns

✔R ✔ ✔ ✔

✔ ✔ ✔ ✔ ____–____ ✔
            shopping

✔ ✔ ✔
✔ ✔ ✔ ✔ ✔ ✔ ✔
_____

7.

Momma ✔ ✔
—————
Mum

✔ ____–____   ____–____   ____–____   ____–____
     got   some   potato   chips

al | ✔   ✔ ✔ ✔
————
along

✔ ✔ ✔ ✔ ____–____ ✔
            shopping

✔ ✔ ✔
✔ ✔ ✔ ✔ ✔ ✔ ✔
_____

8.

Momma   ✔ ✔
—————
Mum

✔ ✔ ✔ ✔
_____

9.

and | al| SC ✔ ✔ ✔
—————
along

✔ ✔ ✔ ✔ ____–____ ✔
            shopping

✔ ✔ ✔
✔ ✔ ✔ ✔ ✔ ✔ ✔
_____

10.

✔ ✔ ✔
✔ ✔ ✔ ✔
_____

11.

✔ ✔ ✔ ✔
and ✔ ✔ ✔ ____–____ ✔
——
he   shopping

✔ ✔ ✔
✔ ✔ ✔ ✔ ✔ ✔ ✔
_____

13.

Momma ✔ ✔
—————
Mum

✔ ✔ ✔ ✔
_____

14.

✔ ✔ ✔
✔ ✔ ✔ ✔ ____–____ ✔
            shopping

✔ ✔
_____

15.

ow ____
—————
YOW
_____

16.

✔ ✔ ✔ ✔ ✔ ✔ ✔

THE TERRIBLE DAYS OF MY CAT CALI

Written and Illustrated by William Haggerty (1990).

TAPE EXAMPLE #16

page 1

Once my cat bit me on the nose when I was
asleep. And once she came back on Friday
and did nothing, just sit down in some shed.
Then she came home.

page 2

Once my cat climbed on the screen. After my
cat climbed on the screen, she went upstairs
and got under the covers in my mother's bed
and slept for one hour.

page 3

After she came out of the covers, she ran
downstairs and purred at the basement door.
Instead of going in the basement door, she
cried at the front door and ran around the
house two times. Then she chased after a
motorcycle. She came back home and she was
hungry.

page 4

And today she ran away, but my brother found
her. She made us late for Reading!

MY CAT CALI

1.

✔ ✔ ✔ ✔ ✔ ✔ ✔ ✔ ✔ ✔
✔ ✔ ✔ ✔ ✔ ✔ ✔ ✔
✔ ✔ ✔ ✔ ✔ ✔ and | SC ✔ ✔
　　　　　　　 in　|

✔ ✔ ✔ ✔

2.

✔ ✔ ✔ ✔ ✔ ✔ ✔ ✔
✔ ✔ ✔ ✔ ✔ ✔ ✔

✔ ✔ ✔ ✔ ✔ ✔ ✔ ✔ ✔R
✔ ✔ ✔ ✔

3.

✔ ✔ ✔ ✔ ✔ ✔ ✔ ✔
✔ ✔ ✔ ✔ ✔ ✔
and | R^2 | SC ✔ ✔ ✔ ✔ ✔ ✔ ✔
instead |

✔ ✔ ✔ ✔ ✔ ✔ ✔ ✔
✔ ✔ ✔ and | the | SC ✔ clo | SC ✔ ✔
　　　　　then |　　　chased |

✔ ✔ ✔ ✔ ✔ ✔ ✔
✔

4.

✔ ✔ ✔ ✔ ✔ ✔　cat | R　✔
　　　　　　　 brother |

✔R sh | ✔ ✔ ✔ ✔ ✔
　　she |

APPENDIX B

Some Questions to Explore

You might try these out in another teacher's class, which tends to reduce the accountability concerns of the students. It will give you a feel for what it is like to get a genuine response. Coming in as a visitor it is easier to establish ignorance.

If I asked you to [*name an activity*], how would you go about it?

If I asked John to [*name an activity*], would he need to ask me any questions about it?

Can you tell me all the things you do in your writing time in class?

What did you do in your reading time today?

When you read this chapter of the book to me, could you explain what you are doing and thinking?

Can you give me an example of a situation in which you might do that?

Could you describe how you wrote this piece, starting from when you were deciding what to write about?

If I were listening in on kids' discussions about this novel, what kinds of comments do you think I might hear?

Have you read any hard books lately? Choose one. What was it that made the book hard?

Suppose you had to try to read a chapter of your social studies book for a quiz at the end of the week but you lost your book. You found it again with only an hour or so left to study. What would you do?

Do you find some reading harder than others? Can you give me some examples? What makes x harder than y?

Are there different sorts of reading?

What sorts of reading do you like best? Can you give me some examples?

Are you really good at some types of reading (writing)? What is it that makes you good at that?

You mentioned two different types of writing. Are there any other types of writing?

You mentioned x writing and y writing. How are they different from one another? When you are writing (reading) them, what would you do differently?

I'm interested in all the different kinds of stories kids like to read. Can you think of different types that you and other kids might like to read?

Do you find that you like some books better than others? What is it that makes some books more satisfying to you?

Are any of the kids in the class especially good readers/writers? What do they (he/she) do that makes them good readers/writers?

Suppose you had a pen pal in the same grade in a different school and you wanted to find out about him as a reader. What questions would you ask him?

Are there ways a writer can make a story more interesting/easier to read [or . . .]

Why did you choose your book?

This new draft of your story is quite different from the first one. It's almost a different story. How did you decide to make the changes?

When you were halfway through the book you seemed to be quite excited about it but now you are telling me you did not enjoy it. What changed your mind? If you were the author, how might you have changed it to keep the reader excited all the way through?

What would you like to learn so you can become a better writer?

What is something you have learned to do in writing (reading)?

APPENDIX C

Form for Recording Alphabet Knowledge

Name _____   Date _____

F	S	g	j
W	L	y	e
T	A	z	r
D	M	k	q
H	I	n	b
X	C	v	u
G	J	o	p
Y	E	f	s
Z	R	w	l
K	Q	t	a
N	B	d	m
V	U	h	i
O	P	x	c
		a	g

Confusions: _____

_____

Comments: _____

_____

Record correct response with a check mark (✔), no response leave blank, and record what the child says in the case of errors. Count as correct: letter name, appropriate sound, or word beginning with the appropriate sound.

APPENDIX D

Sample Reports of Children's Development

Dear Mr and Mrs. Williams:

Thank you for bringing Samantha to the Reading Lab for evaluation last Wednesday (9/23/90). I understand your concern over her reading performance and I have considered your comments and those of the school in some detail as part of my evaluation of Samantha's performance. I feel absolutely confident, however, that she is a very capable reader for her age. Indeed, were she somewhat older I would still be positive about her reading. I base this on my observations of her reading parts of several books for me, including: *Lazy Lions, Lucky Lambs* (Patricia Reilly Giff), *Stone Fox* (John Reynolds Gardiner), and *Anastasia Krupnik* (Lois Lowry). These are books that I would expect average readers in second, fourth, and sixth grades, respectively, to read comfortably. Samantha managed them all. While I do not think that Samantha can generally manage sixth grade material, particularly textbooks, she managed *Anastasia Krupnik* quite well.

On the *Diagnostic Reading Scales* (a test devised by G. Spache, 1981), I tested Samantha on the third and fourth grade levels, both of which she read and understood well. I stopped testing at that point simply because there appeared to be nothing to be gained by taking a first grader beyond that level. It was already clear that she is more than competent.

While reading for me, Samantha showed evidence of all the characteristics of a strong reader. She predicted what words were likely to come next and what was likely to happen next in the story, and she checked her predictions from the print. When she made a mistake that conflicted with later text, she reread and corrected herself. She has a strong sense of the level of meaning to expect from her reading. Samantha is also very competent at figuring out words she has not seen before. She used a range of methods to do this and she used them with the flexibility we expect of good readers.

Finally, the fact that Samantha chooses to read independently at home is very important. This makes me very confident that Samantha should have no trouble in school as far as her reading goes. If any problems arise, I should be happy to discuss her progress with her teacher or whomever is concerned.

Sincerely,

Stewart James
The Reading Lab

GEORGE WASHINGTON
ELEMENTARY SCHOOL

Name: Leslie Jennings   Evaluator: John Smith

Parents: Steven & Mary Jennings   Position: Reading Teacher

Address: 3 Alba St., Crane, 12345

Age: 10

Grade: 4   Report Date: 3/25/90

Date of Birth: 2/22/80   Teacher: Stanley Jones

Leslie is an outgoing, and extremely verbal fourth grader. She has recently transferred to George Washington Elementary School. A psychologist has been working with her since last summer at her family's request. The specific problems cited in the referral are: an immature writing style, weak word attack, poor spelling memory, and inadequate editing and revising.

We have so far had six sessions together, two of which were individual sessions. Leslie is very positive about our classes, and she is eager and cooperative. She says that she likes to read, and is happy to do so in class, but does no reading at home. Writing, however, is not her favorite thing to do, and she is often reluctant.

Academically Leslie had been very successful up until the third grade, when her grades and self-confidence apparently began to erode. Both her previous teachers and her parents expressed some concern about a pattern of difficulty. They felt that Leslie's difficulties with expressing herself in writing might be contributing to the problem.

The reading program at her previous school incorporated a great deal of phonics work into a basal reader program. The writing program encouraged fluency, with a secondary concern for mechanics.

Mr. and Mrs. Jennings' main concern now is whether Leslie can match her writing skill to her verbal skill. If so, how, and if not, why not?

Running Records

Date	Text	Accuracy	Self-Corrections
2/3/90	*Tales of a Fourth Grade Nothing*	94%	1:4
2/5/90	*Mr. Popper's Penguins*	93%	1:5
2/10/90	*Super Fudge**	98%	1:5

---

*In other words, when Leslie read Super Fudge on February 10, she made only 2 errors in every 100 words she read, and she corrected 1 in every 5 of her errors by herself.

Reading Behaviors

- ☐ Leslie reads with fluency and expression.
- ☐ She predicts both what words will be next in the sentence and what will happen next in the story.
- ☐ She monitors and self-corrects from both print and meaning.
- ☐ She rereads words, phrases, sentences, and even paragraphs when she has lost the meaning of the text.
- ☐ Her understanding of what she reads is excellent. She can retell a story (or exposition) with considerable detail, and she can construct main idea and summary statements.
- ☐ Leslie analyzes unknown words, even long ones, quickly and accurately.
- ☐ She uses the context to determine the meaning of unknown words.
- ☐ Her retellings after silent readings are as good as after oral readings when she understands that the purpose is to entertain the audience or, in the case of exposition, for her to check her recall of what she read.
- ☐ Leslie has an excellent vocabulary.
- ☐ She sometimes reads a little too quickly and loses the meaning.
- ☐ She does not always attend to the actual print well, particularly skipping the ends of words.

Writing Behaviors

- ☐ Leslie's ideas flow well when the topic is appropriate, but she often finds organizing her ideas to be difficult.
- ☐ She can write several paragraphs on a topic.
- ☐ She shows ownership of her work.
- ☐ She can read paragraphs back easily.
- ☐ She is a good phonetic speller (she can represent all sounds in words). However, frequently she does not do this.
- ☐ Leslie recognizes some spelling errors in context, more out of context, and can correct some when brought to her attention. However, her errors are often inconsistent.
- ☐ While she knows many conventions, she often ignores them. For example, she produces many run-on sentences, and splits words inappropriately at the end of the line. However, her capitalization, and much other punctuation, can be good.
- ☐ She does not generally attend well to revising and editing.

Examples of Leslie's writing are provided at the end of this report.

Comments

Leslie is a capable reader, and has most of the skills of a good writer. Her general avoidance of writing has meant that she is not automatic at many of the skills she has acquired. Thus, when she has to consciously attend to more than one of these at once, inconsistencies develop.

Teaching Suggestions

Try to increase the amount of writing Leslie does. Generally avoid focusing on print detail in her writing for a while except for specific information that she requests. Focus on responding with interest to what she has to say, and helping her to expand that, so that she can begin to be selective. It is important to affirm the quality of the thoughts she is communicating. Try to increase her confidence in herself as a person and as a writer. It is important to allow enough time for Leslie to find and correct her own errors. When she revises her writing, ask her to read it out loud, pointing to each word as she reads since she sometimes reads more words than are there.

[First draft of original poetry by Leslie Jennings]

3/4/90
As I sit in my bed and ponder to my self I think of the
Sounds of the night. A chicit an animal walking by and cars
rouin by. Oh what a wende wonderful world we have if we did
not fight the world would n be as peasful as the night.

[A personal experience story by Leslie Jennings]
My Birthday

First draft (3/8/90)
   Befor the gests came my sister my mother and me were
running arown geting ready for the gests.
   When Jessica came she was a human dart bord
next Courtnaney came she was a girl from the fifties,
then Meg and Crusten came Meg was an Ice skiter
and Kristen was an baceball player. Next Christy
came she was a split persanality. Then Elena came
she was a little red riding hood. Next sussana cam-
e she was a skier. I was a punk and my sister was
a girl fram fiflys girl. Manida came as a flower Child.

Final (third) draft (3/19/90)
   Before the guests came my sister, my mother, and me
were running around getting ready for their arrival.

First Jessica came, she was a human dart board. Well, she really didn't have any darts, but she did have an awful lot of balloons! Take a look at this . . .

[PICTURE]

Next Courtney came, she was a girl from the fifties, then meg, and kristen came. Meg was an ice skater and Kristen was a baseball player.

Next Cristy came, she was a split personality.

[PICTURE]

Then Elena came she was little red riding hood, and Melinda came as a flower child. Now look at this . . .

[PICTURE]

Next Sussana came, she was a skier. I was a punk and my sister was a girl from the fifties.

When the guests left I played with my toys. Then I missed my friends. But when I went to bed I thought of next year and my next birthday!

Name: Dan Jones   Parents: Mr. & Mrs. Jones
Date of Birth: 10/11/81   Address: 2 Spring St.,
School: PS24   Berlin, NY 54321
Grade: 3   Evaluator: Joan Waterson
Teacher: Ms. Brown   Report Date: 5/2/90

I. GENERAL INFORMATION

Dan is now completing his first year at PS24. Throughout our remedial reading sessions he has shown enthusiasm for reading and writing. He seems very much interested in helping himself to become a better reader and in working toward this goal with determination and persistence.

II. ASSESSMENT PROCEDURE

Assessment has been ongoing over the year using observations, running records of oral reading, and samples of writing.

III. EVALUATION—READING

A. Established Behaviors

1. Dan has a positive attitude towards reading.
2. He extends his reading by comparing what he is reading with other books and to his own experiences.
3. He makes predictions regularly, both at the sentence level and at the story level.
4. Dan shows signs of independence and persistence in figuring out new words. He uses a marker or finger to cover up parts of words.
5. He is flexible and persistent in his attempts to figure out unfamiliar words. He uses a phonetic approach; breaks words into syllables, and sometimes compares the word with other words (e.g., pric/pecurl-er/pecareful for peculiar).
6. Dan keeps track of his reading to make sure it is making sense. Sometimes he corrects the errors he discovers.
7. When he loses the meaning, he often goes back to the beginning of the line to try again.
8. When he reads a word incorrectly, the word he substitutes is usually similar in printed form to the correct word, particularly in the first and last letters (e.g., scarely/scarcely or rested for restored).
9. When Dan is asked to reread a line or page, he can usually find any

errors he made on the first reading if they caused a disturbance in meaning.

10. After silent reading of easy text, he can retell the story and discuss the story in terms of what was and was not said by the author.

B. Emerging Behaviors

1. Dan is beginning more regularly to correct his own reading errors when they conflict with the print.
2. He matches words to print more accurately, and he omits and inserts high frequency words less often.
3. Dan shows increased attention to print. He remarks on punctuation and the use of capitals, and he can talk about the similarities between the printed word and his oral reading error.

IV. CURRENT PROGRAM AND FOLLOW-UP RECOMMENDATIONS—READING

A. Focus of Instruction

My main objective in working with Dan this year has been getting him to attend to print detail to preserve the meaning of the sentence and story. I went about this in the following ways:

Feedback on Print.   When Dan read a word incorrectly in his oral reading, I directed his attention to the print by asking, "Does that look right?" or "What letters would you expect to see?" Dan is very capable of analyzing words, comparing his response to the printed word, but needs continued guidance and practice to make this behavior automatic.

Cross-Checking Cues.   This remains one of Dan's weaker areas. His oral reading errors are often from one source, either they make sense *or* look right. When he was confident that a response was graphically correct I would encourage him to put it back in the sentence to check on meaning. Prompts such as "Does that look like _____ ?" then "Would _____ make sense here?" were given.

After he figured out a difficult word I sometimes asked how he did it. If he mentioned the meaning, I asked if there was another way he could tell. When he discussed print I praised him for finding two ways to figure out the word. Towards the end of the year he was able to give both print and meaning cues without any prompting. I suggest these strategies be continued because, although

Dan has shown progress here, he does not consistently cross-check his responses.

Monitoring. At all times Dan was encouraged to think about what he was reading, to make sure it was making sense. I emphasized this point by doing frequent meaning checks as he read orally. I asked him at the end of almost every page, "Did everything make sense on that page?" In cases where he substituted a word that disturbed meaning but did not mention it when asked, it was necessary to use a follow-up prompt such as "Was there a hard part on this page?" Often this would bring him to his error immediately.

I cannot overstate the importance of expecting Dan to be responsible for the meaning of what he reads. Strategies such as the ones used and any others that further this goal are strongly recommended.

Use of a Word Marker. To slow down Dan's too-fluent language response, to direct his attention to the print, and to reinforce proper directional behaviors, a special marker was devised. It was long enough to underscore an entire line of text and wide enough to cover the one or two lines beneath it. At its center was a black line to underscore each word as he read across the page. A handle extended from the center point so that Dan could manage the marker with one hand and use the other to hold his book. This proved to be a very effective way of improving his one-to-one word matching ability. I think he should continue using a marker or his finger until he can read as accurately without it.

Locating His Errors. To encourage independent reading habits, Dan was given the opportunity to locate his uncorrected errors. When he was not able to find the errors, I would reread what he had read and ask him to find the discrepancies. This gave him additional practice in focusing on the print and made him more aware of the kind of errors he makes.

Monitoring Comprehension. As Dan read along, we constantly checked his predictions against new information we gathered from print. Revising predictions when necessary was stressed. We sometimes wrote them down to keep track and crossed them out when they proved to be incorrect. This was another way of demonstrating the importance of checking on oneself.

B. Materials

Dan read a lot of books that were easy for him. Starting each session with a pleasurable, meaningful reading experience has been a worthwhile procedure. Besides providing him with a successful encounter with books, this period of "warming up" on easy text has given him the opportunity to practice positive reading behaviors that will move him towards becoming a self-improving reader.

Books by Arnold Lobel and others containing five or so short stories were favored over the more lengthy easy books because it was satisfying to Dan to complete two stories each time.

Because Dan enjoys comparing characters and events in books with one another, it has been most worthwhile searching for books with a common thread. He has particularly enjoyed humorous stories where the unexpected often happens, as in *The Stupids Step Out, All of Our Noses Are Here,* and *The Witch, the Fairy and the Magic Chicken.*

The relationship between two friends was another basis for comparison, as in the *Frog and Toad* books, *Hound and Bear,* and the *Monster* series.

Stories on troublemakers (*Bad Thad, Awful Alexander,* and *Today was a Terrible Day*), their deeds and their intentions, led to many stories from real life that were recorded as future writing topics.

Mysteries were used for silent reading. He enjoyed sharing his predictions with me, then reading to see if he was right or not.

Short poems and rhyming stories were also read to help direct his attention to print through metered verse. We reread stanzas from his favorite poems for accuracy and expression. However, Dan did not show the same enthusiasm towards the poetry that he held for many of the other books.

Books I recommend for Dan include *Frog and Toad All Year, Frog and Toad Together* by Arnold Lobel and the *Monster -series II* books for easy reading. *The Stupids* and *The Stupids Die* by Harry Allard are others he may enjoy.

V. EVALUATION—WRITING

A. Established Behaviors

1. Dan shows enthusiasm towards writing when he chooses the topic.
2. He maintains his own topic list in his writing folder, adding and deleting topics when necessary.
3. Dan can compose independently for ten to fifteen minutes.
4. He presents his thoughts in a logical order.
5. Dan is willing to attempt words he does not know how to spell. He can produce a consonant framework for most of these.

B. Emerging Behaviors

1. Dan revises his first draft spontaneously while writing. He has made changes in phrasing, punctuation, and spelling.
2. Dan rereads his first drafts spontaneously upon completion.
3. He can add and delete information properly to clarify the meaning of the piece.
4. Dan can make changes to sentence structure on his own. In a story

containing repeated use of "and," he reread and deleted the word when it was used improperly. He also adjusted punctuation accordingly.

5. Dan gives unknown words careful consideration. He underlines those that he is not satisfied with for a second look.

VI. CURRENT PROGRAM AND FOLLOW-UP RECOMMENDATIONS—WRITING

A. Focus of Instruction

Dan did not lack enthusiasm for writing. Neither did he lack the skill to get his ideas down on paper. However, he did not reread his work critically. This became my main writing goal, and my instructional activities toward that end included the following:

Modeling.   When Dan wrote, I wrote. When we finished, I would suggest rereading our work silently and making any changes that would make our stories better. As I reread, I crossed out information, used arrows to insert information, and generally did a lot of "messing up" of this first draft. After this, we would share our stories and talk about the revisions we made. I praised Dan's efforts to make his story better.

When he was satisfied with a story, I evaluated it in terms of content and structure. If there seemed to be a problem that he did not see, I wrote a story with an overemphasized, similar problem to work on jointly during our next session. Dan was always full of suggestions on how to best solve each of our problems. Some of the questions we addressed were:

- ☐ Does my story have a beginning, middle, and end?
- ☐ Are my sentences in the right order?
- ☐ Are there sentences that repeat or don't belong in the story?
- ☐ Did I use "and" too much?
- ☐ Did I check spelling and punctuation?

These were written on a piece of construction paper and were referred to often. A lot of time was spent improving my stories. I consider it time well spent as he began to look at these things in his own writing.

Encouraging Independence.   My aim at all times during Dan's writing and revising was to convince him that he could trust his own judgment. He was given a writing folder and took control of choosing his own topics, which came from our discussions of books and his personal experiences. I suggest giving Dan the opportunity to select his own topics because he has so many stories that he wants to share.

Part of helping Dan to become independent included giving him ample time to do things for himself, such as correct or revise his own work without any prompting from me. Often he would write quickly, finish before I did, and announce that he was done, knowing that I expected him to read his story as soon as he had finished. When I told him I was not finished and continued writing, he either added to his story or reread it.

To foster independence I tried to give him strategies that he could use to help himself such as the ones below:

- ☐ *Rereading.* Only you can make your story better. Give yourself the chance to do this by rereading carefully. Use your marker and take your time.
- ☐ *Run-on sentences.* Be on the lookout for too many "ands." Underline them if you think you have a problem. Read each sentence out loud with the "and," then without it, as two sentences. Decide which sounds better.
- ☐ *Spelling.* When you're not sure of a word, say it out loud slowly. Write the sounds you hear. Look at the word you've written. If it doesn't look right, try it differently somewhere else on the page.

In general, whenever he was not sure about something, I took that as a sign of progress and brought it to his attention.

Having modeled all phases of the writing process, I felt comfortable giving Dan control of his folder. At this point he had unfinished stories in different stages of composition and revision and took responsibility for deciding what to work on each day.

In addition to these activities, I found it very important for Dan to share his work with the other students in the class and for them to share theirs with Dan. This gives him a broader, more detailed notion of audience and helps to illustrate to him the need to check his work. It also gives him the opportunity to share work that he is proud of.

BOOKS READ THIS YEAR

(Extensive list of books)

Index